From Revolution to Politics

From Revolution to Politics

Chinese Communists
on the Long March

Benjamin Yang

Westview Press
BOULDER, SAN FRANCISCO, & OXFORD

Westview Special Studies on China

Published in 1990 in the United States of America by Westview Press, Inc., 5500 Central Avenue, Boulder, Colorado 80301, and in the United Kingdom by Westview Press, Inc., 36 Lonsdale Road, Summertown, Oxford OX2 7EW

Library of Congress Cataloging-in-Publication Data
Yang, Benjamin.
  From revolution to politics : Chinese communists on the long march
/ Benjamin Yang.
     p.   cm.—(Westview special studies on China)
  Includes bibliographical references.
  ISBN 0-8133-7672-6
  1. China—History—Long March, 1934–1935. 2. Communism—China—
History. I. Title. II. Series.
DS777.5134.Y36   1990
951.04′2—dc20   89-49475
                                                                    CIP

Printed and bound in the United States of America

The paper used in this publication meets the requirements
of the American National Standard for Permanence of Paper
for Printed Library Materials Z39.48-1984.

10   9   8   7   6   5   4   3   2   1

To My Father,
Who Died a Communist

CONTENTS

TABLES AND MAPS

ACKNOWLEDGMENTS

My personal interest in the political history of the Chinese Communist Party can be traced back nearly twenty years to a period during the Cultural Revolution when I was confined in the First Model Prison of Peking. There, only Mao's writings, not even those of Marx and Lenin or the official *People's Daily*, were allowed to be read by the prisoners. To kill time before meals, I scanned through the four-volume *Mao Zedong xuanji* five or six times. Needless to say, Mao's writings are CCP history and politics.

Between 1973 and 1974, while I was staying in the countryside in Shandong receiving "re-education" from the "poor and lower middle class peasants," I managed to write a lengthy book entitled *Politics and Chinese Politics*. The book was essentially a criticism of the radical revolutionary line running amok at the time; an entire chapter was devoted to the history of the Communist Party. I sent the original manuscript to Chairman Mao, together with a long cover letter. There was no response, of course. I wonder if the manuscript is still kept somewhere in the General Office of the CCP Central Committee.

Three years ago a friend of mine, Ross Terrill, introduced me to Harrison Salisbury, who was then preparing for his own unique Long March through China. It was my acquaintance with Salisbury that eventually aroused my intention to pursue that same subject, although using a somewhat different approach. During my recent visits to China, I conferred with a number of scholars, officials, students, and friends who helped me in various ways— in fact, the majority of them are Communist Party members. I am grateful to all of them, especially to the late Professor Hu Hua, not only for their assistance with my research on specific historical issues but also for the general impression they left me with: that the Communists have indeed been undergoing a profound transformation in line with the central theme that this study attempts to elaborate on.

I have for years benefited from Benjamin Schwartz's benevolent concern as well as from Roderick MacFarquhar's meticulous guidance. A simple "thank you" is not enough to express my deep gratitude to them both. I assume all they expect of me is that I myself work harder and write better, and here I promise I will try my best not to disappoint them now and in the future.

John Fairbank's works guided me conveniently to literature previously produced in the West on the Chinese Communist movement in the 1930s, and Tatsuo Yamada's writings and personal communications brought to my attention a number of Japanese articles of relevance. At various stages of writing and revising, I showed the manuscript to Parks Coble, Catherine Hartford, Michel Oksenberg, Anthony Saich, John Schrecker, and Frederic Wakeman and received encouragement and suggestions from them. Nevertheless, my own ignorance and stubbornness make me solely responsible for any flaws yet remaining in this book.

To all the authors referred to in the following chapters and notes, I am greatly indebted for their information and conceptions, despite the fact that I may have expressed opinions at variance with some of theirs. Fully realizing the various difficulties in working on Chinese Communist history and politics, I hate to see myself finding fault with other authors. If I have been guilty of this occasionally in this academic study, I can only excuse myself with the following quote from Confucius: "*dangren burang*," literally, "One should not compromise wherever the principle of humanity is concerned." With the same attitude in mind, I look forward to any possible criticism of this volume.

Benjamin Yang
Cambridge, Mass.

1

INTRODUCTION

How many prominent scholars and politicians have attempted to characterize the essence or *zeitgeist* of the contemporary world? It has been ascribed a host of labels, including "the age of crisis," "the age of reconstruction," "the age of proletarian revolution," and "the age of disorder under Heaven." I would propose that our age should still be understood essentially in terms of the political confrontation between capitalism and communism, despite the archaistic hues the two terms may carry. Indeed, there are few crucial issues in our world that cannot be shown to relate, directly or indirectly, to such confrontation.[1]

The Chinese Communist Party (CCP) plays a particularly conspicuous role in international communism in at least two respects. First, the CCP represents a country with one tenth the land mass, one fifth the population, and one half the organized Communists on earth. More important, the CCP has emerged as a distinctive outgrowth of the Communist movement. It followed a unique path to the victory of revolution, debated sharply with and then split from the Soviet Union, and is now advocating a dramatic reform policy known as "open door to the world" and "two systems in one country." Simply put, it has become an indicator of a fundamental change in the Communist world.

Historical studies serve as one of the most convenient approaches to understanding the CCP's emergence as a unique variant of communism. It is particularly interesting to investigate the mid-1930s—the period of the Long March—in which the CCP went through a process of drastic transformation: hundreds of thousands of Communist troops traveled thousands of miles from South China to North China; and the Communist Party went through a basic change in status and character. The importance of the Long March can hardly be overemphasized, either historically or politically. Older Communist leaders have frequently referred to it as a turning point in CCP history; even now, fifty years later, survivors of the Long March are still in control of China, as I have shown statistically elsewhere[2]; and new Chinese leaders are calling their drive for economic modernization the "New Long March." The Long March has become a symbol of CCP history, just as the Great Wall is a hallmark of ancient Chinese civilization. The importance of the Long March as subject matter also stems from the fact that although this extraordinary epic has drawn much admiration from military commentators and journalists (among whom Harrison Salisbury is the latest and most reliable in view of historical accuracy), few serious academic works have yet dealt with it, either in China or the West.[3]

Definitions

While it was under way in late 1934 and early 1935, the Long March had not yet been so named. The Communists called it the "Western Expedition," because the Central Red Army was withdrawing from its Soviet base in Jiangxi province and moving toward the western provinces.[4] In the eyes of the antagonistic Kuomintang (KMT) army, what the Communists were doing could only be mockingly regarded as the "Western Flight."[5] Ironically, the first appearance of the term Long March, or *changzheng*, was in a speech of Chiang Kai-shek referring to his Nationalist troops in pursuit of the Communists. According to Xue Yue—the KMT general who commanded the Second Route Army to have pursued the Central Red Army all the way from Jiangxi in October 1934 to Sichuan in June 1935—Chiang made the following remarks of approbation after Xue had finished his duty: "Throughout Chinese history, no army whatsoever has ever before been recorded as completing such a Long March of more than 20,000 li. Now we have one, and this is achieved by none other than our Second Route Army."[6]

As for the Communists, it was only a few months after the Central Red Army, or the First Front Army, concluded its part of the Long March that Mao Zedong began to adopt the term. In his famous speech after the Wayaobao Conference, Mao said: "Speaking of the Long March, one may ask: What is its significance? We answer that the Long March is the very first throughout Chinese history, that it is a manifesto, a propaganda team, and a seeding machine. . . . A new situation emerged soon after the Long March ended."[7] These statements not only marked the introduction of the term Long March into the Communist lexicon, but also demonstrated that Mao considered the arrival of his own Central Red Army in northern Shaanxi the conclusion of the Long March, even though while he was making this speech in late December 1935, two other Red Army groups were still struggling to complete their own Long Marches.

Whether out of respect for historical reality or simply for political purposes—since the Long March soon became a symbol of honor and glory for the entire Party and Army, and hence for all those involved—the later official account extended the duration of the Long March to October 1936 in order to include the expeditions of the Second and Fourth Front Armies. The starting date of the Long March nevertheless remains the date when the First Front Army set forth from the Jiangxi Soviet. In the official version, therefore, the Long March is now dated from October 1934 to October 1936.[8]

A logical problem, however, must be brought up. If the Long March pertains not only to the First Front Army but also to other Red Armies, then not merely one but several Long Marches were undertaken. The starting date of the Long March, considered as a general historical period, must be accordingly modified. As a matter of fact, Zhang Guotao's Fourth Front Army and He Long's Third Army left their original base areas, the Eyuwan Soviet and the Xiangexi Soviet respectively, and embarked on their military expeditions as early as October 1932 as a result of the KMT's Fourth Suppression Campaign. As some historians have legitimately argued, this should be regarded as the real beginning of the Long March.[9]

The end date for the Long March is no less controversial. The union of the three Red Army groups at eastern Gansu in October 1936 did not necessarily mean the conclusion of the Long March, because simultaneously 20,000 Red Army troops—which constituted two thirds of the Fourth Front Army and almost one half of the entire Red Army—were just crossing the Yellow River and setting forth on the "Western March" toward Xinjiang. After undergoing extreme difficulties and hardships, this Western Route Army was eventually destroyed in Gansu in early 1937. Unless success should be taken as the prerequisite for inclusion, the Long March should not be considered as ended until this moment. For all these reasons, the Long March is defined in this study as a historical event spanning the period from late 1932 to early 1937.

Leaving concrete dates and events aside, the Long March can be defined in a broader and more abstract sense. It can be understood as an event in which the Chinese Communists went through an overall transfer from South China to North China. Not merely a single episode involving a single Communist group for a brief period, it included a complex series of events involving all major Communist forces over an extended span of time. Although the highlight of the Long March is doubtless the performance of Mao's Central Red Army between its departure from Jiangxi and its arrival in Shaanxi, the earlier withdrawals of other Red Armies from their base areas should be included as the indispensable prologue, and the destiny of the Western Route Army as the epilogue to this historical event. In the ensuing chapters, the term Long March will generally be used in this broad sense. It comprises a number of discrete 'Long Marches' conducted by several different Red Army groups from the autumn of 1932 to the spring of 1937.

Themes

Two basic questions, whether explicitly raised or not, can be found in almost all the previous literature on CCP history and politics in general and that of the 1930s in particular: What caused the Communist Party's rise to power in China and Mao Zedong's rise to power within the Communist Party? What made the Soviet movement rise and then fall in the 1930s and Mao, concurrently, fall and then rise? Answers proposed to these questions have been divergent and even contradictory.

Although he is primarily interested in studies of the CCP during the Sino-Japanese War, Chalmers Johnson, in his pioneer work on relationships between peasant nationalism and the Communist Party, attempts to interpret the CCP's earlier defeats and later successes in a general sense. Professor Johnson writes:

> In other words, from 1921 to 1937 Communists failed in China because the Chinese people, in general, were indifferent to what the Communist Party had to offer. After 1937, it succeeded because the population became receptive to one particular kind of political appeal; and the Communist Party—in one of its many disguises—made precisely that appeal: it offered to meet the needs of the people for leadership in organizing resistance to the invader and in alleviating war-induced anarchy in the rural areas.[10]

Ilpyong Kim, another influential author, offers a rather different explanation. In his book on Communist politics in the Jiangxi Soviet in the early 1930s, Kim concludes that "the Communist leaders of the Kiangsi Soviet period were successful in creating and operating an effective political system and in mobilizing the peasant masses under the Soviet rule," and their "evacuation of the Kiangsi Soviet base in 1934 probably was primarily the consequence of military failure, not of a lack of mass support."[11]

Both factual and logical problems can be found in Johnson's argument. It can hardly be taken for granted, first of all, that the entire 1921 to 1937 period was a simple failure for the Communists, either in view of the CCP's periodic upsurges in 1921-1926, 1928-1933 and 1936-1937 or in view of its general growth in strength throughout the period. Moreover, given that the CCP witnessed a steady growth between 1937 and 1949, the Liberation War (1946-49) may not be taken simply as a smooth extension of the Anti-Japanese War (1937-45), nor was it simply, as Johnson says, that "as a result of the Communist Party's leadership of the resistance, the Party obtained a mass following that it subsequently used to conquer all of China"—but this discussion will be better supported in the final chapter.[12] Finally, in a war period such as the 1930s, mass support, a vague term in itself, is only an indirect and quantitative factor. It must be transformed into the overall political and military strength, if it is to become decisive for one warring side or the other. Instead of considering it as a direct factor (following this line of inference, one may arrive at an even more provocative notion that the victorious KMT must have enjoyed more mass support than the defeated CCP in the early 1930s), mass support must be seen as playing into the overall military contest with the KMT in deciding the destiny of the CCP.

The Communists' evacuation from the Jiangxi Soviet in 1934 was apparently a consequence of their military failure. Problematically, Kim prefers a clear-cut distinction between political conditions and military affairs. He seems to believe that the Communist leaders of the Jiangxi Soviet succeeded politically but failed militarily. This is actually a position the CCP leaders maintained in early 1935; they later changed their opinion. While granting military affairs due importance, one should not ignore how and to what extent the military process was shaped by Communist policies of mass mobilization, social organization, administrative operations, ideological propaganda, and enemy disintegration. More generally speaking, the relationship between the political line and the military line should be under question.

In his classic study of the Communist Party and the rise of Mao, Benjamin Schwartz attempts to outline the basic strategy by which Mao brought the Communist Party to success. Under circumstances defined by incessant splits and wars within the ruling classes, and given the existence of a mass base, a Communist Party organization, a Red Army, favorable terrain, and sufficient economic resources, an autonomous regime of the Communist Party could not only survive but also grow. These ideas, as expressed in a report by Mao to the Party Center in 1928, are regarded by Schwartz as the main features of Mao's strategy in the Jiangxi Soviet years.[13] Although it underwent some statesmanlike refinement, according to Schwartz, Mao changed little in the basic strategy in later years. Schwartz connects this outline with Communist success in China, saying: "Such, I think, are the main lines of the strategy which, in conjuncture with favorable external circumstances, was finally to lead the Chinese Communists to victory."[14]

Nevertheless, a number of historians hold different views on this issue, believing that the strategy of Mao and the Communist Party between the Jiangxi Soviet period and the Sino-Japanese War changed significantly. Shanti Swarup ascribes the CCP failure in the Jiangxi Soviet to its excessive social programs and its success in the Anti-Japanese War to a combination of social and national revolutions.[15] Similarly, Tetsuya Kataoka attributes the Communist victory in the late 1930s and the early 1940s as much to the previous strategy of conducting a peasant war and employing the countryside to encircle the city as to the later juxtaposition of both rural and urban lines.[16]

Although a more precise definition of Mao's general strategy may be needed, I would agree with Schwartz that Mao's basic opinions on making the Communist revolution in China were already established by the Jiangxi Soviet years, and that there were no fundamental changes after this time. Nonetheless, a few points are worth noting. It should at least be admitted that Mao's position within the Communist Party had risen from that of an ordinary Party and Army leader in Ruijin to that of the dominating figure in Yan'an. Hence, since Mao's strategy became the Party's strategy in the latter period, the Communist Party as a whole must have undergone a shift during the 1930s. Mao's own policy positions, it must be added, had also changed significantly between the early and late 1930s. From rebelling against the KMT to uniting with the KMT, from a slogan of "Soviet government" to a slogan of "people's government," from the policy of land distribution to the policy of rent control—these changes are important enough to be considered strategic. What had not yet changed—and I assume this is also Schwartz's essential argument—was Mao's basic mode of thought, which I would term political realism, in contrast to the revolutionary idealism pursued by the earlier Party leaders. Schwartz alludes to the statesmanlike refinement of the Party's political line in the years following the Long March, and he is certainly right to point out that this change was for the Communists no more than some titular alteration. It was perceived as formal rather than substantive shift.[17]

Historical truth, however, does not always lie in historical actors' own perceptions. This case brings to mind the well-known slogan "Chinese learning for substance and Western learning for function" launched by Zhang Zhidong and his Confucian colleagues a century ago regarding national reform in China. It equally seems that Mao and his comrades' united front policy resembled something like "Communist revolution for substance and Chinese politics for function." But just as the former Confucian slogan rose from the historical imperative presented by the substantially superior Western powers, and later history had proved the very opposite view—Western learning became the substance while Chinese learning was left for function; so the Communist slogan arose from historical necessity presented by the contemporary domestic and international situations, and so too Communist history has also generated the opposing view—politics became the substance and revolution was left for function. The 'statesmanlike' turned out to be the *statesmanship*, without which the Communists could hardly have won their final victory.[18]

The present study attempts to demonstrate that the mid-1930s were a time of transformation from revolutionary idealism to political realism in the general orientation of the CCP leadership or, if one prefers, a time of politicization of Chinese Communism. This shift was contemporaneous with Mao's ascent to power in the CCP Center during the period of the Long March, and it was this transformation that had provided the subjective strength which, in conjunction with fortuitous and extraneous factors, culminated in the Communist victory in China in the late 1940s.

Historians have attempted to compare the Jiangxi Soviet period with the Yan'an period to see if there were changes in the Communist Party, and if so, of what nature. But the Long March, which linked the two periods, was the change in itself. Of course, the Long March can be taken just as a temporary interlude between two well-defined historical periods in the Communist movement. At the time, it was indeed considered something of abnormality by both the CCP and the KMT—the Communists were all the time attempting to open new base areas and return to their 'normal' revolutionary activities, while the Nationalists were all the time aiming to wipe out the Communists and return to their 'normal' political rule. But normality and abnormality are scarcely distinguishable in modern Chinese history. The Long March may therefore, perhaps more appropriately, be treated as a historical period in its own right.

Sources

Quite a number of monographs on the Jiangxi Soviet in the early 1930s have been produced in Western literature, which led John Fairbank to suggest that "these studies may have wrapped up the subject until new evidence appears."[19] Generally speaking, these studies contain some defects in historical accuracy. They rely in varying degrees on two limited sources: CCP documents obtained by KMT army in the suppression campaigns, and memoirs of ex-Communists who emigrated from China.

It should be recognized that the Communists were defeated but not destroyed in the 1930s and only those documents—newspapers, journals, notices, and announcements and the like—which were widely circulated among local cadres and peasants in the Soviets were likely to have fallen into the hands of Nationalist troops. Such documents may be sufficient for studies of the Communist movement from a social or ideological point of view, but for any historical survey of policy making and power relationship within the Communist leadership, which most previous studies have focused on, more concrete and substantial information is needed. There is, for example, Derek Waller's careful work on the two national Soviet congresses, in 1931 and 1934; but for the two Party conferences—the Gannan Conference of the Central Soviet Bureau and the Fifth Plenum of the Central Committee— which immediately preceded the Soviet congresses and actually blueprinted their procedures and resolutions, no adequate and accurate information is provided.[20]

Sources in the form of memoirs are even less adequate: they are all dependent on the memories of old men recalling events several decades earlier and influenced by their concern with their own political positions. In his memoirs entitled The Red Army and I, for example, Gong Chu claims to have been the Chief of General Staff in the Red Army Headquarters from May to July 1934. Had this been true, his account of the military situation around the Guangchang Battles in April-May 1934 would have been trustworthy. In fact, Gong never occupied so high a position in the Red Army; his false claim can be explained by anything but a serious concern for historical studies.[21]

As for the Long March period, documentary sources were even more meager until recently. Due to the military situation, no periodicals—like Red Star, Red China and Struggle of the Jiangxi Soviet years—could possibly have been produced. Also as an army group on a military expedition, the Long Marchers were more cautious and efficient in destroying their documents so that few could fall into KMT hands or, one might say, they were less careful and efficient in preserving these papers for future reference.

On the other hand, there is a monumental stock of Long March tales in the form of reminiscences published in China, such as those included in the numerous volumes of Red Flags Fluttering and A Single Spark Can Start a Prairie Fire. Most, if not all, articles of this category are short pieces composed in the name of lower ranking Communist cadres and Red Army soldiers of the time, all with the purpose of describing "heroic people and heroic deeds." These sources might work well enough for some journalistic writings, though subject to all kinds of ambiguity and inaccuracy; for historical research, they prove at least as misleading as useful.

Partly for these reasons, among the dozen or so important Party and Army conferences on or higher than the front army level during the Long March, only one or two had become subjects of historical studies in the past. Consequently, all historians could offer their readers was a vague story of the Zunyi Conference, full of flaws, and a mention of the Maoergai Conference—which actually pertained to another occasion, the Shawo Conference, while the real Maoergai Conference was entirely unknown. Referring to Mao's rise in power at the Zunyi Conference, John Rue writes:

Early in January 1935 they reached Tsun-yi, a small town in northern Kweichow. There Mao, supported by dissident military leaders, insisted that an enlarged conference of the Politburo be called for the purpose of reorganizing the Revolutionary Military Council. The conference was held, and Mao was elected chairman of the Council, replacing Chou En-lai, who remained on it but with greatly decreased power. Yeh Chien-ying was dropped off, as was Teng Fa, the head of the security police. No one was appointed to the new

Council to represent the police. Liu Po-ch'eng replaced Yeh as chief of staff; Chu Teh continued as commander-in-chief and Wang Chia-hsiang as political commissar.[22]

An almost identical description can be found in other writings at the time.[23] But in fact, the whole story told here is too sensational to be taken as evidence for an appropriate understanding of intraparty power relationships. In this single paragraph, there are as many as a dozen factual errors. Any general conclusions based on such sources can scarcely be expected to be more accurate.[24] What seems problematic here is not merely a matter of inaccuracy stemming from a shortage of documentary sources, but the larger question of historical approach. A Japanese scholar, Noriyuki Tokuda, presents a sharp contrast in his *Political Dynamics of Maoism*. Although it contains no factual discoveries and although it is burdened with the jargon of physics—the terms "collective cohesion force," "primitive accumulation of authority," and "takeoff of charismatic leadership," figure prominently in the book—Tokuda offers a story of Mao's rise to power as a gradual, complicated, less dramatic but more credible, historical process.[25]

Chinese Communists began to work seriously on their own history (in response to Mao's call) during the Rectification Movement at Yan'an in the early 1940s. From the very beginning, their studies had been a mixture of political statements and historical references. In April 1945, on the eve of the Seventh National Congress, the Party Center passed the formal "Resolutions on Several Historical Problems." From that time until Mao's death in 1976, official historians in China strictly followed these resolutions, assuming two basic objectives in their studies: externally, to verify the Communist Party's victorious though painful struggle with domestic and foreign reactionary forces; internally, to confirm Chairman Mao's successful but tortuous struggle with rightist and leftist opportunist trends. Although many episodes in the Party history—such as the Li Lisan line, the five suppression campaigns, and the union and split of the First and Fourth Front Armies—had appeared in various publications, they were without exception couched in vague and abstract terms for immediate propaganda purposes.

After Mao's death and especially in more recent years, as the general political climate in China becomes more tolerant of academic studies, CCP history has gradually come under somewhat more objective scrutiny. A large number of documents, memoirs, and even analytical articles have been produced for both the foreign and Chinese reader. During my summer visits to China in 1984 and 1986, I came across a few thousand original documents on CCP history, most of which were unknown in Western literature. One to two hundred of them are referred to in this study. (By the term "original documents," I mean public announcements, internal instructions and communications, journals and pamphlets, military telegrams, conference resolutions and recordings, individual diaries and so on—any contemporary records of contemporary events.) I regard it as one of the basic purposes of this study to employ these newly available documentary sources to introduce and clarify the most significant historical facts concerning the Long March.[26]

Another group of new sources used in this study are reminiscences and memoirs of veteran Communists in China who participated in the historical events of this study and are recalling their personal experiences. In terms of historical accuracy, memoirs of Communist leaders in China differ little from those of ex-Communists outside China. They are all marred by blurred memories and partisan biases. But since now more than one person addresses the same issue, cross-checking becomes possible. In order to establish some historical occurrence accurately, double or even multiple checks on these memoirs should be made. Where this is impossible, reliance on one piece of evidence is accepted with due reservation.

Plenty of secondary literature on the Long March has recently been produced in China. Although many of these writings still carry a strong propagandistic tone, they are far more academic now than in the Mao era. Comparing some representative works recently published in China with those published outside it, the former have generally been far more accurate and comprehensive than the latter. The obvious reasons are that a large proportion of these works in China are written collectively, and that some official historians may have access to more archival documents than their public acknowledgements indicate. After all, CCP history is their own history.

The main body of this study consists of factual descriptions and interpretations in an attempt to offer a systematic account of the Long March and so provide fresh information on, and analyses of, power relationships and strategic orientation in the CCP. While remaining attentive to any shifts in Communist ideology and practice, this study starts and proceeds by accepting the conventional definition and distinction between revolution and politics: the former represents a drastic mode of change of the social or national *status quo*, and the latter stands for the art or science of running the state power. The concluding chapter is devoted to elaborating the dichotomy between revolution and politics in a broader and less conventional sense and hopefully can illustrate not only some patterns in the CCP history in question, but also in Communist politics in general. As both the establishment of historical facts and theoretical interpretations are in order at the present moment, I am well aware that the study of Chinese Communist history and politics may be among those academic subjects too complicated for anyone to accomplish either objective perfectly. Factual and analytical mistakes may occur in the work of one who realizes this situation, but without such a realization they are even more likely to appear. In this regard, Benjamin Schwartz's recommendation of an approach of "humble agnosticism" seems to me as valid now as it was three decades ago.[27]

2

SOVIET REVOLUTION IN SOUTH CHINA

A brief account of the Communist movement immediately prior to the Long March period seems necessary for two reasons. First, it will provide a background to the Long March which, after all, represents the low water mark of the Soviet revolution's confrontation with the Nationalist government in one sense, and the high drama of it in another. Second, this account will offer a general survey of salient events of the period in itself. Careful readers will find that some points of this survey may differ widely with established ones. In my opinion, quite a number of topics of CCP history in the late 1920s and the early 1930s are also in need of reconsideration due to the recent discoveries in mainland China.

The Conclusion of the Communist-Nationalist Collaboration

In view of partisan relationships, 1923-1927 was the period of collaboration between the Communist Party and the Nationalist Party. From the national point of view, the last two years of the KMT-CCP collaboration saw the Great Revolution or the Northern Expedition against the northern warlord regime. As the Northern Expedition was successfully proceeding in 1927, bloody conflicts erupted between Communists and Nationalists and brought their collaboration to an unhappy end. The whole process can easily be understood as a repeated pattern of power struggle commonly found throughout the history of Chinese politics: Collaboration makes possible a joint action against the common enemy, whereas completion of the project renders the collaboration unnecessary.[1]

Even now, Nationalist historians generally recall the Northern Expedition as a great success and propose that it would have been a still greater, if not perfect, victory, if not for the sabotage of the Communists.[2] Official historians in the People's Republic, however, regard the Northern Expedition as a disastrous failure as a result both of the KMT's betrayal of the revolution on the one hand and the CCP Center's rightist line on the other.[3] While any detailed treatment of this subject is beyond the scope of this study, some general observations seem in order.

That the KMT won great successes during the Northern Expedition seems indisputable. When the campaign started in July 1926, the KMT controlled no more than a small base area centered around the city of Canton in Guangdong province and a few armies amounting to less than 100,000 men. In early 1927, the KMT military forces had expanded to four army corps, each consisting of about 100,000 soldiers, and their dominion included most of the provinces of South China. By the end of the campaign in late 1928, all the major warlords in China were either defeated or had bowed to KMT rule; the Nanking government was legitimately established throughout the country and its military forces swelled to eighty armies with total forces of more than 2,000,000 men.[4]

But a deeper investigation of this period unearths points of divergence from the Nationalist line. Though the Northern Expedition was carried out under KMT leadership, it should be remembered that the CCP played an indispensable role in its success. Besides the high morale among the expeditionary troops created by Communist propaganda during these years, there are more concrete forms of Communist contribution. The fermenting peasant movement in Guangdong, Jiangxi, and Hunan provinces, for example, supplied the expedition with an inexhaustible source of recruitment; and the uprising workers made the seizures of big cities such as Changsha, Wuhan, and Shanghai look more like political demonstrations than military engagements. All these mass organizations were largely due to Communist efforts.[5]

Moreover, the abrupt unification of the country proved little more than a superficial success and created for the KMT government, many substantial problems, which quickly flared up after the alleged national unification. The admission and pacification of warlords through peaceful negotiations helped the KMT with a smooth takeover of state power in 1928 but left intact numerous autonomous domains all over the country. In reality, only about a fourth of the military forces and five or six provinces in the Yangtze Valley were directly controlled by the Nanking government; the others remained under the influence of various military cliques, like those controlled by Li Zongren, Yan Xishan, Feng Yuxiang, and Zhang Xueliang. As a result, Chiang Kai-shek faced one civil war after another between 1928 and 1930.[6]

At the social level, its shift in attention from mobilizing the worker-peasant masses to cooperating with the capitalist-landlord elite in order to bring the state under normal political rule alienated the KMT from the masses. Particularly in the countryside, the Chiang government never succeeded in establishing any regular administration below the county level and could not achieve, as Sun Yat-sen had hoped, any significant agrarian reforms.[7] Thus, the CCP became the revolutionary spokesman of workers and peasants and the most potent challenger to the KMT regime in the following decade.

Official Communist historians who consider the first CCP-KMT collaboration and the Northern Expedition a failure can find substantial evidence to support their views as well. From April 1927 when Chiang Kai-shek started the Shanghai Coup and the Purification Campaign, until December of the same year when the Canton Commune was smashed, tens of thousands of Communists deserted or were executed. The labor unions and peasant associations sponsored by the CCP, which at one time claimed to have several millions of members, were virtually extinguished in a few months. Above all, these events contradicted the Communist leaders' expectations and left the Party Center headed by Chen Duxiu in a state of helpless confusion, so that the Communist failure was graphically depicted even in their own behavior.[8]

Viewed more broadly, however, the years from 1923 to 1928 cannot be labeled a total failure for the Communist Party. Even a simple calculation shows their general growth in strength and influence. In 1923 at the Third Congress, the CCP had just over 400 members; two years later in 1925, its membership had increased to 1,000. Mainly during the first phase of the Northern Expedition, the CCP membership swelled to 57,900, according to the records of its Fifth Congress in early 1927. The collapse of the alliance with the KMT diminished CCP membership to about 40,000, as reported at the Sixth Congress of the CCP in mid-1928. Notwithstanding temporary ups and downs, the entire period of the CCP-KMT collaboration and the Northern Expedition was still one of obvious Communist upsurge.

Less apparent but more important was a potential change in the character and orientation of the CCP brought about by its participation in the Nationalist revolution. Before the collaboration started in 1922, the CCP was "only a small group of intellectuals who knew little of Marxism and social movement," as Henricus Sneevliet, the Comintern agent in China at the time, scornfully noted.[9] After joining the Nationalist Party, and particularly after the reorganization of the KMT in 1924, the CCP became a force in the national political arena. A number of Communists assumed high positions in governmental administration and military functions. Unlike the Communist leaders of the first generation, such as the former Peking University professors Chen Duxiu and Li Dazhao, younger Communists like Mao Zedong and Zhou Enlai were groomed as professional politicians and military leaders in the mid-1920s. The political experience and interests accumulated during the CCP-KMT collaboration and the Northern Expedition transformed the Communist Party and developed in it the capacity to compete with the Nationalist Party in bidding for state power.

If a relative assessment may help comprehension of the impact of the first CCP-KMT collaboration and the Northern Expedition upon the Communist and the Nationalist Parties—each side may be understood as successful in some ways and unsuccessful in others—then definite judgments can be formulated concerning some other political forces and individual politicians. The northern warlord regime, as represented by Duan Qirui, Wu Peifu, and others were clearly the losers of the period. Although the influence of old warlords would continue for years and new warlords would reappear in less obvious forms, warlordism as a transitional phase between traditional imperial monarchy and modern republican government ended by 1927. In this regard at least, there is a sense of progress in modern Chinese history.[10]

The assumption that the destruction of its collaboration with the Nationalist Party was for the Communist Party but a downward curve along a general line of growth would by no means excuse Chen Duxiu, the Party's General Secretary, from being a lost politician. Chen gave up his leading position soon after the KMT left-wing government at Wuhan adopted an anti-Communist stance in July 1927. Later, he more openly expressed his protest against the Comintern mandating of CCP cooperation with the KMT. He went even further in the following years by refusing to attend the Sixth Congress of the CCP at Moscow and publishing a statement bitterly attacking Stalin's brutal bureaucratism in the Soviet Union and the CCP's reckless strategy of armed rebellion in China.[11] All these actions may be justified from a personal and moral point of view, but not from a political one. Following this line of argument, Chen could only arrive at the conclusion that he himself should not have taken part in political activities and become the sponsor of the Communist Party from the very beginning. At any rate, after 1927 Chen resigned from the CCP leadership and concluded his political career.[12] The political maturity of the CCP—which may be understood as its primary achievement of that time—was obtained through Communist Party's abandonment of Chen or Chen's abandonment of the Communist Party.

Armed Rebellions and Soviet Establishments

As soon as the "banning cover" of the KMT-CCP alliance was lifted, the organizational and ideological influences the Communists had built up among workers, peasants, and soldiers naturally burst out in the fierce confrontations with the KMT. The later months of 1927 and the next two years (1928 and 1929) witnessed a dozen armed rebellions organized by the Communists, mainly in South China. Although most of them suffered defeats or setbacks at the hands of the superior KMT troops and although none could have achieved its goal of winning back a nationwide revolution

Territory Bases of the Communist Party in South China, 1930–1932

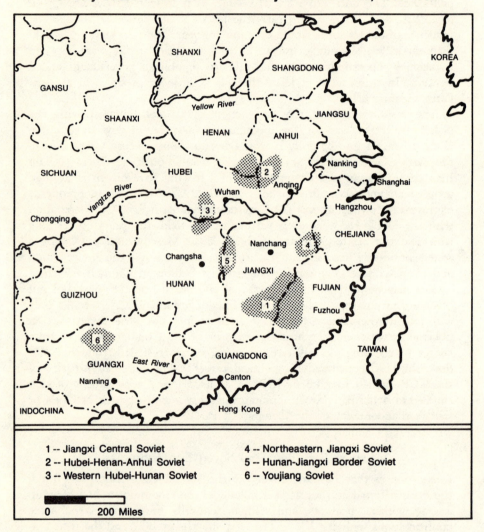

1 -- Jiangxi Central Soviet   4 -- Northeastern Jiangxi Soviet
2 -- Hubei-Henan-Anhui Soviet   5 -- Hunan-Jiangxi Border Soviet
3 -- Western Hubei-Hunan Soviet   6 -- Youjiang Soviet

0   200 Miles

immediately, these rebellions can be understood as modestly successful in the sense that they brought forth to the CCP an entirely new prospect: the creation of military forces led by the Communists and of revolutionary bases held by the Communists. Space allows only a brief introduction of some most outstanding armed rebellions and establishment of Soviets which had strategic impacts on the Communist movement at the time of their inception or in the years to follow.

While other approaches to understanding the Communist rebellions in the late 1920s are possible, here their relationship with the CCP leadership is taken as the criterion by which to classify these rebellions into one of two groups: either the early, large-scale uprisings directly organized by the Party Center or the later, smaller ones sponsored by local Communist cadres. Generally speaking, the results of both types of rebellion were more or less the same: the formation of military bases in the countryside. However, if success or failure of a political action is defined on the basis of agreement or disagreement between its original objective and its final achievement, then the uprisings of the first type failed because they were intended to produce a national revolution and none achieved such a goal. Uprisings of the second type, on the other hand, were often a modest success since they were designed simply to create power and influence on the local level, which some of them indeed did. In other words, the 'Communist rebellion' of the late 1920s was just transformed into the 'Soviet movement' of the early 1930s, no more and no less.

The Nanchang Uprising, the first and biggest, started in August 1927, involving three armies of about 20,000 men in total. In October on their way to Swatow—a port city on the southeast coast from which the Communists thought they could easily receive Russian aid and create their own Northern Expedition—the insurgent troops were fatally defeated by the combined forces of the Guangdong and Guangxi armies. Most rebel leaders who were closely related to the Party Center abandoned their troops and fled to either Hong Kong or Shanghai. Of the survivors, 2,000 retreated westward under the command of Zhu De. After several months of humiliating but necessary affiliation with Fan Kaisheng—commander of a local army and a friend of Zhu—at Shaoguan in Guangdong, Zhu eventually moved to join forces with Mao Zedong in the Jinggang Mountains at the Hunan-Jiangxi border in April 1928.[13] The united efforts of Zhu and Mao resulted in establishment of a Red Army and a rural military base, from which the later Jiangxi Soviet eventually grew. As for Mao, he brought to the Jinggang Mountains the remnants of the Autumn Harvest Uprising in Hunan in September 1927. Before his union with Zhu, Mao had owed the preservation of his troops in the Jinggang Mountains in large part to an alliance with two local peasant troops led by Wang Zuo and Yuan Wencai. Thus, an affiliation with local military forces helped both Zhu and Mao survive, but only subsequent Soviet construction would provide the dynamic power for their rapid rise in the future.

Another group of the Nanchang Uprising survivors—less than 1,000 men—entered the Dongjiang area in Guangdong in early October 1927, under the guidance of division commander Dong Lang. Encouraged by the arrival of strong reinforcement troops, the native Peasant Revolutionary Army headed by Lin Daowen rose up in their third attempt at rebellion and immediately captured two county seats—Haifeng and Lufeng—in late October. Soon afterwards, the Party Center appointed Peng Pai as the secretary of the CCP Special Committee of Dongjiang Prefecture and proclaimed the founding of the Haifeng and Lufeng Soviets.

With the arrival of another defeated division from the Canton Uprising in December 1927, the Dongjiang Soviet had become, in the eyes of the Party Center, the most precious and promising achievement of the movement until the final destruction of this base in February 1928. In its heyday, this base area possessed two divisions of armed forces and controlled a territory of four counties. Partly because of its unfavorable geographic location—sitting on the east coast, it proved more easily attacked by the Nationalists than aided by the Russians, and partly because of its poor leadership—Peng Pai was a Communist veteran experienced in social organization but unversed in military leadership—the Soviet was crushed. Peng fled to Shanghai, passing the Party secretary position back to Lin Daowen and leaving a small contingent of guerrillas commanded by Gu Dacun to fight in the mountains. Despite the heroic effort of Lin and Gu, the Dongjiang Soviet permanently lost its vigor and vitality in the Communist movement.[14]

Just as the Party Center's military confidence was dampened by the debacles of the Nanchang Revolt, the Autumn Harvest Uprising, the Canton Commune, and the Dongjiang Soviet, interest in armed struggle was aroused among local Communist cadres. A new group of Communist uprisings, less ambitious but more appropriate, occurred from late 1927 onwards. These uprisings were organized by native Communists in response to the general call, but not under the direct leadership, of the Party Center. Fang Zhimin's uprising in northwest Jiangxi was among the earliest. Contrary to some historians' allegations, Fang did not work in any salient Party capacity until he became the secretary of a 'five-county committee' in charge of a peasant uprising in his native county Yiyang. The uprising broke out at the end of 1927 and, after the initial dislocations in early 1928, the peasant rebels created a regional Soviet government headed by Fang and a regiment of the 'worker-peasant revolutionary army' under Shao Shiping. From middle 1928 to early 1930, the Northwest Jiangxi Soviet underwent slow but steady expansion under the close scrutiny of the CCP Jiangxi Provincial Committee but with only minimal involvement of the Party

Center.[15] Shielding the Jiangxi Soviet from KMT attacks seems to have been one reason for Fang's slow growth, but being familiar with the local conditions ensured his continuous survival.

Another significant uprising initiated by local Communist cadres occurred in Huangan and Macheng, both in eastern Hubei. Led by native Communists Fu Xiangyi, Pan Zhongru, Wu Guangjie, and Wang Shusheng (among others), the insurgent peasants captured the two county seats and formed a Soviet government and a revolutionary army in late 1927. The rebels were put down as quickly as they rose up. Less than a hundred men survived to flee and hide in the Dabie Mountains until May 1928, when they came out to rebuild a Soviet base in Guangshan with a division of armed peasants. A year later, when this division grew strong enough to assume the title of the 7th Red Army, it aroused the Party Center's interest. Army commander Xu Xiangqian was sent down to assume leadership. In the adjoining regions of southern Henan and western Anhui two more peasant rebellions arose, respectively in Shangnan in May 1929 and in Liuan and Heshan in January 1930. Each uprising produced one division subordinate to Xu Xiangqian's army. Thus in the two years between 1928 and 1930, the Hubei-Henan-Anhui border area—or the Eyuwan Soviet— rose to become a major strategic base of the Communist movement.[16] Its potential for future growth proved even greater. From a defensive point of view, this area standing between North China and South China could possibly mitigate military pressures from both the KMT Central Army and the northern warlords, while offensively it could seek expansion in the vast northern and eastern regions and attack in the western and southern directions along the Peking-Hankou Railway and the Yangtze River Valley.

In January 1928, Zhou Yiqun and He Long retreated to their home towns on the Hunan-Hubei border to promote a peasant rebellion. They arrived at Jianli in western Hubei and gathered together a few local forces scattered in the countryside but failed to capture the county seat. They led the troops to western Hunan, where He Long was born and had stayed as an army officer for several years before the Northern Expedition. Helped by former subordinates and acquaintances, He expanded his troops to 3,000 men and captured the county of Sangzhi in March 1928. In the face of local army and police attacks, however, the patched together Communist forces lost two consecutive battles. Zhou escaped east to return to Hubei alone, while He led the remaining troops of about 100 men west to the Hunan-Hubei border, where he fought back and forth for the next two years. In May 1929, the Hunan-Hubei border base covered two entire counties and parts of others. The troops were named the 3rd Red Army. In the meantime, Zhou managed to establish another Soviet base in Honghu of Hubei and the 6th Red Army.[17] Up to mid-1930, this broad area was regarded as an important Soviet domain, second only to Mao's Jiangxi

Soviet. The creation of the Western Hunan-Hubei Soviet (Xiangexi Soviet) should be largely credited to He Long's personal relations and influences in the area. And yet, as a Nationalist officer newly converted to Communism, He seemed too much accustomed to both abiding by old military norms and ignoring political work on the one hand, and too ready to comply with Party Center directives without adequate independent initiatives on the other. Such a situation probably contributed to this base area's lacking the vitality and momentum of some other Soviets.

The Pingjiang Uprising, led by Peng Dehuai and Deng Daiyuan in July 1928, revitalized an old strategy of Communist rebellion: to incite mutinies within the KMT armies. Peng was a regiment commander in a KMT local army and, through the agitation of Deng, a Communist agent, he led his entire regiment of 3,000 men to join the Communists at the city of Pingjiang in Hunan. A three month-long clash with the government troops reduced Peng's 5th Red Army to no more than 2,000. In November, Peng and Deng decided to transfer their main force to unite with Mao and Zhu in the Jinggang Mountains. The remaining troops were placed under Huang Gonglue's command to conduct guerrilla warfare; later they established the Hunan-Hubei-Jiangxi Soviet.[18]

Further to the South, two more mutinies occurred in Baise and Longzhou of Guangxi under the leadership of Deng Xiaoping, Zhang Yunyi, Yu Zuoyu and Li Mingrui. The Baise Uprising brought about the Youjiang Soviet and the 7th Red Army in late 1929, while the Longzhou Uprising set up the Zuojiang Soviet and the 8th Red Army in early 1930. For a short while, the two Red Armies totalled about 8,000 men occupying a vast territory of a dozen counties. But because the whole area was isolated from other Communist forces and thus countering Nationalist pressures on all sides—and perhaps also because Deng Xiaoping was the special commissioner entrusted by the Party Center with the general responsibility and thus appeared more interested in bringing the troops north to the Communist mainstream than maintaining a single base area in the distant south, the Youjiang and Zuojiang Soviets were from the beginning in a state of flux.[19]

Exceptionally and yet reasonably, two peasant uprisings occurred in Shaanxi province, one in Qingjian in November 1927 and another in Weinan and Huaxian in April 1928, and constituted some rare cases in North China. These rebellions were thoroughly defeated and did not result in formation of any enduring Soviet bases or regular Red Army units until after 1930. The early Communist leaders in this province included native Shaanxians Du Heng, Yang Guodong, Liu Zhidan, Xie Zichang and others. Their local acquaintance with people and armies sustained their continuous guerrilla activities in a few rural spots, though geographic isolation from the central Communist movement hindered rapid expansion.[20]

Features and Patterns of Soviet Revolution

Contemporary Communist politicians and later historians have discussed a variety of factors justifying the formation and expansion of the Soviet movement in China in the 1930s. By consensus, these factors can be assigned to one of two categories: objective conditions and subjective efforts. The first category may include the jealousy and rivalry among various military factions in the Nationalist government, and the political vacuum and autonomy of the Chinese countryside. Of these conditions, the latter seemed less apparent but more portentous. For much of Chinese history, the rural society remained a domain independent of the state government and one offering various possibilities for peasant rebels, secret associates, local despots, bandits and warlords to challenge the government's authority. These possibilities were turned—through the sophisticated agitations of Communists—into the dazzling reality of a mass revolutionary movement.

The Chinese Communist Party was never a monolithic entity, and Chinese Soviet movements in different areas might vary widely in nature. In a different sort of study, these divergences within the Soviet movement might be a subject matter of focal attention. More interesting for the present study, however, are the common features that can be found in the Soviet movement in the late 1920s and early 1930s in general.

Party Leadership. The need for exclusive leadership of the Communist Party over the Chinese revolution was one of the basic lessons the Communists had learned in the late 1920s, and would stress throughout the 1930s.[21] The leaders of the Nanchang Uprising were scolded after its failure for continuing to apply the name of KMT Revolutionary Committee; Mao Zedong upheld only the banner of the Communist Party at the Autumn Harvest Uprising; the Canton Uprising called for establishment of a municipal Soviet or Commune—all these gestures marked a process of ever increasing emphasis on the CCP's independent leadership. By 1928, this phase had already left a clear mark on Communist jargon: freshly converted Communist officers He Long and Peng Dehuai would need to recite such amiable remarks as "Listen to the Party's words" and "Follow the Party's steps." Apart from showing a strong determination to separate from and fight against the KMT, the emphasis on the CCP's sole leadership intensely stimulated Marxist-Leninist type ideological propaganda, social and economic reform, mass mobilization, militant organization, and strict discipline—especially among military leaders and local cadres.

The terms 'Communism' and 'Communist Party' were in the vocabulary but beyond the comprehension of ordinary peasants and soldiers. The Communist Party was an association of the poor, and Communism meant each poor man could get a piece of land—this might be the extent of their understanding.[22] Nonetheless, even this limited understanding could be a sufficient justification for them to join the Communists in building up revolutionary bases, and fighting against the Nationalist government with high spirits and enormous energy.

More significant than its ideological implications were the practical functions of the Communist Party. The Party system played an efficient role as an internal agency. After entering a new location, the Red Army would first get in touch with underground Party branches to gather information and obtain supplies of material and labor. Before leaving an old site, at the very minimum it would make arrangements for a secret Party network for future reference. Within the Soviet base and the Red Army, Party members functioned as leaders, supervisors, agitators, and model workers and fighters; they thus became, in their own words, "a core force" and "vanguards," rallying the masses around them to carry out the Party Center's orders.

Army Build-Up. The necessity of armed struggle or the application of military force was another basic lesson the Communists had learned during the period following the CCP-KMT collaboration—in which their loose mass organizations were crushed by the strong Nationalist troops in a few months, with little competent resistance.[23] After 1927, the military confrontation with the Nationalist Government was apparent, and there was no need to chant repeatedly on the necessity of military struggle; creating a new type of armed force capable of effectively conducting the war and making the revolution became a far more pressing concern.

The revolutionary character of the Red Army was later summarized by the Communists in the 'three basic relations': between military tasks and political work, between the army and the people, and between the officers and the soldiers. Those in the army were taught to be not only a combat unit but also a revolutionary propaganda team, a political organization and an economic production unit. They were taught that they were fighting not merely to win battles, but to liberate the oppressed classes from the exploiting classes and the Chinese nation as a whole from the imperialist powers. To enhance political control in the Red Army, the political commissar and CCP committee systems were implemented: extending from the platoon to the army headquarters, they supervised military leadership at each level. The army was to serve, unite with, and never encroach on the property or rights of the people. Strict 'dos' and 'don'ts' were instituted as policy in the Red Army: from "Fill up the people's water pail before you leave" to "Don't take a bath in a female's sight."[24] Everyone in the Red Army, officers and soldiers alike, were supposed to be equal comrades; the same uniform and the same pension were assigned to everybody, and regular meetings were to subject both officers and soldiers—theoretically, if not in practice—to constant criticism and self-criticism.

Soviet Construction. The Russian term 'Soviet' was first included in the Communist lexicon during the rebellion in Dongjiang in October 1927, and it was later adopted by all the other Communist groups. When first encountered, this term puzzled the peasants, some even took it to be an individual leader's name.[25] However, the feeling of mystery and awe engendered by this foreign word also evoked respect and honor, much like the response of their ancestors to the names Buddha and Jesus. Once they got a clearer idea of its practices, the peasants threw themselves into the Soviet movement with amazing enthusiasm.

Ideally speaking, the Soviet, or representative council of workers, peasants, and soldiers, was supposed to be a fully democratic system enabling all laboring masses to participate fully in government administration and policy making.[26] Actually, leaders of the Soviet at the county or base area level were normally appointed by the Party and the Army from above and functioned as a regional government with little involvement of the mass of peasants in the village, let alone workers and soldiers. Nonetheless, the new government system introduced a more collective form of administration than had ever before existed. On the lower levels of district, township and village, peasants elected their own Soviet chiefs and thus enjoyed considerable opportunities for administrative participation. There the Soviet functioned more like a residential or professional association.

Thus the Soviet system served as a bridge, linking the Communist Party and the Red Army on the top with social organizations and mass movements at the bottom. Whether or not the Communists really meant to create a better, or more democratic, government system remains debatable, but it seems incontestable that the Soviet played a very active and positive role in the Communists' consolidating their revolutionary bases and mobilizing the peasantry to support their rebellious warfare.

Land Reform. The uneven distribution of land ownership—a phenomenon not unique to any particular area, nor to any particular age—had inculcated in the Chinese peasants a psychology of land cultism which might have transcended their economic needs; few rural rebellions in Chinese history won decent successes without calling for some kind of land reform to attract poor peasants. The serious concern of the Communists with land reform can be recognized in the resolutions of almost all CCP Center conferences at that time.[27] In fact, the entire decade from 1927 to 1937 was termed by the Communists the period of the Land Revolution, or more bluntly, the Land War.

Although there had been constant debates within the Party and Army leadership over an appropriate attitude toward the middle and rich peasants, the basic principle of confiscating the landlords' property (primarily the land itself) and distributing it to the poor peasants had never been questioned in any agrarian reform program of the CCP in the early 1930s. That seemed already enough. Together with the Soviet government apparatus, the land reform policy served as the very basic foundation from which the Communists were able to propagate their "mass line" and conduct their "people's war" in the countryside.

The Communists faced a number of important questions at this juncture, questions that were neither easily raised nor easily answered. Should the Party leadership be, or had it ever been, ideologically or politically exclusive? Could the competence of the Red Army be considered as proportional to its revolutionary zeal? Should, or did, the Soviet system aim for democratic participation or power concentration? Were land reform and the mass line the magic wands which would instantly bring about a victorious national revolution? Ultimately, should these revolutionary operations be considered sacred ends, or merely the secular means to other, perhaps less exalted, goals?

But after making even a superficial comparison between the positions of the CCP and the KMT regarding the above mentioned issues (keeping in mind the facts that until the early 1930s the KMT could not reach down with its Party branches below the level of the provincial capital; KMT troops, with all the characteristics of a professional government army, had nothing to do with the common people or the social affairs of the countryside; KMT administration at the local level remained basically a "one-man-one-government" system, in which the provincial governor, the prefecture commissioner and the county magistrate remained in full charge with assistance from only a few clerks; and the land reform issue was even more out of the question for the KMT), it seems clear that all the revolutionary features and strategies of the Communists substantially enhanced their political strength and gave them a significant edge in their military competition with the Nationalists.

On the other hand, it should also be recognized that any increase of strength of one party did not necessarily ensure victory in the war. Defeats and victories in war are determined by the relative strengths, and exertions of these strengths, of both warring parties. Far from being a self-contained entity, the Soviet movement actually constituted one side in a civil war. Its rise and fall, or the patterns of the war, were decided not only by the strength and efforts of the Communists but also, perhaps even primarily, by those of the Nationalists who were wielding state power.

Until early 1930, both the Red Armies and the Soviet bases were rather small, active in only certain isolated spots, mostly in the South. No substantial strategic connections had yet been established among the base areas, and the Red Army as a whole had not yet reached a position of direct engagement with the KMT Central Army. Each Red Army and Soviet base had to compete with the KMT military forces within their province: the local militia, the security police, and the provincial army.

The military system of the KMT government was extremely complex, and it varied from one time and place to another. For the purpose of this study, attention is limited to the South and the Central South, the area where the KMT Central Government wielded great influence and also where the CCP rebellion was most active. Before its reorganization in 1930, the biggest KMT military unit was the army, and the basic mobile unit was the regiment. Apart from the KMT Central Army of about 500,000 soldiers which were directly controlled by Chiang Kai-shek as a national mobile force, there were approximately 2-3 armies, 6-9 divisions, and 18-27 regiments in each province, totaling some 60,000 to 90,000 soldiers.[28] These troops were normally under the command of the provincial governor and based in the provincial capital and some prefectural seats. To guard the county seat, there was no regular army but instead the security brigade and police squad, averaging 300 to 500 men. Down in the district level were local militia sponsored by the local gentry and landlords. As their counterparts, in each Soviet base area the Communists would have a regular Red Army of 1,000 to 5,000 men fighting on the prefecture/county level, a Red Guard brigade of 50 to 200 on the county/district level, and some Youth Guard contingents in the towns and the villages.[29]

Content (or inert) with military normality, the KMT provincial armies would stay in the cities where they were deployed, leaving the Communists to agitate the peasants, set up the Soviets, and clash with local militias and security police in the countryside. Without the intervention of the provincial army, the Communists would gradually annihilate the local militia, expand their armed force and territory, and then make an attempt at the county seat. Often failing in the face of the security police, the Communist rebels had little to lose; once they succeeded in taking over a county seat and wiping out a security brigade, it would become a definite victory with important implications.

After one or more county seats fell into the Communists' hands, a 'bandit suppression campaign' would be organized by the provincial government or, if it happened in a border area, by the concerned provinces. In the late 1920s, seldom could any Red Army win over a whole KMT army or annihilate a whole KMT regiment. Defeated by the larger and better equipped KMT troops, the Red Army would retreat to the sub-county level or transfer to another location. The KMT offensive troops would recover the lost county seats or expel the Communists: in either case, they would happily declare a victory and quickly withdraw, leaving the Communists to recover their old base or create a new one later.

Military contradictions and conflicts within the Nationalist regime created the most advantageous conditions for the Communist rebels. Whenever a war broke out between the KMT Central Army and other KMT military cliques, most of the provincial armies would be transferred to the front and the rest would converge to protect the provincial capital, leaving the prefecture and county levels without regular garrison troops. Under these circumstances, the Red Army could use the opportunity to occupy new territory and recruit new troops.

A general survey of the KMT-CCP confrontation up to the early 1930s shows that the Nationalist government in the Communist-infected provinces of South and Central South China remained in relatively stable military control. When the Communist forces became a serious threat, the provincial army would set out on a suppression expedition. It won more individual battles than it lost; in a full suppression campaign they almost always succeeded. Nevertheless, they could seldom uproot all the Communist forces and influences in a specific area. Relying on their close links with peasant masses, attractive agrarian programs, high morale and strict organization, the Communist rebels would soon recover their strength and emerge with even greater momentum.

More through adaptation to the existing conditions than the ingenious inventions of particular leaders, the Red Army adopted the strategy of guerrilla warfare. When a strong attacking force approached, the small Red Army would necessarily step back a bit, engaging with the KMT troops in the countryside; Red Army men would move around to make some nibbling counterattacks, and when the enemy troops began to withdraw, they would naturally pop out of hiding and chase the enemy. These kinds of guerrilla strategies and tactics were more or less applied by all the Red Army groups in their incubative years—not merely by Mao's Jinggang Mountain troops.[30]

Mao Zedong and the Jiangxi Central Soviet

At the Emergency Conference of the Party Center in Hankou on August 7, 1927, Mao Zedong and Peng Gongda were both elected alternate members of the Politburo and dispatched to Hunan to organize the Autumn Harvest Uprising—Mao as the special commissioner of the CCP Central Committee and Peng as the secretary of the Hunan CCP Committee.[31] Frequent Communications between the Party Center and the Hunan Committee in the following month, as published later in *Central Newsletters*, show the former's high admiration for and then deep disappointment with the latter at the time.[32] Mao did make a timely arrival at the provincial capital of Changsha after the August 7 Conference, and instead of staying in Changsha handling meetings and papers, he immediately left for the countryside of eastern Hunan. As it happened, the wishful projects of province-wide uprisings planned by Peng Gongda and his coterie were abortive everywhere except the Hunan-Jiangxi border area where Mao had gone.[33] This does not mean that Mao himself created any armed forces or initiated any peasant uprisings. Although he had indeed been appointed by the provincial committee as a division commander in early September 1927, this appointment was only titular and anyhow was soon abolished. By that time a division of 'the Worker and Peasant Army' had already come into existence in the Hunan-Jiangxi border, consisting of two regiments of former KMT soldiers and two regiments of rebellious peasants and workers. The Autumn Harvest Uprising was no more than a "calling together" of some extant troops, first to seize the nearby county seats and then to attack the provincial capital. It was only after the failure of their initial operations that Mao came in to collect the survivors at Wenshi, reorganized them at Sanwan, and directed them to retreat eastward into Jiangxi. Under Mao's leadership, the newly named '1st Division of the Worker and Peasant Revolutionary Army' arrived at the Jinggang Mountains in October 1927.[34]

Mao's retreat to Jiangxi after the Autumn Harvest Uprising might have been motivated by contingent factors, and his alliance with Wang Zuo and Yuan Wencai at the Jinggang Mountains might have been fortuitous. Mao could hardly be so opportunistic as to have allied with Wang and Yuan as two 'local bandits'—a version which some CCP politicians once proposed with subtle reluctance, but which KMT historians always seem ready to accept. In fact, Wang and especially Yuan were leaders of two of the numerous 'peasant self-defense brigades' which had emerged during the Northern Expedition years. Clashing with the local landlords and defying the KMT government authorities, these peasant troops were ideologically and practically inclined to join the Communists. Wang and Yuan can therefore be called 'local bandits' only in the sense that the terms might be applied to all Communists, as KMT historians also claim.

In April 1928 Zhu De led his own troops and a peasant army from southern Hunan to join forces with Mao in the Jinggang Mountains— partly on the Party Center's instructions and partly for Zhu's military defeats in Hunan earlier that year. The united 4th Red Army was immediately founded with Zhu as the general commander and Mao as the Party representative. The Army had about 10,000 men and consisted of six regiments: two of Zhu's men, two of southern Hunan peasants Zhu had brought with him, one of Mao's men and one of Wang and Yuan's Jiangxi natives.[35] In the next three months, Mao and Zhu used the vastness of the Jinggang Mountains as the central base from which they dispatched some army units to the surrounding counties, developed Party organizations there, mobilized the peasant masses, carried out land reforms, and built up a Soviet government.

Almost as a rule, friction would follow unification. The Hunan CCP Committee wanted the 4th Red Army to return for another uprising; the peasants from southern Hunan wanted to go back home; and Zhu De's men wanted their independence. The two regiments of southern Hunan peasants had run away by late May 1928. In late July, when the joint forces of the Jiangxi and Hunan Armies approached for a suppression campaign, Zhu De departed with his two regiments to Hunan. Mao was left helpless. But through the initial split and defeat and the subsequent reunion of the 4th Army, Zhu and Mao developed a more mature and stable relationship. The troops of Zhu and Mao were finally merged into one army unit so that one could scarcely tell whose troops belonged to whom. September 1928 to January 1929 was for the 4th Red Army and the Hunan-Jiangxi border base a period of smooth and rapid growth.[36]

In November 1928, Peng Dehuai and Deng Daiyuan led the 5th Red Army of about 1,000 men to the Jinggang Mountains. Peng claimed in his memoirs that he decided to come to the Jinggang Mountains because he respected Mao's abilities. In fact, the Party Center's instructions and the 5th Red Army's unfavorable situation might have had more to do with his decision. Peng was appointed vice commander of the 4th Army and Deng vice Party representative. In January 1929, when another suppression campaign (jointly sponsored by the provincial governments of Jiangxi, Hunan and Fujian and including about 12 to 18 regiments of 25,000 to 35,000 men) approached, Peng and Wang Zuo were left to defend the Jinggang Mountains while Mao and Zhu led the main forces to fight outside the base. Leaving aside possible factional motives, this military arrangement stemmed from the notion that if Mao and Zhu could win a decisive battle on the external front, the encircling KMT troops—especially those of the Jiangxi army—would necessarily withdraw from the Jinggang Mountains. Thus not only would the encirclement end, but the enemy troops could be sandwiched between Peng and Wang from behind and Zhu and Mao in front.[37]

Instead of reaching Ji'an and winning a decisive battle, the main force of the 4th Red Army commanded by Mao and Zhu was trounced by the Jiangxi army at Dayu on their way to southern Jiangxi. After this they lost three consecutive battles before winning one at Dabodi in February 1929. They were forced to move further south to the Jiangxi-Fujian-Guangdong border and naturally were unable to fight their way back to the Jinggang Mountains. Fortunately, a war between Chiang Kai-shek and Li Zongren, the Guangxi warlord, broke out in May and all the KMT troops were called back at once. Under the advantageous conditions of the Chiang-Li War, with the coordinated CCP local forces in western Fujian led by Zhang Dingcheng, Deng Zihui and others and those in southern Jiangxi led by Liu Shiqi, Li Wenlin and others, Mao and Zhu managed to establish a new and bigger Soviet base in the Fujian-Jiangxi border area centered in the city of Ruijin.[38]

Left alone to defend the Jinggang Mountains, Peng Dehuai's troops suffered immensely in January 1929. Eventually he and his 300 men broke through the enemy's siege to flee south. Peng met Mao and Zhu at Ningdu in southern Jiangxi in March. Mao offered an apology for what had occurred in the Jinggang Mountains; Peng would not accept. He gathered his troops and returned north. The first union of Mao and Peng was thus ended, unpleasantly and yet not with open hostility. Peng resumed his title of the commander of the 5th Red Army and recovered the Hunan-Jiangxi border base in April. He moved back to the Hunan-Hubei-Jiangxi border in July, where he was warmly welcomed by his old subordinate Huang Gonglue. In October, Peng dispatched part of his army to southern Hubei. In less than six months, the 5th Army occupied three base areas and expanded its troops to more than 3,000 men.[39]

By the later months of 1929, the Jiangxi Central Soviet had assumed its preliminary shape. In a normal sense it consisted of four loosely connected Soviet bases in western Fujian, southern Jiangxi, the Hunan-Jiangxi border and the Hunan-Hubei-Jiangxi border. This area constituted the backbone of the Soviet movement in China. In this area were three influential Communist forces: the 4th Red Army of Mao and Zhu, the 5th Red Army of Peng and Deng, and the local Party, Soviet and Army personnel. Potentially, Mao was the most powerful and authoritative figure in this broad area, but it was through the Li Lisan adventure in 1930 that the Central Soviet was formally established, along with Mao's general leadership.

For many years in China, official historians have taken the 'two-line struggle' as the basic theme of CCP history. In the Jiangxi period, Mao was assumed to have represented a correct line in opposition to the Party Center's erroneous leftist line. Some observers outside China tried to avoid recitation of official Communist versions but were unable to improve upon them. As a result, they would drift freely in the central current established by Communist historians. They were likely to say that throughout the period of 1927-1935 Mao had persistently built up his own military domain in opposition to the Party Center, both organizationally and politically. To such vague and abstract questions as "Had Mao been against or for the Party Center in the Jiangxi Soviet years?" however, there can be no simplistic positive or negative answer. More valuable historical studies should examine how to surpass this superficial level and probe into the depth where historical figures participating in historical events are less statuesque but more truly alive.[40]

In view of Mao's stature in the CCP, the early Jiangxi years saw him descending from the Party Center down to the local Party branch. Mao was among the founders the Communist Party in 1921, and he became a member of the Central Committee at the Third National Congress in 1923. He entered the Politburo in 1927 on the eve of the Autumn Harvest Uprising. After this, Mao seems to have fallen to even lower local levels, first the commissioner to a province, then the secretary of a front committee, the Party representative in a Soviet base, the political commissar in a Red Army, and so on. But needless to say, this process of demotion was at the same time promotion from a titular position to an actual power holder.

Mao's power rise in the Soviet and the Red Army was due not only to his own capability and efforts but also to the Party Center's influence and assistance. In September 1927, Mao was able to summon together the defeated troops of the Autumn Harvest Uprising under his leadership in Wenshi mainly because of his seniority in the Party. In April and November 1928 it was on the Party Center's instructions that Zhu De and Peng Dehuai came to the Jinggang Mountains and thus decisively enhanced Mao's strength. Zhu then had 9,000 men in contrast with Mao's 1,000, but once again Mao's reputation and seniority in the Party helped him gain the upper hand in the union of these forces at first; his capability made him a dominating figure only later. A similar situation can be found in the formation of the 1st Army Corps in February 1930 and the First Front Army in August 1930. For the Party Center, Mao might look like a man with strong military power, but in the eyes of the Red Army rank and file, Mao was the symbol of the Party Center leadership. This dual function may serve as a key to understanding Mao in the early Jiangxi Soviet years.

Up until early 1930 Mao's relationship with the Party Center was somewhat loose, indirect, and infrequent. His communication with the Party Center was normally through the local Party organizations, and occurred only a few times each year. In these communications Mao was interested in the conditions of his own Red Army more than in national or international affairs. The latter were raised only in connection with the former. As for the Party Center, although as the supreme authority it did issue instructions and suggestions, it seldom made any mandatory demands which might substantially influence Mao. In fact, the Party Center sometimes did not even know Mao and his roaming troops' whereabouts.[41] Simply put, Mao could not receive either much concrete assistance or much direct interference from the Party Center. The Party Center might serve as a spiritual inspiration for his men and, in return, Mao would occasionally donate to the Party Center some financial aid in the form of gold or silver through some secret routes from the Soviet to Shanghai.

Common revolutionary objectives and ideology brought the Party Center and Mao many common interests. After all, they were all Communists. The disagreements and contradictions between them stemmed in part from the disparity of their respective positions: the Party Center as the supreme leadership was more concerned with national and international conditions and with broad theoretical arguments whereas Mao, as the leader of a rebellious army fighting in the rural areas, was mainly responsible for local matters of practical concern.

Both the Party Center and Mao talked about the high tides of the revolution, but for the former these pertained to Marxist-Leninist analyses of the world situation, while for the latter they meant the plausibility of expecting another war to break out between the KMT generals and the warlords. Both were talking about the land reform, but while the former took it as an ultimate end of eliminating the 'feudal system', the latter took it as an expedient method to draw the peasants into his military operation. At times Mao was no less anxious than the Party Center to take over Jiangxi province and some large cities, but at other junctures he was reluctant to do either. Mao called for a policy of total confiscation and equal distribution of land to win over the masses in a newly occupied area at one time but stressed the necessity of applying milder agrarian policies in order to improve social stability and economic productivity in the Soviet base at another; he stressed the Party leadership over the military struggle, but he also stressed the military priority over anything else; he credited the peasants as the main force in the Chinese Revolution, and he also scorned the peasants' conservatism and narrow-mindedness. Within the general framework set up by the Party Center and followed by all the Soviets and the Red Armies, Mao's ideas and remarks changed from time to time and from place to place. Underlying these seeming inconsistencies was his political realism—in contrast with the Party Center's revolutionary idealism. In the Jiangxi Soviet years, as Mao reached political maturity, so did his general strategy for Communist revolution: to carry out military struggles to gain state power, nothing more and nothing less. All the other economic, social and ideological measures were necessary, but their necessity arose solely from their usefulness for achieving this primary goal, not for any merit of their own. In other words, social revolution was only a means and not the end; the final end was to defeat the Nationalist Government and take over the national political rule.

As history has witnessed, this strategy of Mao's indeed corresponded with the political reality in China and also the true interest of the Communist Party. Just as the Party Center gradually moved from Shanghai toward the Jiangxi Soviet, so the strategy of the Party Center as a whole gradually moved toward the strategy of Mao. While both Mao and the Party Center might have followed the same general direction, it was Mao who took the lead at each step and at each moment during the whole process. Thus at any specific step or moment, they might contrast with or even contradict each other.

The Adventure of the Li Lisan Center

The Sixth Congress of the CCP, convened in Moscow in July 1928, had two basic premises: that military confrontation with the KMT government had become an unchangeable reality for and an unquestionable policy of the Communist Party, but equally that reckless putschism as pursued by the Qu Qiubai Center had suffered defeats—Soviet movements born out of the armed rebellions would require more time to pay off. These two somewhat contradictory premises synthesized in the moderate nature of the Sixth Congress which can be identified in the resolutions as well as in the new Party Center leadership adopted at the congress. Thus elected or selected to the Politburo were seven veteran Communists: Qu Qiubai, Su Zhaozheng, Xiang Zhongfa, Zhou Enlai, Cai Hesen, Zhang Guotao and Xiang Ying. Li Lisan, Peng Pai, and a few others were on the candidate list. After the Congress Zhang Guotao and Qu Qiubai remained in Moscow as CCP delegates in the Comintern; Su Zhaozheng also stayed at Moscow for treatment of severe pneumonia. All the other CCP leaders went back to Shanghai by various routes.[42]

Soon after the Sixth Congress, however, political situations both at home and abroad began to change in favor of a more radical line. The later months of 1928 witnessed a steady growth of the Red Armies in the Soviet bases, which brought the Communists an entirely new prospect. Even more decisively, Bukharin—the Comintern leader who supervised the CCP Sixth Congress—was gradually becoming a target of Stalin's attacks for his "rightist tendency" and "rich peasant line." A leftward trend against the moderate nature of the Sixth Congress traveled to the CCP Center, and first materialized in the form of Li Lisan's conflict with Cai Hesen. In November 1928, the debate resulted in leftist Li's replacement of rightist Cai as a Politburo member and head of the Propaganda Department. Cai was called to Moscow, and Li stepped into the leading circle.[43] Among the four Politburo members now at home, Xiang Zhongfa and Xiang Ying were proletarian figureheads, the real power was shared between Zhou Enlai and Li Lisan.

From the reorganization of the Politburo in November 1928 to the Second Plenum in June 1929, Zhou maintained the upper hand; the moderate line of the Sixth Congress was basically preserved. Meanwhile, the anti-rightist wind blowing from Moscow kept pushing the sail of the CCP Center in Shanghai. As the Stalin-Bukharin struggle heated up, the period between June 1929 and April 1930 marked the second phase of the CCP Center's shift in line.[44] Zhou lost ground to Li, which resulted in a competitive period during which the moderate Zhou and the radical Li stood on a more or less equal basis. Some evidence for this analysis lies in Xiang Zhongfa's confession:

At the Second Plenum in September 1929, there were some arguments between Li Lisan and Zhou Enlai. They quarreled again two days after the Plenum. Though I did not quite support Li, I was not able to dissuade him. Afterwards, both the men often were at odds, and I always played the role of mediator and conciliator. After January, 1930 their quarrel grew even more intense. Unable to solve the problem, Zhou decided to leave for Moscow and make a report to the Comintern.[45]

Between Zhou's departure for Moscow in April 1930 and the CCP Third Plenum in September 1930, Li gained full control of the Party Center and his radical line reached its zenith. Up to that point, as Schwartz points out, the Comintern's influence had facilitated Li's ascent to the leading position and the CCP Center's adoption of Li's radical line.[46] In May 1930, Li Lisan convened two national conferences: one of the Red Army for concerted attacks on the large city of Wuhan and another of the Soviet delegates for the establishment of the Soviet Republic of China. On June 11, the CCP Politburo passed its famous (or infamous) resolution calling for the take-over of one or more provinces. The resolution is full of such extravagant statements on Chinese and world situations in Marxist-Leninist dogmas as:

> The various forms of contradictions and conflicts among the imperialists, now focused in China, are likely to sharpen and result in incurable economic and political crises, in ceaseless imbroglios among the warlords, in the collapse of the ruling class's foundations and in the increasing turning of the working class and the broad toiling masses toward revolution to seek their own emancipation. China is the weakest link in the ruling chain of world imperialism; it is the place where the volcano of the world revolution is most likely to erupt. Thus at the present time of ever aggravation of revolutionary crises all over the world, it is possible that the Chinese revolution will break out and the world revolution follow immediately.[47]

As the Li Lisan Center was seriously putting the radical line into practice, the Comintern leaders began to worry that Li might have gone too far. On July 16 Li sent a letter to the Comintern demanding formal approval of his entire strategy. A week later a reply did come. The Comintern's directive of July 23, 1930 to the CCP Central Committee was, as Hsiao Tso-liang points out, a signal of divergence between the Comintern and Li Lisan's radical operation.[48] Between the lines in this document, the Comintern leaders expressed a strong doubt that there was already a "nationwide revolutionary situation in China" and therefore intended to discourage, though still in vague terms, the CCP Center's strategy of attacking large industrial cities all at once.[49]

The Comintern's directive arrived just as Peng Dehuai's 5th Army Corps captured the provincial capital of Changsha, on July 28th. Li Lisan was very excited. Two Politburo conferences were quickly held August 1st and 3rd. The Comintern's instructions were scornfully rejected; the Comintern's agency in Shanghai—the Dalburo or the Far East Bureau—was blatantly condemned; and the Soviet Union was required to dispatch troops to help make the Chinese Revolution which was, after all, an important, if not the most important, part of the world revolution.[50]

The Comintern received the surprisingly good news of Changsha, celebrated it, and might have regretted its earlier conservative stand in the July 23 letter. A few days later, when Li Lisan's protest came, Changsha was already lost. The celebration was over, but resentment against Li Lisan remained. The pressing demands from Li Lisan, the loss of Changsha, the protest of the CI Far East Bureau, and the consultation with moderate Zhou Enlai at Moscow—all these led the Comintern leaders to the decision that Li's excessive operation should be checked. Zhou Enlai and Qu Qiubai were sent back to China in late August 1930.

The warfare at Changsha became the final judgment of Li Lisan's political destiny. From August 24 to September 12, Li desperately summoned all the major forces of the Red Army for another assault on the city. It lasted for weeks but eventually failed. Changsha could not be so easily taken, Li Lisan's leadership could. The Third Plenum was held in September, in which the Li Lisan adventure as a general policy came to the end.

Many authors of CCP history write about the disastrous failure of Li Lisan's line, but few have attempted to explain what this failure really represents. It is true that what happened in the latter months of 1930 was against Li's expectation and anticipation—Li lost his political fortune in September and was called to trial in Moscow in December. But in order to understand such a failure we should also judge it from a more impersonal angle. It must be ascertained, first, whether the Communist movement in China developed or retreated during Li's reign, and then in either case, whether Li's policy negatively or positively affected the process. Looking at the Li Lisan leadership as a whole, it seems that it was not as detrimental and destructive as has been commonly assumed—at least from the viewpoint of development of Red Armies and Soviets, which obviously represented the true momentum of the Communist Party at the time.

In June 1929 there were only two or three Communist troops bearing the title 'army', while the others could only be termed 'divisions' or 'regiments'. The Red Army troops totalled between 10,000 and 20,000, scattered in various places. The regular Red Army troops lacked discipline and weaponry, while the local Red Armies could only conduct 'hit and run' guerrilla raids. By early 1930 the entire Red Army had grown to 7 or 8 armies, 40,000 to 50,000 strong; and by June 1930, to 15 to 20 armies with 60,000 to 80,000 troops. In early August, when the Party call for a strategic attack on big cities, the Red Army amounted 10 to 15 armies totalling 80,000 to 100,000.[51]

Before 1930 no Red Army dared challenge a full KMT brigade of 2,000 to 3,000 men in a single battle nor did any Red Army troops dare to challenge and capture a city bigger than a prefectural seat. During and after 1930, they were able to do both. In other words, their fighting capacity and expertise developed from the ability to defeat the local police on the county level without the provincial army's interference to the capacity to overcome the provincial army on the provincial level without the KMT Central Army's interference.

Apart from the favorable conditions for the Communist rebellions or, more precisely, the outburst of the huge war among Chiang Kai-shek, Yan Xishan and Feng Yuxiang, there should be little doubt that the encouragements and instructions of the Li Lisan Party Center definitely contributed to the rapid growth, in quantity and in quality, of the Communist military forces in early 1930, especially among Red Army groups bearing a strong tradition of localism and conservatism.

The general growth of the Red Army during the Li Lisan leadership does not suggest that those Red Armies which followed the Li Lisan line all enjoyed equally rapid expansion or vice versa. In the Jiangxi Soviet, Peng Dehuai's 5th Red Army followed the Party Center's call more actively than Mao's 4th Red Army. Peng enlarged his troops from 1,000 in June 1929 to 3,000 in November 1929; from 5,000 in April 1930 to 8,000 in June 1930; and finally to 15,000 in August 1930. He took Changsha and lost it but recruited more than 7,000 soldiers. Mao's 4th Army was not quite eager to answer Li Lisan's call. At the same time, Mao's troops grew less rapidly from about 3,000 in June 1929 to 15,000 in August 1930. His troops would have been even smaller than that had they not absorbed Huang Gonglue's 3rd Army in June 1930, which originally was part of Peng's 5th Army.[52]

The Red Army in the Xiangexi Soviet was the most active. According to the Party Center's instructions, He Long's 3rd Army and Zhou Yiqun's 6th Army were combined into the 2nd Army Corps in May 1930. Soon after they abandoned their home bases and crossed the Yangtze River to begin joint attacks on Wuhan and Changsha. Eventually He and Zhou lost two thirds of their 20,000 soldiers. Xu Xiangqian's 1st Army in the Eyuwan Soviet's activity increased its strength from 3,000 in June 1930 to 6,000 in September 1930. After 1930, the Eyuwan Soviet replaced the Xiangexi Soviet as the second largest Communist base.[53]

Following this line of research, the need for a more balanced assessment of the positive and negative impacts of the Li Lisan line as well as its relations with the upsurges and setbacks of Communist forces arises. Taking the above listed facts into consideration, we should at least dispel the assessment of the Li Lisan leadership as an utter failure. The tragedy of Li as an individual lies in the fact that he was too obsessed with revolutionary fantasies to realize the real political relations he was necessarily involved with in China and in Moscow.

Another interesting but controversial subject is Mao's relationship with the Li Lisan line. The left and right trends represented by Li and Zhou within the Party Center and the ever increasing leftward course of the Party's general line through several stages should be kept in mind to avoid falling into superficial and unbalanced judgments. The exchange of two letters between the Party Center and Mao has been often referred to as evidence of confrontation between Li and Mao.[54] Now that the originals of letters are available, a more precise study becomes possible.

The letter of the Party Center to the Front Committee of the 4th Red Army dated February 7, 1929, was most probably drafted by Zhou Enlai, who was head of the Department of Organization and the General Office of the CCP Center at the time. This letter judged the current situation as still one of "stalemate between the revolutionary and the reactionary," called for leaders to "work on and win over the broad masses" as the Sixth Congress required, and suggested that Mao and Zhu let the troops and the 4th Army be divided into small squads in the countryside.[55] The April 5 letter of the Front Committee is a reply, obviously written by Mao in person, complaining that the Party Center's "evaluations of the objective condition as well as our subjective strength are both rather pessimistic" and stand for offensive activities to take over the entire Jiangxi in one year.[56]

It should be obvious that these letters show that at that period Mao criticized Zhou's conservative stand in the Party Center and supported, though perhaps equivocally, Li's radical position. As mentioned before, the upsurge of the Soviets and Red Armies in 1929 had indirectly facilitated Li's radical position in the Party Center. To be fair, Mao's main concern in the letter was his own army's strategic operation and not the factional relations within the Party Center. It should be further noted that the Party Center's letter was written in February 1929, right after the 4th Red Army's loss of the Jinggang Mountains base, and that the Front Committee's reply was issued in April 1929, after the 4th Army's rehabilitation in southern Jiangxi and western Fujian. These immediate military situations might also have influenced their respective—pessimistic and optimistic—positions.

From June to September 1929, Mao left the 4th Red Army and remained idly in western Fujian for three months as a result of joint opposition of Zhu De, Chen Yi and others. Chen Yi left Jiangxi for Shanghai. He met with Li and Zhou and gave them a detailed report on the 4th Army. Chen was instructed by both Li and Zhou that Mao's leadership in the 4th Army should be firmly supported. Returning to the Soviet base, Chen brought back a letter of instructions from the Party Center. In December Mao chaired the Ninth Conference of the 4th Army: the famous Gutian

Conference. The Party Center's letter, presumable drafted by Zhou Enlai, purported to guide and control the Soviet base and Red Army.[57] By interpreting the Party Center instructions to stress Party discipline, proletarian leadership, political work, etcetera, Mao attempted to consolidate his own leading position in the military in the 4th Army and stengthen his authority in the local Party and Soviet cadres.[58]

In his article "A Single Spark Can Start a Prairie Fire" or his personal letter to Lin Biao, (who was then a brigade commander in the 4th Army) on January 8, 1930, Mao complained about the "bad influences" of Party Center's "rightist spirit" as expressed in its February letter, but he seemed quite satisfied to find that "Since then, the directives of the Party Center have by and large been appropriate." Apart from the fact that Mao here pretended to be an infallible authority in evaluating the Party Center leadership even before one of his subordinate officers, the article shows that Mao remained, as previously, in favor of Li Lisan's radical position and against Zhou Enlai's moderate position.[59]

In February 1930, Mao still benefitted from the Party Center's radical line in Red Army reorganization and concentration. He employed the anti-rightist slogan to persuade the local cadres and officers to hand over their own power, and he was formally appointed Secretary of the General Front Committee in charge of general affairs in the Central Soviet area. It was not until later, when the Li Lisan Center ordered all the Red Armies, Mao's included, on a military expedition that Mao began to be at odds with Li.

The Party Center's or Li Lisan's basic idea was to bring all the Red Army troops under more concentrated leadership and then transfer all mobile forces to make an attack on Wuhan. Mao had no objection to the first action and thus the General Front Committee was formed with Mao as its head, but he did not support the second action for obvious reasons. Instead of transferring his troops to the north, he distributed them to the south and the east. To excuse himself to the Party Center, he referred to three brigades of the KMT army blocking the way north and concluded that "the 4th Army is unable to take the route north at this moment." Moreover, Mao drew up a three-month plan for distributing all his troops into the countryside of southern Jiangxi and western Fujian. "Under the present circumstances," Mao argued, "it would obviously be a sheer militarist line to concentrate our main forces on large combat actions, and it would obstruct the great task of mobilizing the masses and expanding the Soviets."[60]

The more directly Li Lisan tried to operate the 4th Army, the sharper the conflicts between the Party Center and Mao became. In April 1930 the Party Center warned Mao that "the 4th Army has been extremely slow in expanding its forces and the results are extremely unsatisfactory. The main reasons for such a situation are that first, you were unaware of your strong attachment to a conservative stand, and thus did not decide to quickly expand your forces; second, your untimely decision to distribute your forces to militarize the peasants; and third, you did not try all different ways to mobilize the peasants to join the Red Army troops."[61]

There must have been something in the Party Center's instructions which practically impressed Mao. Indeed, his 4th Army had not been aggressive enough and had not expanded as fast as some other Red Armies, particularly Peng Dehuai's 5th Army. Peng followed the Party Center's call more vigorously and therefore grew more aggressive than Mao. Between February 1930 and June 1930, Peng tripled his troops and took over a number of large and medium-sized cities.

On June 15, 1930, the Party Center, in even harsher terms, scolded Mao for being too conservative and urged his troops to turn north immediately. Ten days later, Mao suddenly changed to the other extreme. He summoned 36 senior officers in the 1st Army Corps, signed and published two solemn announcements, declaring an immediate northern expedition to capture Wuhan on June 25, 1930. Amazingly, Mao attached his own signature to the announcements with the self-appointed title of 'Chairman of the Chinese Worker and Peasant Revolutionary Committee'.[62] He left Tingzhou in Fujian, presumably to attack Nanchang. He stayed near Nanchang for a few weeks but undertook no serious military operations. In late July, soon after hearing the news of Peng's capture of Changsha, Mao quickly directed his troops to Hunan and meanwhile wrote to the Party Center in an strikingly bold tone:

> We regard the present situation as one of inevitable collapse of the KMT regime. After He Jian's disastrous defeat by the 3rd Army Corps, the situation will definitely be more shaky. My 1st Army Corps is to destroy the enemies and take over Changsha, Yuzhou, and Wuhan, to establish a vast Soviet base in the three provinces, and to promote the nationwide rebellion. . . . We hope that the Center will immediately issue us orders regarding the composition of a government and the organization of a general headquarters.[63]

It seems very obvious from the above quotation that Mao was asking the Party Center for a higher command position. He got the position. As the 1st Army Corps arrived in the city of Yonghe, Mao met Peng's 3rd Army Corps, retreating from Changsha. At the Party Center's behest, the two troops were combined into the First Front Army with Zhu as general commander and Mao as general political commissar. Naturally, Mao had to make another attack on Changsha, but he followed Li Lisan's order in word rather than spirit. After besieging Changsha for a couple of weeks, fighting a few skirmishes in its suburban areas and finding it hardly surmountable, Mao directed all the troops back to his Jiangxi base. Although the second attack on Changsha failed from the Li Lisan Center's point of view, Mao maintained his position as the General Political Commissar of the First Front Army—which comprised the two major forces of the Red Army, his own 1st Army Corps and Peng's 3rd Army Corp, totaling more than 30,000 men.[64]

During Li Lisan's two years of leadership in the CCP Center, the only period of direct confrontation between Mao and Li was from April to June 1930, when the latter tried to directly command the former's troops. Except for this, Mao acted, intentionally or not, in conformity with the Li Lisan Center or, more specifically, the radical trend of Li within the Party Center. Born in the same area and known to each other since childhood, Mao and Li had a personal relationship more intimate than that with any other Party Center leaders. Above all, it was by dint of the Li Lisan adventure that Mao had been promoted from a leader of one army to that of an army corps and then to that of a front army in less than half a year, and that Mao eventually ended his three-year seclusion from the central leadership to reclaim a position in the Party Center.

Considering his strategy and position in general, Mao did appear as an opponent to the Li Lisan leadership, as far as he would go against any Party Center authorities. On the one hand, the relations between Mao in the 4th Army and Li in the Party Center reflected the complicated internal, political relations of the Communist Party, in which the interests and behaviors of a constituent unit did not always accord with those of the general leadership. On the other hand, there existed a clear difference between Mao and Li in fundamental thought—the former being a political realist, the latter a revolutionary idealist.

3

THE FOURTH SUPPRESSION CAMPAIGN
AND THE LONG MARCH

Of all the wars between the central government and the local military cliques after 1927 (all under the banner of the KMT), the one between Chiang Kai-shek on one side, and Feng Yuxiang and Yan Xishan on the other, was the greatest. It lasted half a year—from May to November 1930—and spread over more than ten provinces, mostly in North China. Chiang committed nearly all his regular troops: 1,000,000 men; Yan and Feng fought with 600,000. As a result, 200,000 of Yan and Feng's troops surrendered; 200,000 were killed or wounded; the remaining 200,000 were forcibly enlisted in Chiang's army. The victorious Chiang side lost 100,000 at the most modest estimation.[1] These rough statistics serve as a convincing explanation for the rapid growth of Communist strength in 1930 in the South without serious interference by the Nationalist government. They also help explain why soon after the war ended Chiang could shift his attention to the South and start a series of suppression campaigns against the Communists.

With the Dongjiang Soviet destroyed and the Zuojiang and Youjiang Soviets abandoned, the Communist movement as a whole moved farther north toward the Yangtze Valley. The numerous Soviet bases had by late 1930 coalesced into three strongholds: the Jiangxi Central Soviet, the Eyuwan Soviet, and the Xiangexi Soviet, located respectively south, north, and west of cosmopolitan Wuhan. While the Party Center was attempting to sort out the organizational and ideological dislocations caused by the downfall of the Li Lisan leadership and to regain control of its subordinates, the Red Armies were left free to manage their own affairs. Eventually, they all retreated to their old bases. In exchange for their offensive expeditions, they now faced a defensive battle against a developing KMT retaliation.

The First Three Suppression Campaigns

Compared with the huge armies of Feng Yuxiang and Yan Xishan, the tiny Red Army did not seem worth much worry in the eyes of Chiang Kai-shek. After all, it was only a few tens of thousands of peasant rebels scattered over a few spots in the countryside. Naturally, Chiang did not originally label his military action against the Jiangxi Soviet in late 1930 the "*First* Suppression Campaign"; he scarcely supposed it would need any successors. Moreover, because of certain political considerations, he only put the governors of the few most concerned provinces—Jiangxi, Anhui, Hunan, and Hubei—in charge of their own anti-Communist affairs. Only in Jiangxi, where the Red Army was supposed to be the strongest, were some non-native troops added to the campaign.

A field headquarters was formed in Jiangxi with Lu Diping, the provincial governor, as commander-in-chief. Under Lu's headquarters were three army routes, altogether 10 divisions totalling 100,000 men. Among them, the central route of four divisions was commanded by Lu himself. The other six divisions did not take an active part in the campaign. In the central route, Luo Lin's division was left to guard Ji'an and the other three divisions of Gong Bingfan, Zhang Huizan and Tan Daoyuan, altogether about 30,000 men, were designated offensive forces. Their combat strategy was to drive straight into the Soviet territory and overcome the Red Army by swift attacks.[2]

Withdrawing from the Changsha expedition, the First Front Army captured Ji'an, a prefectural seat in western Jiangxi, in early October, 1930. Although slogans like "the victory in Ji'an symbolizes the victory in the whole Jiangxi province" were still chanted, Mao had already returned to his old idea of accumulating strength in rural areas rather than making attempts on big cities.[3] The city of Ji'an was soon given up. On October 30, a joint conference on the General Front Committee of the Red Army and the Action Committee of Jiangxi Province was held at Luofang. At the Luofang Conference, Peng Dehuai's 3rd Army Corps was criticized for implementing the Li Lisan line in attacking Changsha but was also highly praised for its smooth acceptance of the correct line under the present General Front Committee leadership.[4] Both the criticism and the praise were necessary for Mao to consolidate his authority in the newly founded First Front Army. By the time the Nationalists started their First Suppression Campaign, there were about 40,000 men on the Communist side belonging to two Army Corps and generally under Mao's command. They gathered around Donggu, a rural town in the western Jiangxi mountains.

On December 22, 1930, the General Front Committee issued a manifesto entitled "Eight Favorable Conditions for a Grand Victory." In this interesting and important document, two fundamental features of Mao's general strategy throughout his military career in the Jiangxi Soviet period are established: first, the policy of abandoning part of Soviet territory to lure the enemy troops deep into the base area where the Red Army could enjoy the most favorable conditions: support from local peasants, familiarity with local terrain, etcetera; second, the policy of conducting mobile operations to concentrate superior forces in order to destroy part of the enemy forces, defeating the rest one by one. This new strategy marked an evolution from guerrilla activity to mobile warfare.[5]

The First Suppression Campaign started with the Jiangxi Soviet in early December 1930. Lu Diping put Gong Bingfan's Fifth Division in front and his own troops, Zhang Huizan's 18th Division, behind. The two divisions constituted the focal point in the general assault of the Red Army at Donggu. Gong's division started off immediately, but Zhang's 18th Division did not follow as closely as it should have. To his great surprise, Gong did not meet much resistance, and took Donggu easily. The major forces of the Red Army gave up the town and moved away. Gong telegraphed the field headquarters at Nanchang and also reported the victory to Chiang Kai-shek. He was promptly awarded by Chiang a prize of 10,000 silver dollars.[6] Xie Muhan, then the Chief of General Staff in the Field Headquarters, described subsequent events as follows:

> Zhang Huizan did not lead his 18th Division to advance according to the schedule. He remained in place on December 17 and approached Donggu late in the morning of December 21. In the mist of a heavy fog, Zhang mistook Gong Bingfan's troops for the Red Army. An intense fight took place between them and lasted for four hours with wounds and casualties on both sides. Despite Zhang's apology after the incident, Gong still thought Zhang did this deliberately out of jealousy for his success and awards. Gong transferred his troops to Yinfu at his own will to get away from Zhang's command. Zhang was much angered and stopped further communication with Gong. Consequently, the formerly planned 'focal point' was null and void.[7]

A few days later Zhang fell into the Red Army's ambush ring in Longgan. Outnumbered by some 20,000 Red Army troops, Zhang's division of 7,000 was annihilated and Zhang himself captured. The Red Army quickly shifted to attack the nearby Tan Daoyuan's 50th Division and won another decisive battle. With all his own troops either lost or beaten, Lu Diping could no longer continue his leadership, and the period of the Nationalist Army's rearrangement meant the victory of the First Anti-suppression Campaign for the Red Army.

The Second Suppression Campaign did not begin until three months later because of the slow transfer of northern troops to the southern battlefield. He Yingqin, the Minister of War, was named commander-in-chief. Under his leadership were all *zapaijun* (miscellaneous forces), most of whom were former Feng and Yan troops recently brought from the North to Jiangxi. Altogether, there were five routes, 20 divisions and about 200,000 men, of which eleven divisions—110,000 men—directly took part in the fight.[8] Wang Jinyu's 5th Route Army and Sun Lianzhong's 26th Route Army were also brought to the campaign and assigned a salient role. Wang's conversation with his chief of staff before the campaign seemed frank enough to show his own motive and morale:

> We miscellaneous forces have never had a home base of our own. Whenever our troops are moved, all our belongings must be thrown away. You know such bitter experiences. This time Generalissimo Chiang promises to appoint me the governor of Jiangxi after the war. O.K. We'll soon have a home and a bright future, and will never be worried about getting things with no place to stock them. Let's do our best.[9]

Actually, the same position Wang looked forward to had also been promised by the Generalissimo to another general of the miscellaneous troops, Sun Lianzhong. Whether the two generals really wanted to do their own best on the battlefield remains questionable, but it seems obvious that neither of them wanted to see the other do his best.

The KMT's general strategy adopted in the Second Campaign, "Be aware of every step and push forward together," required that each of the attacking troops advance slowly and safely toward the center of the Jiangxi Soviet and that all of them maintain close coordination on their way. Clearly, such a strategy was the result of the lessons drawn from the previous campaign and suited to the incoherent condition of the miscellaneous armies. The previous campaign had reduced the Red Army's forces a bit, but its victory had helped Mao consolidate control of both the Red Army and the local Soviet. The recordings of the General Front Committee conferences available now show Mao's undisputed authority and indispensable role in the Red Army by early 1931. All conferences were without exception chaired by Mao. A common topic of these conferences was how to transfer and concentrate the Red Army to make the most decisive battles.[10]

The Second Campaign began with the First Front Army—almost all its 30,000 men—hidden in the mountain adjacent to Donggu for twenty days, waiting for the enemy's arrival. Such a military maneuver was only possible for the Red Army, with its strict discipline and good relationship with the local people.

As Gong Bingfan led his Fifth Division from Futian toward Donggu, he wondered why "for three days no traces of the Red Army could be found; all around everything seemed as quiet as the dead." The troops continued on their way. "Directly under command of the division head-quarters were 1,000 men. Following the guard battalion was the headquarters with 40 or 50 horses and three sedan chairs—the division commander, the vice-division commander, and the chief of staff each seated in one. At the end was the logging battalion with mules and carts. All these constituted a slender column running for five or six li along the rocky path."[11]

In this manner, Gong's division moved into the Red Army's encirclement in the mountains, fired on by overwhelmingly superior Red Army forces from all sides. Within a couple of hours, the whole division was destroyed and Gong himself was captured by the Red Army. He had kept making emergency calls at the critical time, but all the Nationalist generals Gong contacted by telegraph refused to come for rescue under various excuses.[12] In the next three days, the Red Army swept from west to east and conducted three consecutive battles, defeating one KMT division in each. Ten days later, it reached Guangchang and fought with the KMT troops there, getting an upper hand in the battle but failing to capture the city. Marching further east, the Red Army overcame the city of Jianning and smashed another KMT division. At the end of May 1931, most of the KMT forces withdrew and left the Red Army to celebrate its victory.[13] This campaign may be taken as a perfect illustration of Mao's strategy: "lure the enemy troops deep and annihilate them one by one." In addition, the campaign showed that the Red Army could defeat a weak and isolated miscellaneous force on an equal basis. With enemy forces larger in number, or when attacking a fortified city like Guangchang, they might not be so successful.

The Third Suppression Campaign commenced soon after the second. This time Chiang decided to assume general command in person and brought five divisions of his own Central Army to the battlefield. Altogether there were 22 divisions: 250,000 men. Three 'thrusting armies'—two on the left or eastern front commanded by He Yingqin and one on the right or western front by Chen Mingshu—consisted mainly of KMT Central Army troops and were assigned with a task of swift assault. The combat strategy for the Third Campaign was much like the one applied in the First Campaign. Essentially, it was to employ superior armed forces, advance in several routes, drive straight into the Soviet base area, swiftly break up the Red Army's main forces, destroy the Soviet government, and then gradually exterminate Communist influences.[14]

After their victory in the two previous campaigns, the general situation had changed in favor of the Communists. The Soviet regime expanded and the Red Army greatly consolidated its forces, and this new condition brought a possibility of modifying the old military strategy. The essential question was whether it was still necessary to surrender Soviet territory and allow the enemy to drive in so deeply. At the conference of the General Front Committee convened at Kangdu before the Third Campaign, even

Mao deemed it possible to expel the enemy at the outer edge of the Soviet. In his speech, Mao stated: "This time we may be able to beat the enemy before it gets its foothold. This seems possible by now."[15] The Kangdu Conference, held on June 22, 1931, also marked a phase of political maturity for Mao and the CCP, though the term "political maturity" here may seem more like a euphemism for political plotting. Aware that there existed a situation of military equilibrium and strategic interaction among the KMT Central Army, the Guangdong Army and the Red Army, Mao proposed:

> Normally Chiang Kai-shek would take a defensive position toward Guangdong and fight the Red Army first. But provided the Guangdong Army went to attack Changsha, Chiang Kai-shek would first fight Guangdong regardless of the Red Army threatening Wuzhou. At the present moment, therefore, we should not push toward Wuzhou anymore. Even if the enemy troops withdraw from Nanfeng, we should only dispatch some small units there. We should deploy our troops at remote and out-of-way locations so that Chiang will take a defensive position with us and turn to fight the Guangdong Army.[16]

The early stage of the Third Suppression Campaign seemed quite satisfactory from the KMT's point of view. By the end of July, 1931, despite strong resistance from the Communists, the Nationalist troops had managed to capture almost all the important cities and towns and control most territory of the Jiangxi Soviet. The Red Army retreated to Ruijin in June and then shifted to the Donggu area at the center of the base area. At first, the Communists attempted a breakthrough from Futian and a shift to the east for a surprise attack at the enemy's rear. But finding that their plan exposed and the enemy's front line strengthened, they were forced to retreat to Xingguo, where an open space of about ten square miles was available for them to gather together.

From there, the Red Army tried and succeeded in another breakthrough. Making a quick attack on the weakest army—the Third Thrusting Army—it defeated divisions led by Shangguan Yunxiang and Hao Mengling. Moving further east, they fought Mao Bingwen at Huangpi. Close pursuit from behind and the strong blocking force in front then caused Mao to turn to the west again. Mao managed to return to Xingguo in August 1931. "By the time the enemy discovered this fact and shifted west again," Mao recalled, "our troops had already had a fortnight's rest, whereas the enemy, hungry, exhausted and demoralized, were no good for fighting and so determined to retreat."[17]

In fact, the reasons for the KMT withdrawal are not entirely in line with Mao's allegation. From Huangpi to Xingguo is only about 200 li: one or two day's walking distance. Besides, the Red Army had thus far fought only three miscellaneous troops. The real factors accounting for the KMT's withdrawal were more complicated. The attempted assassination of Chiang at Nanchang in June, the rebellion of the Guangdong and Guangxi armies in August, and the intrusion of Japanese troops in Northeast China in September were more decisive to Chiang's decision to withdrawal than his loss of a few battles to the Red Army.[18]

The main difference between the Third Campaign and the previous ones is that by this stage the Red Army's combat capacity surpassed that of the KMT provincial and miscellaneous armies. With concentrated forces, favorable timing and terrain, the Central Red Army could even defeat one division of the KMT Central Army in a single battle. The strategy adopted by the Red Army had finally developed from small-sized guerrilla activities to large-scale mobile warfare. Its essential features were the retreat to the base rear to avoid reckless fighting at the front, the concentration of the main forces to break through a weak point in the enemy attack line, and the ability to expand a partial success into an overall victory. But it does not mean that the Mao strategy was always workable. Had the Third Campaign continued longer and the KMT's main forces managed to hold their captured cities and towns in the Jiangxi Soviet, without departing to chase the Red Army or withdrawing to cope with the warlord rebels and the Japanese invaders, a stalemate situation would have most likely been generated, resulting in mutual reduction of both sides in protracted warfare. For the weak Communist side, without hope of reinforcement, such a situation would obviously have been dangerously detrimental. Based on the events of the middle of the Third Campaign and those to come in the Fifth Campaign, the above assessment should be taken as more than a simple hypothesis.

At the time of the earlier suppression campaigns in Jiangxi, the provincial armies in Anhui and Hupei were engaged with Xu Xiangqian's Fourth Front Army in the Eyuwan Soviet and He Long's 3rd Red Army in the Xiangexi Soviet, respectively. These two Red Armies did not win much until the KMT army shifted its attention to the Jiangxi Central Soviet in the Third Campaign. In the later months of 1931, a national military equilibrium between the Nationalist troops and the Communist troops came into existence, which soon created a dilemma for the Nanking Government. Without gathering its troops to fight the Red Army in the Jiangxi Central Soviet the KMT could hardly succeed there, but transferring so many troops into that particular area would leave other Red Armies and Soviet bases opportunities for rebellious actions. At the end of 1931, the Fourth Front Army in the Eyuwan Base grew to 30,000 men while He Long's 3rd Army expanded to 20,000 men. The total Red Army manpower jumped to about 100,000 troops, already reaching the size of an average warlord army. Needless to say, its military and political potential was incomparably greater than that of any local warlord and clique.[19]

The Transfer of the Party Center
from Shanghai to the Soviet

Although the Li Lisan line may have had an ambiguous effect on the Red Army and the Soviets in the countryside, it had a salient adverse impact upon the urban work of the Communist Party. At the height of the Li Lisan adventure, all CCP branches and left-wing organizations, including the Youth League and the Labor Union, were combined into 'Action Committees' for immediate revolts in the cities. After the Communists' failure, the Red Armies could flee back to their rural bases while these Action Committees in the cities had to stay and bear the brunt of direct retaliation from the Nationalists. The period following the downfall of Li Lisan was one of fierce intraparty struggle. This facilitated the KMT's apprehension of the Communists. He Mengxiong and his comrades in the Jiangsu CCP Committee, the most powerful provincial committee at the time, were arrested and killed right after the Fourth Plenum in January, 1931. Gu Shunzhang, the head of the CCP secret agency, Xiang Zhongfa, the CCP General Secretary, and other Communist leaders were arrested in the early months of 1931. Some were killed and some defected. Almost all the secret liaison spots of the CCP were exposed, and the Party work was seriously jeopardized. Xiang Zhongfa's confession gives a vivid account of the CCP strength in the cities in June 1931:

> All Communist Party members, excluding those in the Soviet areas, total approximately 20,000 at this moment. The great majority of them, though still included in this calculation, are merely formal figures and without any actual function. . . . In Shanghai, there are 580 Party members, 270 Youth League members, and 470 Labor Union members. The monthly membership fees are only 270 copper dollars in total. From this point we can see their weakness.[20]

In a certain sense and to a certain extent, the upsurge of the Soviet movement and the escalation of the military struggle improved the CCP position as a whole but aggravated the problems of the Party Center in Shanghai. As the civil war between the CCP and the KMT intensified, the Nanking Government promulgated martial law, which made leftist activities in the cities extraordinarily difficult. Telegraph facilities made communication between the Party Center and the Red Army in the Soviet more efficient, but at the same time made it all the more vulnerable. Whenever a secret communication line was discovered and broken, it was the Party organization in the cities that suffered most.[21]

The CCP's failure in urban work left the Party Center in the position of a simple liaison relaying instructions from the Comintern to the Soviets.

It gradually degenerated into a cumbersome burden rather than an efficient leading apparatus. The Comintern as the general supervisor had less factional biases, which were obsessing the CCP leaders, and therefore could more easily see through the above described situation. It was the Comintern's initial suggestion that prompted the CCP Center to consider a transfer to the rural Soviets soon after the Fourth Plenum in early 1934.[22]

The Party Center was forced to move to the Soviet, but it also descended to the Soviet and Red Army came to assume leadership. From the Soviet and Red Army point of view, since all of them were more or less created and consolidated under the slogan of Party Center leadership they would naturally pass their power over to the Party Center. Of course, frictions and conflicts were inevitable. Normally, the newly arrived Party Center leaders could initially obtain the titles of general leadership; they then would proceed to strengthen their power by applying ideological standards to judge and purge former Soviet or Army leaders. Flaws and faults were always there to be picked up—political as well as organizational. Through their years of practical work in the countryside, most Soviet and Army cadres were liable to have committed such errors as abuse of power, expropriation of wealth, licentious behavior, or factional activities. Some of these "errors"—such as the "warlordism" of using whips and sticks to drive the soldiers on the battlefield—seemed impermissible from an ideological viewpoint but had proved necessary from a practical standpoint. All in all, there was a profound contradiction between the revolutionary ideals held by the Party Center leaders and the political reality faced by the Red Army officers and Soviet cadres.

The Party Center underwent numerous changes after the Fourth Plenum in January, 1931. In April, Zhang Guotao, Shen Zemin and Chen Changhao left Shanghai for the Eyuwan Soviet; Ren Bishi, Wang Jiaxiang and Gu Zuolin went to the Jiangxi Central Soviet; and Xia Xi and Xu Fugen went to the Xiangexi Soviet. Wang Ming returned from Moscow to Shanghai; Xiang Zhongfa was apprehended in June; further reorganization brought Bo Gu and Zhang Wentian into the Party Center and the Politburo in July. Finally in October 1931, Wang Ming left once more for Moscow and Zhou Enlai for the Jiangxi Soviet. The Party Center had turned into a mixture of returned students and worker-cadres without much authority. It was called provisional, and so it was indeed.[23]

As a local Soviet and Red Army leader, Mao might be in need of two types of people from the Party Center in Shanghai: technical personnel such as telegram operators, ammunition mechanics, and medical experts, and field commanders with professional military training such as Ye Jianying and Liu Bocheng. What Mao did not need—and never asked for—were political leaders. He needed practical clerks, not ideological bosses. Although from a practical point of view Mao did not need Party leaders, their arrival at Mao's Red Army and Soviet brought him some positive consequences in view of intraparty relationship; and it represented a gift or reward as much as a threat.

For years, Mao was supposed to be under the jurisdiction of the local Party system wherever his troops were deployed, though the stronger his Red Army troops grew, the more ambiguous this disciplinary issue became. The relations between the 4th Red Army and the Special Committee of Southwest Jiangxi were in just such a condition from early 1929 to late 1930. In August 1930, Xiang Ying was appointed Secretary of the Yangtze Valley Bureau and concurrently, Secretary of the Wuhan Action Committee. Next, Zhou Yisu was sent to the First Front Army as a representative of the Yangtze Valley Bureau. He was the first standing commissioner to Mao's troops and was soon appointed a member of the General Front Committee. Now that the commissioner of a multi-provincial bureau was with him, it seemed as though Mao's General Front Committee had legitimately jumped out of the control not only the local Party committee but also the provincial Party committee.

At the suggestion of Pavel Mif at the Fourth Plenum, the Central Soviet Bureau was formed in January 1931. Zhou Enlai was appointed its secretary but could not immediately leave Shanghai for this duty. In his stead, Xiang Ying as the acting secretary dropped his position in the Yangtze Bureau and moved to the Jiangxi Soviet in in December 1930. Mao, as a member of the Central Soviet Bureau, was formally brought under Xiang's leadership. There, Mao was for the first time directly challenged by Xiang, who was a Politburo member and had equal seniority to Mao. Nevertheless, partly because of the general trend against the Li Lisan line, in which Xiang had at least played an ambiguous role, and partly because of the great victory of the First Suppression Campaign, Xiang had to acknowledge Mao's position, for example, in the Futian Incident.[24]

A Communist leader with a worker origin and a reputation in the labor union movement, Xiang could hardly hold his leading position in the Jiangxi Soviet simply by virtue of his title. He could only stay at the rear, managing the routine work and leaving Mao at the front with the Red Army—as free as ever before. In April 1931, a Party Center delegation came to attend the Enlarged CCP Conference in the Jiangxi Soviet. After the Congress, the three delegates—Ren Bishi, Gu Zuolin and Wang Jiaxiang—remained in the Jiangxi Soviet and joined the Central Soviet Bureau.[25] Since the three newcomers had little experience—and little interest—in military affairs, they also stayed at the Ruijin office quarters. Their first target of criticism was not Mao with the Red Army at the front but Xiang Ying in the Party and Soviet at the rear. The Central Soviet Bureau under Xiang's leadership was bitterly scolded as having "a compromising line" and a "rightist tendency", its resolution on the Futian Incident was, moreover, failed to make clear that the incident was "a counter-revolutionary rebellion."[26] Ironically, the conflict between Xiang and Ren led to Xiang's replacement by Mao as Acting Secretary of the Central Soviet Bureau for a while after the April conference. But it soon became clear to the Party Center commissioners that Mao was true power holder in the Army and Soviet and thus the main obstacle to the Party Center's authority and strategic line. After the military emergency in the Third Suppression Campaign was over and as more Party Center personnel crammed into the Jiangxi Soviet, Mao was criticized at the Gannan Conference of the Central Soviet Bureau in early November 1931. In the First National Congress of the Soviet immediately following the Ganan Conference, Mao attained the chairmanship of the Central Government of the Chinese Soviet Republic but lost his command in the Red Army: the First Front Army was dismissed, and so was Mao's General Political Commissar within it.[27]

In December 1931, Zhou Enlai arrived at the Jiangxi Soviet and assumed the position of Secretary of the Central Soviet Bureau. Zhou Enlai's arrival brought Mao face to face with the power challenge of a man who not only had high seniority but also rich military and political experience. In the long run, it also saved Mao from a total loss in his political fortunes. Zhou was politically poised enough to protect and not to eliminate Mao so long as Mao's influence in the Party and Army remained useful to the Communist cause in general. This attitude of Zhou toward Mao became even more apparent after Bo Gu and the Party Center arrived at the Jiangxi Soviet in early 1933. From that time, there appeared a kind of multiple power relationship which persisted until the end of the Jiangxi Soviet period in late 1934. As Kim points out, there existed three types of power indicators: Bo, the power holder; Mao, the opposition leader; and Zhou, the mediator.[28]

Before these Party Center leaders' arrival in 1931, nobody in the Jiangxi Soviet could match Mao's authority in the Party or in the Army, in seniority or in capability. His authority in the Red Army was even more unchallengeable. As one group of Party Center leaders after another came to the Jiangxi Soviet, Mao had to share power with and lost power to them. But this problem should be viewed from another angle: the transfer of the Party Center from Shanghai to Jiangxi represented a reward for Mao's success in the past and provided a chance for direct competition for the Party Center leadership in the future. In this respect, Sheng Yueh's insightful view is helpful:

> The move of the CC of the CCP to Kiangsi is an important event in its
> history. It marked a new phase in the struggle between Mao Tse-tung and
> the 28 Bolsheviks. Viewed from one angle, the move of the CC of the CCP
> to Jui-chin [Ruijin] somewhat weakened Mao's leadership in the Central Soviet

area and placed him temporarily in an unfavorable position. But viewed from another angle, the move of the CC of the CCP from large city in China to an isolated area in inland China meant that the CC could not root its support in a workers' movement and therefore had to rely on the support of the armed forces led by Mao. Generally speaking, armed force is the most vital instrument needed to establish or overthrow a regime. Without direct control of the armed forces, Ch'in Pang-hsien and his faction were helpless to oppose the rising power of Mao Tse-tung, who finally defeated them.[29]

The Fourth Suppression Campaign and the Fourth Front Army's Long March

The Red Army in the Eyuwan base, with three divisions of only 2,000 men, did not attract much of the attention of the Li Lisan Center in early 1930. This was actually lucky for them, as there were no strict orders from the Party Center requesting them to attack the big cities. Despite the losses of some Red Armies during the period of the Li Lisan adventure, the First Red Army grew to 6,000 strong. After the Third Plenum of the Party Center in September 1930, Zeng Zhongsheng was sent from Shanghai to the Eyuwan Soviet to be the Secretary of the CCP Committee and the Chairman of the Military Sub-Council in this base area. Zeng carried out a policy later labeled as a compromising line. He tried to correct the obvious mistakes of the Li Lisan line while attempting to rally the local cadres for a smooth development.[30] From Winter 1930 to Spring 1931, the 1st Army was reinforced by the 15th Army and reorganized into the 4th Red Army with 10,000 men. The 4th Army succeeded in breaking two suppression campaigns, conducted mainly by the Nationalist troops in Anhui, and increased its forces to 20,000. It occupied a base area with a population of 1,800,000 and became the second largest Communist force.[31] The rapid growth of the Eyuwan Soviet and the 4th Army came to the attention of the Party Center. In April 1931, Zhang Guotao, Shen Zemin and Chen Changhao were dispatched to the Eyuwan Soviet. The Eyuwan Sub-Bureau of the CCP Central Committee was formed with Zhang as the secretary taking overall responsibility. Besides their membership in the Sub-Bureau, Shen was appointed Secretary of the CCP Committee and Chen Secretary of the Communist Youth League in the Eyuwan base area—or "Eyuwan Province" as the Communists formally called it.

Zhang Guotao was a veteran Communist, well known as a dissident in the Comintern. He might not have looked too highly upon young student-leaders like Wang Ming and Bo Gu. But in early 1931, when he returned from Moscow and faced the new situation, he declared his full support of the new Party Center, though his motives might be a bit more complex. This is clearly shown from Zhang's statement published in *Honest Words* on March 5, 1931:

There still exist within our Party many unprincipled, factional biases of the petty bourgeoisie which confuse the two-line struggle. The rightist elements and the remnants of Li Lisanism try to use these biases to cover up their anti-Comintern actions. They openly or covertly stand against the alleged Chen Shaoyu faction. What they actually do is stand against the Party Center and the Comintern by means of opposing Chen Shaoyu, because Chen Shaoyu and his followers are the great comrades who are firmly carrying out the line of the Comintern and the Party Center.[32]

Zhang Guotao entered the Eyuwan Soviet in April 1931. Either in line with his true political approaches or—less apparently but more likely— because of his power interests, Zhang immediately started a 'two line struggle' within the local Party and Army. In this endeavor, Zhang clearly applied his appointment in the Party Sub-Bureau and the Party Center's new line as his most powerful weapon, despite the denials Zhang makes in his memoirs: "I was a man who had deep resentment against the Comintern and especially against Stalin, and I was not trusted by them. How could I use the Comintern's name as a magic wand? I could never and I would never shout the 'correct line' of the Comintern to scare and conquer those 'local reds.' "[33]

In fact, he did. Zhang proclaimed the formation of the Sub-Bureau and abolished the former Eyuwan CCP Committee in May. Zeng Zhongsheng's position as secretary of the committee was automatically abolished. Zhang also dismissed Yu Dusan from his position as Political Commissar of the 4th Red Army, and temporarily transferred Zeng to take Yu's place, "on the condition that Zeng fully admitted his mistakes and agreed to carry out the Party Center's line in the 4th Army, the Sub-Bureau approved his appointment as the political commissar in the 4th Army."[34] All these changes were instituted under the 'correct line' of the Comintern and the Party Center; it could not possibly have been otherwise.

In the summer of 1931, the KMT army started its Third Suppression Campaign against the Jiangxi Central Soviet, and had to take a defensive position towards the Eyuwan Soviet. Both to support the Jiangxi Soviet and to achieve its own expansion, the 4th Army undertook a southern expedition. Now fierce conflicts erupted between the 4th Red Army and the CCP Sub-Bureau.

Under the leadership of Xu Xiangqian as commander, and Zeng Zhongsheng as political commissar, the 4th Red Army set off with six regiments. In early August, it destroyed one KMT regiment and took Yingshan. After resting for two days, the 4th Army marched southwest to Xishui and Luotian towards Wuxue on the Yangtze River. It concluded two successful battles, defeated six enemy regiments, and took a few more counties in eastern Hubei. At the same time, however, consecutive messages came from the Eyuwan Sub-Bureau, ordering the 4th Army to turn east and attack Anqing in Jiangsu.[35]

The 4th Army leaders appealed directly to the Party Center, arguing on the impracticality of moving so far from the base area to attack a big city like Anqing. Failing to win any sympathy from the Party Center in Shanghai, Zeng Zhongsheng called back his troops but at the same time raised even stronger arguments: Yingshan to Anqing was about 400 li in a mountainous region where no Party organization had ever existed; the Red Army lacked rear transportation means, porter services, intelligence agents and local cadres; it would be insane for a single division of the Red Army to capture Anqing and threaten Nanking; what, if any, difference was there between the present order to capture Anqing in a month and Li Lisan's previous order to capture Wuhan in two weeks?[36]

In a letter of the 4th Army headquarters to the Party Center, Chen Changhao was particularly criticized. This reflected the fact that Zhang would rather like to use Chen, a young returned student versed in theoretical polemics but lacking political experience, to wrest power from the old cadres in the Eyuwan base and win the sympathy of the Party Center controlled by the returned students. On November 3, 1931, the Party Center made a decision to stand openly for the Eyuwan Sub-Bureau against the 4th Red Army:

> The Fourth Army disobeyed the decision of the Military Council and deliberately changed the military plan; it ignored the correct instructions of the Sub-Bureau and convened non-party meetings to stand against the Sub-Bureau, distributed its own decisions to the local Party branches and lower army units, and bypassed the Sub-Bureau to make reports directly to the Party Center in order to deceive the Party Center. All these constitute serious anti-Party mistakes.[37]

Chen Changhao was quickly despatched to Yingshan to take over Zeng Zhongsheng's position. Following this action came a huge anti-counter-revolutionary movement in the Army and the Soviet. Zhang Guotao himself admitted that "about 600 were arrested, of whom one third were army men. More than 100 of them were punished—30 or so were put to death and 100 sentenced to various terms."[38] In a report of the Sub-Bureau to the Party Center, it was said that "by now more than 600 reactionaries are under arrest. Among them are 100 in northwest Anhui, 200 in Huangma and 300 in the 4th Army."[39] A month later, Chen Changhao reported in a speech that "this time we have eliminated 1,000 reformist traitors and 1,600 rich peasants and bad elements."[40]

In both the dimension and the manner, the intraparty struggle in the Eyuwan Soviet was even fiercer than in the Jiangxi Soviet. One of the causes of this intensified situation may be that most of the Party and Army leaders being eliminated such as Zeng Zhongsheng, Yu Dusan, and Xu Jisheng, had themselves been sent by the Party Center to take over power from the local cadres. Thus they lacked the strong capacity Mao possessed in the Jiangxi Soviet to resist the newcomers. Another possibility is that the Eyuwan Soviet did not have several equally strong political forces balancing with one another as in the Jiangxi Central Soviet.

It is hard to tell how much the anti-counterrevolutionary movement influenced the military process. In a moral sense, the movement was ridiculous in its true unreasonableness. Few, if any, victims of the movement were guilty as charged. Nevertheless, it seemed that the movement had indeed spurred the combat spirit of the Red Army. At any rate, with these "counterrevolutionaries" hidden inside, the 4th Army had won great victories and grown rapidly in the past. After their elimination, the Fourth Front Army continued these successes.

On November 7, 1931, just as the First National Soviet Congress was held in Jiangxi, the Eyuwan base area opened its own congress entitled "the Second Congress of the Eyuwan Soviet." On the same day, the Fourth Front Army proclaimed its founding; it consisted of two armies of about 30,000 men. All these actions constituted possible competition with the Jiangxi Central Soviet and the First Front Army.[41]

From December 1931 to May 1932, the Fourth Front Army successfully conducted the battles of Huangan, Shangcheng and Sujiafu and broke up another suppression campaign. The Sujiafu battle lasted for 48 days, and turned out to be a giant victory. The Red Army besieged 6,000 KMT troops in the city of Sujiafu. When Li Shiding, a provincial army commander, hurried to the rescue, the Red Army ambushed and annihilated his troops and took him prisoner. The KMT troops inside the city surrendered. All in all, the Red Army wiped out 30,000 enemy troops and, the Fourth Front Army increased its strength to 50,000 troops.[42]

As soon as a truce was reached between the KMT government and the Japanese invaders at Shanghai in May 1932, Chiang Kai-shek started the ambitious Fourth Suppression Campaign against the Communists. As a national strategy, the Fourth Campaign attempted first to deal a fatal blow to the Eyuwan and Xiangexi Soviets in the north, and then shift attention to the Jiangxi Soviet in the south.

Chiang himself assumed the general command at Wuhan Headquarters in charge of military operations against the Eyuwan and Xiangexi Soviets. Summoned to the campaign were three routes of the army made up of both provincial and central armies. The left route was to cope with the Xiangexi Soviet base while the central and right routes, 22 divisions and five brigades totalling 250,000 men, were to attack the Eyuwan Soviet. Advancing step by step from the west, the east and the north, the KMT troops attempted to press the Red Army south to the Yangtze River for a showdown.[43]

The Red Army in the Eyuwan base took the same strategy as before, leaving the 25th Army to defend the eastern front and placing the main force of the 4th Army to attack in the west. It tried to repeat its strategy of "besieging the city to destroy the reinforcements." This time, however, the enemy proved too overwhelmingly superior for the Communists to confuse, and their formerly successful strategy had the opposite result. The 4th Army operated around Macheng for a month in July and August, yet could not break into the city. Meanwhile, KMT General Xu Yaoting destroyed the 25th Army, captured the city of Heqiu and cut deep into the Soviet from the eastern front; while on the northern front, Chen Jicheng's troops drove close to Qiliping; and on the west, Wei Lihuang's troops approached Huangan. With the three enemy columns driving into the heart of the Soviet, the 4th Army withdrew from Macheng.[44]

After giving up its siege of Macheng, the 4th Red Army moved to defend Huangan. There, it fought a battle with Wei Lihuang's column from August 11 to 13. The battle cost each side a few thousand lives, but finally the KMT army took over the city and the Red Army had to retreat again. Shifting its main forces to the north, the Red Army fought another battle at Qiliping, which had been one of the centers of the Soviet for years. The Qiliping battle from August 15 to 18 turned out to be the fiercest and most decisive. All the 4th Army forces joined the battle, to the extent that "staff personnel, political workers, and even cooks all picked up rifles and went to the front."[45] On the KMT side, there were two columns led by Chen Jicheng and Wei Lihuang, altogether five or six divisions. Again, the battle played to a stalemate with each side losing about 3,000 men. The KMT army eventually captured Qiliping, along with some other cities and towns in the area. The 4th Army was compelled to retreat again, this time east into western Anhui. At Jinjiazhai, Xu Xiangqian's 4th Army joined Cai Shenxi's 25th Army. Another fight took place in Xinji and ended no better for the Communists.

Altogether, the Fourth Front Army had fought four or five big battles with the Nationalist Army from July to September 1932. In each battle, both sides lost two thousand men or more. For the Nationalists, this was affordable; for the Communists it was fatal. Now it was time for Zhang Guotao to telegraph the Party Center imploring a general mobilization of all Red Armies and people of other Soviet bases to support the Eyuwan Soviet and the Fourth Front Army. The Party Center in Shanghai could do no more than pass this message on to the Jiangxi Central Soviet and the First Front Army. The Jiangxi Soviet and Army leaders Zhou Enlai, Mao Zedong and Zhu De, offered some coordinated attacks in the north. At the same time, they lectured, authoritatively and scornfully, that instead of distributing its forces to protect so many points the Fourth Front Army should shift its main forces to some suitable places and deal a hard blow on one enemy unit, defeating the others one by one.[46] Talk is cheap. By the middle of September, when Jinjiazhai (another center of the Eyuwan Soviet) was lost, the Communist leaders began to think of abandoning the base for a long distance expedition.

In late September 1932, Zhang Guotao gathered all the troops in western Anhui, took a detour through the southern front and reached Hekou in eastern Hubei in early October. Some skirmishes in the Hekou area with the pursuing enemy reduced the Red Army to less than 20,000 men. Cai Shenxi, the commander of the 25th Army, was killed in one of the battles.[47] The Eyuwan Sub-Bureau held an enlarged conference at Huachaiban on October 11. All the participants agreed that this Fourth Campaign had so far failed, and a strategic shift had to be made. Tentatively, they decided that the 25th Army and the Eyuwan CCP Committee should remain in the base area to conduct guerrilla warfare, while the main force of the 4th Army and the Eyuwan Sub-Bureau would strike outside the base. It was hoped that the 4th Army would soon find a chance to move back when the intruding enemy left.[48]

Deep in the night of October 12, 1932, the bulk of the Fourth Front Army, three divisions of 20,000 men, crossed the Peking-Hankou Railway between Guangshui and Weijiadian and hurried toward the west. Its immediate objective was to move further away from the pursuing enemy. When it reached Suixian in Hubei on October 16, a conference of senior military cadres was held to decide the next step. Some stood for a counterattack in northern Hubei followed by a fight back to the Eyuwan base, while others proposed going south to join He Long's 3rd Red Army in the Xangexi Soviet. Neither of the proposals seemed feasible: the first was obviously too risky and the second was precluded in that the 3rd Army was itself in big trouble at that juncture. The final decision was no decision. The Fourth Front Army would continue to run west, leaving aside any long term plans.[49]

Knowing that the Red Army had left its Eyuwan base, Chiang Kai-shek began to reorganize his army. As his strategic objective in the Fourth Suppression Campaign was simply to deal a hard blow to the Eyuwan Soviet as preparation for a concentrated assault at the Central Soviet, Chiang spared no more than four divisions to chase the Fourth Front Army. Chiang put them all under the command of He Chengrui, the governor of Hubei, and instructed the local troops in Hubei and Henan to intercept the Red Army on its way.[50]

On October 19, the Fourth Front Army arrived at Zaoyang on the Hubei-Henan border, where it engaged several times with the pursuing KMT troops and the Henan army led by Liu Zhenhua, who apparently had an idea of preventing the Red Army from entering his domain. The Communists suffered further losses on the battlefields, but more horribly, they had to abandon their sick and wounded comrades, who amounted to a few thousand. In a letter of the Party Center to the Eyuwan Committee later, the situation was vividly described:

> Your treatment of the sick and wounded soldiers was simply an unforgivable crime. At first you tied them up and attempted to desert them; then again you locked them in a temple to desert them; finally, you took away their food supplies and distributed them among yourselves. Because of all these actions, only 2,000 of the 10,000 sick and wounded could eventually get back to the Soviet area.[51]

In early November, the Fourth Front Army reached the Manzhou Pass on the Hubei-Shaanxi border, where the Communist troops clashed with Xiao Zhichu's Hubei army and then with Yang Hucheng's Shaanxi army. They broke through the blocking line and burst into Shaanxi. Obviously out of tactical urgency rather than any strategic objective, they drove deep into the heart of Shaanxi, reached Lantian and Ziwuzhen in the vicinity of the provincial capital, Xi'an. After a fight with Yang Hucheng's troops in Ziwuzhen, they were forced to turn back south and reached Chenggu in early December, 1932. Now it was up to the Communists to formulate serious decisions for a long-term plan.[52]

The Party Center was clearly unhappy with the Fourth Front Army's evacuation of the Eyuwan Soviet base, even more so with its running so far to the west. On November 27, the Party Center instructed the Fourth Front Army to stop running west and open a new base area on the Henan-Hubei-Shaanxi border and ready itself for a counterattack. Later, the Party Center warned that it would openly denounce the Fourth Front Army if it continued westward.[53] Moreover, suspicions and protest arose from within the Red Army itself. Zeng Zhongsheng, Zhang Qiuqin, and others planned to send an envoy to the Party Center with a petition against Zhang Guotao and Chen Changhao. As Zhang Guotao recalled, "They created all kinds of fuss and rumors, saying that going west, far from other Soviet areas, would be hopeless."[54]

In his memoirs, Zhang Guotao claimed that it was according to a well-planned schedule that the Fourth Front Army deliberately undertook a feint attack into Shaanxi and then turned back to Sichuan. This claim seems unfounded. It was most probably the urgent military situation in front of them and the pressure from within the Party and Army that eventually brought the Fourth Front Army to northern Sichuan.[55] In early December, 1932, two more senior cadre conferences were held at Gucheng and Xixiang in southern Shaanxi. At the first conference, the cadres decided that the Army should stop going west; at the second one, they decided to move to Sichuan before winter came. In the next ten days, the Red Army climbed over the Qinling and Bashan mountains, and entered northern Sichuan. It took, and settled in the city of Tongjiang. Its troops had been reduced by that time from 20,000 to 15,000 by its three-month Long March.[56]

All kinds of advantages awaited the Red Army in northeast Sichuan at that moment. The KMT Central Army had already begun its Fourth Suppression Campaign against the Jiangxi Central Soviet and had consequently called back most of its troops then in pursuit of the Fourth Front Army. Yang Hucheng's Shaanxi army had neither the intention nor the legal right to follow the Red Army into Sichuan. At its present location, the dreadful economic condition of the masses and the weakness of the local military forces—owing to the decades-long conflicts among the Sichuan warlords—facilitated an explosive growth of the Red Army. On December 29, 1932, the Revolutionary Committee of the Sichuan-Shaanxi Base Area was founded; in early February, the First Congress of the CCP and the First Soviet Congress were convened; a new Soviet base was born.[57]

Just as the Fourth Front Army was settling in northern Sichuan, the Party Center began to publicly denounce Zhang Guotao's western flight. On January 5, 1933, the Eyuwan CCP Committee submitted a report to the Party Center protesting Zhang Guotao's rightist tendency, patriarchism, and flightism. The report, co-signed by all the leading figures of Eyuwan CCP Committee with Shen Zemin taking the lead, noted on the evacuation of the Eyuwan Soviet:

> In our view, this action [evacuation from the Eyuwan Soviet] was in direct opposition to the Comintern's instructions, to the Party Center's orders to the Fourth Front Army, and to the correct line as expressed in the Central Bureau's telegrams and other papers concerning the mobile war. It was nothing less than a rightist opportunist flight. Those responsible for this rightist opportunism were Comrades Guotao and Changhao. Comrade Guotao should be held particularly responsible because of his consistent opportunistic tendency witnessed by his behavior in the Nanchang Uprising and his attitude in the Soviet area now.[58]

On March 15, the Eyuwan CCP Committee received a reply from the Party Center, saying "After a careful review of your work in the Fourth Campaign, we think that the Party in the Eyuwan base had indeed committed extremely serious mistakes. We think it is an extraordinary mistake that you decided on October 11 to allow the Red Army to leave the Soviet area. This wrong decision laid a basic foundation for the Fourth Front Army's western flight."[59] It is important to note that this telegram was addressed to Shen Zemin in the Eyuwan base area, not Zhang Guotao in northern Sichuan. By that time, Zhang had already firmly established a new base and therefore the Party Center tried not to blame him too much. Since the Party Center seemed as yet unwilling to recant on its former criticism of the Fourth Front Army's actions, the blame was shifted to Shen Zemin and his Eyuwan CCP Committee.

Comparing the situation faced by the Fourth Front Army after losing the Eyuwan base with that of the Central Red Army two years later, one may ask why there had been no change in leadership in the former, as happened with the latter. It seems even more incredible, given that Zhang had been opposed by the Party Center. Among the possible explanations, two are worth noting. Zhang's quick success in northern Sichuan helped to smother grudges and silence dissenting voices. More importantly, the Eyuwan Sub-Bureau was not like the Party Center, and any decision to change the present leadership could not be immediately reached. Dissidents like Zeng Zhongsheng and Zhang Qiuqin had to appeal to and wait for the Party Center's decision in order to abolish Zhang Guotao's leadership in the Fourth Front Army and the Eyuwan Sub-Bureau. The Party Center thus worked as a buffer. In late 1932, the Party Center was not yet entirely discontented with Zhang Guotao, but by the time it began to scold him seriously—in early 1933—Zhang's ordeal was already over.

The Fourth Suppression Campaign and the Third Red Army's Long March

An integral part of the Fourth Suppression Campaign personally conducted by Chiang Kai-shek was aimed at the Xiangexi Soviet. The military process in this area bore a great deal of resemblance to that in the Eyuwan Soviet: both began and ended around the same time, lasting from May to November 1932, and both had the same consequences—KMT troops successfully occupying base areas, while the Red Armies were compelled to embark on flights or Long Marches.

Thanks to the engagement of the KMT army with the Jiangxi Soviet in the Third Campaign, and with the Japanese invasion from late 1931 in Manchuria to early 1932 in Shanghai, the Xiangexi Soviet also enjoyed a period of smooth growth. Under the political leadership of Xia Xi and Guan Xiangying and the military command of He Long and Duan Dechang, the Communists managed to establish a fairly large V-shaped area of influence running from south to north and cutting through Hubei. The southern tip around the Honghu Lake at the Yangtze River was their home base. The northern mountainous region served as a vast guerrilla zone, though it was in the central area that they captured such numerous strategic cities as Yingcheng, Tianmen and Qianjiang, and there they constituted a direct threat to the provincial government. The whole Soviet—before the Fourth Campaign in May 1932—covered about 20 counties. The Communist troops, under the title of the 3rd Red Army, consisted of three regular divisions with 15,000 men in total and a number of Red Guard brigades numbering more than 10,000.[60]

The KMT suppressing troops, some 100,000 of them, were named the Left Route Army with He Chengrui, the Hubei governor, as the commander-in-chief. At He's disposal were five divisions of his own provincial army which constituted the eastern column; some troops of the neighboring Sichuan army together with some local security brigades formed the western column. Their basic strategy was to use the Eastern Column, commanded by Xu Yuanquan, to make slow and steady intrusion while deploying the Western Column of Wang Lingji as a defensive force.[61]

The first month's engagement was focused on the central area. In the face of attacks by the superior government army, the Red Army gave up one city after another and retreated step by step westward, though none of the battles at this stage were decisive. By June 1932, the Communists were compelled to make a serious decision as to their strategy in coping with the situation. After fierce debates, a final decision was reached: He Long would lead two divisions to fight outside in the north while Duan Dechang would lead one division and some local forces back south and fortify a strong defense line in the Honghu base.[62] Thus, two lines—one offensive and external, and the other defensive and internal—were formed. Provided the Red Army could win a victory at the outside line, the KMT troops would naturally withdraw from the southern Soviet base.

Two battles at the northern front in the Jingshan area in July 1932, ended with no success for the Red Army. These battles lasted several weeks and each side suffered losses of several thousand men. Once again, for the government, this amount was a comparative pittance; while for the Communists, this meant a reduction by almost one-third of their entire regular forces. The Red Army was pushed back to the Honghu base.[63]

In these critical days, the 3rd Army received instructions from the Military Council in the Central Soviet suggesting that "the Third Army should immediately concentrate all its forces, pick out and break up one weak point of the enemy while applying the local forces and massive guerillas to delay other points. In this way, it can defeat the enemy one by one." This reminder proved as helpless to He Long as it had to Zhang Guotao.[64]

August and September did not witness any big losses for the Red Army. One time, Duan Dechang's troops even annihilated an entire KMT brigade at Xingou. Nevertheless, the enemy steadily drew tight its encircling knot and the Red Army's troops were slowly squeezed away. He Long took the lead to burst through this encirclement and flee north to the Dahong mountains. Following him were Duan Dechang and other smaller units of the Red Army and the Red Guards, leaving the Honghu Soviet toppled in late October. The surviving Communist forces, 10,000 in total, managed to gather together in Suixian of northern Hubei. A meeting of the most responsible Party and Army leaders was held to discuss the situation and future strategy. With the Nationalist troops pressuring them from three directions, they unanimously resolved that the only way to save the troops from destruction was to flee further north. After a quick reorganization and preparation, the 3rd Red Army set off on its Long March in early November, 1932.[65]

Because this expedition of the 3rd Red Army was more a desperate flight than a heroic feat—it meant more shame than glory for He Long, who was later to become a high ranking commander in the Communist army—few participants feel comfortable recalling it in detail. Information on this event is thus incomplete and inaccurate. The limited sources available only allow for some sketchy descriptions. In mid-November 1932, He Long and his troops left northern Hubei and entered southern Henan. They were guided by a piece of map torn from a high school geographic textbook.[66] They vaguely hoped to run into the Fourth Front Army or some local Communists on the way. What they encountered instead was a strong Nationalist division deployed on the Hubei-Henan border under the command of Ma Hongkui. The Communists had to detour west and entered Luonan of Shaanxi province at the end of the month. After some frictions with the enemy troops in that district, Liu Zhenhua's division of the Northwestern Army, they were forced south. In December 1932, He Long directed his men into eastern Sichuan where the political and military conditions proved as unfavorable as anywhere. They did not induce any significant recruitment or find sufficient respite to work on a new base, and had to keep marching and fighting. Eventually, in January 1933, the 3rd Army arrived at Shihe on the Hubei-Hunan border. The three-month-long march cost almost one half their troops.[67]

The Hunan-Hubei border had been He Long's home base for three years before his 1930 adventure attacking Wuhan. Here, the returned Red Army could easily find what He called "old relations" and get resettled after the tedious expedition.[68] As the military situation became less urgent, the intraparty struggle was resumed under the name 'anti-counterrevolutionary movement.' Partly as the natural result of the military failures of the past months—disagreement and contradiction among the leaders, desertions and betrayal of local cadres, and so on—and partly as a result of some personal issues for the top leaders, especially Xia Xi and He Long, this movement was carried out with an unprecedented intensity and cruelty. Most high ranking leaders, including Wan Tao, the former Political Commissar of the 3rd Red Army, Duan Dechang, the founder of the Honghu Soviet, the political commissars of all the three divisions and the chairmen of almost all the county Soviets were labeled counter-revolutionaries and executed. Although Xia was himself one of the returned students, he showed no mercy to his former classmates.[69] As a mockery of his revolutionary radicalism, Xia went so far as to have abolished all the Communist Party organizations within the Red Army and all the Soviet systems within the base area, presumably to purify the Party and the Soviet.[70]

Though this old Soviet base might provide the Communists favorable conditions to salvage the crisis, it also showed them some potential problems which prevented any hopes of rapid expansion: the whole area was physically and mentally exhausted by the incessant revolution and war. In autumn 1933, when another KMT suppression operation approached, the 3rd Army had to flee to the Qianjiang area of eastern Sichuan. After roaming around the Hunan-Sichuan border for several months, it arrived at northeast Guishou in early 1934. Its troops had by then shrunk to just 3,000 men. Even He Hong, the simple-minded Communist loyalist, realized that "we could not act like this any more . . . A wild pheasant has his nest on top of the mountain and a white crane has her cave at the river's bank. We, the Red Army, also need a home base."[71] A conference of the Xiangexi Sub-Bureau was convened on June 19, 1933, at Fengxianxi, a village on the Hunan-Guizhou border. Resolutions were passed that the Party and Soviet system should be rehabilitated and a new base should be established in eastern Guizhou. The anti-counterrevolutionary movement was halted and opportune policies like that of allying with native peasant rebels or "the celestial army" and protecting middle peasants and small merchants were adopted.[72] Competing with the local armed forces, the 3rd Army eventually managed to found a new base under the title of the Hunan-Hubei-Sichuan-Guizhou (Xiangechuanqian) Soviet, where it barely sustained its existence until fortune brought Ren Bishi's Sixth Army Corps to the area later in October, 1934.

For a general assessment of this first phase of the 3rd Red Army's Long March from the Honghu Soviet to the Xiangexi Soviet and eventually to the Eastern Guizhou Soviet, some conclusive remarks can now be made. Among the three major Communist forces in the 1930s, the 3rd Army was the weakest. Its smooth expansion in 1931 was due to the KMT Central Army's engagement with the Central Red Army and the Japanese invaders, and the provincial army's attention to the Fourth Front Army in the Eyuwan Soviet. Left to compete with local police forces, the 3rd Army could win victories and grow, but when the multi-provincial troops of the KMT approached in the Fourth Campaign, it proved beyond its military capacity to win the match. The 3rd Army's strategy of sending the major force to offend outside and leaving the minor force to defend inside proved ineffective.

Further, the evacuation and expedition of the 3rd Army was a direct consequence of its military failure. It stemmed from a desperate effort to survive, rather than any constructive objective. The fighting capacity of the 3rd Army had dropped to such a low point in late 1932 that it could not even overcome local security forces. This condition partially explains why Zhang Guotao and Xu Xianqian successfully founded a new base in northern Sichuan while He Long and Xia Xi could not do the same in eastern Sichuan.

Returning to the Hunan-Hubei border helped He Long temporarily survive—by dint of reliance upon his old acquaintances—but He and Xia Xi could scarce expect rapid development in this base area. Revolution requires new locations with fresh materials and new people with fresh militant spirits—things generally lacking in an old area.

Finally, after their eastern expedition at the Li Lisan period in 1930 and, particularly, their Long March following the Fourth Campaign in 1932, He Long's troops had by and large lost their political momentum. He himself was an army man obsessed with military pragmatism, without any independent revolutionary imagination. Xia Xi, on the other hand, was too ideology-minded to fit his ideas to practicable reality. The inability of these leaders to coordinate their two extremes substantially contributed to the defeat and collapse of the Xiangexi Soviet.

The Fourth Suppression Campaign
in the Jiangxi Central Soviet

After the First CCP Conference of the Central Soviet Area and the First National Soviet Congress were convened at Ruijin in November 1931, three distinguished institutions were formally established. The Party or the Central Soviet Bureau was formed with Zhou Enlai as secretary and Ren Bishi and Xiang Ying as vice secretaries. The Soviet or the Central Government of the Soviet Republic was set up with Mao Zedong as chairman and Xiang Ying and Zhang Guotao as vice chairmen. The Army or the Central Military Council with Zhu De as chairman and Wang Jiaxiang and Peng Dehuai as vice chairmen was finally established.[73]

The real mechanism of the Communist leadership might have been quite different from the formal appointments listed here. Practically speaking, there were two types of leadership performance at the time: the 'front work' moving together with the Red Army, and the 'rear work' staying at Ruijin. Aware of the importance of the war, Zhou chose to follow the Red Army as the representative of the Central Soviet Bureau and left the general political leadership to Ren Bishi and Xiang Ying. Therefore, most documents issued in the name of the Central Soviet Bureau in 1932 were drafted not by its secretary, Zhou, but by its vice-secretaries, Ren, and less often, Xiang. Such a situation is important even in view of documentary studies of that period.

Inspired by the formation of new leadership and by the Ningdu Revolt (in which an entire KMT army of 20,000 came over to the Communist side in December 1931), the Red Army initiated a combat by attacking Ganzhou, the center of southern Jiangxi, in January 1932.[74] Defending Ganzhou was only one KMT brigade led by Ma Kun and some local security forces totalling 7,000 men. Ma's garrison troops were well-prepared and the city firmly fortified. Peng Dehuai's regular Red Armies and Chen Yi's local troops of 30,000 men besieged Ganzhou for more than a month and made four explosive assaults, but they could not break into the city. Instead of capturing Ganzhou, an entire division of the Red Army was captured by the enemy.[75]

After the failure in Ganzhou, the army corps system was reinstated. Obviously, it proved inefficient to put all the army units directly under the command of the Military Council. A military conference was held in Jiangzhou in March 1932 to review the previous actions and plan future maneuvers. Since he was not responsible for the Ganzhou battle, Mao naturally lodged strong criticisms. After the Jiangkou Conference, Mao was designated supervisor of the First Army Corps. Instead of going to southern Jiangxi, as the Military Council required, Mao directed the First Army Corps to Fujian. He succeeded in capturing Zhangzhou, a large port city of Fujian. At the same time, the western route of the Third Army Corps was fighting in South Hunan, not as successfully as the First Army Corps. In July 1932, the First Front Army was re-established with Zhu as General Commander and, after certain hesitations, Mao was rehabilitated as the General Political Commissar, presumably at Zhou's recommendation.[76]

Taking advantage of the engagement of the KMT Central Army with Zhang Guotao's Fourth Front Army, Mao transferred the Red Army to northern Fujian-Jiangxi border and achieved some victories in the Nanfeng area. In late September, however, Mao stopped moving north. Deliberately rejecting the possibility of cooperation with the Fourth Front Army may be too negative a description of Mao's purpose. But Mao was certainly uneager to rescue Zhang Guotao at the risk of his own army, nor was he obedient enough to follow the Central Soviet Bureau's order. At the Ningdu Conference of the Central Soviet Bureau in early October, 1932, Mao became the central target of criticism. He was scolded by almost all the participants, especially Xiang Ying and Ren Bishi. Zhou Enlai played a decisive, though unobtrusive role at the Ningdu Conference. Although he too was unhappy with Mao's autocratic control of the Red Army and arrogant displays of independence from the Party leadership, Zhou did not agree to expel Mao from all leadership. Consequently, Mao was sent back to the Soviet government and lost contact with the Red Army from that point on.[77] In late October, the Red Army moved further northeast for offensive actions. It won some small battles under the collective leadership of Zhou Enlai, Zhu De, Wang Jiaxiang and Liu Bocheng—who replaced Ye Jianying as the chief of general staff at the Ningdu Conference.[78]

As soon as the military operations in the Eyuwan and Xiangexi bases ended, the KMT began its offense against the Jiangxi Soviet. He Yingqin continued as commander-in-chief. Under his general headquarters were three route armies. The Central Route Army, headed by Chen Cheng, consisted of 40 divisions of 400,000 men, among which Chen's own 10 divisions of about 150,000 men took part in the combat while other divisions remained at the rear as reserve forces.[79]

The Red Army had 60,000 regular troops in three army corps and 20,000 local troops. Zhu De was styled General Commander as before, and Zhou Enlai substituted for Mao Zedong as General Political Commissar and the most authoritative figure at the front. But for various reasons, among which Zhou's conciliatory personality was most apparent, the General Headquarters of the First Front Army assumed a more collective nature within its leadership and a less independent position from the superior Party organization now than it ever had before.

Full of militant enthusiasm and short of military knowledge, the newly arrived Party Center leaders adhered to an all-round offensive strategy, even when the Fourth Suppression Campaign was already started. They demanded that the Red Army besiege and capture the city of Nanfeng. Thereupon, disagreements between Zhou Enlai and his Army commanders at the front and Bo Gu and his Party Center leaders at Ruijin occurred in early 1933. In two telegrams dated January 13 and February 7, 1933, Zhou raised mild objections to the Party Center's orders and proposed a withdrawal from the Nanfeng besiegement. As a reflection of the power relations within the Communist leadership and an indication of Zhou's personal character, his telegram issued on January 13, 1933 seems the more interesting. After listing detailed reasons for calling off the troops from Nanfeng, this telegram ends as follows:

> Zhu, Wang and the other comrades here all agree in my above opinions. But the Party Center keeps sending us orders to attack the city and that is very different from the strategy as expressed in my previous telegrams. I myself would always like to think that destroying the enemy, particularly its main forces, should be a precondition to capturing a city. After the enemy is destroyed, we can just stride into the city, no matter how strong its fortifications may be. Otherwise, if we keep attacking the city but cannot take it quickly, it will be exactly what the enemy wishes to happen at the present time. I expect from you—the comrades working in the Party Center—an answer as to whether my above plan is acceptable or not. Given no answer after

tomorrow, I will have to make the decision myself and at the same time ask for instructions from the Party Center.[80]

The Party Center did not approve Zhou's plan at first, but after attacking the city for a few weeks without success, the Red Army had to give up its attempt at Nanfeng. The first phase of the Fourth Campaign saw a few clashes at the northwest edge of the Jiangxi Soviet base in February, 1933. Then, willingly or unwillingly, the Red Army gradually retreated to the Lichuan area. Three divisions of the KMT army led by Chen Cheng marched from Yihuang toward Guangchang. Chen planned to begin a full-fledged strategic attack, after taking the city of Guangchang.[81]

Two KMT divisions, the 52nd under Li Ming and the 59th under Chen Shiji, rushed into the ambush of three Red Army corps at the Yihuang area in late February. The Red Army destroyed Li Ming in several hours, then shifted to attack Chen Shiji. In two days, two KMT divisions of 15,000 men were annihilated. It took a couple of weeks for Chen Cheng to reorganize his troops and resume their southern move. In the same manner, another division, the 11th, which was Chen Cheng's own favorite troops, was badly beaten by the Red Army. After these losses, the Campaign could hardly continue any longer.[82] Encouraged by their easy victories, the Red Army quickly turned to counterattack the enemy. Two army corps were ordered to encircle and attack the city of Le'an. Despite their absolute superiority in strength over the KMT garrison forces—5,000 to 2,000—they could not break the enemy defense. Instead, the Red Army lost as many as 2,000 men before it quit.[83]

At the end of March, 1933, the KMT formally called off the Fourth Campaign, leaving some troops to defend the few strategic cities. In the meantime, the Red Army proclaimed a great victory and marched back to its inner base. Since all the victorious battles occurred in the outer edge of the Soviet area, the new strategy was well authorized. It seemed that the Red Army did not have to surrender the Soviet territory to lure the enemy inside anymore. The Red Army could expel and destroy the enemy "outside the gate of the Soviet country." The Campaign was also a justification for the new Party Center leadership: Mao did not participate in the battles, yet even larger victories were clinched.

In impartial estimation, it seems that the CCP's victory was achieved because the Fourth Campaign in the Jiangxi Soviet was but a transitional phase between the KMT's operation in the Eyuwan and Xiangexi bases and its operation in the Jiangxi Soviet, and also because the number of KMT offensive troops directly involved in the Campaign was not as superior to the Central Red Army as in the two previous cases. The situation was never so grave for the Jiangxi Soviet, and the Party Center leaders were inaccurate in ascribing the victory to the new offensive and forward strategy.

When Mao was still alive and in power, official historians in China used to claim that the Central Red Army's victory in the Fourth Campaign was due to the legacy of Mao's original strategy. That is not quite true either. Of the two essential features of Mao's strategy—luring the enemy into the Soviet base to fight on the interior line, and concentrating main forces to destroy a part of the enemy in a mobile war—Communist leaders rejected the first and kept the second. Had they accepted Mao's former strategy completely, they would certainly have lost a large part of their territory but the victory could hardly have been greater than what they actually achieved.

From the Nationalist standpoint, the Fourth Suppression Campaign as a whole could be viewed as reasonably successful in two senses: the KMT wiped out two of the three major Communist bases, and it learned bitter lessons—it had to take the Red Army more seriously and it had to change its military strategy. Chiang Kai-shek had held the idea that by putting his Central Army into battle, he could automatically win. The victories in the Eyuwan and Xiangexi Soviets enhanced his confidence. The failure in the Central Soviet shocked him, aroused his attention, and created in him a serious attitude to the forthcoming operation. The CCP leaders in the Jiangxi Soviet earned pride and glory from the Fourth Campaign, and it seemed as though they might never lose. They were victors, and assumed that they would continue to be so by just doing the way they had done. In fact, the disparity in mentality between the Communists and the Nationalists can be taken as a starting point from which to explain their different approaches and achievements in the Fifth Campaign to follow.

4

THE FIFTH SUPPRESSION CAMPAIGN AND THE LONG MARCH

The Fifth Suppression Campaign represented the climax of the military struggle between the Communists and the Nationalists in the 1930s. It ran a full year, from October 1933 to October 1934, and involved more than a million troops fighting in a dozen fierce battles and numerous small skirmishes. The Campaign deserves a book-length monograph in itself. The confines of this book only allow for a general account of the episode, pinpointing the military situations and strategies of the Communist Party at various points of development.

Studies of the Fifth Campaign illustrate the relationship between politics and military affairs. In one respect, the Fifth Campaign constituted a civil war whose outcome was eventually decided by the execution of armed forces. The Communists failed in the Campaign mainly because the Bo Gu Center stressed political impact nearly to the negligence of military affairs. From another point of view, the Fifth Campaign may be seen as a national political process potentially decided by the manifestation of each party's overall appeal. One of the prime reasons for the Nationalists' victory in the Fifth Campaign resided in their conscious effort to create a broad and solid political platform from which to effectively stage their military performance.

The Start of the Fifth Suppression Campaign

Even before it began, the Fifth Campaign had become the subject of intensive military preparation and political propaganda on the parts of both the KMT and the CCP. On the Nationalist side, the Fifth Suppression Campaign distinguished itself from all the previous ones in the way it was conducted. The Nationalists finally devoted their full attention to the Communists, and they had developed a new strategy for dealing with their tenacious enemy.

As an initial change, Chiang Kai-shek stressed a slogan concerning the general policy for the Fifth Campaign: "Seventy percent politics plus thirty percent military affairs."[1] This meant to create a solid political condition which previous campaigns had lacked. Further, in order to concentrate all attention on the Communist rebellion, the KMT reached a compromise with the Japanese invaders in North China. In May 1933, an agreement was signed by the KMT government and the Japanese army at Tanggu. The Tanggu Agreement allowed the Japanese de facto control over all Chinese territory north of the Great Wall. In return, the Japanese promised not to undertake any further southern advance. A buffer zone between the Great Wall and the Yellow River was established: military forces from either side were forbidden to enter.[2] For the same purpose, the age-old *baojia* or household registry system was applied throughout the country, particularly stringently in the Communist-infected provinces so that government control could reach the grassroot level and cut off the Communist links with the local peasantry. Strict laws were adopted boycotting the Soviet economy. No material goods whatsoever were to be smuggled to the Soviet area, and anybody trading salt, medicine, or food with the Communist rebels would court severe punishment. In the urban communities, besides the harsh rules established regarding publications and public activities, the "New Cultural Movement" was initiated to inspire national patriotism and Confucian ethics in defiance of Communist ideology.[3]

In the KMT army, German advisors were hired to teach modern techniques of field command; and modern weaponry—especially heavy guns, airplanes and communication instruments—was bought to re-equip all the Central Army troops.[4] A military training program was initiated at the Lushan Mountain in June 1933, with Chiang as the director and Chen Cheng as his deputy. After three sessions, all the 7,500 officials ranked platoon leader or higher had completed the program.[5] Their knowledge of military technology was greatly improved. Moreover, they were taught, in Chiang's own words, "to revitalize our revolutionary spirit—which had been dead; and to rehabilitate our revolutionary cause—which had been lost." All army officers were thus required to wear the same uniform, eat the same food, live in the same camp, and fight on the same front as the rank and file did.[6] Under military pressure and political persuasion by the Nanking government, all KMT military cliques and provincial armies were drawn into direct or indirect actions against the Red Army. In fact, this situation was possible thanks to the Communists themselves, who had by then become a serious threat to the common interests of all KMT military wings, diminishing their internal tensions.

In October 1933, a giant combat project was put into action. Chiang personally assumed general command in the Nanchang Field Headquarters, under which four army groups were formed in the four directions. The

Northern Route Army was the main offensive force of the project, concentrating its attacks, as before, from the north to the south. Under the command of Gu Zhutong, it contained 38 divisions totalling 400,000 men, most of whom belonged to the KMT Central Army. For the blocking or defensive forces, Chen Jitang was assigned the role of commander of the Southern Route Army in charge of nine divisions—this time composed mainly of troops from the Guangdong Army. He Jian, with his 14 divisions of the Western Route Army, was to confront the 6th Red Army Corps at the west bank of the Gan River. He was moreover placed there to obstruct the Central Red Army in case it attempted a westward escape. The Eastern Route Army—under the leadership of Cai Tingkai and containing his six divisions—was placed so as to check the Red Army from the Fujian side. Later, after Cai's abortive revolt in early 1934, Jiang Dingwen took charge of the eastern front and transformed this army into another attacking route.[7]

The Fifth Campaign directly involved more than sixty regular KMT divisions, or about 600,000 soldiers. Including such special troops as air force, artillery, communication, transportation and loggery, the total was actually more than 750,000. After taking into account the local security brigades and police squads of the four or five provinces, nearly one million troops were involved in this Campaign—at least this was the Communist claim.[8] To make the situation more graphic, it should be noted that the combined strength of encircling KMT troops amounted to as much as one third of the entire population of the Jiangxi Central Soviet.

Regarding the new strategies the KMT adopted in the Fifth Suppression Campaign, much emphasis—perhaps too much emphasis—has previously been placed on the connection of the Nationalists' victory to their blockhouse construction. For this reason, a few points need to be clarified. The blockhouse policy did not have as much to do with Chiang's German advisors—such as Von Seeckt and Von Falkenhausen—as some writers claim.[9] This was in fact an old method: first experimented with by middle rank officers such Dai Yue and Liu Weiyuan in the early 1930s, it was later suggested by senior leaders, He Yingqin, Zhao Guantao and others at the Lushan training program, and was eventually accepted and propagated by Chiang.[10]

Meticulous attention was paid to the allocation, construction, and protection of blockhouses. Normally blockhouses were located at high spots difficult to approach but open enough to make full use of firepower. They were thickly walled with stone and concrete, and in capacity varied from housing a squad of a dozen men to accommodating a battalion of several hundred.[11] The basic objective of the blockhouse policy was to cope efficiently with the Red Army's mobile warfare. The strategic location of a blockhouse made it impossible for the Red Army to pass by. To take it would cost them strength and time. More often than not, the blockhouse keepers could hold on long enough for reinforcements to come for the rescue along the highway linking one blockhouse to another. From 1933 to 1934, the KMT army constructed about 15,000 blockhouses all around the Jiangxi Central Soviet base, a territory of but 10,000 square miles.[12]

Chiang also adopted a new combat strategy in the Fifth Campaign, which he conceptualized as "strategic offense and tactical defense."[13] All army units were required to advance one step at a time, tightly encircling the Soviet area from all directions and finally squeezing the Red Army for the showdown. In Chen Cheng's words, this was to "dry the pool to catch the fish." This strategy was supplemented or completed by the "blockhouse policy" and the "highway policy." Whenever the army reached its destination, it would build blockhouses at all strategic points. Then highways would be built to connect blockhouse strongholds with one another and with the rear reserve forces. No troops would rush to seize new areas before the places they had taken were perfectly consolidated.[14]

While the Nationalists were carefully planning the Suppression Campaign, the Communist leaders were for their part busily engaged in two projects: an intraparty struggle generally termed the 'anti-Luo Ming line,' and a massive movement of land investigation. Both actions seemed necessary and beneficial in the view of the newly arrived Party Center led by Bo Gu and Zhang Wentian. It was an endeavor to strengthen its leadership, politically and organizationally. Neither, however, was particularly beneficial in bringing about a measure of preparation for the forthcoming military showdown with the KMT.

Luo Ming was the Acting Secretary of the Fujian CCP Committee from March 1932 to January 1933. At the early stage of the Fourth Campaign, Luo expressed his opinions about the current situation and the Party's work in two articles. After suffering from repeated assaults of the KMT, he reported, people in western Fujian were characterized by a mood of panic and fatigue. "A lot of masses at the border area went up to the mountains and then came back down again, saw a peaceful time and then faced a fearful one. It became very hard to call them together for meetings and military actions. Seeing the enemy advancing day by day, the masses, local Party, and government cadres lost their confidence in any active offenses against the enemy."[15] According to Luo, these phenomena were not merely due to such problems as shortage of political agitation, anti-counterrevolutionary effort, mobilization of class struggle, or enforcement of the Party's leadership. "It should be clear that although all the above factors are indeed valid, the most crucial matter is the inappropriateness of our military command. More concretely, it is due to the Party's lack of skillful operation of military struggle. . . . The Party had been too mechanistic in its military leadership; it is useless to develop the same plan and apply the same measure to different counties and districts."[16] Luo stood against the Party Center's blind call for an "all-round offensive strategy" and an "all-out military recruitment." Based on his assessment, Luo argued for more flexible military strategies suitable to local conditions. For local Red Armies and new Soviet bases like those in his western Fujian, he suggested that policies different from what the Party Center stipulated should be implemented. He did not think, for instance, that he could fulfill the army recruitment quota assigned in the area under his jurisdiction.[17]

Luo raised his opinions merely from a local point of view without a clear intention of challenging the Party Center and its political and military line in general. He might have been quite accurate in his depiction of the depressing situation in western Fujian, where intense warfare had lasted several years, wearing out the peasants' revolutionary enthusiasm and material resources. But Luo was definitely unwise to openly test the tolerance and authority of the new Party leaders. He was immediately castigated by Bo Gu and Zhang Wentian in the most militant Marxist-Leninist terms.[18]

The military victory in the Fourth Campaign immensely reinforced the Bo Gu Center's political position before all the opposition elements. Then the Party Center shifted its spearhead of offense to the intraparty front, so to speak. The anti-Luo Ming repercussions spread to the CCP branches in Jiangxi, where Deng Xiaoping, Mao Zetan, Xie Weizun and Gu Bo were singled out. They were charged with sympathy for the Luo Ming line and with factional activities. In the central Soviet government, Deng Zihui and He Shuheng were criticized for their "pessimism"; in the Red Army, Tan Zhenlin and Xiao Jinguang were punished for their "defeatism".[19]

Detailed studies of the anti-Luo Ming line have been provided by Kitada Sadao, a Japanese historian. Like many other historians, Kitada claims this movement was actually aimed against Mao Zedong. Such claim may be true in a final analytical sense but not in a practical one. Few of the "Luo Ming-liners", and in particular Luo himself, had any intimate relations with Mao, and the attacks on them had little direct impact on Mao's position. Besides, it should be noted that the anti-Luo Ming campaign in the Jiangxi Soviet was far less extensive and unreasonable than the anti-counterrevolutionary movements in the Xiangexi and Eyuwan Soviets.[20]

The Land Investigation Movement also needs a more profound appraisal than that often supplied. In fact, what most concerned the Communist leaders in the movement was how to appropriately employ the land problem as a measure to create a favorable revolutionary atmosphere to the advantage of their political and military objective. Aims to improve the peasants' livelihood or even to increase economic productivity in the Soviet were secondary. The peasants were excited by land distribution, their obvious material gain, but discouraged by the prospect of joining the Red Army and losing their lives, just as clearly their physical loss. When they eventually learned of their loss to their gain, their militancy began to abate. The Communist leaders then had to recharge their revolutionary enthusiasm through land investigation and redistribution. But if this land reform was overdone, social chaos and economic setbacks would occur to the disadvantage of the Soviet regime and the war. In such a case, the slogan of anti-leftist trend would be raised instead. From June to September 1933, land investigation was carried out vehemently, and many 'middle peasants' were reclassified as 'landlords'. October to December 1933 was a rehabilitation period, in which landlords became peasants again. From January to February 1934, there was another period of anti-rightism and anti-rich peasants. Only the ever aggravating military situation brought these oscillations to an end.[21]

In conclusion, it seems that the anti-Luo Ming line in leading circles and the land investigation movement among the masses in 1933 might have temporarily created a militant mood, but such a mood could hardly be regarded as a durable, favorable condition for the Fifth Campaign. Although they were outspoken about the forthcoming war, the Party Center leaders did not have any solid, suitable plans in military affairs in general and in combat command in particular. Instead, they simply imposed one army recruitment drive after another, which either failed due to the ever-growing size of quotas, or resulted in quickly patched and incompetent troops. They knew little more than just loudly chanting the slogan "overall positive offense," which seemed useful in amusing themselves during peace time but proved useless in overcoming the enemy in war time.[22]

Incidents in Fujian, Conferences in Ruijin, and Battles in Guangchang

The first phase of the Fifth Campaign—that is, October and November 1933—was marked by active offenses of both sides in the same Lichuan area, northeast of the Central Soviet. The result might be claimed a victory by both the Nationalists and the Communist—the former succeeded in taking the strategic city of Lichuan and the latter destroyed one enemy division at Xunkou. The actual situation was stalemate. But in the sense that such a stalemate should in time work to the benefit of the militarily superior KMT side in the long haul, it could be deemed an evil omen for the Communists.[23]

On November 20, a large scale army revolt suddenly burst out from within the KMT camp at Fujian. Sponsored by Chen Mingshu, the former Minister of Public Transportation, and Cai Tingkai, the General Commander of the 19th Route Army, the so-called People's Republic of Fujian and the People's Productive Party proclaimed their formation and their anti-Chiang stance. Under their control were six divisions of KMT troops at the eastern front and a large number of police units in the province, some 100,000 soldiers. Although the revolt was the reasonable culmination of conflicts between the army led by Chen and Cai and the Chiang's Central Army, it came as a great shock. Chiang quickly transferred eleven divisions of his northern route troops to cope with the emerging situation, leaving the Fifth Campaign dormant for the next two months.[24]

Reviewing the Fujian Revolt, all historians agree that it offered the Communists a golden opportunity to win over the Nationalists in the Fifth Campaign. They further allow that the Revolt did not serve the Communists very well or the Communist leaders failed to take full advantage of this event. But on whom the blame should rest—if indeed there is blame to be assigned—remains an arguable question. On more than one formal occasion, Mao Zedong stated that the left-opportunist CCP leaders at that time were wholly responsible, naively rejecting a military alliance with the Fujian rebels to fight Chiang's troops. This assertion is accepted by some historians.[25] Others insist that it was Mao who adamantly opposed any active cooperation with the 19th Route Army; and for this blunder Mao was given a disciplinary punishment by the Comintern and the CCP Center.[26] Until the Communist archives are opened and all records (if any exist) of the Politburo and Military Council conferences from September 1933 to February 1934 are released, there is no way of judging between these accounts. Using my own researches with presently available sources, judging from the personalities and dispositions of Mao and other CCP leaders as evidenced elsewhere, and with a general knowledge of CCP history—which I characterize as a complex process of continual readjustment rather than a monolithic, static set of responses and ideological poses—I will present my own understanding of the situation.

The Communists knew of 19th Route Army's plans for revolt several months before the defection occurred. In order to start an open mutiny against the KMT Central Government, Chen Mingshu and Cai Tingkai realized, soberly enough, that they needed military allies. They tried the Guangdong warlord Chen Jitang first and received only an ambiguous reply. In September 1933, they sent a secret envoy directly to the Jiangxi Soviet base to negotiate. Chen Gongpei met Peng Dehuai at the western Fujian front. As a battlefield commander, Peng naturally welcomed the idea of turning foe into partner. He treated Chen well, but had no role in deciding the matter. He had to report it to his superiors, the heads of the General Headquarters of the Red Army, Zhu De and Zhou Enlai. The instinctive reaction of Zhu, Zhou and other military leaders was ecstasy. The Party Center headed by Bo Gu and Zhang Wentian at Ruijin was informed of the incident by the Red Army headquarters. Neither militarily experienced nor politically prudent, they could be easily moved by the surprising good news. In a happy and excited mood, the General Headquarters was instructed to send a telegram message to Peng Dehuai scolding him for lack of sufficient hospitality to the distinguished Fujian guests.[27]

When the envoy plenipotentiary of the Fujian government and the 19th Route Army did come for treaty talks a month later, the Communist leaders were cooler and more serious. Mao Zedong, Zhou Enlai and Zhu De, as leaders of the Soviet government and the Red Army, received Xu Hongming and his aides, but Bo Gu as leader of the Communist Party did not condescend to meet the representatives of an obnoxious "People's Productive Party." Mao was a type of politician whose pragmatic resourcefulness could easily turn to sensitive suspicions. In all likelihood it was at this moment that Mao admonished his colleagues not to show too much eagerness and rush into allying with the Fujian rebels, and that he proposed to bargain for all good terms to the benefit of the Communist side. This attitude was accepted by the Party Center, not because Mao had dominating power yet, but because what he said sounded rather sensible—to the inexperienced any suggestion would sound sensible—to Party leaders like Bo Gu and Zhang Wentian.

After several days of close negotiation between Zhou Enlai on behalf of the Soviet Government and the Red Army and Xu Hongming on behalf of the Fujian People's Government and the 19th Route Army, a preliminary agreement was finally signed on October 12, 1933, the essential contents of which are quoted as follows:

1. Both sides shall immediately stop military actions and draw a provisional demarcation line over which neither side shall station any main forces. The 19th Route Army must take all measures to expel or extinguish any forces which may obstruct the execution of this agreement in Fujian and in the border area between Fujian and the Soviet.
2. Both sides shall restore their relations of import and export trade according to the principle of mutual aid and cooperation.
3. The Fujian government and the 19th Route Army shall immediately release all political criminals in prison.
4. The Fujian government and the 19th Route Army shall allow all revolutionary activities, such as social organization against Japanese imperialism and all militarization of revolutionary masses, and grant freedoms of publication, speech, assembly, association and strike.[28]

Obviously from the agreement, there were a lot of political and economic demands from the Fujian side by the Communists. As for the urgent military affairs, it did not mention anything in any positive terms other than a simple truce between the two sides. Mao might have thought of employing a harsh stand to keep the Communist Party's superior position in this alliance, but the Bo Gu Center as a whole took each item on the paper seriously and kept on criticizing the Fujian Government for not fulfilling the above promises in the next month.

As the KMT Central Army drove into Fujian and won a few decisive battles with the 19th Route Army in Jian'ou and Yanning, the loosely patched Fujian People's Government collapsed in short order in late December, 1933. It was at this juncture that Mao sensed the urgent need for military action, less for rescuing the Fujian rebels than for taking full advantage of the urgent situation. He suggested that the main forces of the Red Army make immediate offenses from northeast Jiangxi to Zhejiang.[29] The Party Center changed its position too, but in the opposite direction. Consulting with the Comintern and the Shanghai Sub-bureau and appealing to the Marxist-Leninist doctrines of proletarian revolution and class struggle, they decided to adopt an even more antagonistic stance toward the Fujian government. At the very least, this was a waste of time. As Braun puts it, "the Politburo and the Military Council discussed almost for a month how the political situation should be correctly assessed and which military orders should be issued, rather than acting vigorously."[30]

After it toppled, the Communist leaders continued to deride the Fujian government until they found themselves in the face of an ever fiercer assault by the KMT.[31] Of course they did not totally forget to take advantage of Cai Tingkai's misfortune. They tried secretly to buy Cai's leftover troops, but were firmly rebuffed.[32] All the Communists had gained from the incidents in Fujian was perhaps a month's free time, during which they managed to hold two national conferences to satisfy their vainglory and compete for power within the Communist Party, the Soviet Government, and the Red Army.

From January 15-18, 1934, the Fifth Plenum of the Sixth Central Committee was convened at Ruijin, with full and alternate Central Committee members and delegates from some provincial Party committees as participants. According to Braun, Mao deliberately avoided attending the conference. He introduced a note of discord into the meeting by stating that his poor health would not permit his participation. Actually, Mao did not attend because he felt that he, as Chairman of the National Congress and the Central Government of the Chinese Soviet Republic, should present the report on the Soviet governmental work, and was offended when Zhang Wentian was entrusted with such a responsibility.[33] Here it is only appropriate to make an evaluation of the political report and an account of some organizational issues concerning this Plenum.

With the urgent situation of the Fifth Suppression Campaign in mind, it is obvious that Bo Gu's political report to the Fifth Plenum, entitled "Current Situations and Tasks of the Party" and accepted as the general resolution, is an exemplary piece of what Mao called *benben zhuyi* or "bookwormism"—heavily worded but inappropriate to the practical conditions. The revolutionary situations both at home and abroad were said to be excellent; the policies of both the Comintern and the CCP were held to be impeccable; and the major task of the Party was nothing more than continuously fighting against those "right opportunists" who did not acknowledge this excellence—these constituted the central themes of Bo's speech. As for forthcoming war, he had little to say about concrete military strategy or tactics, but repeated a wishful slogan: "consolidate and expand the Red Army and fulfill in as short as possible period of time the goal of creating one million steel and iron soldiers."[34] Given the military urgency of the situation in January 1934, it is amazing that not even a formal report or resolution on military affairs appeared during the 5th Plenum. Power relations within the Party Center, it seemed, had become the focal point of attention.

At the Fourth Plenum, held in January 1931, neither Bo Gu nor Zhang Wentian were elected members of the Central Committee. Only a few months later, both jumped in rank to members of the Politburo. With most Communist leaders away, what remained in Shanghai in 1932 were only three or four members of the Politburo—barely enough to sustain a provisional Party Center. When this institution moved to the Jiangxi Soviet area and merged with the Central Soviet Bureau in January 1933, it still could not proclaim itself as the Party Center. It was sometimes called the Central Soviet Bureau, and other times the Central Bureau of the CCP. Apparently, the newly promoted leaders lacked a sense of security regarding their stature within the Party. A Central Committee plenum could certainly solve that problem. At the Fifth Plenum, a new Politburo of the CCP Central Committee was formally established.

Following the Fifth Plenum was the Second National Congress of the Soviet regime, which lasted for ten days, from January 22 to February 1.

Table 4.1 The CCP Politburo in Early 1934

Full Members: Bo Gu, Zhang Wentian, Zhou Enlai, Xiang Ying, Wang Ming,

Chen Yun, Kang Sheng, Ren Bishi, Zhang Guotao, Mao Zedong, Zhu De,

Gu Zuolin

Alternate Members: Liu Shaoqi, Wang Jiaxiang, Deng Fa, Kai Feng

The Standing Committee or the Secretariat:

General Responsibility Bearer: Bo Gu

Members: Bo Gu, Zhang Wentian, Chen Yun, Zhou Enlai, Xiang Ying [35]

The Second Congress was in all ways a showy demonstration of the Soviet movement. A giant auditorium was constructed and decorated specifically for this occasion; the ceremony included a military parade and a salute of gunshots; the schedule was designed to promulgate the constitution, the code of laws, the government with various ministries, and so on. In sum, no effort had been spared in depicting the Soviet as a formal national state rather than the shaky rebellious base it actually was. The Soviet organ, *Red China*, reported that as many as 693 delegates and 83 alternate delegates came to attend the Congress from all over China, in addition to 1,500 guests from the world.[36] However, the last figure at least was ridiculously exaggerated, or it must have pertained to those curious peasant watchers.[37] To make this national state more authentic, the Congress stipulated formation of a ministry of foreign affairs in the government and nomination of all the Soviet bases as provinces, though none of the few Soviet bases had ever been so large as one third of an average province and all of them were encircled by vast KMT territory and superior KMT troops. As far as the Second Congress was related to the Fifth Campaign, although its formalization of governmental stature might have promoted the recruitment campaign for the Red Army and the material support of local communities to the war, the Congress laid out the hampering precondition that the Red Army adopt the positional defense of the Soviet Republic as its prime objective and central strategy.

Contrary to some studies of this event, I believe that the Second Congress was a success rather than a failure for Mao Zedong as a Communist politician. The leading role of Mao throughout the Congress was too conspicuous to ignore. The entire performance became almost a one-man show. Mao proclaimed the opening of the Congress on January 22 and enjoyed congratulations from all circles. On January 24-25, Mao presented the main speech, which had about 40,000 Chinese characters—the longest of Mao's writings, and also the longest CCP formal document thus far. After two days' study and discussion of his speech by divided groups of delegates, Mao showed up again to make remarks on January 27, commenting on some views brought about in the discussions and criticizing others. The next few days were devoted to reviewing and planning specific government jobs, conducting an election, and reorganizing the Soviet leadership. On February 1, Mao announced the triumphant conclusion of the Congress.[38] The Congress reaffirmed and consolidated Mao's image in the eyes of the masses, the cadres, the Comintern, the Soviet Union, and even the antagonistic KMT as the quintessential symbol of the Chinese Soviet movement. Mao's speech at the Congress and several other articles by Mao were quickly compiled into a book in Moscow—the first publication of *Selected Works of Mao Zedong*. With the Soviet movement acknowledged as the major achievement of the Communist revolution, Mao's position as its representative could scarcely be denied.[39]

Waller gives a reasonably comprehensive description of the Second Congress in a monograph, but his understanding of the Congress as a landmark of Mao's 'demotion' in the Communist leadership needs more depth of comprehension. To indicate Mao's jeopardized position, Waller sharply divides the 17 members of the Presidium of the Central Executive Committee into Maoists and the Returned Students, and counts Zhu De, Lin Boqu and Fang Zhimin as of the former faction and Xiang Ying, Zhang Wentian, Bo Gu, Zhou Enlai, Li Weihan, Deng Fa and others as of the latter. He uses Zhang Wentian's appointment as Chairman of the Council of People's Commissars to illustrate Mao's dismissal from practical leadership in the Soviet government, and the takeover of the returned students-leaders. The real situation was more complicated, even in terms of factional alignment and power distribution.[40]

In summary the two conferences marked essentially more failure than success for the Communists as far as their position in the Fifth Campaign was concerned. Neither of them had much positive impact on the military situation in the Fifth Campaign, which would prove to be the most decisive standard for judging their fate and destiny at that time. Temporarily, the conferences wasted some of their time and chances. In the long run the failure was more insidious: they had helped reach a general condition, if not exactly a military strategy, from which the defeat of the Red Army in the Fifth Campaign proceeded.

From the standpoint of the intraparty struggle, however, the influence of the two conferences was ambiguous. Politically and, to a lesser extent, organizationally, Bo Gu and his men legalized their overall leadership by means of the two conferences. For Mao and his confederates, though these events marked a further demotion in a certain sense, they consolidated their position in another way. Mao remained Chairman of the Central Executive Committee for the Soviet Republic and became a full member of the Politburo. He did not suffer any direct criticism either at the 5th Plenum or at the 2nd Soviet Congress, as he did in the Ningdu Conference. In fact, except for a few cases, it is seldom that any individual Communist leaders could be identified as pro-Mao or pro-Bo. Most of them would keep changing their positions according to the times and issues. In a real sense, the only victory the incumbent Party Center leaders could claim was the assurance that should the Red Army prevail militarily, they would be well-off; in this case Mao would probably, though not necessarily, be further downgraded. If they could not, then Bo would bear the responsibility and Mao would most likely rise. Thus, the battlefield of intraparty struggle was moved to the battlefield of Guangchang shortly after the conferences, where the decisive fight between the KMT army and the Communist army would at the same time become the decisive struggle between Mao and Bo.

None of the Red Army corps commanders were called back from the front to attend the Party or Soviet conferences, but the busy engagement of the General Headquarters leaders in Ruijin at that time made it impossible to conduct any large strategic maneuvers. In January 1934, the 3rd Army Corps made a hesitant advance at the eastern front without much success. The 1st Army Corps was ordered to advance at the western front and then to shift to the north where, unable to break the enemy defense, it retreated quickly.[41] The KMT Central Army captured Fuzhou in the middle of January and immediately resumed their attacks on the Red Army from both the northern and the eastern directions with greater momentum and higher morale.

Though versed in Marxist quotations and revolutionary slogans, Bo Gu had neither much experience nor much self-confidence in military affairs. He had to rely on or leave to Zhou Enlai the military command until October 1933. Zhou was a person accustomed to hard and careful work at routine matters, but not to the defiance of his superior on the one hand, nor to the stringent tactical demands of his subordinates on the other. Zhou in his turn depended heavily upon the commanders in the army corps for military affairs. This situation changed totally when Otto Braun, the military advisor of the Comintern to the CCP, came to Ruijin in October 1933.[42] Bo Gu trusted Braun for various reasons, and Braun indeed knew too well of modern warfare and military technique. Since defense of the Soviet state had already become the entrenched strategy, there was no need of any more strategy. All that left to do was figure out how to arrange such a defense tactically and technically. The Braun concept "short swift thrust" was in itself not so much a strategy as a tactic, but because no well-planned strategy existed, it assumed strategic importance.

Braun's faith as a German Communist in the world revolutionary cause was as admirably strong as his faith in his own military profession as a German soldier. He set to work right after the close of the Soviet Congress, strict to himself in taking each route of KMT troops into meticulous attention and equally strict with the Red Army commanders, making them obey every directive he gave. Each squad and each artillery had to take the exact location shown on his combat maps. Military command was for Braun a physical science, not a liberal art as it was to Mao.[43]

In two months' face to face confrontation with the KMT troops the Red Army could not win any decisive battles. On the contrary, it had to withdraw its defensive line further to the south. The KMT troops did not attempt any quick or long distance pursuits; they patiently built up blockhouses in the occupied areas, connected them with highways and formed a thick and broad blockhouse network on the northern front. Then they began to press slowly but steadily southward. By mid-March 1934, they approached the city of Guangchang, about 150 li directly north of Ruijin.

Fierce fighting took place in Guangchang and vicinity in late April. It consisted of a dozen battles and lasted two weeks. Eventually, the Communists lost 5,000 men and had to give up the entire area. May 1934 saw the KMT army's successful capture of Longgang, Guangchang and Jianming and its creation of a new deep-cut offensive line from the north. The situation appeared more appalling for the Communists.[44]

In view of military strategy and tactics, the Guangchang battles brought what Mao later criticized as "the pure defensive line" to full application and a decisive test. Though Zhou Enlai and Zhang Wentian had written several articles on the Guangchang battles, neither of them—most especially the latter—were directly involved. Before the battles took place a field headquarters was formed.[45] Bo Gu assumed the post of Political Commissar of the Headquarters with the effect, if not the purpose, of removing Zhou Enlai from direct military responsibility. Since Zhu De as the General Commander of the Field Headquarters was as ever a figurehead, Bo Gu would now exert decisive power. Furthermore, since Bo himself knew little of military affairs, Braun became de facto leader for the Guangchang battles. The policy and slogan of "red blockhouse vs. white blockhouse" was formulated. Accordingly, several layers of fortification were built up, each with an intensive array of man- and fire-power. When the KMT troops approached, a human wave tactic was employed—i.e., one wave of Red Army soldiers after another would thrust outwards, driving toward the enemy's strategic points or command quarters for a swift counterattack over a short distance. Sometimes they succeeded and knocked off a certain number of KMT troops. Other times they failed in the face of the enemy's superior forces and reinforcements. Even when they succeeded they could only maintain their defense line intact as usual. Once they failed, they had to give up the defense line and retreat to the next one. Thus the general result was their successive retreat from one defensive line to another and their abandonment of one place after another. In this manner, as Peng Dehuai recalls, the city of Guangchang was eventually lost:

Attacking Guangchang were seven enemy divisions, in addition to one brigade of artillery troops for explosive offense and thirty or forty airplanes for bombing. Backed up by their turtle shells (blockhouses), they marched forward step by step. Each step forward was limited to 1,000 to 2,000 meters, safely under the cover of fire power. Firmly taking their foothold, setting their fortification up and arranging their fire power well, they would take another step. Six or seven planes bombed the Red Army front in shifts. In each day's bitter fight, our army thrusted several times without success. Nearly 1,000 men would die. The whole battalion assigned to defend what Otto Braun called "a permanent stronghold" was wiped out. All died martyrs—not a single man came out alive. Seeing this fact, they [the military leaders] eventually allowed a withdrawal and gave up their plan of defending Guangchang.[46]

More or less similar descriptions of the Guangchang battles can be found on the KMT side. Most historians, aware of the differences between the military strategy in the Guangchang battles and that in the previous campaigns, attempt to establish some connection between the different strategies and their respective consequences. Otto Braun offers a unique version of his own. Reluctant to admit it as a failure, Braun tries to ascribe the loss of Guangchang to Mao's attitude to the Party Center, "obey in words but resist in deeds."[47] Braun's views as the general commander on the spot should be very much treasured, but his direct responsibility for this historical episode makes the above assertion less credible.

Strategically important as it was, Guangchang might not be so crucial as is commonly assumed. In the first three anti-suppression campaigns the Communists had lost this and many other cities and yet they won the war after all. Only this time the fact that the Communist leadership took the defense of Guangchang as a life and death matter and cried so loudly before and after the event in itself made the Guangchang battles something really important. In other words, the loss of Guangchang was a decisive failure for the Communists psychologically more than practically. It left open the gate to Ruijin, the capital of the Soviet, less than it left open the gate to the overconfident heart of the Party and Army leadership. Arguments over responsibilities in the past followed, as did an adjustment of military strategies for the future.

The Anti-Japanese Vanguard Brigade and Its Northern Expedition

In May and June 1934, the KMT troops were biting deeply into the Central Soviet. Three attacking columns of Gu Zhutong's Northern Route Army captured Guangchang, Longgang and Jianning, and pressed toward Shicheng, a city about 100 li north to Ruijin. Jiang Dingwen's Eastern Route took Liancheng and moved westward toward Tingzhou; and Chen Jitang's Southern Route took Junmenling, threatening Huichang at the south of the Soviet capital. Defending the Soviet from inside the base area had proved unsuccessful and would seem unpromising. A need of basic strategical changes became a subject of consideration for the Communist leaders in general and Zhou Enlai in particular. The first indication of such changes was the dispatch of the Anti-Japanese Vanguard Brigade in early July 1934.

Long Marches of the Red Army in South China in 1934

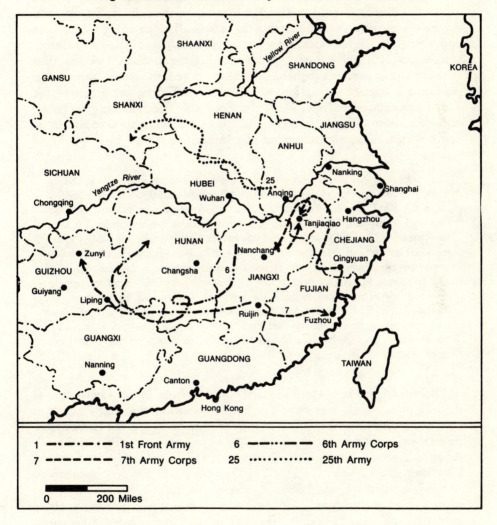

On July 7, the 7th Army Corps assembled in Ruijin according to an urgent order from the Red Army headquarters. Renamed the "Anti-Japanese Northern Expeditionary Vanguard Brigade", it immediately set out eastward toward Fujian province. This Vanguard Brigade consisted of three divisions, numbering 7,000 men in total. Its top rank leadership included Xun Huaizhou as the Commander, Le Shaoying as the Political Commissar, Su Yu the Chief of Staff and Liu Ying the Director of the Political Department. All these appointments were in fact the same as the 7th Army Corps. The only change in the leadership was that a representative of the Party Center named Zeng Hongyi was sent to supervise general affairs.[48] A few days after the Anti-Japanese Vanguard Brigade embarked, the Ruijin government published a solemn declaration, signed by Mao Zedong on behalf of the Soviet government and Zhu De, Zhou Enlai and Wang Jiaxiang on behalf of the Red Army. The declaration contains an eloquent appeal to the entire nation's patriotic sentiment against the Japanese invasion:

> It goes beyond any doubt that we will not give up our present anti-imperialist revolutionary base which we have created through countless bloody struggles with the KMT bandits. But on the other hand, the Soviet government and the Red Army can by no means bear to see our Chinese nation fall into the hands of the Japanese imperialists, to see all China be sold out by the national traitor and thief the KMT, to see the Chinese masses be killed and raped by the imperialists, and to see the Anti-Japanese Volunteer Army in the Northeast fighting singlehandedly without any support. Therefore, despite the urgency of the decisive fight we are now undertaking in front of the outnumbering KMT bandits and despite all kinds of difficulties and hardships, the Soviet government and the Red Army have made the utmost determination to dispatch this anti-Japanese vanguard brigade to march to the north and fight against the Japanese.[49]

The title "Anti-Japanese Vanguard" was nothing but a catchword, as Braun admits in his memoirs. The urgent situation the Red Army was then facing seemed too obvious for both the Nationalist and the Communists themselves to believe that there could be any direct connection of the 7th Army Corps' expedition with resistance of the Japanese invader.[50] A few years later in an article, Liu Ying, the Director of the Political Department of the Vanguard Brigade, recalled some of the instructions issued by the Party Center at the time. The Vanguard Brigade was required "to drive deep into the enemy's rear and expand massive guerrilla activities there, and to establish new bases where the enemy's rear front could be decisively threatened."[51] In other words, the 7th Army Corps' maneuver was a partial and belated experiment of the project which had been discussed among the Communist leaders previously, namely, to fight outside and harass the

KMT's rear in order to distract and extract the KMT troops suppressing the Central Soviet.

Leaving the Soviet cities, Ruijin and Tingzhou, the 7th Army Corps struck east toward the heart of Fujian. Under the leadership of brave and capable 24-year-old commander Xun Huaizhou, the Red Army quickly broke through the blockade line and successfully took cities such as Jiangliu, Datian, and Longxikou. Then it forced its way across the Min River and cut deeper into the province. On August 1, a fierce battle took place at Shuikou between the Red Army and the KMT garrison troops, and resulted in the latter's stampede. Following the enemy's retreating steps, Xun directed his men to approach the provincial captial of Fuzhou. For a while, the Red Army even pierced into the downtown area.[52]

Shocked by the abrupt intrusion of the Red Army, Chiang Kai-shek immediately transferred troops to rescue Fuzhou. With two more regular KMT divisions added to the defense force, it grew beyond the capacity of one Red Army corps to break the fortified city. Eventually Xun Huaizhou had to call back his attacking troops. In September the Vanguard Brigade swept along the eastern coast to the north. Picking up and dropping Luoyuan and Ningde, it entered Zhejiang and occupied Jiangyuan. Although it received some reinforcement from the Communist guerrillas at the Zhejiang-Fujian border, the Army Corps was reduced to 4,000 men by late September.[53] The failure to achieve any significant strategic purpose and the sad news of the Central Red Army's plan of evacuation from the Central Soviet aroused confusions among the 7th Army Corps leaders as regards their next moves. The Party Center representative, Zeng Hongyi, suggested that the Army Corps be dissolved into small guerrilla units to fight furtively in the mountains and wait for any future opportunities, but the Army Corps commander, Xun Huaizhou, could not accept such a pessimistic idea and stood for continuing the northern expedition. A military conference was held at Changshan in Zhejiang, but neither side was able to dissuade the other. With the strong support of his army subordinates, Xun gained an upper hand and directed the main force of 3,000 men to Chongxi in northwest Jiangxi in early October.[54]

In mid-October 1934, a message came from the Party Center and the Military Council demanding that Fang Zhimin, Chairman of the Northwest Jiangxi Soviet, should go to resolve the debate within the 7th Army Corps and reform the Anti-Japanese Vanguard Brigade. Fang and his men reached the 7th Army Corps at Chongxi, where a joint conference was convened immediately. At the Chongxi Conference, Fang Zhimin played the role of supervisor and mediator. Both Zeng Hongyi and Xun Huaizhou were mildly scolded and definitively demoted. Zeng was deprived of his command of military affairs and re-appointed secretary in the Northwest Jiangxi Soviet, while Xun was reassigned as commander of the 19th Division, newly formed from the 7th Army Corps. The 7th Army Corps and Fang's own 10th Army were combined into one unit entitled the 10th Army Corps under the sole leadership of Fang Zhimin.[55] On October 24, 1934, the reformed Anti-Japanese Vanguard Brigade left the Northwest Jiangxi base for its northern expedition, or the second phase of its Long March. The top rank leaders of this sector of the Red Army in late 1934 can be found in Table 4.2.

Table 4.2 The Anti-Japanese Vanguard Brigade in October 1934

The Political Committee

Chairman:	Fang Zhimin
Members:	Fang Zhimin, Liu Chouxi, Luo Shaohua, Tu Zhennong, Liu Ying

The 10th Army Corps

Commander:	Liu Chouxi
Political Commissar:	Luo Shaohua
Chief of Staff:	Su Yu
19th Division Commander:	Xun Huaizhou
20th Division Commander:	Liu Chouxi
21st Division Commander:	unknown[56]

Turning his grudge with his comrades into fierce anger against the KMT enemy, Xun led his own troops to start the northern expedition. They climbed the Yuhuai Mountains, defeated two regiments of the Zhejiang army at Changshan and got as near as 90 li to the provincial capital of Hangzhou. From there they turned northwest and cut into Anhui, passed through Jingde and Jingxian and directly threatened Wuhu, one of the most strategically important cities along the Yangtze River.[57] At the same time, the bulk of the Anti-Japanese Brigade under the leadership of Fang Zhimin took a more direct route from northwest Jiangxi and arrived at southern Anhui in early December. Fang called Xun back to the general headquarters for a more united operation. The whole army of 10,000 gathered together at Shangkou of Anhui in the middle of the month.[58]

After the Central Red Army's evacuation from the Jiangxi Central Soviet, Chiang Kai-shek could easily summon a large number of his troops to cope with the Anti-Japanese Vanguard Brigade. According to Wang Yaowu, the KMT general to whom the later destruction of Fang Zhimin's army was mainly accredited, seven or eight KMT divisions and a number of independent brigades totalling 200,000 troops took part in this military campaign. The security troops and local police of Zhejiang and Anhui were ordered to block and intercept the Red Army in their respective provinces.[59]

The Red Army stayed in Tangkou for two days and then continued marching northward. As the KMT's chasing troops were distressingly close, Fang Zhimin and his commanders decided to strike back before going any further. On December 14, 1934, a decisive battle took place in Tanjiajiao. Although the Red Army managed to ambush a KMT brigade led by Wang Yaowu, they could not have dealt a destructive blow to Wang's troops. After a day's fierce engagement, 300 Red Army men were dead, including— worst of all—the 19th Division commander Xun Huaizhou. Fang Zhimin had to issue an order to withdraw.[60]

The defeat in the Tanjiajiao battle and the death of Xun Huaizhou dampened the Red Army's morale and caused various problems within their leadership. Roaming around the counties of Shitai, Taiping, Dongzhi and Jimen in southern Anhui for another month or so, Fang Zhimin could not see any hope or purpose in going further north and began thinking of a return to his home base in northwest Jiangxi for a respite. He certainly did not take into full account the fact that by that time the Northwest Jiangxi Soviet was firmly occupied by the KMT troops and their intensive blockhouse networks constructed throughout this small base area.[61]

On January 10, 1935 the Anti-Japanese Vanguard ended its northern march and started its southern flight. The pursuing enemy kept biting its tail on the way, while local forces hit its head for good measure. Under the command of Fang Zhimin, Su Yu and Liu Ying, 700 Red Army men barely succeeded in sneaking through the KMT blockade. The remaining 2,000, led by Liu Chouxi and Wang Ruzhi, were cut off and left at the northern side of the Yuhuai mountains. To fulfill his duty as the general commander, Fang was determined to turn back himself to be with the majority of his army. A few more skirmishes reduced Fang Zhimin and Liu Chouxi's 2,000 men by half in late January. As the enemy encirclement drew tighter, they dispersed into small groups, hiding among forests, bushes and grasses and awaiting their fate. Wang Yaowu gives a vivid description of the Red Army's appalling situation at that moment:

After my troops set out, I heard sporadic bursts of bullets. The dispersed Red Army men, hiding in the mountainous woods, exposed to the bitter winter cold and suffering from starvation and thirst for several days, were hardly able to rise from the ground. Some of them wanted to lift their rifles to shoot the approaching KMT troops, but their frozen fingers could not bend the trigger. Some strove to throw hand-grenades, but they were too weak to pitch them out of their palms. They totally lost their fighting capability. The Red Army soldiers searched out by each regiment in my 1st Brigade looked pale and skinny, their hands and feet were full of chilblains and their lips full of blisters for lack of drinking water.[62]

On January 29, 1935 Fang Zhimin, Liu Chouxi and Wang Ruzhi were captured near the blockade line in Dexing of Jiangxi. Later, Fang and Liu were executed in Nanchang, while Wang betrayed his Communist faith to save his skin. This long march of the Anti-Japanese Vanguard Brigade, which lasted for seven months and covered four provinces, ended tragically. In custody at Nanchang, Fang reviewed his own errors in military command which he believed had caused the failure of the Anti-Japanese Vanguard. The following quotation from *A Brief Account of My Revolutionary Experience*, written by Fang in the Nanchang prison, witnesses his noble and fair—perhaps more than fair—appraisal:

> Morning. I wake up but do not yet get out of bed. The right time for recalling the past. Among the memories, the most anguishing is this failure of the 10th Red Army Corps. I did not quite understand what had gone wrong at the time, but now it seems crystal clear. Where were the errors? what caused the failure? if I had done not this but that, how could the troops have been defeated? and how could we have been captured? I start swearing at myself and occasionally hitting my body with my own fist: "Damn you, the stupid dumbbell!"[63]

In point of fact, Fang's northern expedition had a red herring or scapegoat function and was doomed to fail. It was originally designed by the CCP leadership to risk his men in order to divert the KMT's attention from the Central Soviet. After the main forces of the Red Army gave up their Central Soviet and began the Long March, Fang's handful of troops were left as the helpless prey of the overwhelming KMT army. The real significance of Fang's activities, for better or worse, might be that they did attract a large amount of Nationalist troops to the east and thus facilitated the Central Army's action in the west from late 1934 to early 1935 and, moreover, they left a few hundred survivors commanded by Su Yu and Liu Ying who were to become an ingredient of the New Fourth Army after the outbreak of the Sino-Japanese War in the late 1930s. The tragedy of Fang Zhimin as an individual Communist leader is that he was not informed of his real mission at the beginning and he was not fully aware of the true effect of his actions at the end.

The 6th Army Corps and Its Western Expedition

Despite the sensational intrusion of Xun Huaizhou's Anti-Japanese Vanguard Brigade into Fujian, July 1934, did not see any drastic change in the intensifying situation in the Central Soviet. Only two or three Nationalist divisions were transferred from the Eastern Route to reinforce Fuzhou. The Northern Route, which constituted the main direction of assault, was scarcely affected and its two columns led by Xue Yue and Chen Cheng kept pushing southward, tightening the encirclement. By the end of the month, the Red Army dispatched another army corps to attempt an exterior operation. Chosen for this operation was Ren Bishi's 6th Army Corps at the western front.

Because of the shortage of sufficient documentation on the early stage of Ren Bishi's western expedition and also because of the shortage of historical studies of this seemingly unimportant episode—unimportant unless seen in the context of the Red Army's general strategy—there have been some controversial presentations even among Chinese Communists themselves. In a recently published biography of Ren Bishi, for example, an official Chinese writer says "before the Central Red Army's Long March, Comrade Ren Bishi received the Central Committee's instruction and led the Red Army in the Xianggan border to break through the enemy's blockade and start on the western expedition. The main task of his troops was to promote and facilitate the Central Red Army's Long March and function as a vanguard unit."[64] The KMT general, Li Jue, who was fighting the Red Army at that time, shared this same conceptualization. In his memoir, Li recalls that he and his colleagues did not know the real purpose of the 6th Army Corps until it had passed Hunan and entered northern Guizhou, and "it was only . . . [then] that we realized that the abrupt action of the 6th Army Corps' western expedition was to test the conditions in Hunan, Guangdong, Guangxi, Guizhou and Sichuan for the main forces of the Red Army and act as the vanguard unit of the Long March."[65]

As will be discussed in detail later, the Central Red Army had not reached any definite decision on the Long March when the 6th Army Corps set out its western expedition in late July and early August. The Party Center's dispatch of the 6th Army Corps on an expedition was as yet only based on the idea of transferring some troops to fight outside the Central Soviet to distract the enemy's encircling troops so as to allow the main forces of the Red Army to overcome the enemy inside the Central Soviet and thus save the home base. This purpose can be clearly understood from the tasks the Central Committee assigned the 6th Army Corps' operation. The 6th Army Corps was asked to fulfill a three-staged project: 1. To break through the enemy blockade line to reach the Guidong area in southeast Hunan and carry out partisan activities there. 2. To arrive at

Xintian and Jiyang of southern Hunan, carry out partisan activities there, and work on a Soviet base. 3. To go across the Xiang River and strike into the center of Hunan and expand the base area there.[66] Intensive activities of the 6th Army Corps in central Hunan would thus compel the Hunan army to rearrange its military forces and spoil the KMT's strategy of gradually tightening the encirclement of the Central Soviet and facilitate the victory of the Red Army inside the Jiangxi Soviet.

Another neglected factor leading to this expedition lay in the fact that by the end of July 1934, the precarious situation in Ren Bishi's Hunan-Jiangxi border area made remaining there with his troops impracticable. The 6th Army Corps was formed in June 1933. Three divisions, located in two separate regions west of the Central Soviet: the 16th Division to the north, and the 17th and 18th divisions to the south, were joined in its composition. In the Fifth Campaign, they were all under attack by He Qian's Western Route Army and suffered immensely. In July 1934, the base county of Yongxin was lost and the Red Army had to retreat to the southern side of the Jinggang Mountains.[67] Left to their own devices, they probably would have decided to disperse into the mountains to carry out guerrilla warfare. If they were to come up with a new strategy, they could go east across the Gan River to join the Central Army. Had it been a year before, the Party Center might have invited the 6th Army Corps to the Central Soviet as it did with the 10th Army of the Northwest Jiangxi Soviet. But in July, when the Central Soviet itself was facing a critical situation and pondering its own way out, the 6th Army Corps was ordered to undertake a western expedition instead.

On August 7, 1934, all the troops of the 6th Army Corps—except the 16th Division which remained in the Hunan-Hubei-Jiangxi border area, and a few local army units which were left in the Hunan-Jiangxi border area—gathered in Suichuan of Jiangxi province in order to depart. Five days' fighting and marching brought the 95,000 Communist troops to Guidong in southeast Hunan, where the top leadership of their western march was announced.

Informed of the Red Army's escape to southeast Hunan, Chiang Kai-shek ordered Chen Jitang of Guangdong, Bai Chongxi of Guangxi and He Jian of Hunan to intercept and pursue. The Guangdong army displayed some reluctance to act: the Red Army was not trespassing its territory. The Guangxi army made a move in the north: a fear of the Red Army's entry into its domain gave it a sense of purpose. He Jian was downright enthusiastic: it was in his home province that the Communists were currently encroaching. Two divisions of the Hunan army quickly approached the spot under the command of Liu Jianxun. Under this pressure, instead of following the Party Center's instruction to undertake guerrilla activities in southwest Hunan, the 6th Army Corps had to proceed to the second stage

Table 4.3 The Sixth Army Corps on the Long March
in August 1934

The Political and Military Committee

Chairman:	Ren Bishi
Members:	Ren Bishi, Xiao Ke
	Wang Zhen

The 6th Red Army Corps

Commander:	Xiao Ke
Political Commissar:	Wang Zhen
Chief of Staff:	Li Da
17th Division Commander:	Xiao Ke
Political Commissar:	Wang Zhen
18th Division Commander:	Long Yun
Political Commissar:	Gan Siqi[68]

of the original plan ahead of time. They rushed further west, passed beyond Shukou, Dongjiang, Zhenxian, Yizhang and Guiyan and reached Xintian in southern Hunan in front of the Xiang River.[69]

The 6th Army Corps was, according to the original plan, supposed to carry out guerrilla activities in southern Hunan and then go across the Xiang River to strike into Xipu and Xinhua in central Hunan. But with two enemy divisions closely following from behind and five regiments guarding the river ferries in front, the Communist troops could fulfill neither of the tasks without perilous consequences. After some trial and failure at both tasks, they had to move still further southwest, leaving Hunan for northern Guangxi. The Guangxi authority sent Liao Lei with two divisions to intercept the Red Army, which then passed over northernmost Guangxi and arrived at Chengbu and Daodong at the southwest corner of Hunan in early September.[70]

The further west the 6th Army Corps went, the more tenuous its connection to the Central Soviet became, and the more meager its possibilities for strategic influence on the Central Red Army situation. Orders from the Military Council came requesting, ever more insistently, that the 6th Army Corps should stop moving west. "The most appropriate location for the 6th Army Corps' operation is the mountainous region of Chengbu, Suining and Wugang in the Hunan province," the September 8 order of the Military Council read, "the 6th Army Corps should remain in that region at least until September 20, destroying the enemy's units smaller than a brigade and developing the Soviet movement there."[71] It is obvious that the true sense of this order was that the 6th Army Corps should risk its own existence for the sake of the Central Red Army in the Central Soviet. Accordingly, the 6th Army Corps decided to stay in southwest Hunan and fight with the upcoming enemy.

To coordinate all the KMT troops in these southern provinces, Chiang Kai-shek appointed He Jian as Commander-in-Chief. On the battlefield, Liao Lei assumed solitary command of the joint forces of the Hunan and Guangxi armies. The situation worsened considerably for the Red Army.[72] In September 1934, the 6th Army Corps had several clashes with the enemy, winning some battles but losing still more. In early October, when the 6th Army Corps had to run west again, they headed for the Liping area of eastern Guizhou where the KMT forces seemed weak.[73]

The fact that the 6th Army Corps could have successfully arrived at eastern Guizhou had much to do with the selfishness of the Hunan and Guangxi armies. Both followed the Red Army into Guizhou with a plan of sending the "Communist monsters" as far away as possible from their home provinces: neither wanted to be intensively engaged in fighting. As soon as they found the Red Army proceeding deeply into Guizhou, they were content to stop and set up their own defense lines, conclusively preventing the Communists from turning back. The Hunan and Guangxi armies remained there until late in October, 1934 when they were suddenly called back to fight with the Central Red Army, whose Long March had just begun.[74]

Just as the 6th Army Corps arrived at Wongan in eastern Guizhou, Xiao Ke and Ren Bishi received another telegram from the Military Council once again forbidding their going west. The 6th Army Corps stopped for a few days, at a loss for any strategic orientation. On October 7-8, they engaged in a fierce battle with the local army, in which the Red Army lost six or seven hundred soldiers and the 18th Division Commander, Long Yun. The troops in total were reduced to less than 4,000.[75] On October 10, Ren Bishi and Xiao Ke telegrammed the Central Military Council. Instead of asking for any instructions, Ren and Xiao simply informed the Military Council of their decision to divide their troops into two columns and move to join He Long. After two weeks' tedious march and hard struggle, the 6th Army Corps reached Yinjiang at the Guizhou-Sichuan-Hunan border, where it ran into He Long's 3rd Red Army.[76]

As both the 6th Army Corps and the 3rd Army were under very precarious conditions, and as neither was strong enough to hold any ambition against the other, both groups seemed truly happy with their union. A celebration rally was immediately held at Yuyang of Sichuan province. A month later a joint Party and Army leadership was established. As the only Politburo member and the commissioner of the Party Center, Ren Bishi naturally became the secretary of the CCP committee and the political commissar of the Army headquarters. For his military seniority and reputation in the Red Army, He Long assumed command of the Army headquarters. To put both the troops on an equal basis, the 3rd Army resumed its former title of the 2nd Army Corps, and the joint forces amounted to 7,000 soldiers.[77]

With the benefits of political consolidation and military solidarity—thanks to Ren Bishi and He Long respectively—and with most of the regular KMT troops drawn back to the east to confront the Central Red Army, the united 2nd and 6th Army Corps grew rapidly in this multiprovincial border area. By the end of 1934, Ren and He developed their armed forces to more than 10,000 men and built up a base with a population of one million people. To a certain extent, both the troops recovered their previous military capacity and political momentum.

Decision Making on the Long March in the Jiangxi Central Soviet

Until now, the question as to when and how the Communists reached their decision to abandon the Central Soviet and start the Long March has been a riddle for almost all historical writers. Owing to the intrigue of personal relations involved in this subject, especially relations between Mao Zedong and Zhou Enlai, official historians in China have not yet been 'mind-free' enough to touch such a subject. The references available to Western historical writers, apart from articles published in the Communist journals at that time, were memoirs of some former Communists, among whom Warren Kuo and Gong Chu were the most outstanding.

Despite stylistic differences, Kuo and Gong tell a similar story. An enlarged conference of the CCP Politburo and the Military Council was convened soon after the defeat in the Guangchang battles; finding it impossible to defend the Central Soviet from inside, the Communist leaders decided to break through the KMT encirclement and shift to fight outside; the expeditions of the 6th and 7th Army Corps were therefore designed as preparation for the general evacuation in October.[78]

Suspicions should be aroused when we find that Warren Kuo (or his informant, Chen Ran) was only a middle level Communist cadre at the time and was thus not qualified to attend the alleged Politburo conference, enlarged as it might be. As for Gong Chu, though his position in the Red Army was much higher, purposeful distortion of some historical facts in his *The Red Army and I* and *General Gong Chu's Memoirs* should lead the careful reader to doubt his other accounts. The publication of Otto Braun's memoir in 1975 has thus far provided the most concrete and comprehensive information on this subject. Certainly errors and biases can also be found in his account, but Braun was indeed one of the supreme decision makers at that time and at least he does not blatantly spin fairy tales.

The idea of breaking through the KMT blockade and fighting into the exterior area had been raised from the very early stage of the Fifth Campaign, but with the important difference that the idea was proposed in a positive and offensive sense at that time, not in the more passive and defensive sense in which it was to be considered later. In early May 1934, the Communist leaders held one or more conferences to review the Guangchang battles. Attending the conference were Politburo members and Military Council members available in Ruijin. There were some arguments among Zhang Wentian, Bo Gu and others, but discussion centered on settling responsibilities in the past rather than making plans for the future, around tactical matters rather than strategic plans.[79] The Front Headquarters of the Guangchang battles was dismissed and Bo Gu lost his position as the Political Commissar in the Front Headquarters. Zhou Enlai, as the Political Commissar of the Red Army, resumed his position in charge of general military affairs. By creating a more effective defense, and winning more battles within the Soviet base, Zhou thought, the Red Army might defeat the Nationalist suppression in a protracted war.[80] At the same time, as Braun faced blame for the Guangchang defeat, he attempted to defend his military slogan of "short, swift strike," which became almost the trademark of his whole command. He wrote several articles to promote this policy and persuaded some Army Corps leaders—notably Lin Biao and Peng Dehuai—to do the same. Though neither Lin nor Peng was particularly fond of Braun and his slogan, they both agreed and each published an article on *Revolution and War*.[81] Peng and Lin probably took this action as a chance to show their allegiance to the Comintern and the Party Center as an abstract whole without much knowledge of the subtle discord already emerging within the Party Center.

As the KMT attacks continued in May and June, shifts in military operation assumed a more fully strategic nature. In July, the 6th and 7th Army Corps were sent to fight in the enemy's rear. This indicated a basic change in Zhou Enlai's mind—the change from an intention of winning the campaign by winning each battle to that of sacrificing some Red Army units by sending them out to divert the enemy, so that the major forces could break the encirclement from inside the base area. The Communist leadership was reluctant to give up the Central Soviet and wanted to save it even at a rather discouraging cost. It was not until the middle of August, when the 6th and 7th Army Corps failed to bring about any drastic change in the situation that the subject of a wholesale evacuation was given serious consideration. Braun gives an important description of the process of decision making of the Long March in his memoir:

> The Politburo requested me to draft a new quarter-year plan for August to October. It was revised by Chou En-lai, approved by the Standing Committee of the Politburo, and transmitted in outline to the ECCI by way of Shanghai. The preparation of this plan triggered the first serious difference of opinion between me and Chou En-lai. My original thought had been to penetrate the blockade line with the 3rd Corps, but otherwise to maintain a strategic defense in the interior of the Central Soviet Area. I felt that this would guarantee the return of the main forces, although this was certainly problematical in view of the enemy's many-layered fortifications belt. At the very least it might preserve the Soviet Area as a very strong guerrilla base in the long term.
>
> Now Chou En-lai vehemently urged the evacuation of the entire Soviet Area, including all institutions, rear-line services, installations, and a large part of the independent and local units intended for mobile and guerrilla warfare in the interior of the Soviet Area and its border district. Po Ku negotiated a compromise in which Chou En-lai, who directed the entire operation, retained the upper hand. The number of persons to be evacuated was only slightly lowered—10 to 20 per cent according to my estimates.[82]

Braun does not give the exact time of the discussed occurrence, but since this was shortly after the 6th Army Corps' western expedition, it was probably sometime in the middle of August. This assumption can find support in one of Zhou Enlai's articles entitled, "A New Victory in a New Situation," published in *Red Star*, August 18, 1934. The article calls as clearly as possible for "strategic transference." In its essential section, Zhou wrote, "We must resolutely thrust our way into the rear of the enemy, strike into the remote rear of the enemy . . . to create a new situation and not to return to this old Soviet again."[83]

Zhou's article, as well as publications of other Communist leaders at that time, was written and published not to confirm a decision already accepted by the Party Center, but to lobby, so to speak, for support in order to get his position accepted. At this moment all we can judge of the procedure of the decision of the Long March is this: in mid-August, after some debate between Zhou and Braun, the decision was made by the three heads, Zhou, Bo, and Braun; soon afterwards it was discussed and confirmed by the Standing Committee, Zhou Enlai, Bo Gu, Zhang Wentian, Xiang Ying and Chen Yun. Then an outline report was sent to Moscow. In late August, members of the Politburo and Military Council were notified of the decision. It was for this purpose that Mao was called back from the south to Ruijin. In early September the Army Corps commanders were informed "so far as they were concerned with executing certain maneuvers in their area of jurisdiction."[84] It was not until late September and early October that the lower level officials learned of this decision, but they still had the jump on the rank and file, who knew of it only when it was put into action in mid-October.

The public disclosure of the Long March occurred in an article of Zhang Wentian in *Red China*, September 29, 1934. The title of the article was, ironically, "All for the Defense of the Soviet." The article claims a possibility of retreating from and surrendering the Soviet in one particular place in order to win the victory of the Soviet all over the country.[85] As opposed to Zhou Enlai, whose articles at that time merely dealt with military affairs, Zhang Wentian in his article implies his stand in the intraparty struggle. He labeled all these who still held the view of defending the Soviet within the Soviet as opportunists. By that time at the very latest, Zhang was openly showing his disagreement with the leading circle.[86]

To protect the confidentiality of the military schedule and to avoid disagreements within the supreme leadership, a so-called "Three-Man-Group" was formally established to carry out the evacuation operation, with Zhou taking full charge of all details of general arrangements.[87] The arrest and betrayal of the secretaries—Li Zhusheng and Sheng Zhongliang (Sheng Yueh)—of Shanghai Bureau revealed to the KMT the Red Army's intention of evacuation, but helped the Party Center in Ruijin get rid of the Comintern, waiting for whose approval would have at best delayed the schedule. Both the above factors made it necessary and possible to begin the evacuation a bit earlier. The Central Army embarked on the Long March in mid-October 1934.[88]

Mao Zedong's position and performance at the end of the Jiangxi Soviet period constitutes another mystery in many historical writings. It has been dramatically mistaken in some studies. In this respect, Gong offers another sensational story referring to Mao before the Long March. According to Gong Chu, Mao was exiled together with his wife to Yudu at the southernmost part of the Jiangxi Soviet, and he was thus deprived of all his positions and functions. He could not attend any Party and Army meetings; no persons from senior leadership paid him any attention anymore. A vivid description of a casual meeting between Gong and Mao is provided in his book. Gong recalls that on the way to his appointment as the general commander of the Southern Jiangxi Military District in September 1934, he happened to notice Mao from among a crowd. Gong says that at that time he had just received a special pension of ten dollars and therefore bought a fat hen and two pounds of pig feet. He let one of his guards send all these things to Mao's residence to be cooked by Mao's wife, and at 9:00 p.m. he himself went to have a drink with Mao. Then to the highlight of the drama:

> Wine is something that can easily stir up one's true emotions. We recalled the old days in the Jinggang Mountains. Mao uttered a long sigh and said, "Comrade Gong, since I joined the revolution, I have been expelled from the Party Center three times and had been punished with severe warnings eight times. This time they put all the charges of failure against myself alone. Gone are the days of us old Jinggang Mountain comrades now!" While talking like this, sorrowful tears rolled down his cheeks. He coughed softly, his face looked even more skinny and pale as reflected by the glimmering light beams from a soybean oil lamp, and he was extremely distressed.[89]

Gong's version of Mao's status in the summer of 1934 has been passed from one writer to another, and each one tacks on his own fripperies. John Rue concludes that Mao was not merely exiled but probably jailed in Yudu.[90] It is true that in the early months of 1934 Mao no longer played any decisive role in the Party and Army leadership. In the Soviet government, he was overshadowed by Zhang Wentian. But Mao's actual situation, not to say his potential influence, was by no means so wretched. As a member of the Politburo and the Military Council, Mao was informed of all the important Party and Army decisions and entitled to attend the supreme Party and Army conferences. In the Soviet government he shared leadership with Zhang Wentian, and he had his part of power in this field. Since all the government work was actually in the service of the war, Mao might be said to have no decisive power, but then neither did Zhang in this sense.[91]

After the Guangchang battles, when the military situation went on an irrevocably aggravating course and the military leadership was concentrated in the three men, Mao first avoided attending the conferences and then left the capital for the south—all on his own initiative. Checking several memoirs, it seemed that Mao made two trips in the period between the end of Guangchang battles and the beginning of the Long March. After attending the Military and Politburo conference in May, he left for Huichang, south of Ruijin. Passing through the city of Huichang, Mao wrote the well-known poem "Huichang".

Huichang—after the *ci* "Qing Ping Le"
(Summer 1934)

Dawn in the east just begins to break:

Do not say that too early we march,
Over all green hills we shall trample before growing old.
The views are especially good on this side.
The high peak outside Huichang walls
stretches ridge upon ridge into the eastern sea.
Our fighting men point to south Guangdong and gaze,
Where the landscape seems even more green and rich.[92]

It may not be sufficient to establish Mao's entire frame of mind just by reading one piece of poetry. Nevertheless, here we can hardly find Mao's overwhelming distress and depression as portrayed by Gong. On the contrary, the work reflects the author's strong will and high aspirations. There in the Huichang region Mao met Soviet cadres and Red Army officers and issued instructions whenever he stayed. In late June he came back to Shazhouba, the Soviet government seat near Ruijin. He stayed there and joined the discussions of the 6th and 7th Army Corps' maneuvers. Even if his signature of "the Declaration of the Anti-Japanese Vanguard" could be merely a matter of formal procedure, Mao's interview with *Red China* correspondent, published in that journal on August 1, 1934 should be persuasive enough to show his presence and function.[93] The quick fall of Jianning and Liancheng prevented Mao from making his trip to the eastern front. Therefore, he left his family in the Ruijin suburbs and set out for the western front of Yudu together with his service staff in early August. This trip was not a happy experience not for political reasons, but due to Mao's physical condition. He contracted a serious disease and lay in bed for more than a week in early September. Dr. Nelson Fu, the Director of Central Hospital of the Red Army was specially sent—obviously by the supreme leadership—to treat and take care of him. Mao was called back to Ruijin soon after he got well, just as the Communist leaders were planning the general evacuation.[94]

Refuting Gong's story is easy, but the real purpose of Mao's two trips to the front is harder to explain. I would support Braun's view that Mao intentionally avoided any further involvement with the military situation for the purpose of intraparty struggle. In Chinese history, modern as well as ancient, such political schemes have been played by quite a number of resourceful politicians.[95] It should be clear that from early 1934 onwards Mao had firmly established himself as the opposition spokesman. If the incumbent Party and Army leaders could fare well in front of the KMT, then they would also be well-off in the Party leadership. If they could not win the Fifth Campaign, they would hardly prevent Mao from rising up again. In Mao's own words, "The only thing for me to do at such times was to wait."[96]

In reality, Mao was not alone in his opposition to the Party and Army leadership. The deterioration of the general situation on the one hand and the concentration of the supreme leadership on the other hand had caused discontent among other high ranking cadres, among whom Zhang Wentian and Wang Jiaxiang were the most crucial. As Braun admits, the "Central Triad" of Mao Zedong, Wang Jiaxiang, and Zhang Wentian had already come into formation in the summer of 1934, in confrontation with the "Military Troika" of Bo Gu, Zhou Enlai and Otto Braun himself.[97]

5

MILITARY LINE VERSUS POLITICAL LINE: THE ZUNYI CONFERENCE AND THE RISE OF MAO

In January 1935—three months after the Long March was underway—the Chinese Communists crossed the Wu River and arrived at Zunyi, Guizhou. They stayed in Zunyi for about two weeks and held an enlarged Politburo conference there. The importance of the Zunyi Conference in CCP history and particularly in Mao Zedong's political career has aroused the interest of many Chinese and Western historians. In turn, their numerous reflections on this event have greatly enhanced the importance of the Conference, perhaps at the loss of a sense of perspective. Moreover, the large volume of writings on the Zunyi Conference contain a variety of basic errors on the Conference: errors regarding its composition, procedures, resolutions, and most importantly, its essential nature. Elsewhere I have dealt with identification and verification of the factual details of the Zunyi Conference[1]; this chapter will mainly be concerned with a general review of the Conference as one episode in the development of CCP history and as one phase of Mao Zedong's political and military career.

Early Phases of the Long March

The variety of claims as to the starting date of and the total number of initial participants in the Long March undertaken by the Central Red Army (the First Front Army) in the Jiangxi Soviet nearly rival the number of sources in overall quantity. Reviewing these versions and the relevant source material, one should realize that the controversy over the first question is concerned less with an identification of a particular time than with a proper definition of the term 'start of the Long March.'

On October 10, 1935, instructions for preparation and mobilization for 'a strategic transfer' were issued in the name of the Central Government of the Soviet Republic and the General Political Department of the Red

Army. At the same time, some units of the Red Army Headquarters were ordered to leave their office buildings in Ruijin and move a bit to the southwest. On October 16, the main Red Army forces of the 1st and 3rd Red Army Corps finished their preparation work—reorganization and mobilization—and marched swiftly toward the enemy blockade line.[2] On October 21, the 1st Corps took Xintian, and two days later the 3rd Corps took Gupi. Thus the KMT's first blockade line was cut open. Meanwhile, the Party Center and the Military Council sped through the Xintian-Gupi line, turned west and crossed the Dao River. With three dates—the 10th, the 16th and the 21st—all eligible as the starting date, the last one, in which the actual move of the central leadership and the entire army group took place, seems perhaps the most appropriate.

As for the number of initial participants, the figure 100,000 should be dismissed: Zhou Enlai and Otto Braun both later admitted it was used only for the purpose of deceptive propaganda. The true figure, according to Braun at least, should be 75,000 to 81,000; the official Chinese version cites 86,000 as the most accurate estimate. Since Braun's estimation was the total strength of the 'Central Army Group,' he may not have included those peasant volunteers and hired porters. The figure 86,000 thus seems most reliable.[3] Braun also inadvertently forgets to mention that one regular Red Army division, eight independent regiments, and some local forces—totalling 30,000—were left at the disposal of Xiang Ying and Chen Yi to continue fighting within the Jiangxi Central Soviet. The leadership of the Red Army at the beginning of the Long March are shown in Table 5.1.

Even if, as Braun insists, the military engagements in the previous year did not substantially jeopardize the strength and morale of the Central Red Army, the evacuation of the Central Soviet was clearly a result of military defeat. At the beginning of the Long March, besides a strong desire to escape from the KMT encirclement and preserve the Red Army from destruction, the Communists did not have any long-term plans as to where to go or what to do, as Mao himself admitted. One may also say that they had too many vague and fanciful ideas to be taken as having any definite ones.[5]

After breaking through the first blockade line, the Red Army marched directly west, reaching the Jiangxi and Hunan border in late October. In the next month, they proceeded in three columns: the 1st and 9th Army Corps formed the Left column, and the 3rd and 8th Army Corps formed the Right column; these two columns were to clear the way from both sides. The command column of the Party Center and the Military Council stood at the middle with the 5th Army Corps protecting it from behind. Lying ahead of them was the second blockade line, running from Guidong to Rucheng in southeastern Hunan.[6]

Table 5.1 The Central Red Army on the Long March, October 1934

Central Red Army Headquarters

    General Command: Zhu De

    Political Commissar: Zhou Enlai

    Chief of General Staff: Liu Bocheng

    Director of Political Department: Wang Jiaxiang

    Active Director of Political Department: Li Fuchun

First Army Corps

    Commander: Lin Biao

    Political Commissar: Nie Rongzhen

Third Army Corps

    Commander: Peng Dehuai

    Political Commissar: Yang Shangkun

Fifth Army Corps

    Commander: Dong Zhentang

    Political Commissar: Li Zuoran

Eighth Army Corps

    Commander: Zhou Kun

    Political Commissar: Huang Xin

Ninth Army Corps

    Commander: Luo Binghui

    Political Commissar: He Changgong

First Column of the Military Council

    Commander and Political Commissar: Ye Jianying

Second Column of the Military Council

    Commander and Political Commissar: Li Weihan[4]

The Rucheng and Guidong region was the exact territory that the 6th Army Corps had passed over two months earlier. The legacy of the Central Red Army received from the 6th Army Corps in this and other places seemed more negative than positive. Though the CRA could benefit from the information sent to them by the 6th Army Corps through radio communication, it had to face the even stronger fortified resistance which had been built up by the Nationalists in response to the intrusion of the 6th Army Corps. Fortunately, this time the Communists' strength was also enhanced.

The 1st Army Corps successfully took Chengkou on November 3, just as the 3rd Army Corps moved to the south of Rucheng. With the Nationalists' Guangdong army withheld from the south and their Hunan army from the north, the Command Column of the Red Army hurried through the blockade line on November 8. Li Hanhun, a general of the Guangdong army, managed nonetheless to bite off part of the Red Army's rearguard forces on November 10, and dealt the 5th and 9th Army Corps some heavy losses near the city of Yanshou. This was the first defeat of the Red Army on the Long March, and Mao used this situation to criticize the Party leaders. As for Chiang Kai-shek, the battle helped him realize the Red Army's intention. Before then, Chiang was not yet quite certain whether the Communists were making a feigned attack or a wholesale evacuation.[7] Now it became clear that the Communists were conducting a long-distance transfer, and on November 13, Chiang formed an ad hoc headquarters to cope with the new situation. He Jian of the Western Route Army in the Fifth Suppression Campaign became the commander-in-chief of the 'Bandit Pursuit Army.' Under He's leadership were not only the entire Hunan army, but also twelve divisions of the former Northern Route Army led by Xue Yue. From that time until the autumn of 1935, Xue's troops of the KMT Central Army served as the spearhead which chased the Red Army's rear all the way while local troops of each province which the Red Army reached served primarily as the checking force.[8]

While Chiang rearranged his troops, the Red Army continued westward, leaving behind another blockade line along the Wuhan-Guangzhou railway after some clashes with the local garrison troops in Liangtian and Yizhang, and entering southern Hunan in mid-November. In the Liwu and Lanshan region, the Communists gained a couple of days to decide their next move. Two months earlier, when the 6th Army Corps reached the same location, Ren Bishi and Xiao Ke had contemplated forcing through the Xiang River near Lingling to open a Soviet base in central Hunan. Such a possibility was instantly ruled out by the Central Red Army. The leaders of the Central Army had originally thought to establish a new base in the Hunan-Guangxi border; when they arrived it appeared impossible to do so. The Party Center and Military Council leaders were psychologically reluctant to accept the idea of moving to appeal directly to other Soviet bases and Red Armies, but instead hoped to establish a new base of their own in strategic coordination with the other Soviets and Red Armies. Partly for this reason, Mao at that time advocated an engagement with the KMT army before moving any further. Mao's proposal had the support of Zhang Wentian and Wang Jiaxiang in the military conference, but was rejected by a majority of voters, including Zhou Enlai, Bo Gu, Zhu De and Otto Braun. The final decision was avoid fighting with the enemy and go across the Xiang River to the further west.[9]

The crossing of the Xiang River turned out to be the fiercest engagement on the Long March. Disagreements among the central leaders and slow motion of the Command Column delayed the military action, so that by November 25, three groups of encircling Nationalist armies—altogether 15-20 divisions numbering 200,000—had taken their positions. First, the Hunan Army led by Liu Jianxun came from the north and reached Juanzhou, a city at the bank of the Xiang River. Second, the Guangxi army led by Bai Chongxi awaited the Communists in Guanyang and Xing'an, another city on the river bank (about 100 li south of Juanzhou). Finally, trailing the Red Army's footsteps from the east side were Yue Xue's troops, directed by Zhou Hunyuan.[10]

In response to this positioning, Lin Biao's 1st Army Corps was reassigned to the Right Column while Peng Dehuai's 3rd Corps replaced it as the Left Column. The 1st Army Corps failed to capture Juanzhou but managed to secure a portion of the river bank to the south of the city. The 3rd Army Corps did the same at Xing'an in the north. By November 27, the Red Army temporarily controlled a stretch of the Xiang River about 60 li in length, ready for the Command Column to cross.[11]

According to Nie Rongzhen, the Political Commissar of the 1st Army Corps, the Command Column of the Party Center and the Military Council were on that day located at Wenshi, 160 li away from the Xiang River. If the Command Column could have kept the same speed as other combat troops, it could have passed the River in one day. Unfortunately, the Command Column could only crawl 40 to 50 li per day and it thus took four days to reach the Xiang River.[12] The 1st and 3rd Army Corps commanders urged the Party Center leaders to speed up the crossing whereas the latter insisted that the former hold on the opening.[13] During the four days from November 28 to December 1, intensive fighting led to serious losses for all the Red Army troops defending the open corridor for the safe passage of their headquarters. Thanks to their bitter sacrifice—as well as to the Guangxi army, which stepped back a bit from the southern front to prevent Yue Xue's Central Army troops taking advantage of the situation in order to intrude into the Guangxi territory—the Party Center and the Military Council eventually crossed the Xiang River.[14] The sacrifice on the

Red Army side also included two divisions of the rearguard 5th Army Corps and the breakup of the 8th Army Corps. All this, in addition to the previous losses, reduced the Red Army's strength from their initial 86,000 to 40,000 after the Xiang River battle. Only Braun does not regard this as a significant failure. While admitting all the extent of the losses in those Red Army units, Braun concludes in reference to the Xiang River battle:

> The greatest loss occurred within the newer army units composed, in accordance with Chou En-lai's evacuation model, and primarily made up of inexperienced recruit volunteers. General Headquarters estimated that these units lost up to 50 percent of their men by the time the city of Li-P'ing in eastern Kweichow was captured. In the reserve division, the figure stood at 75 percent. . . . Casualties in the main forces, that is, the veteran divisions of the 1st, 3rd, 5th and 9th Corps, remained within modest limits.[15]

The above allegation is another example of the impregnable spirits of this German soldier. Though the casualty numbers might not be so high as some historians, such as Jerome Ch'en,[16] have claimed, the Xiang River battle was indeed a devastating fiasco for the Communists. The heavy losses reported sustained by Red Army were corroborated by KMT reports.[17] The following is an eyewitness account of the battle by Yan Daogang, chief secretary in Chiang Kai-shek's command headquarters at the time:

> The pursuing campaign on the Hunan-Guangxi border lasted about two weeks, from November 21 to December 2, 1934, and the intensive engagement was only one week or so. Participating in the campaign were twenty to thirty divisions. During this period, the fighting attracted all Chiang Kai-shek's attention. Telegrams and messages flew to and from the Command Headquarters. The battle ended as a grand victory on the part of the Nationalist army. . . . Nevertheless, Chiang was still not quite satisfied, blaming the Guangxi army for moving back from the battlefront so that the Communists were able to escape their total destruction.[18]

Leaving the Guangxi and Hunan armies behind and throwing their own cumbersome machines and equipment away at the eastern bank of the Xiang River, in early December 1934 the Red Army found itself in a much easier situation in the southwest corner of Hunan. As the entire army moved further away from the Jiangxi Soviet base and entered the strange southwest highland, however, the growing uneasiness in the rank and file as to where they were going and what they were doing was once again brought to the attention of the Communist leaders. After describing difficulties in army recruitment, Nie Rongzhen then recalled:

Another big difficulty was how to maintain and increase the troops' spirit and morale. The key problem was how to explain to the officers and soldiers the future of the Red Army or where we are heading for. They kept bringing this question to us. At first, we just answered 'transfer.' But the further we went, the less the word 'transfer' could serve as a satisfactory answer to the suspicions and doubts harbored in their hearts. After crossing the Wuhan-Guangzhou Railway, we were compelled to give them the definite answer that we were to unite with the 2nd and 6th Army Corps.[19]

Actually it was not just the soldiers who needed the reassurance of a definite answer, but the Party and Army leaders themselves needed the comfort of this idea. Thus when the Red Army reached southwest Hunan in early December, the plan to turn north to join He Long and Ren Bishi emerged out of a temporary propaganda slogan. For a short while, this plan seemed desperately necessary to the entire Red Army, but it was abandoned before long, not by the Communists but by the actions of the Nationalists. Instead of following Chiang Kai-shek's order to hurry down south to combine forces with Zhou Hunyuan at Xinning and make a joint pursuit at Chengbu, Xue Yue cleverly suggested that both his and Zhou's troops move northwest to Wugang, Hongjiang and Zhijiang to wait for the Red Army there.[20] This made the Red Army's plan of turning north for a union with the 2nd and 6th Army Corps practically impossible.

A Politburo conference was held in Tongdao at the southwest tip of Hunan. There, heated debate sprang up over opposing proposals offered by Otto Braun and Mao Zedong concerning the future movements of the Red Army. Braun proposed waiting on the spot until the KMT army passed to the west and then going northward to join the 2nd and 6th Corps, and Mao stood for marching further west to open a new base in northern Guizhou. This time, Zhou Enlai transferred his support to Mao, shifting the balance. Braun's proposal was rejected. On December 15, the whole army arrived at Liping in Guizhou. During their two day stay in Liping, the Red Army reorganized its troops. Since the 5th and 8th Army Corps had both suffered substantial losses in the Xiang River battle, the two units were combined into one and the title of the latter abolished. Another Politburo conference was held, and the commanders of the 1st and 3rd Army Corps, Lin Biao and Peng Dehuai, were invited to participate. Mao's proposal of moving to Guizhou was formally adopted. Apart from the decision to open a new base in northern Guizhou, the Liping Conference also touched upon the matter of intraparty contradictions. It was resolved that as soon as a proper time came, the Politburo would hold an enlarged conference to review the experiences and lessons of the Fifth Campaign.[21]

Liping was the last point at which the Central Army followed the former route of the 6th Army Corps. From that point the 6th Army Corps had, under Party Center instructions, turned to the north and united with the 3rd Red Army. Now the Central Red Army, not bound by any superior leadership, decided to move further west in search of new prospects. Whether they could successfully establish a new base in this barren highland region seemed a matter of secondary consideration; the military vacancy in Guizhou could at least alleviate the heavy pressure of the last two months and allow them the respite they badly needed.

Two weeks of uninterrupted hiking brought the Red Army troops to the edge of the Wu River on New Year's Eve, 1935. Xue Yue's army lay far behind them in western Hunan. In front of them was Zunyi, the second largest city of Guizhou, poorly protected, as an easy prize. As 1934 ended, so did the first phase of the Central Red Army's Long March. At the cost of one half of their troops, the Communists had survived the Nationalist blockades.[22]

The Convocation of the Zunyi Conference

With the KMT Central Army remaining in the vicinity of Hungjiang and Zhijiang in Hunan, the Red Army only confronted the local Guizhou army in late December 1934. In terms of size and fighting capacity, the Guizhou army was by no means equal to the Red Army. After more than two years of internal warfare, Guizhou reached a barely unified form in 1934 under Governor Wang Jialie. Knowing that the two divisions of his provincial army could not hope to cope with the Red Army, Wang followed the Communists to northern Guizhou without challenging them. Then Wang intentionally called his own men back to the south to defend the provincial capital of Guiyang and, if necessary, to flee east to Guangxi.[23] Stationed in northern Guizhou was another KMT general, local warlord Hou Zhidan, with one division and a few guarding squads, no more than 10,000 men of which 4,000 or 5,000 were scattered at a dozen ferry spots along the 200 li long bank of the Wu River. Only one battalion was deployed at Zunyi, the center of this region.[24] On January 1, 1935 the vanguard unit of the Red Army reached Jiangjie at the southern bank of the Wu River, while the Command Column was left about 100 li behind at Houchang (now called Caotang). While the squad of engineers was constructing raft bridges and the other troops were celebrating the new year, the Communist leaders held a Politburo conference. The resolution of this Houchang Conference reaffirmed the plan to establish a new Soviet base on the Guizhou-Sichuan border. "Our first target is the northern Guizhou area centered around Zunyi," the resolution states, "and then we should gradually expand into southern Sichuan. This is our focal task at this moment."[25]

Another sentence in the resolution reads, "as for the military policies and the decisions of time and location of battle, the Military Council will give a report at the upcoming Politburo conference."[26] Here are two noteworthy points: a Politburo conference dealing with military affairs was already planned before the Communists entered Zunyi; and the Party Center leaders seemed interested more in discussing the current military work than in reviewing lessons of the past, obviously saying little for their sense of responsibility.

Despite some dramatization of these episodes, the successful crossing of the Wu River and the seizure of Zunyi were for the Red Army really a forgone conclusion. Both the Guizhou army and the Red Army realized this before their actual engagement.[27] The 2nd Division of the 1st Army Corps took two ferry spots in Jiangjie and Sunjiaji on January 2. Hou Zhidan was smart enough to have abandoned his troops and escaped apprehension by the Communists, though to little purpose: his cowardly conduct led to his arrest and execution at the hands of the KMT a few months later. Following the enemy's retreat, the Red Army quickly took Zunyi. To be more accurate, the schedule of the Red Army's entry into the city is as follows: January 7, the city was taken by the 1st Army Corps; January 8, the General Headquarters of the Red Army entered; January 9, the Military Council and the Party Central followed. Under the circumstances, no high level CCP conference could have possibly been convened before January 9, 1935, let alone January 6, which has been commonly regarded as the starting date of the Zunyi Conference until very recently.[28]

The first thing the Communists did in the city of Zunyi was to form a garrison headquarters headed by Liu Bocheng and Chen Yun. Then they announced lenient policies toward urban residents and enterprises as well as harsh disciplinary codes for the Red Army units and soldiers. The former category included such items as "no troops can reside in any shops" and "without permits of the political organs and careful checks, no confiscation of local gentry's property can proceed," while the latter category forbade any troops (except those from security bureaus and political departments) from entering the city and warned "against anybody urinating and defecating messily in the city or its suburbs."[29]

Later, the Communist leaders undertook more substantial work. They resumed and reformed the city's administrative system to bring an orderly life to the populace, dispatched and distributed the troops to the surrounding strategic posts. Needless to say, the Communists never forgot their Communist propaganda.[30] Though having their own purposes, these maneuvers could also be seen as general preparation for the forthcoming Politburo conference. The Zunyi Conference was not regarded as rushed or harsh a coup d'état as some may believe.[31]

A telegram from Zhou Enlai to Liu Shaoqi and Li Zhuoran has been found to be the most convincing evidence indicating the starting date of the Zunyi Conference. It reads, "Shaoqi and Zhuoran: The Politburo conference will be held on the fifteenth, and you should hurry to the city of Zunyi tomorrow, the fourteenth (24:00 hours, January 13)."[32] More careful studies lead to the conclusion that the Zunyi Conference most probably began in the evening of January 15.[33]

Aside from the service personnel, body guards, Wu Xiuquan (who acted as an interpreter to Otto Braun), and Deng Xiaoping (the record keeper), eighteen Party and Army leaders formally participated in this enlarged Politburo conference. The participants had been chosen on the basis of two criteria: full or alternate Politburo membership and/or army corps central or army corps military leadership. Table 5.2 lists the participants at the Zunyi Conference.

While all the full and alternate members in the Politburo legitimately attended the Conference, three of the eight army corps leaders were either absent or left out. As the 1st and 3rd Army Corps were the main forces of the Red Army, so their four leaders were called to the Conference, even though Lin Biao and Nie Rongzhen were not yet Central Committee members. The 5th and 9th Army corps were new and weak troops, therefore their leaders, with the exception of Li Zhuoran who was a Central Committee

Table 5.2 Participants at the Zunyi Conference

Full Politburo members:

    Mao Zedong, Zhu De, Chen Yun, Zhou Enlai, Zhang Wentian,

    Qin Bangxian

Alternate Politburo members:

    Wang Jiaxiang, Deng Fa, Liu Shaoqi, He Kequan

Central Military leaders:

    Liu Bocheng, Li Fuchun

Army Corps leaders:

    Lin Biao, Nie Rongzhen, Peng Dehuai, Yang Shangkun, Li Zhuoran

Military advisor from the Comintern:

    Otto Braun [34]

---

member and the Political Commissar of the relatively stronger 5th Army Corps, were not invited to attend. Even the selection of participants indicates that the Zunyi Conference was convened with a blend of serious political and military considerations and that it reflected the real power structure of the CCP and the Red Army at that time. Furthermore, the urgent situation made possible a transformation of focus from political orientation to military necessity.

It is interesting to note that the official version of the Conference includes Deng Xiaoping and Wu Xiuquan as participants at the Zunyi Conference. Actually, Deng was at the time neither a Politburo member nor a senior military leader and he could hardly be considered qualified to participate. He attended, as noted above, simply as the record keeper. Similarly Wu, as interpreter for Otto Braun, really also belonged to the service staff. An obvious explanation for these flaws lies in the fact that both Deng and Wu are presently CCP leaders and official Chinese historians are not too reluctant to let academic accuracy yield to political discretion.[35]

Maintaining their routine work, the eighteen Communist leaders convened in several night sessions from January 15 to January 18. The conference proceedings can be roughly divided into four phases. The first phase consisted of three speeches made by Bo Gu, Zhou Enlai, and Mao Zedong respectively. None of the speeches is extant now, but it should be clear that the basic agenda for the conference was set as these three attitudes toward the current leadership—defensive, neutral, and offensive—were presented.

Bo Gu chaired the conference and spoke first. As the head of the Party Center, he presented a general political report on behalf of the Politburo. A fairly large portion of his speech was a verbose recollection of the political victories and progresses the Party had allegedly made in the past year. Regarding the Communists' undeniable failure in the Fifth Suppression Campaign, he attempted to excuse the Politburo and himself by stressing the difficulties and hardships of confronting a million KMT troops.

Zhou Enlai was the second speaker to produce a military or supplementary report on behalf of the Military Council. Although he was not the Chairman of the Military Council, Zhou had been for years the Party Central leader in charge of military affairs. He said more about the military errors of the Party and Army leadership but could not acknowledge these errors as an incorrect military line. Mao Zedong had no such qualms. As the Conference's third speaker, he did not hesitate presenting a long and well prepared speech which eloquently reviewed and criticized the military line of the Politburo and the Military Council.

The second phase marks the beginning of a turn toward Mao. Following the speeches of Bo, Zhou, and Mao were some other Politburo members. Their exact order is not as clearly documented and thus difficult to determine.

It would most likely be the following: Wang Jiaxiang, Zhang Wentian, Chen Yun, Liu Shaoqi, and He Kequan. The first four (Wang, Zhang, Chen, and Liu) all more or less supported Mao's criticism of the incumbent military leadership. He Kequan was the only clear supporter of Bo and Braun at the Conference.

By this time, the military commanders and non-Politburo members found the discussion heated enough so that they felt the need to show their stands in the debate. Peng Dehuai complained about Braun's reckless military command; Liu Bocheng negatively reviewed past military actions and suggested future maneuvers; Nie Rongzhen added a few words to the same effect. Braun hardly had a chance to respond but just bent his head, grimly and silently smoking in a corner of the meeting hall. The following discussions led ever more in favor of the opposition and its spokesman Mao.[36]

In the third phase Zhu De and Zhou Enlai showed up and made the situation clearer. They joined the majority in criticizing the erroneous military line. Zhou made his second speech not as a representative of the Party or Army organization as he did previously, but as an individual participant. As a member of the Standing Committee of the Politburo with the highest seniority and as the de facto leader in the Military Council, Zhou's posture was regarded as decisive by both sides. Arguing openly at the meeting table, Mao had also been clever enough to conduct some "homework" on Madam Zhou.[37] After Zhu and Zhou aligned themselves with Mao, Wang, and Zhang, there seemed little hope for Bo Gu and his men to win back the situation. No vote was recorded or remembered at the Conference, and its third phase ended in a general approval of Mao's label of the Politburo and the Military Council as bearers of an erroneous military line.

The formal resolution of the Conference and the reorganization of the Politburo and the Military Council of the Party and Army leadership were, legitimately and practically, left for the Politburo to deal with after the military men without Politburo membership were dismissed to return to their army units. The army corps leaders such as Peng, Lin, Nie, Yang and Li departed from the Conference in the evening of January 17, and the meeting of the Politburo members the next morning constituted the fourth and final phase of the Zunyi Conference.

The dismissal of the military commanders from the Zunyi Conference was made out of military urgency at the time. While the Communist leaders were at the Conference, Xue Yue's Central Army already reached Guiyang and Wang Jialie's Guizhou army was starting an attack from the Wu River. In his autobiography, Peng Dehuai recalls that the KMT troops crossed the Wu River to attack Zunyi from the south and he "had to leave for the front before the Conference was over."[38] Recently discovered documents of the KMT archives show the battle referred to by Peng took place between the 3rd Army Corps and the Guizhou army at Daobashui on the afternoon of January 17.[39]

Some practical decisions or resolutions reached at the meeting of the Politburo members on January 18 can be found in a 12-page manuscript that Chen Yun drafted shortly after the Zunyi Conference to communicate decisions of the Conference to the Party and Army cadres (this document is among those transferred from Moscow to Peking in the early 1950s). The following items of resolution, as contained in Chen Yun's manuscript, are essential, though not all inclusive:

1. Comrade Mao Zedong was elected a member of the Standing Committee of the Politburo.
2. Comrade Zhang Wentian was designated to draft the resolution which was to be communicated to the Party branches after its approval by the Standing Committee.
3. Proper assignments of the Party and Army positions in the Standing Committee were to be made later after the Conference.
4. The Three-Man-Group was dismissed and the military leadership was returned to the supreme army leaders Zhou Enlai and Zhu De. Comrade Zhou Enlai was to be the final decision-maker on behalf of the Central Committee in dealing with military affairs. . . . Comrade Mao Zedong was to be his chief assistant.[40]

Another category of resolutions may contain oral decisions and agreements reached through discussions at the Conference. Examples might include short-term military plans and tactics, minor changes in Party and Army positions, reorganization of some army units, and communications with both other Red Armies in rural Soviets and underground Party agents in big cities. The implementation of these resolutions can be recognized in the telegrams, orders, notices and announcements issued by the Party Center and the Military Council soon after the Conference, especially from January 19 to February 8. Although it was distinguished for its reviewing of past experiences and lessons, the Zunyi Conference did not entirely ignore the Party and Army's tasks at the present and for the future.[41]

The Resolutions of the Zunyi Conference as an Analytical Review of Communists' Experiences in Military Affairs

The Zunyi Conference might have lasted a few more days had it not been for the KMT attacks—a situation similar to that the Second Soviet Congress had faced in late January 1934. For the same reason, no formal resolutions were adopted at the Conference. At this stage, documentation leads to the conclusion that two written resolutions emerged from the conference, though they were completed the next month. The first one, entitled "Resolution on Summing up the Campaign against the Enemy's Fifth Suppression" and adopted by the Politburo Conference, contains 14 sections and runs about 15,000 Chinese characters.[42] The second—"Outline Resolutions of the Enlarged Politburo Conference Concerning the Experiences and Lessons Drawn from Smashing the Fifth Suppression Campaign"—adopted by the General Secretariat of the CCP Central Committee contains eight sections and about 3,000 characters.[43] Judging from the wording and contents of the two documents, we surmise the second (Outline Resolution) was a concise message to be distributed among the Party Center leaders while the first (Summary Resolution) was an elaboration of the second for the purpose of broader circulation among the Party cadres and Army officers. The Summary Resolution was doubtless drafted by Zhang Wentian, while the Outline Resolution was probably a joint product of Zhang and Mao. Both documents were drafted in February 1935 on the basis of Mao's speech and Zhang's remarks at the Zunyi Conference.[44]

Unlike some other CCP resolutions which had been presented, discussed and accepted during the conferences and therefore had become an integral part of the conferences to which they pertained, both the written resolutions of Zunyi Conference were produced after the Conference and had no direct influence upon the Conference itself. In other words, their importance is primarily in their usefulness for historical documentation. This section sets as its main purpose the analysis of the contents of the two resolutions as a historical review of the Communists' experiences in military affairs.

1. The Political Line vs. the Military Line

The military line of the Party leadership was labelled "rightist opportunist" by both resolutions because, as the Outline Resolution states more clearly, "the pure defensive line of the military leadership is no other than a concrete manifestation of rightist opportunism." But the two documents unequivocally declare that, despite the *military* mistakes of the Party and Army leadership which caused the failure of the Fifth Suppression Campaign, its political line was nonetheless correct. "Mistakes in military conduct may make all the best supportive work at the rear null and void; all these mistakes should be charged particularly to Comrade Bo Gu," the Outline Resolution informs us, "But at the same time, it should be noted that these are for Comrade Bo Gu only a partial, serious mistake and not a general mistake in political line."[45] Ironically, it seems as though the very correctness of the Party Center's political line—as shown by its success in recruiting more than 100,000 peasants to join the Red Army, mobilizing a massive movement to support the war and thus creating a most favorable "objective condition" to win the Campaign—made their "subjective errors" leading to the military failure, and hence their "erroneous military line" inexcusable.[46]

We should note that after the Rectification Movement in the early 1940s, the CCP Center headed by Mao pronounced a new verdict on the Party leadership from 1931 to 1935. This time the political line of the Bo Gu Center was no longer deemed 'correct' and its military mistakes became an integral part of a now 'leftist opportunist line.' Mainly due to this basic change—and not for any of the other reasons that have been supposed—the Summary Resolution was excluded from inclusion into official editions of *Selected Works of Mao Zedong* in the 1950s.[47]

In Communist terminology, political line equals general line, thus a mistaken political line of the Party Center simply means a mistaken Party Center. When the Zunyi Conference was held, various factors prevented such a harsh criticism of the Party Center. There were the considerations of political credibility and face on the part of individuals. Zhou Enlai, for instance, had been an outstanding member of the Party and Army leadership, and at the Zunyi Conference Zhou was elevated to an even higher position. Zhang Wentian was also politically associated with the Party Center; he had jumped from an unknown figure to a top leader in the Party Center in the past few years, and it was he who drafted the resolution. Even Mao Zedong, despite his opposition status, was the Chairman of the Soviet Republic and had been involved with those papers and slogans praising the Party's political line in the past. Moreover, at the Zunyi Conference Mao did not acquire enough authority to argue against the general line of the Party Center—even had he wished to do so.

On a more practical level, the urgent situation on the Long March made it inadvisable to seek intraparty struggle which might jeopardize the Party and Army's efficient and collective work. The disconnection of contacts with the Comintern, too, facilitated an initial change of the Party leadership on the one hand, but discouraged any attempt to arbitrarily overrule the Party Center and its general line on the other. Further, the existence of Red Armies other than the Central Red Army served as barrier against radical disassociation with the Party Center as a whole.

Although any of the above mentioned reasons might be valid enough, a deeper explanation may be that intraparty relationships in the CCP were most often in a gradual process of development, not a punctuated equilibrium, and the overall conditions at the time of the Zunyi Conference prohibited a radical change of Party leadership. For those who prefer to understand historical events through personal psychological analyses, it should be understood that what Mao expected in the Zunyi Conference was not the expulsion of all incumbent leaders from their functions but rather an adjustment of its function to fit into his own strategy and leadership, as revealed by his efforts in the following years.

As for the harsh denunciation of the Bo Gu leadership in the 1940s, one may of course attribute it to a sinister scheme by Mao. It seems that as soon as Mao held the central power firmly in his hands, he did not scruple to revoke the resolutions of the Zunyi Conference and launch attacks on his opponents. A correct political line now became an erroneous one; rightist opportunism became leftist opportunism. But the more noteworthy question is perhaps, if or in what sense it is just and fair to judge the CCP leadership of 1931-1935 of having carried out an erroneous general or political line.[48]

The basic fact is that under the Bo Gu leadership, the Communists were roundly defeated by the Nationalists, their armed forces reduced, their Soviet territory lost, and their goal of attaining state power retarded. They certainly failed from a military standpoint, and yet the question still concerns the extent of the influence of this military failure on the Party's general situation or the relationship between military and political affairs: how much did military defeats preclude political gains? Could this military defeat be excused for any political slogans and social programs? Mao clearly saw that the primary objective of the CCP, of the Chinese revolution, must be the actual seizure of state power. No credit for a correct general line could or should be given to any leadership which failed to win the civil war—no matter what its ideology and social programs were, or how loudly it proclaimed the revolution.

2. Why the Failure in the Fifth Campaign?

One of the focal points of argument at the Zunyi Conference was how to explain the military failure of the Communist in the Fifth Suppression Campaign in the Jiangxi Soviet. To this question, the two resolutions and Chen Yun's manuscript all provide the same answer. The Summary Resolution states:

> Comrade Bo Gu has in his report overestimated the objective difficulties, arguing that the fifth 'Suppression' could not be smashed in the Central Soviet because of the superior strength of imperialists and KMT reactionaries. He has at the same time underestimated the revolutionary conditions. Thus inevitably, he reaches the opportunist conclusion that it was objectively impossible to break up the fifth 'Suppression' at all.[49]

The Outline Resolution expresses the same thought in even stronger terms: "The main cause leading to the failure to break up the suppression was a subjective one, not an objective one. It was because we committed the mistake of a pure defensive line in military command and disregarded the basic strategic and tactical principles of the civil war in China."[50] Chen Yun's manuscript was prepared to communicate the "spirits" of the Zunyi Conference to the Party cadres and Red Army officers, and it therefore attempted to illustrate the above-mentioned opinions with some hypothetical scenarios: "The enlarged Politburo conference believes that if we could have conducted a correct military command at the time, it would have been absolutely possible to break up the Fifth Suppression Campaign. The situation in China would have been quite different from what it is now; the movement of the Revolution and the Soviets would have favorably developed."[51]

In fact, as Chen Yun points out, Bo Gu did not deny in his report some subjective mistakes in military command, nor did he openly claim that these mistakes were secondary. But such an acknowledgement was apparently insufficient for Mao and and his supporters. Mao wanted a strict admission that the mistakes in military command constituted an erroneous military line, which should be held responsible for the defeat in the Fifth Campaign and the loss of the Central Soviet. With this agreed, Mao would be able to reorganize the current military leadership to his desire.

In Chen Yun's manuscript, "Comrade A (Otto Braun), firmly and entirely objects to any criticism against him."[52] This stubbornness is still to be found decades later in his memoirs, where Braun still insists that the KMT's Fifth Campaign had already been broken as early as July 1934, and even the evacuation of the Jiangxi Central Soviet was not a failure, but a well-planned operation of a well-preserved army.[53]

War is decided by the physical attrition of two or more warring parties. Studies of the military confrontation of the CCP with the KMT in 1927-1934 should pay adequate attention to both sides. For many years following 1927, the KMT was the governing party of the whole of China, while the CCP was only one of several opposition parties. The KMT put up with the CCP as one of many nuisances. The CCP had just one goal, to defeat the KMT and seize state power. The Communist victories in the early suppression campaigns all owed much to these orientations. Once the KMT took the Communist rebellions really seriously, no Red Armies in any Soviet bases were likely to win.

In the Third Suppression Campaign, the KMT troops managed to occupy all the big cities and most of the territory of the Central Soviet. The Communists lost far more than they had in the Guangchang battles in 1934. The KMT's withdrawal at the end of the Third Campaign was primarily due to the emergency caused by the Guangdong and Guangxi revolt in August and the Mukden Incident in September 1931. In the Fourth Campaign, the KMT succeeded in defeating two of the three major Red Army forces. The Fourth Front Army concentrated its main forces on the western front, but could not win a decisive battle before the eastern front collapsed. The KMT encirclement was tight and eventually the Fourth Front Army had to flee west. At the Xiangexi base, the 3rd Red Army tried to station its main forces fighting outside to the north with a minor force defending the Honghu base. Outnumbered by the enemy, neither the exterior nor the interior front could succeed as expected. The 3rd Army also had to leave the base area and embark on the western expedition. The Fourth Campaign in the Central Soviet base was only a transitional phase between the KMT's focal engagement with the Eyuwan and Xiangexi Soviets and the Fifth Campaign against the Central Soviet, and only a small portion of its forces took part in the few battles.

From this summary, it emerges that when the KMT concentrated all its attention and strength on the Fifth Suppression Campaign in late 1933, with one million troops pressing steadily into the Central Soviet from all directions, the situation was, if not hopeless, far more grave than the CCP leaders could have imagined. The resolutions of the Zunyi Conference offered as a hindsight strategy for defeating the KMT encirclement the notion that the Red Army should break through the blockade line and fight at the enemy's rear—a strategy differing not only from the one applied by the Bo Gu Center in the Fifth Campaign but also from that practiced by Mao in the earlier campaigns. The Outline Resolution gives a hint of the suggested strategy:

> Under the present technological conditions, the only method of fighting against 'blockhouseism' is mobile warfare—that means not merely remaining behind the blockade line and waiting for the enemy troops to approach and then wiping out them in large numbers, but transferring the Red Army outside to the vast rear regions without blockhouses and compelling the enemy troops to leave their blockhouses to engage our troops in a mobile war.[54]

Neither of the resolutions offers concrete ideas as to when and how the Red Army could have broken the KMT blockade line and reached the enemy's rear areas. Only two years later in his "On the Strategic Problems of China's Revolutionary War" (perhaps the first systematic expression of his military and political philosophy, and a talented blend of his realistic calculation and romantic imagination), Mao attempted to fill this gap.

> At the time of the Fujian Revolt, two months after the commencement of our anti-suppression campaign, the main forces of the Red Army should undoubtedly have thrust into the Jiangsi-Zhejiang-Anhui-Jiangsu region, with Zhejiang as the center, and swept over the length and breadth of the area between Hangzhou, Suzhou, Nanking, Wuhu, Nanchang and Fuzhou, turning our strategic defensive into an strategic offensive, menacing the enemy's vital centers and seeking battles in vast areas where there were no blockhouses. By this means we could have compelled the enemy, which was attacking southern Jiangxi and western Fujian, to turn back to defend its vital centers, to break its attack on the base area in Jiangxi and render aid to the Fujian People's Government.[55]

Mao's proposal has some merit, but an intimidating series of 'ifs' are mines in the path to victory. To flesh out the scenario, if a) such a maneuver had been conducted in November or early December 1933, when the Fujian Revolt was still in its heyday; and if b), the combined forces of the 1st and 3rd Army Corps had been dispatched to drive from Jianning, Lichuan and Taining into northeast Jiangxi; and if c), they had been reinforced with Fang Zhimin's 10th Army and continued driving deep into central Zhejiang[56]; and if d), they had successfully caught one or more key cities—such as Hangzhou, Wuhu and Nanking—and thus compelled the KMT Northern Route Army to turn back; and if e), the Red Army had then managed to destroy several Nationalist divisions; if further, f) and g), the 19th Route Army in Fujian had kept steadfastly fighting the KMT Central Army on the one hand, and being friendly with the Red Army on the other, and if h) and i), after the Red Army's departure from the Jiangxi Soviet Chen Jitang had not attempted any invasion from the southern front nor He Jian from the western front, and if j), the Red Army had then successfully swept back to Jiangxi and a depressed Chiang Kai-shek proclaimed a halt to his suppression campaign—then there would have been a perfect materialization of Mao's strategy. Unfortunately, each of these 'ifs' could just as easily become an 'if not.'

Following this line of wishful speculation, it would be possible to win the Fifth Campaign for the Communists in an even easier way, as Peng Dehuai actually imagines in his memoir. Referring to the unsatisfactory battle at Tuancun Xunkou in late 1933, Peng says: "Since four enemy regiments were already annihilated in Xunkou, if the 1st and 3rd Army Corps had worked closely together, the Tuancun Battle would have become a decisive victory and we would have destroyed another 12 enemy regiments. With 16 enemy regiments destroyed, the Fifth Suppression Campaign could not have continued anymore."[57] Unfortunately, the situation at the time was not quite so simple, even from a military viewpoint.

As previous experiences showed, even had the 1st and 3rd Army Corps been combined, they would hardly have the joint capacity to break and capture a well-guarded city like Ji'an, Ganzhou or Lo'an, to say nothing of Hangzhou and Nanking. Even if they could break through the blockade line into the eastern region, it might not be beneficial for them to stay in these "white areas." With so many KMT troops following them, the Communists would hardly be able to establish a new base or achieve significant recruitment, and their own strength would most likely diminish. Supposing the Fujian Revolt were quickly pacified or enlisted by Chiang Kai-shek, and the Jiangxi Soviet were taken by Chen Jitang and He Jian, then the Red Army would have to fight with the KMT Central Army at the lower Yangtze Valley or the eastern coast. The consequence would be far more precarious. In a miniature form, the Anti-Japanese Vanguard

Brigade of Xun Huaizhou and Fang Zhimin had experimented such a maneuver. Another proposal of Mao raised in the same article was essentially as follows:

> After a year's fighting, although it had become inopportune for us to advance to Zhejiang, we could still have turned to strategic offenses by directing our main forces toward Hunan, that is, by driving into central Hunan instead of just passing through that province to Guizhou. In this manner we could have attracted the enemy troops from Jiangxi into Hunan and destroyed them right there.[58]

Mao refers here to the situation in June or July 1934, after the Guangchang Battles. In his view, the main forces of the 1st and 3rd Army Corps should have taken the same action as the 6th Army Corps. Actually, Ren Bishi did earnestly try this strategy. After gathering at southern Hunan, Ren attempted to cross the Xiang River from Lingling and drive into central Hunan, but this ended up with a hopeless failure. It should also be noted that even if the 1st and 3rd Army Corps had reached central Hunan as imagined by Mao, they could hardly have diverted all the Nationalist forces. He Jian's Western Route Army was not an offensive force but mainly a defensive one already in Hunan. Gu Zhutong's Northern Route Army would most probably have continued its attacks; the Jiangxi Soviet would be lost for sure; and central Hunan might not be so favorable for the Communists. The same appalling situation might have occurred: the Red Army could not find time to establish a new base or recruit new troops under heavy military pressures in a strange land. As the military situations in early 1935 witnessed, it was not so easy to achieve either of these purposes, even when Mao himself assumed the leadership.

Unlike historical facts, historical analyses are at best still guesswork. In this sense, neither Mao's hindsight strategy nor our critical study of this strategy should be taken as definitely valid. In fact, what had brought about the military result was primarily a contest of strength rather than a selection of strategy and tactics. In other words, the generally superior strength of the KMT side remained the most decisive factor in assuring the Red Army's failure in the Fifth Campaign. From this estimation, two interesting points may be noted: first, Bo Gu was right when he attributed the CCP's failure in the Fifth Campaign to the superior strength of the KMT; second, Mao's being deprived of direct leadership or responsibility in the Fifth Campaign should be regarded as his lucky fortune, as it opened the route on which to challenge and seize power from the present Party and Army leaders.

3. The Pure Defense Line vs. the Offensive Defense Line

The resolutions of the Zunyi Conference put in sharp contrast the two military lines, the highly praised "offensive defense" line and the downgraded "pure defensive" line. The first recommends that "our strategic line should have been battle-deciding defense or offensive defense—concentrate superior forces, select the enemy's weak points, apply mobile warfare, confidently to destroy a part or a large part of the enemy force, then break other parts one by one and finally smash their encirclement."[59] As for the second one, the resolutions describe it: "In the Fifth Anti-suppression Campaign, however, a pure defensive or positional defensive line was adopted instead of the battle-deciding defensive line, coupled with the tactic of 'short, swift thrusts.'" In order to compare and contrast the main features of the two military strategies, we can draw the following list of comparison according to Mao's description.[60]

The Pure Defense:	*The Offensive Defense:*
Distribution of forces	Concentration of forces
Positional warfare	Mobile warfare
War of attrition	War of annihilation
Battle of protraction	Battle of quick decision
Short, swift thrusts	Big retreat and big advance

Since Mao's proposals for the Fifth Campaign were no more than hypotheses, there is no surety that different results might have ensued had they been adopted. Perhaps it is safer to leave the wishful thinking to those who would prefer by it, and turn back to some questions of verifiable facts, as Wu Tien-wei has done in his admirable work on the Zunyi Conference. Was the CCP military strategy in the Fifth Campaign really the same as charged by the Zunyi Conference resolutions? More to the point, were there any basic differences between the strategy implemented in the previous campaigns and the strategy applied in the Fifth Campaign? If there were, how much did they positively or negatively affect the military processes for the Communists?[61]

The first three anti-suppression campaigns were all conducted under Mao's direct command with basically the same strategy. Facing the approaching KMT troops, the Red Army would willingly or unwillingly give up its Soviet territory and retreat into the base area; then they would furtively concentrate their main forces and manage to catch one or more enemy divisions either by ambush or surprise attack; afterward, the KMT army would withdraw and leave the Red Army to celebrate its victory. The Fourth Campaign was different in that this time the Red Army chose the outer edge of the Soviet base as the battlefield; while the Nationalist troops began entering the Soviet, the Red Army ambushed to destroy two enemy divisions there.

At the initial stage of the Fifth Campaign in 1934, the Central Soviet had assumed such high prestige as a formal state that it became impossible to think of surrendering its large territory to lure the enemy in, nor would the KMT's new strategy of blockhouses seem to allow the Red Army to do so with any benefit. The loud slogan "Never give up an inch of Soviet land" raised by the CCP Center during the Fifth Campaign was intended for propaganda purposes, and it also reflected the common opinions and general positions of the Party and greatly influenced the military action of the Red Army.

It was at the time of the Guangchang battles that the military strategy adopted by Bo Gu and Otto Braun emerged in sharp contrast to that of Mao. Under the slogan "Defend Guangchang, the gate to the red capital" and calling for "short, swift thrusts," the battles became sheer positional defense, and the "pure defensive line" came to full implementation— excepting the distasteful title. One positional battle followed another, and each battle cost two to three thousand Red Army men; one city after another was lost, and the loss of each city would make the next one— closer to the capital—seem more necessary to defend. Hence progressive slogans "Defend Jianning," "Defend Yiqian," and "Defend Shicheng." The entire strategy was certainly different from the one applied by Mao in the first three campaigns in 1931, whether out of helpless necessity under the circumstances in early 1934, or due to the influence and desire of Bo and Braun.

Despite Braun's adherence to this strategy, Zhou Enlai and others grew skeptical and began pondering a shift in overall military policy soon after the Guangchang Battles. The 6th and 7th Army Corps were dispatched to fight outside the Soviet in July. From then until the start of the Long March in October, the situation was too diffuse to make a clear contrast between Maoist strategies of the past and those of the Party Central at the present. Both the military conditions and the Communist responses were incomparably different from those of the previous campaigns.

On the basis of the above analyses, the military strategies of the Red Army in the years 1931-1934 can be best understood as a gradually changing system rather than the sharp bouncing back and forth from a correct line to an incorrect line. Nevertheless, with the actual differences as a general background and with the former success and the present failure quite apparent, Mao was naturally entitled to raise the entire issue at the Zunyi Conference, and the Conference would naturally incorporate these contrasts in its resolutions, despite the exaggerations involved.

4. Military Debates on the Early Long March

Since the Communist leaders still considered the Long March part of the Fifth Campaign in January 1935, the resolutions of Zunyi Conference accordingly included the early phase of the Long March in its review of the past military line. The Outline Resolution delivers criticism in two main areas: implementing the evacuation after it had been decided, and conducting the expedition on the Long March. Even after the decision to evacuate was made, it begins by noting, the Red Army kept on fighting purposeless battles with the KMT, consuming immense amounts of Red Army time and strength. Due to inadequate planning and communication, moreover, the evacuation from the Soviet area became a "panic flight" and an "overall house move" without any explanation for the strategic transference to the cadres and masses. In the western expedition as it developed, the critism further points out, the formation of a cumbersome noncombatant command column made marching and fighting extremely clumsy and forced all the combatant troops to function solely as bodyguards. No positive efforts were made to fight the enemy, and thus the Red Army remained continually passive, hit and beaten by the KMT.[62]

In this analysis, the subject dealt with is an even more unique situation, and the leveled criticisms are even less apropos than previously. To begin with the first point, the defense of Xingkuo and Tingzhou up to the very last day before the overall evacuation should not be unfairly criticized— for all the apparent military reasons, this cannot legitimately be termed an aimless and useless fight. From late August 1934 when the final decision was reached up to its inception in early October, moreover, Zhou Enlai was in charge of the entire evacuation. It was neither just nor fair to say that the preparatory work had been a panic rush. Even if this had been the case, it would be primarily due to military failure in the preceding months. Elsewhere, interestingly, the Outline Resolution charges that the decision for evacuation was made in August and should have been implemented immediately: thus the somewhat contradictory criticisms of both too much delay and too quick flight. Neither are the complaints of not consulting and communicating with the cadres and masses particularly well-chosen. Perhaps this reflects more the grudges of Mao and Zhang than the grievances of the rank and file. When he received the decision on the Long March later, Mao himself did not reveal this top secret to even Lin Biao or Nie Rongzhen, to say nothing of consulting with common cadres and masses.[63]

Although it was not entirely unreasonable of the opposition to raise the issue, the hindrance of noncombatant institutions and heavy equipment to military efficiency was not just a thoughtless error. It was mainly due to the initial objective of the Long March that the Communists had brought with them printing machines, bank notes, large artillery, and heavy ammunition. At the time, none of the Communist leaders—Mao included— thought that they would have to move as far away as they eventually did, and they wanted to save these things for probable future use. Finally, as for the charge that the incumbent leaders did not fight any battles on the way but merely adopted a "flightist line," it does not seem just either. From the start of the Long March up to the arrival at northern Guizhou, there was seldom a possibility for the Red Army to engage the enemy offensively. It might have defeated one or two pursuing or blocking enemy units, but that would have cost it some of the precious time at the very best. After the Zunyi Conference, as we shall see, Mao himself tried to win some decisive battles in Guizhou and Sichuan, without any encouraging consequences.

In summary, the charges against the military leadership at the initial stage of the Long March as expressed in the resolutions of the Zunyi Conference were generally unjust. It is almost groundless to label the military operation of that period as the pure defensive line as the resolutions of the Zunyi Conference do. Nevertheless, as the opposition leader, Mao seemed justified in casting this kind of aspersion simply because the incumbent leaders were on the losing end, and they would naturally be accountable for the loss. Positions of political leadership must meanwhile be positions of political responsibility.

Mao's Rise to Power

The general mood of the Zunyi Conference in favor of Mao Zedong did not mean that Mao could take over the Party or Army leadership right away. Such an attempt might have cost him what he actually gained. As a matter of fact, there was no mention of Mao's name in the resolutions of the Conference. Although there were some changes in the Party and Army leadership at the Conference, none of them seemed abrupt or radical. The direct result of the abolition of the Three-Man Group was that Otto Braun lost his position in the military leadership once and almost for all. Soon after the Zunyi Conference, Braun left the Military Council and was assigned to the 1st Army Corps. Bo Gu was another main targets of the Conference. He was dismissed entirely as a military leader and considerably weakened politically.[64]

Despite his large role in the former military line, Zhou Enlai was put in a unique, though temporary, position as "the final decision-maker on behalf of the Party Center in dealing with military affairs." This is one of the many ironies in CCP history. But for Zhou as a person, it did not seem unreasonable.[65] The even larger irony was that though Zhou had for a long time functioned as the decision-maker in military affairs without the formal title, the moment he obtained such a title at the Zunyi Conference Zhou was about to lose this true function to Mao. The simple solution to this puzzle lay in the fact that despite Bo Gu's superior status in the Party and Zhu De's in the Army, their weakness in either military or political work naturally granted Zhou de facto military leadership. Now with the militarily experienced and politically ambitious Mao as his assistant, and under the unfavorable atmosphere that followed the Zunyi Conference, Zhou would be pushed ever further aside.

What did Mao achieve at the Zunyi Conference then? One accurate answer: not that much. Mao became neither Chairman of the Military Council nor Chairman of the Politburo as has been commonly believed in the past, but only a member in the Standing Committee of the Politburo and then an assistant to Zhou Enlai in dealing with military affairs. Another equally true answer to the same question: very much indeed. Mao for the first time in his Communist career became one of the five top leaders of the Party and obtained the right to decide the most important Party and Army activities. More importantly, he won a reputation as the only man who had represented a correct Party line in the past and the one who possessed the potential to lead the Party and Army to victory in the future. In Braun's words, "the Zunyi Conference represented the first and most important step in Mao's usurpation of power in the Party and Army."[66] This first step would gradually lead Mao to supreme leadership in the years after the Zunyi Conference.

Verbal condemnation of the past leadership is one matter, successful practice of the present leadership is quite another. After the Zunyi Conference, successes or failures in military affairs continued to be the final judge of the new Party and Army leadership. Four men led the central military command in early 1935: Zhou Enlai, the bearer of general responsibility; Zhu De, the titular but necessary commander-in-chief; Mao Zedong, Zhou's strategic advisor; and Liu Bocheng, the battlefield tactic designer.

The Zunyi Conference required that two achievements be made. The general purpose of creating a new Soviet base must be a long-range scheme, whearas the immediate objective was to take "defensive offense" toward the approaching KMT troops. The results on the battlefield in February and March 1935, though not at all as good as Mao was expecting—or as good as many Long Marchers later recalled—were barely acceptable. Due to various factors, including the change in leadership and strategy, the Red Army lost some battles and won others. Gradually but steadily, Mao's position improved.

While the Communist leaders were holding the Zunyi Conference and their troops were reorganizing in northern Guizhou, Xue Yue and his 2nd Route Army of two columns in eight divisions (about 100,000 men) entered Guiyang, the provincial capital of Guizhou.[67] Xue first took military command from Wang Jialie, and then urged Wang to begin a northern pursuit of the Red Army. On January 19, two divisions of the Guizhou army forced their way across the Wu River. The Red Army gave up Zunyi with little struggle and shifted to the northwest in three routes. On their way to Chishui on January 20, 1935, the General Headquarters of the Red Army issued a "Combat Plan of Crossing the River," the first important military and political document of the post-Zunyi Conference leadership. This plan consists of three parts: an estimation of the situation, a general combat policy, and initial tasks. As regards the general policy, the plan states:

> The basic policy of this field army is to cross the River from northern Guizhou to land in southern Sichuan, and move into a new area. Employing the 2nd and 6th Army Corps' activities to contain the enemy at southeast Sichuan and maintain cooperations with the Fourth Front Army in northwest Sichuan, we shall thereafter start a general counterattack to break up the enemy's suppression, take over Sichuan and carry out the Soviet revolution in the whole province.[68]

This combat plan suggests that "the key point to fulfill this plan is to catch and control some ferry spots along the Yangtze River," and "in case we meet extreme difficulties and cannot cross the River and the pursuing troops get close, we should concentrate our forces for an abrupt attack on the pursuing enemy and annihilate one or more parts of it."[69] According to this plan, telegrams in the name of the Politburo and the Military Council were immediately delivered to the Fourth Front Army and the 2nd and 6th Army Corps, requesting them to undertake cooperative actions.

Reaching the Chishui River on the Guizhou-Sichuan border, the Red Army encountered far stronger resistance from the Sichuan army than it had expected. The Sichuan army, under the general command of Liu Xiang, had three firmly stationed divisions of six brigades. In addition, six regiments of the Guizhou army were deployed there. The Red Army fought a few battles with the Sichuan army in late January, but none ended satisfactorily. In the battle at Tucheng on January 28, perhaps the worst one, all the Red Army corps took part in fighting, yet they could not defeat the enemy's three brigades and had to leave the battlefield, suffering heavy damage.[70] After that, the Red Army temporarily gave up the idea of crossing the Yangtze River. Instead, they crossed the Chishui River, ran further west, and arrived at Weixin in Yunnan Province in early February 1935.

From February 3 to February 11, 1935, the Red Army stayed in Weixin. Because of the further loss of troops, the Military Council had to order a reduction of divisions to regiments. At the same time, the Politburo work was reassigned and Zhang Wentian formally took over the general leadership from Bo Gu. Both of the resolutions of the Zunyi Conference were composed and distributed among the Party cadres and Army officers at this period.[71]

Presumably following Mao's suggestion, the Red Army sneaked back to northern Guizhou in late February with the idea of engaging the pursuing enemy troops in a few decisive battles and settling in northern Guizhou.[72] The main forces recrossed the Chishui River on the 20th, recaptured Dongzi on the 25th and Zunyi on the 27th. From February 28 to March 1, they had their first successful battle in the Tongzi and Zunyi area. Two divisions of the KMT Central Army led by Wu Qiwei were soundly defeated, and about 3,000 men and 2,000 rifles were lost to the Communists.[73]

In wake of the triumphant battle at Zunyi, the old system of the Front Command Headquarters (FCH) was resumed on March 4, obviously with the approval of Zhou Enlai. Mao was appointed the Political Commissar of the Front Headquarters and Zhu De the General Commander. Since the Front Command Headquarters was to stay with the 1st Army Corps and take charge of military command of all other Army Corps, it would automatically reduce the General Headquarters to practical impotence.[74] Such an appointment enabled Mao to recover his dominant control of the bulk of the Central Red Army, which he had lost at the Ningdu Conference in October 1932.

On the very next day after its formation, the Front Command Headquarters produced a combat order. This March 5th order of the FCH, undoubtedly drawn up by Mao, expresses both the Red Army's strategy at that time and the configuration of Mao's blended personality of romanticism and realism. The order requested that the three Red Army Corps prepare for a grand battle to annihilate Zhou Hunyuan's three divisions. In the last half of the order, Mao writes:

3. All our Army Corps should strive our best to dispose of the two divisions of Xiao and Xie tomorrow the 6th in order to engage Wan's division continuously on the 7th.
4. The general rear staff will be located in the place between Huajiantian of Yaxi and the city of Zunyi.
5. The Front Command Headquarters will follow the 1st Army Corps headquarters to arrive at Baicuokan on the 6th.
PS: Apart from radio telegrams for military reports, our communication will also be carried out by means of bonfire: a big victory, set up with three piles of fire; a small victory, two piles of fire; and stalemate or unfavorable, one pile of fire.[75]

Here we find Mao, in the name of the Front Command Headquarters, daring even to designate the operation of "the general rear staff", or the Party Center and the Military Council. Mao's confidence and eagerness to win some grand battles are also in evidence. But as it turned out, none of the victories were achieved and no enemy troops were defeated on

March 6-7. An engagement did occur ten days later with Zhou Hunyuan's troops at Lubanchang, but it also proved no more than a "one pile of fire" encounter.[76]

In late March and early April, Mao did something awfully wonderful or wonderfully awful. Leaving the 9th Army Corps in the north as decoy force fighting independently for almost a whole month, he himself led the main forces to break through the Wu River and drive southwards into the heart of Guizhou. For a while the Red Army got as close as a few miles to Guiyang, the provincial capital. When Chiang Kai-shek hurried from Chongqing to Guiyang and called the Yunnan army for reinforcement, the Red Army turned southwest and drove into Yunnan.[77]

Even in his later years, Mao still boasted of the entire operation from February to April 1935 as the "proudest moment" in his military career.[78] But at that time not all the Red Army men, nor even his proponents, seemed fully to understand his genius in military command. In the three months after the Zunyi Conference, the Red Army under Mao's command continued to move through Guizhou, Sichuan, and Yunnan. It survived, but was still struggling for survival. Neither of its strategic objectives, creating a new military base or annihilating a large number of the enemy, was achieved.[79] While Mao still adhered his strategy of engaging the enemy troops at the present area, doubts and protests grew among military commanders as well as Party leaders. Bo Gu, Zhang Wentian, Liu Shaoqi, Peng Dehuai and Lin Biao were among the most outstanding grumblers, though most of these men had been supporters of Mao at the Zunyi Conference.[80]

Zhang Wentian, a soft-minded and 'scholar-type' person, thought of relieving Mao of military command at one time and of leaving the Red Army himself for Shanghai at another. Lin Biao was irritated with the apparently aimless and useless roaming. In the name of the 1st Army Corps, he and Nie Rongzheng telegrammed Zhu De, requesting an immediate change in military strategy.[81] He also wrote to the Military Council, suggesting that a new Front Command Headquarters be formed under Peng Dehuai.[82] All this took place in late April when the Red Army was trying to extricate itself from eastern Yunnan. On April 29 the Military Council and the Politburo had to issue an instruction, which offered a politely positive review of the military action in the past months but urged an immediate crossing of the Jinsha River. The Communist leaders began to talk about opening a Soviet base in western Sichuan, though they were still reluctant to admit it as appealing to the Fourth Front Army.[83]

The Jinsha River is the upper portion of the Yangtze River in northern Yunnan province, well beyond the reach of the main forces of the Nationalist army. After seven days of hard struggle, the Red Army reached the northern bank of the Jinsha River. On May 12, 1935, another enlarged Politburo conference was held in the suburbs of Huili. Everybody was excited by the successful crossing of the Jinsha River and the possibility of joining the Fourth Front Army. The resolution of the Huili Conference renounced the previous idea of opening a new base in western Sichuan (where the Conference took place) and proposed moving further north to meet the Fourth Front Army. This was the first time the Party Center leaders dropped the illusion of creating a new base by themselves and had to gamble on relying on a subordinate unit. In other words, they had by then lost all definite ideas as of where to go and what to do except the least preferred alternative of joining the Fourth Front Army and casting any future plans aside. At the Huili Conference, all the anti-Mao moods were suppressed. Peng Dehuai was the central target of criticism, and Lin Biao was bitterly scolded by Mao: "You are nothing but a baby! What the hell do you know!"[84]

Though Xue Yue's troops distantly chased them and the Sichuan warlord, Liu Wenhui, stood in front blocking their way, the Communists were challenged more by the adverse geographic conditions than by the enemy troops in May and June 1935. They climbed over a number of precipitous peaks and crossed several fast flooding rivers along the western Sichuan-Xikang border. On June 12, 1935, they finally ran into the Fourth Front Army at the foot of the Jiajin Mountains. After eight months of marching and fighting, the Central Red Army had not achieved any of its basic strategic objectives. Its troops were reduced from more than 80,000 at the outset of the Long March to less than 40,000 by the time of the Zunyi Conference, and they were now down to about 20,000.[85] The meeting with the strong Fourth Front Army provided the Party Center leaders with some excitement and inspiration, but it at the same time depressed all their original dignity and imagination. With such mixed feelings of illusion and disillusion, the First Front Army joined forces with the Fourth Front Army. Both the Red Army groups embarked on a new phase of the Long March.

6

THE ARMY VERSUS THE PARTY:
ENCOUNTER OF THE FIRST
AND FOURTH FRONT ARMIES

The period June to September 1935 witnessed first the happy union and then the acrimonious split of two major Communist forces—the First Front or Central Red Army (CRA) and the Fourth Front Army (FFA)—in the highlands of western China. Considering the hardships each force had undergone and the difficulties each encountered in facing of their common KMT enemy, it seems hardly credible that these two Red Armies should break up. Further, there were many similarities between the two leaders, Mao Zedong and Zhang Guotao. Both were veteran cadres of the Communist Party; both had conducted armed rebellions in the countryside for years; both looked down upon the 'returned students' in the Party leadership; and both had been criticized for 'rightist opportunism' several times in the previous years.

Before the union, as the two armies were approaching each other in early June 1935, Otto Braun recalls, "Po Ku reacted to this news with mixed feelings. On the one hand he welcomed the prospective union of the Red Army forces. On the other hand he feared that Mao Tse-tung might adopt Chang Kuo-tao's politics, which so closely resembled Mao's recent suggestions, and force them on the Politburo."[1] Bo Gu's prediction proved wrong with precision; events were to move in just the opposite direction. Instead of allying together to make further attacks on Bo Gu and his ilk, these two men fought one another in an even more pronounced and antagonistic manner.

Among the many issues wrangled with in the struggles between Mao Zedong and Bo Gu and between Mao and Zhang Guotao, there exists a fundamental difference. The Mao-Bo conflict was basically over revolutionary policies with a strong theoretical overtone—though practical results in the end decided the theoretical debate. Although it involved the question of internal leadership, the debate was mainly over external relations: how to overthrow the KMT regime and carry out the revolution. On the other hand, the struggle between Mao and Zhang constituted what may be called a pure power clash. Their struggle was essentially for Party clout, however much its rhetoric disputed doctrines of Marxism and Leninism, policies in fighting the enemy, and making the revolution.

Move to the Party Center's Call

Driven out of its Eyuwan Soviet base and relentlessly pursued by the KMT troops, the Fourth Front Red Army arrived in northern Sichuan in late December 1932. It soon became clear that they had hit the right place at the right time, and the next two years saw a dazzling growth of the Communist movement in this province. A densely populated basin located on the southwest highlands and secluded from China Proper, Sichuan is known as the 'State of Heaven' in Chinese history. It is also known as a locale where disorder easily erupted and peace was more difficult to restore. From the downfall of the Manchu Empire in 1911 to the start of the Sino-Japanese War in 1937, Sichuan remained in a condition of military division and civil war. As many as 470 battles were recorded among local warlords and military cliques during the period 1912-1933; that means on average battles twice-monthly.[2]

Mainly as a result of warlordism, the livelihood of the Sichuanese in general and the peasants in particular was on the verge of destruction. Their appalling living conditions can be well understood in the context of what was called the 'pretaxation system' implemented throughout the province. As an excuse for their endless extortion of funds for warfare, warlords in Sichuan competed with one another in imposing 'pretaxes' on the peasant households in their own 'garrison areas.' They would levy one or more years' tax in advance in addition to the annual tax quota due. The snowball rolled heavier and faster so that by the early 1930's a dozen terms of tax were collected in a single year, and in certain areas the peasants were required to pay the tax for the 21st century.[3] To cope with the situation, a large proportion of the Sichuanese peasants gave up crop farming and undertook illegal but profitable opium cultivation. As the situation grew worse, they had to abandon their land and flee their homes. According to the sources available, 24 million people, one third the population of Sichuan, were lost in the four years 1929-1932.[4] Needless to say, these conditions aided the growth of the Communist rebellion.

When the Fourth Front Army arrived in 1932, Sichuan was divided largely among six warlords—each claiming one army and holding a number of counties as his domain. Altogether, there were 500,000 to 600,000 warlord troops in addition to numerous local militias and bandit gangs.[5] Although some warlords might quarrel and fight with one another under a political slogan (usually half-baked), few had any political or moral orientation beyond immediate personal or factional interest—hence schoolmates fighting against schoolmates, native folk against native folk, and relatives against relatives. In October 1932, the civil war in Sichuan assumed the new form of the Liu family feud: Liu Wenhui, the provincial governor; against his nephew Liu Xiang and a few smaller warlords. In December 1932, the fight reached its zenith at the provincial capital of Chengdu. Tian Songyao, the warlord of northern Sichuan and one of Liu Xiang's supporters, transferred almost all of his men to the Chengdu vicinity for a showdown with Liu Wenhui, leaving only 1,000 troops in his home base to be encroached on by Communist intruders.[6]

In Zhang Guotao's memoirs, he stresses that when the Fourth Front Army came into Sichuan, he was determined to abandon the dogmatic pattern of the Soviet and to instead proclaim a new policy of people's government. Zhang claims to have produced a political manifesto entitled the "Three Covenants" or "A Ten-Point Program for Entering of Sichuan," which focused on peaceful coexistence with local troops, maintenance of the present system of government, and improvement of the people's welfare, rather than the previous insistence on establishment of a Soviet regime, distribution of land and other radical revolutionary measures. Allegedly because the Party Center opposed his manifesto, Zhang had to change his position and return to the old Soviet style. Finally, Zhang laments, "A few years later my miscarried idea was picked up by Stalin. The inappropriate policy of the Soviet was abolished; the strategy of the national anti-Japanese united front and the CCP-KMT collaboration against the Japanese invasion was adopted. There were various reasons which made me unable to change the erroneous policy of the CCP at that time, one of them being my own amiable disposition."[7] Careful studies of the relevant events, however, would lead to a more complicated story, of which Zhang's claim is but one part.

Hundreds of documents—mostly secret at the time—have been found concerning the Communist movement in the Sichuan-Shaanxi Soviet in the 1930s, but the manifesto Zhang refers to is not among them. From a contemporary perspective, it seems that the public support of a Communist leader such as Zhang for a plan to abolish the Soviet system would have been too bold to be true. From the evidence of available documents, moreover, the Communists' itinerary from December 1932 to February 1933 would have left very little time for such a basic change of policy. On December 17 they entered Sichuan and set up the Soviet Government of Lianghekou Township; December 21 the Soviet Government of Chipei County was formed; January 6, 1933, the Soviet Government of the Xixiang-Chenggu Border followed. Between January 20 and 27 a pamphlet on "How to Distribute Land" was issued; February 7 the Soviet Government of the Sichuan-Shaanxi Province was founded.[8] All these events and documents show a constant leaning in favor of the Soviet, and the term 'people's government' is nowhere to be found. If there had been a time of declining the Soviet policy, it could only have been some time between December 21, 1932, and February 7, 1933.

Nevertheless, it may well be that when the Fourth Front Army first climbed over the Dabie Mountains and landed in northern Sichuan, beaten in the past and worried about the future, its most urgent consideration was to strive by any means to survive and not to ponder revolutionary tenets. The rank and file might do so without thinking too much, but Zhang as a mature and responsible CCP leader may have considered some alternative to the previous policy under the new circumstances. With various enemy troops gathering about, perhaps it would be better to propose a truce with all and obtain it with some. With the present structures of government standing firm, discretion might advise he acknowledge them rather than call for their immediate overthrow. Without holding a solid military and administrative stand, distribution of land would be impossible and unwise. In this expedient and contingent sense, some moderate measures were brought in and the Soviet system was held back for the time being.

In early 1933, the Party Center had just assumed leadership in the Jiangxi Soviet and the Central Red Army had just begun its victorious Fourth Campaign. The Bo Gu Center could not understand Zhang's position from a practical point of view, nor could it tolerate his position theoretically. It criticized Zhang's behavior almost automatically. On the other hand, Zhang's later shift back from political conservatism back to revolutionary radicalism was not merely at the Party Center's admonishment, but more for reasons stemming from personal interest.

The FFA's call for peace had effects on some of the Sichuan warlords. Tian Songyao, whose territory was directly affected, refused the Red Army's suggestion resolutely and arrogantly, but his remaining troops in northern Sichuan proved no match for the Red Army. To the surprise of both sides, the Red Army brushed away the enemy and took over three counties in less than one month. A new Communist base was easily established. Once the Communists set foot in northern Sichuan, their policy drastically shifted back to radical or left revolutionism. The old government systems were overthrown and the Soviet—or, the Council of Worker-Peasant-Soldier Representatives—was allegedly established from the Sichuan-Shaanxi province down to each county, district and village. Struggles against all reactionary elements and influences were announced everywhere, and land confiscation and redistribution carried out in this area was even stricter than in the Jiangxi Soviet. Able-bodied peasants were drafted into the Red Army while youngsters were organized into the Red Guards and the Youth Corps. All these radical measures were necessary for consolidating and enhancing the

Communist power; they arose from the Fourth Front Army's own practical need and had little to do with the Party Center's mandate.[9]

The conflicts among local warlords invited the incursion of the Red Army and in return, the expansion of the Red Army temporarily mitigated the warlord conflicts. A military agreement was reached among Liu Wenhui, Tian Songyao and Deng Xihou in Chengdu in January 1933. They decided that each of their three armies would be allowed one brigade deployed in Chengdu, jointly guarding and governing the provincial capital. In February, Tian was named 'Supervisor of the Rebel Extermination on the Sichuan-Shaanxi Border' by the Nanking government and returned to his northern Sichuan base to cope with the Communists.[10]

Tian quickly announced the formation of a front headquarters headed by his vice commander and divided his whole army of 60,000 men into three assault columns. On March 8, Tian's army took Bazhong; on March 18, it took Nanjiang; and on April 29, Tongjiang.[11] The Communists were pushed back to the very northern end of Sichuan. But just as Tian had declared the Communists' entire collapse and was aiming for a fatal blow, battles between the warlords at Chengdu began again. Liu Wenhui pushed Deng Xihou's troops out of the city and started an offensive northward up the Jialing River, encroaching on Deng's territory and threatening Tian's rear. Under these circumstances, Tian hastened to transfer his troops back to the southwest. The Red Army took this chance to counterattack. From May 21 to May 24 they beseiged 13 regiments of Tian Songyao at Kongshanba. After three days' engagement, one half of the Tian troops (about 5,000 men) were destroyed and the other half were scattered. Tian's army collapsed. In ten days he lost all he had gained in the three preceding months. In the wake of the enemy's withdrawal, the Communists recovered all the three Soviet counties. Before another twenty days had passed, they had doubled their territory.[12]

A superficial survey may lead to the belief that the Red Army could win victories easily in any enemy-free region, and hence the fewer the KMT troops the easier the CCP's success. This is not quite true. Warlordism in Sichuan actually helped the Red Army in at least two ways: it prevented the KMT Central Army and other provincial armies (like those of Yang Hucheng of Shaanxi and Liu Enmao of Henan) from following the Red Army into Sichuan. Further, the warlords in Sichuan were less competent and more liable to be defeated: military victories over them allowed the Communists to equip their own troops, and it excited and incited the local people to join them. Generally speaking, in order to be beneficial from the Communist standpoint the local military forces could neither be too strong nor entirely nonexistent. As long as the Communists could enjoy an apparent edge in military engagements, it would be fine to have some local troops to fight with. Just such an ideal situation existed in Sichuan in the early 1930s.

After their victory over Tian Songyao, the Fourth Front Army convened a military conference at Mumen in Nanjiang. The Mumen Conference, chaired by Xu Xiangqian, brought the strategy of mobile warfare in this new environment to a more conscious level. Here, it was also decided to expand the four divisions to four armies, each of about 10,000 men. Starting in August 1933, the Communists organized three offensive battles in the south against Yang Sen, to the west against Deng Xihou and to the east against Liu Cunhou.[13] They captured more new territory and obtained substantial material supplies, and did not mind violating the peace agreement they had made with the warlord Yang Sen. By October 1935 the FFA reached its peak of growth in northern Sichaun. The Sichuan-Shaanxi Border Soviet covered 21 counties with a total population of 5 million people.[14] The Fourth Front Army had five armies, organized into 15 divisions totalling 80,000 troops. Its senior leadership is shown in Table 6.1.

As the radical line of the Fourth Front Army facilitated its military and political victory, its victory in Soviet construction and military struggle in return sprialed it into an even more radical tendency. Such a radical trend would proceed to not only an external policy toward the enemy, but also an internal policy toward the comrades in the CCP and Red Army. Beginning June 1933, a political movement against right opportunists and counterrevolutionaries developed. This anti-counterrevolutionary movement in the Sichuan-Shaanxi Soviet and the Fourth Front Army in 1933 presented a kind of mixed picture. At the base level, it pointed to the landlords, rich peasants, bandits, turncoats and other easily recognized villains. Within the elite, Zhang Guotao was determined to punish those who had opposed his leadership in the past or might hinder his authority at the present. Thus we find that senior officials like Guang Jixun and Shu Yuzhang were killed, and Zeng Zhongsheng and Zhu Guang imprisoned.[16] They were without exception labelled rightist opportunists. Here again, Zhang did not seem to accept the Party Center's leftist line reluctantly—on the contrary, he vigorously applied this line to his own advantage.[17]

As the Communists became a common threat to all the warlords in Sichuan and after Liu Xiang won a decisive victory over Liu Wenhui, a new and larger military campaign agianst the Communists commenced in October 1933. Chiang Kai-shek appointed Liu Xiang 'General Commander of Rebel Extermination in Sichuan.' All the Sichuan warlords except Liu Wenhui took part in the campaign, which comprised six routes and approximately 200,000 troops.[18] This campaign was conducted at almost the same time as the KMT Central Army's Fifth Suppression Campaign against the Jiangxi Soviet, and the early developments of both the campaigns are similar: Liu Xiang's armies pressed deeply into the Sichuan-Shannxi

Table 6.1 Leadership of the Fourth Front Army, October 1933

The Revolutionary Military Council of Northwest China

Chairman:	Zhang Guotao
Vice Chairmen:	Chen Changhao
	Xu Xiangqian

The CCP Committee of the Sichuan-Shaanxi Province

Secretary:	Zhou Guangtan

The Soviet Government of the Sichuan-Shaanxi Province

Chairman:	Xiong Guobing

The Fourth Front Red Army

	General Commander:	Xu Xiangqian
	Political Commissar:	Chen Changhao
	Vice Commander:	Wang Shusheng
	Chief of Staff:	Ni Zhiliang
	Director of Political Dept:	Fu Zhong
4th Army:	Commander:	Wang Hongkun
	Political Commissar:	Zhou Chunquan
30th Army:	Commander:	Yu Tianyun
	Political Commissar:	Li Xiannian
31st Army:	Commander:	Wang Shusheng
	Political Commissar:	Sun Yuqing
9th Army:	Commander:	He Wei
	Political Commissar:	Zhan Caifang
33rd Army:	Commander:	Wang Weizhou
	Political Commissar:	Yang Keming[15]

Soviet; by the summer of 1934 the FFA was squeezed to the very northeast corner of Sichuan; it lost almost all the Soviet cities and towns. Some Party and Army leaders began thinking of a flight back to southern Shaanxi.[19]

The warfare in Sichuan ended quite differently from that in Jiangxi. After two months' stalemate around the strategic city of Wanyuan in northeast Sichuan, the Fourth Front Army once again managed a successful break through the weak point of Liu Cunhou's Sixth Route, bursting into the enemy's rear line. In the next week they cut apart the Fifth and Sixth Routes and destroyed 15,000 enemy troops, and recovered most of their lost land. On August 24 Liu Xiang left the command post with his chief of staff and telegrammed Nanking to request resignation.[20] However much Chiang Kai-shek was saddened by the Communist victory in Sichuan, he was at the same time happy for an opportunity to send his own Central Army to control the situation. Chiang summoned Liu to Nanking, reasserting Liu's leading status in Sichuan. Meanwhile Chiang compelled Liu to accept a joint plan of military operation with the Central Army and some armies from other provinces as participants.[21]

The FFA finally won the victory, but this time it proved neither so easy nor so absolute. It lost 30,000 soldiers in the ten-month-long engagement. Although it managed to bring in about the same number of recruits, it could not achieve any drastic growth, in terms of territorial acquisition and army expansion, as it did after the previous war with Tian Songyao. The Communists claimed their military victory was due to their own correct strategies, and tactics such as "condensing the battlefield for a decisive counterattack."[22] The causes were not so one-sided. They were helped along in that the KMT Central Army could not have taken part in the campaign because of its involvement with the Central Red Army in Jiangxi and also because the Sichuan warlords refused all alien troops' entry to the province. The inner conflicts among the Sichuan warlords also continued in itself to exert a decisive influence. Warlords like Liu Wenhui and Liu Cunhou never put all their efforts into the service of Liu Xiang, and even within Liu's own camp, factional struggles (like that between Wang Lingji and Liu Guanyun) showed up at the critical juncture.[23] The high combatant capacity of the Fourth Front Army, which had been cultivated ever since the Eyuwan years, was always the basic asset in the war. In other words, the Red Army was unlikely to be defeated by the Sichuan warlords alone in terms of fighting capacity, reardless of strategic arrangement.

The combat plan drawn by the Central Military Council on January 20, 1935—two days after the Zunyi Conference—had a close bearing on the Fourth Front Army. As the KMT Central Army tried to draw the Sichuan warlords into the national warfare, so did the Central Red Army with the Fourth Front Army. From the Nationalist viewpoint just as from the Communist viewpoint, Sichuan was gradually losing its independent status and being drawn into the national political and military platform of the CCP-KMT confrontation. The January 20 plan states, "Before this field army's crossing the River, the Fourth Front Army should take active operation towards the direction of Chongqing and draw the heavy troops at Chongqing to its side in order to facilitate this field army smoothly crossing the River."[24] Two days later, on February 22, an express telegram was delivered in the name of the Politburo and the Military Council to the Fourth Front Army. The telegram ordered:

> Unless something unexpected happens, we will go across the Yangtze River toward the north in the middle of February. There must be quite a number of fierce battles on the way. The realization of this strategic plan has a close connection with your cooperation. . . . Therefore, you shall immediately concentrate your troops and accomplish all the necessary preparation for launching an offensive operation to the west of the Jialing River as soon as you can.[25]

The plan obviously required that the Fourth Front Army take offensive actions against the enemy troops in Sichuan and thus load them upon its own shoulders in order to help—save is too strong a word—the Central Red Army and the Party Center. In his memoirs Zhang Guotao recalls that after receiving the above telegram, he decided to force across the Jialing River from Cangxi in response to the Central Red Army's maneuver. Once again, the historical data does not credit such a simple assertion. Instead of leading his army to attack Liu Xiang in the south, Zhang actually started the "Southern Shaanxi Campaign" from late January to early March 1935 at ignorance of the Party Center's request. The FFA broke its peace treaty with the Shaanxi army commanded by Sun Weiru, plunged into the Hanzhong Plain and won considerable victories. It stopped its northern assault and drew back to Sichuan, after some unhappy confrontation with Hu Zongnan's troops of the KMT Central Army.[26] The FFA did not move across the Jialing River to the west until the end of March 1935, when the Central Red Army was far away roaming the Yunnan and Guizhou provinces. Reasons for the FFA's going west of the Jialing River in late March 1935 included something more than just obedience to the Party Center or care for the Party Center's safety. At best, it could only be described as a belated answer to the Party Center's call.

In early 1935 the KMT Central Army and some troops from other provinces gathered in Sichuan to assist the the Sichuan army in suppressing the Fourth Front Army. The situation became so grave that Zhang Guotao himself admitted, "we had better give up northern Sichuan on our own initiative rather than be expelled by the KMT." After two years of intensive military engagement, northern Sichuan was already economically and mentally exhausted by the everlasting rebellions or, in Zhang's own terms, it was "a lemon squeezed dry."[27] Zhang was considering a westward move to either open a new Soviet base in Xikang and Qinghai or—if conditions proved unfavorable—to retreat to Xinjiang and the Soviet Union. Finally, to be fair, the idea of joining forces with the Central Red Army might also have been a consideration.

The Fourth Front Army broke across the Jialing River in late March 1935. In the next month Zhang Guotao was busy organizing a thorough withdrawal from the Sichuan-Shaanxi Soviet; he collected all the local forces and concentrated them into five divisions—including one women's division—and picked up all local cadres higher than the township level. Only one district secretary and one battalion commander were left with about 300 men to continue guerrilla activities. The total force, including the Party and Soviet cadres, was more than 80,000. After the Communists' departure, of course, the Sichuan army immediately swarmed in to fill the vacuum.[28]

At first the Fourth Front Army established its headquarters in Jiangyou and Beichuan, then moved further west to Maoxian and Lixian. To cope with this new situation, Zhang Guotao once again proposed a less radical type of reform, this time the "Confederate Government of Northwest China." On May 15 he founded the CCP Special Committee of Northwest China.[29] The inaugural proclamation of this confederate government indeed includes such moderate policies as calling for a union of all minority peoples and fighting Japanese imperialism. Zhang Guotao should be credited for this shift in the general line, which resulted more from his own hard-earned experience than from any instructions he recieved from the Comintern or the Party Center. But two points still stray from Zhang's own assertions. This Northwest government was regarded as part of the Chinese Soviet Republic and not—as Zhang and contemporary Chinese historians claim (though with different purposes)—an open contrast to the Soviet system and the Party Center political line.[30] In the proclamation Zhang's obvious disrespect for the Central Red Army is evident, as is his challenge to the Party Center's authority. "This Northwestern Confederate Government of the Chinese Soviet Republic is now founded just at a time when the invincible Fourth Front Red Army has embarked on its great western expedition and won numerous victories, at a time when the revolution is surging ahead in Northwest China."[31] The proclamation listed victories of other Red Armies, but did not spare one fine word for the Central Army. In the 'No. 1 Announcement of the Northwestern Confederate Government', it went so far as to claim that this government "will lead the gallant soldiers of the Fourth Front Army—which is 300,000 strong—and lead the 26th

Long Marches of the Red Army in West China, 1934–1936

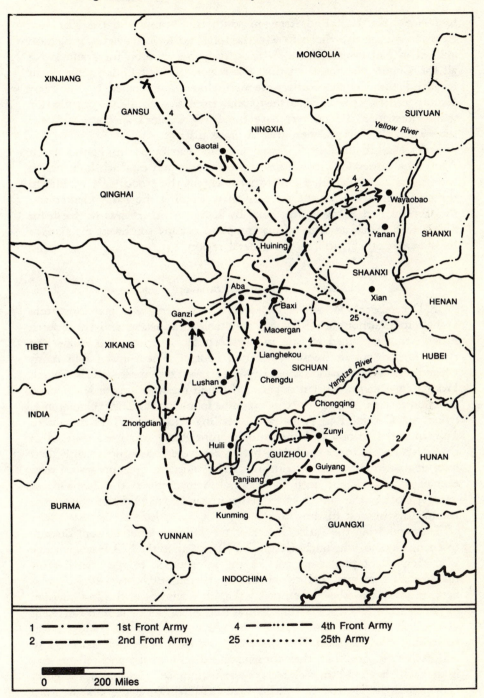

MONGOLIA

XINJIANG

GANSU

NINGXIA

SUIYUAN

Yellow River

Gaotai

QINGHAI

Wayaobao

Huining

Yanan

SHANXI

SHAANXI

Aba

Xian

HENAN

Baxi

Ganzi

Maoergan

TIBET　**XIKANG**

Lianghekou

HUBEI

Lushan

Chengdu

SICHUAN

Yangtze River

INDIA

Chongqing

Zhongdian

Zunyi

Huili

GUIZHOU

HUNAN

Guiyang

Panjiang

BURMA

Kunming

GUANGXI

YUNNAN

INDOCHINA

| 1 | —·—·—· | 1st Front Army | 4 | —··—··— | 4th Front Army |
| 2 | — — — — | 2nd Front Army | 25 | ·········· | 25th Army |

0　　　200 Miles

Red Army, the 29th Red Army in southern Shaanxi and the 39th Red Army in southern Sichuan to win the total victory of sovietizing Sichuan and all of Northwest China."[32] In other words, it took for granted that all the Communist forces in this vast region of West China were under its jurisdiction. These words were naturally not welcomed by the Party Center leaders, especially as they came from a subordinate organization whose formation did not yet have the Party Center's approval and at a time when the Party Center was in grave distress.

From May to June 1935, Zhang Guotao distributed his Fourth Front Army in all directions to capture strategic spots and establish influence in western Sichuan. Whether and to what extent the troops sent by him to the southwest were for the purpose of welcoming the Party Center and the Central Red Army is debatable. By all means, there was no harm for Zhang in dispatching some of his troops to occupy southwest Sichuan, as he did with other parts of this general region.[33]

Union: The Lianghekou Conference

In December 1934, while the Central Red Army was marching from Hunan to Guizhou searching for a suitable destination and the Fourth Front Army remained at ease in northern Sichuan, the two major Red Army forces kept in frequent telegram contact. The Central Red Army needed general information about these southwest provinces, and the Fourth Front Army offered what it obtained through interceptions of KMT radio communications.[34] But in the three months following the Zunyi Conference, when the Central Red Army was wrestling with local KMT troops in Yunnan and Guizhou and the Fourth Front Army was itself engaged in the southern Shaanxi expedition, both sides were too occupied with their own affairs to maintain a faithful correspondence. Few telegrams were exchanged. It was not until the Central Army crossed the Jinsha River and got close to the Fourth Front Army in early May 1935 that the former resumed its interest in the latter.

Telegrams from the Party Center or the Military Council went directly to Zhang Guotao, who might inform Xu Xiangqian in the FFA Headquarters, who then might pass along part of the information to the related army units—each step was conditional. When, therefore, the two Red Armies first ran into each other—presumably the 4th Regiment of the 2nd Division of the First Army Corps of the Central Red Army with the 74th Regiment of the 9th Army of the Fourth Front Army on June 12, 1935—it was something of a surprise. They initially took each other as enemy troops and exchanged fire, then they communicated with bugles and yells. A few hours later they fell into each other's warm embrace.[35] Leaders of the Party Center and the Central Red Army followed into Dawei the next day. On

June 14 a mass rally was held to celebrate the union. Zhou Enlai led the rally; Mao Zedong and Zhu De gave speeches; slogans, musics, songs, and dance performances followed. While the soldiers and cadres were in ecstasies, Mao did not forget to have a private reception of the commander of this FFA unit.[36]

On June 15 Mao and other leaders proceeded north to Maogong, a much larger village. Xu Xiangqian, the General Commander of the Fourth Front Army, telegrammed the Military Council regarding the military situation and operations and also conveyed "the warmest greetings on behalf of the Fourth Front Army" and welcomed "our one-hundred-battle-one-hundred-victory Central Red Army with one hundred thousand times of warmth and sincerity."[37] Li Xiannian, then Political Commissar of the 30th Army of the Fourth Front Army, hurried in to meet the Party and Army leaders. Mao had a private talk with Li as well. The Communist leaders stayed in Maogong for several days, allowing the journey-weathered troops to take a rest and themselves a chance to assess the new situation. From the Fourth Front Army, which had just been back from the northern expedition, the Party Center leaders learned of some current political and military affairs in North China, including the Japanese's further invasion into the North and the KMT's compromise as shown in the He-Utsumei Agreement. Abruptly on June 15, the Party Center put out a statement on the national anti-Japanese war.[38] The immediate purpose of this statement was the Communist Party's announcement of its position in the national political arena. In a later debate of the Party Center leaders with Zhang Guotao, coincidentally, this issue was raised as one of the reasons why the Red Army should go north to fight the Japanese. Xu Xiangqian came from Lixian (where the FFA General Headquarters was located) to Maogong in order to meet with Mao and the Party and Army leaders. But the CRA leaders soon clearly realized that Zhang Guotao was the possessor of the real power in the Fourth Front Army, and no joint decision could be reached without Zhang's attendance.

In all likelihood, the Politburo and Military Council leaders held a conference at Maogong soon after they arrived. The only evidence of such a meeting is a few vague words in Otto Braun's memoirs. But judging from some documents issued in the middle of June 1935, it seems that the Politiburo and Military Council did meet to propose new strategies based on the new information and the new situation. Braun recalls an informal discussion on the subject.[39] The motives of the Politburo and Military Conference in inviting Braun may have been two-fold: to use him as a bridge to maintain contact with the Comintern and the Soviet Union in the future; and also to use him, an envoy of the Comintern, as a symbol of the Party Center's legitimacy in the whole Party and Army.

On June 16 the Party Center sent a telegram to Zhang Guotao, who was in the north at Maoxian, touting a strategic plan to attack the three provinces of Sichuan, Shaanxi and Gansu and establish a Soviet regime along the Min River. One interesting point in this telegram was that instead of addressing him as "comrade," as the Communists usually called each other, Zhang was exceptionally flattered as "your honor" or, literally, "our elder brother."

> Our present plan is that all the troops of your honor and the major forces of this field army should start a large scale attack to the east of the Min River against the approaching enemy, deliver it a hard blow and search for expansion in the area between the Min and Jialing Rivers. Then we will take one part of Shaanxi and one part of Gansu to be locations of flexible strategic operation. Therefore, the key to this plan is to firmly hold Maoxian, Beichuan and Weizhou in our hands and to smash back Hu Zongnan's southern approach.[40]

The purpose of this telegram seems very clear: it required Zhang Guotao to employ his troops to expel the Nationalist army at the north and then strike back eastwards to northern Sichuan. It was hoped that a new Soviet could be opened at the Sichuan-Shaanxi-Gansu border area, which would imply that Zhang should not have given up his northern Sichuan base and moved all his troops from the east to the west to meet the Central Red Army at all. The next day a reply came from Zhang which stressed the impossibility of fighting back to the east and suggested either marching further westward or turning to the south. Zhang's plan was to employ the CRA to fight back to the Chengdu area. In other words, the Central Army should not have come so far to the north. After several telegram exchanges without any agreement, the Party Center requested that Zhang come to Maogong immediately to discuss and help decide the matter.[41]

The Central Red Army continued moving north and arrived at Lianghe-kou; it was there that Zhang eventually came—escorted by a cavalry squad of guards and aides—on June 24, 1935. A tall platform was set up; a big audience gathered; Mao, Zhou, Zhu, and other Party and Army leaders waited in the heavy rain.[42] Zhang himself recalls, "As soon as I saw them, I dismounted and ran forward to embrace them, to shake hands with them. After many years of bitter separation and hardship, we were united here again. Our joyful mood was beyond description. Mao Zedong stepped onto a table and gave me a welcome address. Then I gave a reply speech to salute the Party Center and express my deep condolences for the hard struggle seen by the First Front Army."[43] On the same day, Zhang was invited to an evening feast with all the Politburo and Military Council leaders. Jokes, wisecracks, and laughter filled the dinner table. Zhang and

Zhu then had a cordial, all-night chat. Zhu praised the heroic Fourth Front Army and commented that as long as Zhou and Mao and Zhang all agreed on any military project or operation, nobody would object. Zhang in turn praised Zhu and the Central Army for their heroic spirit and promised, on behalf of the FFA, to assist them with some soldiers and weapons.[44]

Despite the annoying problems hanging on the time, despite the unhappy experiences to follow, and despite the exaggerations of recent memoirs concerning their divergence, the affection and respect of the two principal Red Army forces—including their two most important leaders, Mao and Zhang—toward each other was genuine and sincere at the moment of their union. Common practical and ideological bonds had for many years linked them. Solidarity was the main feature of the early phase of their contact. Their conflicts did not occur abruptly; the whole event involved a complicated relationship gradually inclining to strain.

On the Fourth Front Army's side, almost all of its top leaders, including Zhang Guotao, Chen Changhao, and Xu Xiangqian, had achieved their leading positions not only by their own efforts, but as a result of the Party Center's assignment. Throughout the years in the Eyuwan and Northern Sichuan Soviets, they applied the Party Center's authority and prestige as a means of consolidating their status in the eyes of local cadres and subordinate soldiers.[45] For officers and men in the FFA in general, the Party Center, the Central Soviet, and the Military Council represented their faith and hope for so many years that their longing for the Party Center had already become a kind of religious creed—a symbol of all their goals. In other words, they were to come to fulfill their spiritual mission. As for the Central Red Army, after several months of tiring travelling and fighting, they were driven to a nearly desperate situation. Their troops had been reduced to about one fifth of the original strength in the past eight months; they lost all their home base and could not found a new one despite their persistent efforts. Now they had suddenly discovered a reinforcement of more than 80,000 troops and a Soviet base already in existence—the FFA was for them a physical savior. Such a feeling permeated the CRA from the top leaders down to the rank and file. The respect of the CRA for the FFA was thus based mainly on practical and material considerations. For whichever reason, both sides were truly happy at the reunion, not merely playing out a sinister scheme or diplomatic ploy. Each side tried to treat the other in the best manner possible; perhaps they did. Between Zhang and Mao there were also separated yet aligned interests: their individual political interests, the interests of the armed forces to which they belonged, and the interests of the Communist Party and Red Army in the face of their general Nationalist enemy.

The morning following Zhang's arrival, the Politburo held a conference. Whether it could be called a Politburo Conference in a strict sense or not, the conference was later on known as the Lianghekou Conference. The purpose of the Conference was obvious: to decide the tasks, especially the military maneuvers, of the Communists after the union. The participants in this Conference (though there are some varied accounts) seem to have been all the full and alternate Politburo members and in addition, the leaders of the Red Army Headquarters. They were: Mao Zedong, Zhang Wentian, Zhou Enlai, Bo Gu, Zhu De, Wang Jiaxiang, Liu Shaoqi, Kai Feng, Deng Fa, Liu Bocheng, Li Fuchun, and Zhang Guotao. Otto Braun might have been invited to participate as well as Xu Xiangqian. Deng Xiaoping attended the Lianghekou Conference, as he had the Zunyi Conference, as the recordkeeper. Less probable attendees were army corps leaders such as Peng Dehuai, Yang Shangkun, Lin Biao, and Nie Rongzhen.[46]

As the man in charge of general military affairs, Zhou Enlai chaired the Conference, meaning that the Conference was not just a political conference, but focused primarily on military objectives. Zhou was the choice, morevoer, because he was an indisputable veteran Party and Army leader even in the eyes of Zhang Guotao, unlike Bo Gu or Zhang Wentian whose chairmanship might have made Zhang uneasy. Nevertheless, Zhang Guotao and Mao Zedong were the two key figures. Zhou analyzed the present situation and proposed that—as the Party Center leaders in the Central Red Army had decided in advance—the Red Army should temporarily set up a military base at the present location, and it would go north as soon as possible. Since this was the first meeting of leaders of the two Red Armies, although the main topic of discussion remained where they should all go and what they should do, the underlying problem was how to bring the two armies under a united or, at the very least, a coordinated leadership. Later, it was clear that the resolution to go north did not bother Zhang Guotao nearly as much as the fact that it was resolved without his consent.[47]

The Lianghekou Conference dealt with three urgent military problems such as strategic policy, operational maneuvers, and army leadership. Regarding policy, Zhou reported that the two Red Armies had had different strategic goals before their union: the FFA had wanted to go west through Xikang; and the CRA had wanted to go east across the Min River. Now neither plan seemed appropriate, so the Party Center proposed that the joint troops first go north to southern Gansu and then open a new Soviet base on the Sichaun-Gansu-Shaanxi border.[48]

Zhou Enlai's report was a compromise, but it obviously favored the Central Red Army. Zhang Guotao and Mao Zedong were the next speakers. Zhang objected to Zhou's proposal on behalf of the Fourth Front Army. Zhang argued that since about 130 enemy regiments were now placed on the eastern front, there should be no reason for the Red Army to tangle there. To the north, vast grasslands and high mountains lay in their path and the distance was great; what was more, Hu Zongnan's Central Army, amounting to more than 20 regiments, stood directly in the way; even if the Red Army could pass these barriers and reach its destination, it would be too depleted to compete with the local forces and create a new Soviet. Therefore, Zhang proposed moving a little west, taking western Sichaun and Xikang as the temporary base to defy Hu Zongnan, backing onto the Tibet highland, and then trying to either move northwest to reach the Soviet Union or turning south to attack Chengdu, according to future changes in the political and military situation. Mao supported Zhou's proposal, of course, but he argued for its adoption in far stronger terms. Mao suggested that the Red Army not only move to the north immediately, but also destroy Hu Zongnan and capture the city of Songfan. He demanded that the united command be decided and appointed solely by the Politburo Standing Committee and the Central Military Council, neither of which included any member of the Fourth Front Army.[49]

All in all, nonetheless, the Conference proceeded peacefully and politely. When Zhang gave his speech, Mao and others quietly took notes. Though the majority of the participants pronounced themselves in accord with Zhou's position, all of them had to face the fact that Zhang was not just one participant with one vote, but the representative of the dominantly strong Fourth Front Army. The Conference concluded with no definite resolution, but in a lukewarm manner as Mao said "How about leaving the matter for further consideration?"[50]

Zhang Guotao left Lianghekou for Maoxian right after the Conference, and Zhang Wentian was entrusted with the task of drawing up the resolution. The Resolution of the Lianghekou Conference as it exists was not presented and adopted at the Conference. Though the Resolution showed a clear preference for the Politburo or the Central Red Army, it still was a product of mediation and compromise. Altogether the Resolution has five items, and the first three are translated below.

1. After the union of the First and Fourth Red Front Armies, our strategic policy is to apply our main forces to attack at the north, to destroy the enemy in a large numbers in mobile warfare, to take over southern Gansu first and then to create the Sichuan-Shaanxi-Gansu Soviet Base. Thus, we will put the Chinese Soviet movement on a firmer and broader base foundation or foothold in order to strive for victory in the northwestern provinces and eventually in all China.

2. To realize this strategic policy, tactically, we must concentrate our main forces to destroy Hu Zongnan's troops, to capture Songpan and control the region north of Songpan in order to achieve a successful march to southern Gansu.

3. One part of the Red Army—a minor part of the Red Army—should be dispatched to the Yao and Xia Rivers to control this region so

that we can back on the vast area of Gansu, Qinghai, Ningxia and Xinjiang provinces, which would be to the benefit of development toward the east.[51]

From the first two items, it appears that the Resolution adhered to the Zhou's proposal on behalf of the Central Red Army. Item 3 was a concession to Zhang Guotao's proposal of a western operation. As regards the military command, the Conference decided that it must be unified and it should be concentrated in the Military Council. Zhang Guotao was appointed as vice chairmen in the Military Council; all the Red Army troops were to be organized into three routes: the Left, the Central and the Right, commanded respectively by Lin Biao, Peng Dehuai and Xu Xiangqian. It should be noted that the CRA, with one sixth of the joint forces, controlled two thirds of the regular positions, while the FFA's five-sixths had merited one third.[52]

The Communists headed north after the Lianghekou Conference, though not as quickly as the Resolution mandated. They crawled only 200 li in the whole month from mid-June to mid-July, 1935. There might be other explanations for this slow motion, but the most obvious reason was the discrepancy between titular leader Mao in the Party Center and power holder Zhang Guotao in the Fourth Front Army.

Clash: The Conferences at Luhua, Shawo, and Maoergai

The spectacular upsurge of the Fourth Front Army in late 1934 and the triple-edged threat of the Red Armies to Sichuan in early 1935—the Second and Sixth Army Corps from the southeast, the Fourth Front Army from the north, and the First Front Army from the south and southwest—were a good excuse for the KMT Central Army to intrude in the province, thus ending its age-old seclusion from national affairs.[53] It is hard to say whether Chiang Kai-shek's real purpose was to pursue the Communists or control the Sichuan warlords. Perhaps they figured equally in his mind. In December 1934, Chiang ordered Hu Zongnan's troops to enter northwest Sichuan and appointed He Guoguang (Director of the First Bureau of the Ministry of Defense of the KMT Central Government) as the head of an advisory group to supervise the military affairs in Chengdu. Soon after, the Sichuan warlords Deng Xihou, Tian Songyao, and Yang Sen publicly delegated their "garrison zones" to the provincial and central government. On March 2, 1935, Chiang flew to Chengdu in person to celebrate the unification of the province and urge an overall reform movement. As either a political end or a military means, Chiang called for government reforms and socio-economic modernization, not merely military unification in Sichuan province. The year 1935 indeed marked significant progress in the modern history of Sichuan.[54]

In the summer of 1935, Chiang spent most of time in Chengdu. He employed the Sichuan army as a defensive force, to be heavily deployed along the Min River, lest the Red Army should surge back to the east. In the northwest, Hu Zongnan's army stretched to Songpan and Zhu Shaoliang (another KMT Central Army general) moved to block southern Gansu. Finally, Chiang summoned Xue Yue's troops to Chengdu as military support to help bring Sichuan under the control of the Nanking government and then transferred Xue to the Wenxian area to check the Communists in northwest Sichuan. Chiang preferred a slow but firm combat project to deal with the Red Army; his basic policy was to cut off the Red Army's material supplies, block its escape, and wear it down in western Sichuan.[55] From the Communists' point of view the military situation did not seem that urgent for the time being; they had enough time to ponder their next step. From June to September 1935, their subject of military affairs served merely as a backdrop for intraparty conflicts.

Though there have been different assertions regarding the exact strength of the First and Fourth Army when they united in June 1935, a careful analysis of the most credible sources shows that the First Front Army had 10,000 to 15,000 men while the Fourth Front Army had 60,000 to 70,000. Their ratio was more or less 1:5, a considerable disparity of strength.[56] In terms of weaponry and material supplies, the FFA was once again far superior. On the other hand, the leaders of the CRA—whether within the Politburo, the Military Council, or the Red Army Headquarters— dominated the Fourth Front Army, despite the initial change after the Lianghekou Conference. In the Politburo, Zhang Guotao was the FFA's only representative. He was one of three vice-chairmen of the Military Council; the chairman and other vice-chairmen were from the CRA. In the General Headquarters there were no FFA men at all.

The rank and file soldiery and lower level cadres and officers in the two Red Armies were those who had showed the greatest and most sincere happiness at their meeting; it was also they who would be most likely to express their disrespect and resentment for one another after their union. They tended to argue over meals and bullets, roads and camps, uniforms and badges, the titles of Chairman Mao and Chairman Zhang, and over a hundred and one other matters.[57] These arguments boiled down to a simple question: which of the two sides, this strong Fourth Front Army or that senior First Front Army, should be superior to the other? Officers and soldiers of the Fourth Front Army regarded the Party Center as a God to whom they prayed, but not a boss they obeyed. For many years the soldiers had been accustomed to obeying their squad leaders and the division commanders had been accustomed to obeying their army commanders. The glory of their own army unit had been their motivating force in fighting the Nationalist enemy and would be the source of the cocky pride with which they defied their Communist allies.

While common soldiers and petty officers seemed like trouble makers, their top leaders were more restrained in manner but more devious in action. In point of fact, most of the riots among the soldiers were incited by leaders for their own factional purposes: the soldiers were often employed to turn initial quibbles into big fusses. The leaders of the First Front Army—partly because they were more solid as a group and partly because they were already the authoritative side—could afford to be more poised and more outspoken. Zhang Guotao, on the other hand, was in a less favorable position in terms of votes and legality in the Party and Army leadership, and he was thus forced to resort to more covert and blunt means. In his memoirs, Zhang recalls that Mao had cultivated a tendency to be suspicious through his years of guerrilla warfare. This may be true, but it might equally be that Zhang was, as Braun describes, "every bit as ambitious as Mao,"[58] and thus bore watching. Through 20 years of political experiences within the Communist Party, both men had become resolute and astute as politicians—unlike Bo Gu, Zhang Wentian and Chen Changhao in the former quality and unlike Zhu De, Peng Dehuai and Xu Xiangqian in the latter. They had both had their ups and the downs, seen the ins and outs, and learned the words and the deeds in the Communist history and politics. They both treasured power in general, power of their own troops and, above all, their own personal power.

The Military Council produced a combat plan entitled "Operation of the Songpan Battle" on June 29. It required that the entire Red Army march north in order to destroy Hu Zongnan's troops and capture the city of Songpan as a pass to Gansu.[59] The Fourth Front Army was at that moment located in the north, closer to Songpan, in a more convenient position to engage the Hu's army. Zhang was naturally reluctant to carry out a plan which he had not voted for and would sacrifice his own men. Instead, the FFA under his control remained quietly in place. Only Mao and his own troops hurried toward the north and climbed over several peaks to reach Maoergai near Songpan.[60] It was up to Mao to lead his men through the FFA deployment and employ them in wrestling with Hu Zongnan at Songpan, if he so desired. Mao did not wish to do this and so had to stop and negotiate with Zhang.

When Mao urged Zhang to take action, Zhang boiled Mao's proposal, "We should fight the KMT," down to his own interest, "We should therefore settle the problem of a unitary military command." Chen Changhao was younger and more outspoken: he telegrammed the Military Council in the name of the Fourth Front Army suggesting that Zhang Guotao be named Chairman of the Military Council in order to concentrate the military leadership. On July 9, the Sichuan-Shaanxi CCP Committee telegraphed the Party Center proposing the appointment of Chen Changhao as Political Commissar of the Red Army General Headquarters. Now leaders in the CRA gave in, though not yet entirely. They turned Chen Changhao down for the while, but appointed Zhang Guotao to be the General Political Commissar on July 18. Under this condition, Zhang left his headquarters at Zagunao, moved one more step north and met the CRA leaders at Luhua, where they had another conference immediately.[61]

The Luhua Conference left no formal resolution. Perhaps indeed there was no written resolution at all.[62] This Conference was sheer bargaining for power. As a result of this Conference Zhang Guotao obtained the de facto control of the Army leadership, as can be seen from Table 6.2 of the military system devised at the conference.

The table itself indicates the promotion of Zhang Guotao and his men. It also stipulated that the General Headquarters had sole authority in military command. In the General Headquarters neither Zhu De nor Liu Bocheng had had or would have any decisive influence. Actually, Zhang replaced Zhou Enlai as the final decision-maker in dealing with the overall military affairs. The Front Headquarters was in charge of combat operations; its commander and political commissar were both from the Fourth Front Army.

As for Mao, his membership in the Three-Man-Group was automatically dropped, his assistantship to Zhou in military affairs was even more out of the question, and his former position as Political Commissar of the Front Headquarters was given to Chen Changhao. In other words, Mao lost all his titles and power in the Red Army. Yet his influence in the Party Center and his role as the spokesman of the First Front Army remained intact, and was perhaps even more firmly, though not formally, established. He was the mastermind in the whole bargaining process. Zhang's real strength had convinced diplomats like Zhou Enlai; his promotion had subdued military men like Zhu De and Liu Bocheng; but Zhang had definitely offended Mao and the returned students as power struggle-oriented persons: they rallied more closely together, though from different angles of political interest and different depths of political thought.

Assuming his post as the General Political Commissar, Zhang had to order the joint troops to move north. The strong spearhead forces commanded by Peng, Lin, and Xu all gathered around the town of Maoergai by the end of July 1935. Zhang himself arrived at the Red Army General Headquarters at Maoergai after the Luhua Conference, while the rear forces of the Fourth Front Army remained in the Zhuokeji area in the south.[64]

Zhang Guotao and his men still seemed dissatisfied with the results of the Luhua Conference. The positions Zhang and his men had obtained were somewhat nominal. There was still no clarification of the relationships

Table 6.2 The Military System of the Red Army After the Luhua Conference

The General Headquarters		
	Commander-in-Chief	Zhu De
	General Political Commissar	Zhang Guotao
The Front Headquarters		
	General Commander	Xu Xiangqian
	Political Commissar	Chen Changhao
1st Army	Commander	Lin Biao
	Political Commissar	Nie Rongzhen
3rd Army	Commander	Peng Dehuai
	Political Commissar	Yang Shangkun
5th Army	Commander	Dong Zhentang
	Political Commissar	Zeng Risan
32nd Army	Commander	Luo Binghui
	Political Commissar	He Changgong
4th Army	Commander	Xu Shiyou
	Political Commissar	Wang Jianan
9th Army	Commander	Sun Yuqing
	Political Commissar	Chen Haisong
30th Army	Commander	Cheng Shicai
	Political Commissar	Li Xiannian
31st Army	Commander	Zhan Caifang
	Political Commissar	Yu Tianyun
33rd Army	Commander	Luo Nanhui
	Political Commissar	Zhang Guangcai[63]

among the General Headquarters, the Military Council and the Politburo; a fully-staffed and well-equipped General Headquarters did not yet exist; Xu and Chen could hardly exercise their command over the army units of the First Front Army. Besides, Zhang, Chen, and their men were not merely interested in the military affairs; as Communists and politicians they aspired to positions in the Party Center. To address these concerns, they requested a conference of the Politburo to discuss political issues.

The Politburo conference which convened at Shawo on August 5-6, 1935, might be considered the most important event in the reunion of the First and Fourth Front Armies. It was the only conference to deal seriously with general political issues. Both sides looked forward to such a conference: Mao hoped to use the majority of the Party Center to compel Zhang to move north; Zhang hoped to use the fall of the Jiangxi Soviet to attack the Party Center's political line and change its leadership. Besides, there was indeed an ever more urgent need for the Communist troops to become more coordinated in military maneuvers in order to face the Nationalist enemy.

Participating in the Shawo Conference were all available Politburo members: Zhang Wentian, Zhou Enlai, Mao Zedong, Zhu De, Bo Gu, Zhang Guotao, Deng Fa, and Kai Feng. On the Fourth Front Army side, besides Zhang Guotao, Chen Changhao, and Fu Zhong (Director and Vice Director of the General Political Department) attended. Military leaders such as Peng Dehuai, Liu Bocheng, Lin Biao, and Xu Xiangqian were not invited partly because of the political nature of the Conference and partly due to their military duties. The balance of power between the CRA and the FFA had clearly changed from that which prevailed at the Lianghekou Conference. Zhang Guotao is perhaps mistaken when he recalls that he and Chen Changhao rode to the conference location and Chen was not allowed in, but he is correct in stating that the resolution had been drafted even before the convocation.[65]

Zhang Wentian chaired the Shawo Conference and read the resolution he had drafted as the general report on behalf of the Politburo. The report criticized Zhang Guotao for abandoning the northern Sichuan Soviet base, for arbitarily declaring the Northwest Confederate Government and, above all, for hesitating to carry out the northern expedition project. Zhang Guotao and Chen Changhao were immediately put in a defensive position. After all, they were the minority in the Party Center and the Politburo.[66]

Zhang Guotao made various excuses for himself and the Fourth Front Army before quickly shifting the topic to the political and military errors of the Party Center and the First Front Army: having lost the entire Jiangxi Central Soviet and the bulk of the Red Army in the Fifth Campaign and on the Long March, how could the Party Center leaders continue to brag about the correctness of their general line?[67] For this part of the discussion, the Conference could only reach a conciliatory agreement. The participants decided to revise the draft resolution, omitting defamations of either side to stress the importance of the entire Party and Army's solidarity. The final Resolution of the Shawo Conference devoted considerable space to this matter.

> The fraternal solidarity of the First and Fourth Front Armies is a necessary condition for fulfilling our historical mission of creating the Sichuan-Shaanxi-Gansu Soviet and establishing the Chinese Soviet Republic. All those tendencies, intentional or unintentional, toward breaking the solidarity of the First and Fourth Front Armies can only be harmful to the Red Army and beneficial to the enemy.
> It should be made clear to each individual comrade that both the First and Fourth Front Armies are constituents of the Chinese Worker and Peasant Red Army, and both were under the leadership of the Central Committee of the Chinese Communist Party. There are only class love and aid between us, not divergence and contradiction. Only in this way can the union of the First and Fourth Front Armies be firm and lasting, can we combine into one unit to defeat our class enemy.[68]

Contrary to its preliminary draft, the Resolution praised the glorious experiences and achievements of both sides—the Party Center's political line was correct and could not possibly be otherwise; the political line of the Fourth Front Army was equally fine—and lauded the excellent situation after the union of the two Red Armies. Since the situation was so favorable, it followed, the whole Army should go north to fight the Japanese and create a Sichuan-Gansu-Shaanxi Soviet. Though it was a matter more of rhetoric than of logic, the northern march was nevertheless reaffirmed at the Shawo Conference. This might be the biggest victory for Mao and the First Front Army at the time.[69]

The Resolution of the Shawo Conference called for fighting against rightist opportunism: "The wavering attitude of rightist opportunism is obvious in most of our troops and it is growing in some of the troops. It is most dangerous to the fulfillment of our strategic task. At present one of the key tasks is to launch a struggle against rightist opportunism."[70] But Zhang Guotao could claim that Mao was a rightist opportunist because Mao did not believe that they were able to defeat the enemy here and hold the Soviet base now. Mao could also protest Zhang's opportunist 'flightism', for Zhang dared not fight Hu Zongnan and go north against the Japanese invaders but rather wanted to stay at their present base or flee to the distant west. In bizarre occurrence, applying the slogan of anti-rightism, Zhang executed his old opponent Zeng Zhongsheng, who had been in custody since 1933 as a victim of the anti-counterrevolutionary movement in northern Sichuan and who had attempted to deliver an petition to the Party Center after the the CRA-FFA union.[71]

Zhang Guotao grew more aggressive when he came to the question of strengthening the Party Center's leadership. He raised a motion to add some of his own men to the Politburo. After some bargaining, Chen Changhao joined the Politburo, while Xu Xiangqian and a few others became the Central Committee members. Even more successful was Zhang's demand for more military leadership. It was made clear that the General Headquarters had the sole right to exercise military command while the Politburo and the Military Council functioned merely as general supervisors. Zhang was entitled to reform the headquarters and reorganize the army system. Soon after the Conference, all the major troops were divided into two routes under the leadership of the General Headquarters and the Front Headquarters respectively.

As a general result of the Shawo Conference, Mao and the First Front Army maintained their titular superiority, while Zhang and the Fourth Front Army gained the upper hand in practical power. In terms of military affairs, Mao succeeded in formally passing his proposal of going north, but Zhang would lead the troops in doing so. Further, a contradiction between the formal Party Center and the substantive Army Headquarters developed.

Now the northern march seemed to have assumed a practical facade. Since most of the rear forces which constituted the Left Route Army were

Table 6.3 The Two-Route Division of the Red Army After the Shawo Conference

---

The Left Route Army: 5th, 9th, 31st, 32nd, 33th Armies

    The General Headquarters

General Commander	Zhu De
General Political Commissar	Zhang Guotao
Chief of General Staff	Liu Bocheng

The Right Route Army: 1st, 3rd, 4th, 30th Armies; Party Center

    The Front Headquarters

General Commander	Xu Xiangqian
Political Commissar	Chen Changhao
Chief of Staff	Ye Jianying[72]

---

still in the south, Zhang Guotao, Zhu De and Liu Bocheng returned to Zhuokeji after the Shawo Conference. They were to reform the General Headquarters and direct the Left Route Army to the north. They brought with them all the radio stations, secret codes, and operation personnel. Communication between the army units and the Party Center, and between the army units and the Military Council, were suspended; all Red Army troops were supposed to contact and obey only the General and Front Headquarters.[73]

Zhang and Zhu did not arrive at Zhuokeji until August 20, 1935. At the same time, the Right Route Army was still at Maoergai, where the Party Center was itself located. The Right Route was supposed to go through Banyou and Baxi, turn northeast to break through the enemy blockade along the Gansu-Sichuan border, and then bend northwest to the Yao River valley in Gansu. The Left Route was supposed to move northwest to Aba and from there either move northeast to join the Right Route, or continue north through the grassland and through the Sichuan-Gansu border and then turn northeast to the Xia River valley also in Gansu. Thus the two routes could meet or draw close at the Yao and Xia Rivers in southern Gansu and create a Soviet base there.[74]

The Right Route Army faced a rather complicated situation from the very beginning of its formation. On the one hand, Xu and Chen of the Front Headquarters were to be responsible to Zhu De and Zhang Guotao in the General Headquarters. On the other hand they were staying with and were responsible to Mao Zedong, Zhang Wentian and Zhou Enlai in the Party Center and the Military Council. Besides, half of the troops of the Right Route, namely, Lin Biao's 1st Army and Peng Dehuai's 3rd Army, belonged to the First Front Army and remained out of their direct control. Furthermore, being assigned in the new army system, their allegiance shifted a bit. They would have been happy to see all the troops to join together for a unified action rather than see themselves left to fight Hu Zongnan alone.

On August 20 another 'enlarged Politburo conference' was held in Maoergai, before the Right Route took off for the north. This conference was most certainly sponsored by Mao himself. Zhu De and Zhang Guotao were both away in the south, and Zhou Enlai was absent due to either his poor health or his dislike for factionalism. In addition to the full and alternate members of the Politburo, the military commanders of army rank or higher (such as Xu Xiangqian, Chen Changhao, Lin Biao, Nie Rongzhen and some others), with the exception of Peng Dehuai and Yang Shangkun (who were with their troops at the front), participated in the Maoergai Conference.[75]

To evade charges of undermining the Shawo Conference, the Maoergai Conference dealt exclusively with military operations. This time Mao Zedong himself acted as both the chairman and the drafter of the resolution. There were three parts to the resolution, which can be summarized as follows: 1. The strategic policy at present must be to go north to capture the Yao River valley centered at Minzhou in southern Gansu and from there possibly to expand influence to the east of Shaanxi and Gansu; 2. The first step is to organize a successful battle to break through the KMT blockade along the Songpan line; 3. It is not appropriate to have the main forces go west of the Yellow River to the far northwest.[76] What seems more noteworthy is the combat which the resolution requests be conducted at Songpan:

> To realize the above strategic plan, the battle in front of us is the most crucial matter. Negligence and defeat in this battle will bring difficulties and even failure to the whole strategic plan. Therefore, in the present campaign we should strive to control the Yao River and especially the eastern bank region, to break the enemy's blockade line along the Lanzhou and Songpan, and put ourselves in a favorable mobile position to continuously win over the enemy. To concentrate as far as is possible our main force in one direction and to conduct combat firmly and bravely are the guarantees of victory in this battle. Opportunist surrender to hardship or taking the path of least resistance will make us lose the battle, and make it impossible for us to realize our general strategy.[77]

Mao's main concern was how to inspire the troops in general, and Chen Changhao and Xu Xiangqian in particular, to fight a battle. On Chen and Xu's part, they had too junior status in the Politburo to raise any objections to Mao's plan, and they actually might feel somewhat contented with their recent promotion in the Party Center and the Army Headquarters. Chen was a young returned student who could be quick tempered but also easily persuaded, while Xu was a Whampoa Academy graduate with a more military than political disposition. Above all, they were currently the commanders of the Right Route Army. Not only did they have to face an inevitable confrontation with the KMT army, they also wanted a successful battle to their own credit. The Maoergai Conference went smoothly, without any serious opposition to Mao, and it seemed like a routine mobilization before a military expedition. Thus after nearly three months of hesitation and argumentation, the Communists eventually left their camps and resumed their northern march, the Right Route Army from Maoergai towards Songpan and the Left Route Army from Zhuokeji toward Aba.

Split: The Baxi Conference

While the Communists were busy quarrelling among themselves, hesitating to make any definite strategic operations, the KMT had time to prepare an encircling movement. By late August about 130 regiments of the Sichuan army were stationed along the Min River to prevent the Communists from sneaking back into eastern Sichuan; behind them were the second layer of defense—the newly arrived Hupei army led by Xu Tingyao. In the south, Yang Sen and Liu Wenhui followed the Communists to occupy Maogong and Fubian. In the north, Hu Zongnan dispatched his troops to guard the Songpan line. Behind him were Zhu Shaoliang and Yu Xuezhong in Shaanxi and Gansu for rear defense. After staying in Chengdu for a month to help Chiang Kai-shek control the political situation in Sichuan, Xue Yue moved to Pingwu and Wenxian to check the Communists from the northeast, lest they flee to southern Shaanxi and meet the 25th Red Army there. There was no KMT army in the west, but that direction was the safest because the barren Xikang plateau presented an absolute obstacle for any troops to stay there for long. In sum, except in the southern direction where Liu Wenhui and Yang Sen followed the Red Army's vacancy to fill in the Maogong area, the KMT simply waited for the Red Army, initiating no offensive moves.[78]

The Right Route Army, commanded by Chen Changhao and Xu Xiangqian and accompanied by the Politburo, left Maoergai on August 21, and plunged into the vast muddy grassland. The 1st, 4th and 30th Armies and the Front Headquarters went ahead, leaving the 3rd Army and the Party Center to follow. Seven days of tedious marching brought them to the area of Banyou, Baozuo and Baxi in the northwestern corner of Sichuan province, where on the grassland trails hundreds of corpses of their comrades were left.[79]

The town of Baozuo lay about 30 li east of Baxi. There, one enemy regiment belonging to Hu Zongnan's KMT Central Army was deployed. As a necessary measure to break open the road to the north, Chen gallantly proposed to employ his own FFA troops to fight a battle at Baozuo. Mao did not object. The 4th Army sieged Baozuo, pretending to take the town; Hu Zongnan sent one division to rescue the garrison troops and engaged the 30th Red Army with the rest of his troops. The combat started August 29 and lasted one day. Both sides lost thousands of men.[80] The KMT division was wiped out, leaving Baozuo for the Communists. Thus the route to the north was broken open. From there, Lin Biao and Nie Rongzhen led the 1st Army further north. The Front Headquarters and the Politburo stayed in Baxi for the next few days waiting for the 1st Army to clear the way ahead and at the same time contacting the Left Route for coordinating operations.

Led by Zhang Guotao and Zhu De, the Left Route started off on August 20 from Zhuokeji toward the northwest. From Maerkang on August 25, they too entered a tough terrain of woody hills and grassland. By the end of the month they reached Aba—about 200 li west of the Right Route at

Baxi.[81] Between them lay the real grassland. Since Zhang Guotao had not taken going north very seriously before, and was not quite certain how to do so now, he stayed on for a few days. When the news of the battle at Baozuo arrived, he felt less happy to know the road to the north was opened than upset that his FFA troops alone had battled and thus suffered so many casualties.[82]

From the Aba area there were two ways for the Left Route Army to enter the north if it so desired. It could either go directly north and pass the Qinghai and Gansu border toward the Xia River, or turn northeast to join forces with the Right Route and then proceed north together toward the Yao River. Both courses had their geographic barriers. Zhang Guotao ordered his men to try going east to approach the Right Route Army. This meant struggling through the vast grassland lying between Aba and Baxi. Worse yet, heavy rains spattered them from August 30 to September 2. They trudged through the grassland for three days and halted before the Gequ River, which was flooding over. They made several attempts at building bridges, but none succeeded. The whole army was stuck in the grassland.[83] This situation reinvigorated Zhang's desire to turn back—not only back to Aba but back to the south. A telegram was issued in the name of the Red Army Headquarters before they turned back to Aba:

1. We inspected the upper part of the river for 70 li and could not find any place to wade across or set up bridges. All the army units had only 3 days' food; the 25th division had only one day's food. The radio ran out of supplies. In face of the endless grassland and unable to go forward, we are idling to death! It was so miserable without a guide. Now we have decided to turn back three days from tomorrow morning.
2. The whole combat strategy is very much affected. So many troops were lost last time at Maoergai when the food supply was cut short. Again [you] require [us] to go to Banyou. Here is the result! Going to the north is not only inopportune, but will cause various difficulties and obstacles.
3. We are thinking of luring the enemy to the north and then letting the Right Route Army take the chance to strike back at the enemy in Songpan. The Left Route Army will also shift to Songpan. This should be immediately decided and carried out.[84]

This telegram sounded uncertain and indecisive. The Right Route ignored it and operated according to the original schedule. The 1st Army set out to the north on September 4 and reached Ejie the next day, while the Front Route Headquarters and the Politburo leaders remained in Baxi. A telegram altercation began between the Party Center in the Right Route and the Army Headquarters in the Left Route. A reply telegram in the name of the CCP Center and the Military Council was delivered to respond to Zhang Guotao or the Red Army Headquarters, insisting that the original plan of going north should not be altered and urging the Left Route to approach Baxi or, at worst, to take the straight northern road and meet the Right Route in Gansu later. On September 8, Chen Changhao and Xu Xiangqian themselves offered Zhang Guotao some mild dissuasion: "We regard it as a principle not to divide our troops, and it seems better for the Left Route to join us rather than turn back to the south."[85]

Zhang Guotao stuck to his notion of returning south. On September 9 the Red Army General Headquarters gave a long and concrete argument backing its new strategy. In essence, the telegram argued that since a part of the Red Army had already driven into the northeast and aroused the enemy's attention, the main forces should take the chance to fight back to the south and defeat the Sichuan army there. It was far more feasible in the author's eyes to create a new Soviet base in Sichuan than in any strange northern provinces.[86]

The telegram went to Chen Changhao and Xu Xiangqian in the Right Route Headquarters. They received it with contradictory feelings. They had been Zhang Guotao's followers for several years in the past and were working as leaders of a subordinate army unit now; these considerations would lead them to stand with Zhang and the General Headquarters. Nevertheless, they were also CCP members and had to dutifully pass the message to the Party Center. A reply telegram from the Party Center was issued in a severe tone.

> Comrade Guotao and also Xu and Chen:
> Chen talked about going south. The Center deems it entirely inappropriate. The Center points out earnestly: going north is the only way out at this moment, whereas in going south we will face extremely unfavorable conditions in terms of enemy layout, geographic conditions, populace, and material supply. It will bring the Red Army to an unprecedentedly difficult situation. The Center insists that the policy of going north not be changed by any means; the Left Route Army should go north immediately. If it is too detrimental to come to the east, you can cross the Yellow River to the west and capture the Gansu and Qinghai border area and expand to the east. Answer us immediately.[87]

Zhang Guotao did give an answer the next day. But the answer was addressed not to the Party Center leaders but only to his men, Chen and Xu in the Front Headquarters. This telegram is still a mystery in CCP history. It has been a big controversy among Chinese historians and politicians. Some believe that in the telegram Zhang ordered Chen and Xu to take action to force Mao and the Party Center to return south. If they refused, violent means would be used. Others contest that the telegram contains no phrases so blunt. Doubtless, though a strict military order, not a mild suggestion, was issued by Zhang to Chen and Xu to turn south, and left the latter a choice of allegience between the Party Center and the General Headquarters. Naturally, Chen and Xu accepted the GHQ's order. Ye Jianying, who worked in the Right Route Army Headquarters as Chief of Staff, was informed of the telegram. He quickly slipped the news to Mao.[88]

At the time, Mao and most Politburo leaders were in Baxi with the Route Army Headquarters, while the sick and bedridden Zhou Enlai and Wang Jiaxiang were with the 3rd Army nearby, a dozen li behind. Mao hurried to see Xu and Chen. Under the ruse of visiting Zhou and Wang for a discussion about the revised operation, Mao secretly left Baxi with Zhang Wentian and Bo Gu, and ran to the 3rd Army's camp. There the Politburo members held an emergency conference on September 10.[89]

Like many crucial historical events, the Baxi Conference left no formal documents but very obvious impacts. In an excited mood, the Party Center leaders just listened to Mao, the "emergency knowhow." There was no time for Bo Gu and Zhang Wentian to consult or even recall any quotations of Marx or Lenin. Mao suggested a secret, immediate flight and the others agreed unanimously.[90] A telegram was sent to the 1st Army asking Lin Biao to stop at his present location and await further instructions. Early the next morning Ye Jianying managed to flee from the Front Headquarters. He and his men even stole some military maps. At dawn the Party Center leaders directed the 3rd Army to take off. They did not, however, forget to telegram an ultimatum to Zhang Guotao:

Comrade Guotao:
1. To implement its own strategic policy, the Center orders you once more to lead the Left Route Army to the Banyou and Baxi area. No objections. No delay. No disobedience.
2. The Center has decided that the Vice Chairman of the Military Council, Zhou Enlai, should take overall command of the whole Right Route Army, and has already ordered the 1st and 3rd Army Corps to concentrate at Luoda and Ejie.
3. The Left Route Army must immediately reply as to its concrete arrangements for the northern march.[91]

Informed of the 3rd Army's departure, Chen sent a letter asking Peng Dehuai to stop. Peng passed the letter to Mao. Mao replied: "Just tell him we will have a chance to meet again." Chen was considering dispatching some men to intercept Peng's troops. Xu Xiangqian was reluctant to do this: "How can it be possible for one Red Army to fight with another?" Li Te, a returned student and Zhang's close follower, rode a horse to the 3rd Army, yelling to the officers and men to obey the General Headquarters and return south. He started a heated argument with Mao. There Li also met with Otto Braun—this time even Braun stood with Mao. Braun was strong and brave enough to pull Li from his horse's back. Their altercation in Russian stunned the entire audience. Nevertheless, Li Te did succeed in calling back most of the Fourth Front Army soldiers except those which were formally combined with the Central Red Army.[92]

One day's nonstop march brought Mao and his followers to the 1st Army in Ejie, where they held a meeting to denounce Zhang Guotao, and from where they started their own northern march. The next day Zhang Guotao held his own meeting at Baxi to denounce Mao. From there his forces turned south back to Sichuan and Xikang. Thus their union, dramatically begun three months earlier, concluded in an even more tempestuous manner.

At the very moment of the split between Zhang's Fourth Front Army and Mao's First Front Army, it seemed too early to pass any judgment on who was right and who was wrong at a practical level—that is, who would have more or less chance to win. This topic will be more profitably discussed in later chapters. But here a brief discussion of the question of legitimacy seems appropriate: in other words, who was right or wrong in view of Party principle and Army discipline? As this is only a discussion and since both sides efficiently argued for themselves, the best focus is a consideration of their opposing views.

Xu Xiangqian gives a vivid summary of Zhang Guotao's challenge to the Party Center, when he later recalls, "To stretch his palms asking for power, to then make defiant claims as being in an equal position, and finally to set up his own Party Center—these constituted the three acts of Zhang Guotao's anti-Party drama."[93] Beyond doubt, throughout the whole process Zhang indeed depended on his military strength to claim political power and defy the Party Center. Zhang had his reasons, though, more worthy than a simple plot. The Central Red Army had been by far the strongest Red Army before; it had obviously declined in the previous two years. As Mao could use this failure to accuse the Party and Army leadership at the Zunyi Conference, why should not the FFA now request the CRA as a whole to bear the responsibility? If the new leadership after Zunyi was really impeccable, why had the CRA troops further decreased in size? As for the final disruption, Zhang Guotao and the Red Army Headquarters had the right to call back any subordinate army unit, while there was no legitimate reason for Mao to play tricks with the Right Route Army Headquarters and coax the 1st and 3rd Army Corps to sneak through the gateway opened by the FFA's sacrifice.

From Mao's point of view, Zhang never admitted that the Politburo and the Military Council were the legitimate leadership of the entire Communist Party and Red Army. What was more, Zhang had participated in the

Politburo conferences, clearly crediting their legitimacy. The plan to go north was resolved in Zhang's presence several times, but at the very last moment, Zhang made the excuse of rains and floods not only to prevent the Left Route Army from joining the Right Route Army, but even to call back the Right Route.[94]

After the split, each side accused the other of committing a line of "rightist flightism," which literally means fear of fighting the enemy or retreat for saving one's skin. This question can be better put this way: for what reasons did they argue for their own strategic orientations? It was not a simple question of going north or going south. In June when they first met, the Central Red Army advocated moving east across the Min River. Later it stood for going north, although the exact direction and goal of "north" changed a few times. As for Zhang Guotao, at first he had no thought of a long distance transfer, but intended to expand influences to the west and south. He had no definite plan; sometimes he considered going south to attack Chengdu; at other times he was for going west to Qinghai and Xinjiang, or for going northwest to Gansu at the Xia River. The lack of a definite strategy plays a major role in Zhang's eventual failure.

Zhang and Mao had both fought with the KMT troops for years—not always infallibly—and both were afraid of the KMT in a certain sense and to a certain extent. Neither side was willing to fight back in the direction from which it had just come: the east for Zhang and the south for Mao; and each side thought that the other side might be facing some less competent enemy, so that Mao thought they could go east back to northern Sichuan, and Zhang thought that turning south to Chengdu was a possibility. While both were fearful of the enemy in this sense, Mao was perhaps more so. The Central Red Army had been chased all the way from Jiangxi to western Sichuan, trying to win some decisive battle to open a new prospect many times without success. It wanted to make a long distance transfer and could hardly imagine staying at the present location or fighting back to the south. Although Zhang's withdrawal from northern Sichuan was partly due to his concern about the KMT's new suppression, he had reasons other than military defeat. He was less beaten, less scared, and thus more inclined to maintain his troops in the Sichuan-Xikang area rather than moving far away to the north. All in all, we might say that Mao was more "rightist" and "flightist" than Zhang, but whether "rightism" or "flightism" should be regarded as a great evil is quite another matter.[95]

7

SETTLEMENT IN NORTH CHINA

It seemed a bit strange, not only to the outsiders but to the Communists themselves, that the Central Red Army led by Mao could have eventually settled in northern Shaanxi, at the foot of the Great Wall. A bit odder too, shortly before the CRA's arrival another group of the Red Army—the 25th Army under Xu Haidong—had just come from the south to the same place. Neither of the Red Armies had scheduled such a destination, but these occasions were not arrived at by coincidence—they were necessary.

After they came to this alien land, the two Red Armies quickly showed their respective military and political dispositions. In terms of specific military affairs per se, there was little difference: both had had to fight with the Nationalist enemy and both had proved quite conscientious and skillful in this. Their political attitudes following the initial military measures, however, differed sharply: the 25th Army turned its military strength in victory toward another anti-counterrevolutionary movement and brought the local Party and Army to the verge of dissolution; the Central Army strived hard to compromise within the new base area and then managed a rapid expansion beyond its borders.

The objective of the two newly arrived Red Army groups was the same: to establish their own position. What differed were their practical approaches, which were indeed profoundly opposed. The 25th Army stuck to the old formula of extreme revolution while the Central Army adopted a new attitude of moderate politicism. There might have been contingent and extraneous factors influencing the decisions of the Communist leaders and the consequences of these decisions; more interesting is the fact that their basic strategy had changed. A new mode of thinking can be seen in the policies and work style implemented by Mao and the Party Center even in the first year of the sojourn in Shaanxi.

From Desperation to Prospect

The break with the Fourth Front Armies in September 1935 constituted one of the most severe tests for Mao as a Communist politician and the

162

Central Red Army as a Communist group. Had Chen and Xu's troops gathered together or been gathered together to intercept him, Mao agreed that he would probably have surrendered and followed Zhang Guotao south.[1] Although such an event was unlikely, Mao took meticulous precautions. He ordered his men in the Party Center and the 3rd Army Corps to depart from Baxi at midnight, not allowing anyone to burn torches or use other lights. They arrived at Axi early the next morning, but did not stop there. They marched north another whole day and reached the 1st Army Corps in Ejie, hungry and tired.[2] While the soldiers were taking a rest, the Party and Army leaders were holding another meeting to cope with the emerging situation.

The situation truly represented, as Mao later recalled, the darkest moment in his political career.[3] In the three weeks after the Baozuo Battle and the arrival of the Red Army at Baxi and Aba, it became clear that the KMT had turned all its attention to the north. Hu Zongnan and Xue Yue's Central Army formed a curved blockade line from the east, northeast, and southeast sides; while further north 200,000 to 300,000 troops were stationed in Gansu and Shaanxi.[4] The bulk of the KMT's forces had been transferred to the north whereas the bulk of Red Army troops had turned back to the south, leaving Mao just two army corps with which to face the appalling situation. In front of the CRA were narrow paths along mountain slopes and river valleys leading to southern Gansu. Even if they could pass through them and reach Gansu, the KMT troops led by Zhu Shaoliang and Yu Xuezhong were there waiting for them.

At the split in Baxi, Mao permitted all the men of the Fourth Front Army in the Red Army Academy and in the 3rd Army Corps to leave if they wished, and most of them did return to their former army group. Two of Mao's troops, the 5th and 9th Army Corps, remained in the Left Route Army, as did Liu and Zhu together with the Headquarter personnel and equipment: altogether 4,000 to 5,000 men were gone. Apparently Mao had lost the game to Zhang. The 1st and 3rd Army Corps at the time totalled about 8,000-10,000 soldiers.[5] In other words, Mao's army was reduced to its size in early 1928—when the 4th Red Army was founded at the Jinggang Mountains—and the present situation was far worse than at that time in terms of the location and strength of the enemy.

There were some positive aspects, of course. Through many years of hard struggle, the soldiers and officers had become tougher and stronger, and the leaders were far more experienced in dealing with political and military affairs. Most importantly, Mao's own position within the Party and Army had entirely changed since the Jinggang Mountains period. Here a distinction must be made between the interest of an individual Communist politician and the interests of the Party and Army as a whole. At the Zunyi Conference, after the Party and the Army had suffered ignominious military defeat, it was the right time for Mao to assume leadership. By the time of the Ejie Conference Mao, through the confrontation with Zhang Guotao, had become the indisputable leader in the Party Center and the Central Red Army. Zhou Enlai, Zhu De, Zhang Wentian and others all showed their weaknesses when faced with this extraordinary challenge: Zhou's tenderness, Zhu's ignorance and Zhang's incompetence. Zhou was a flexible diplomat, Zhu a staunch soldier, and Zhang an eloquent scholar— Mao was a complete politician. An enlarged Politburo conference convened at the village of Ejie in September 1935 saw the Party Center and the Central Red Army in perhaps the worst situation they had yet faced, and Mao in a more influential position than ever before.

The 21 people attending the conference at Ejie included all Politburo members, all Central Committee members, all Military Council leaders, and the four leaders of the 1st and 3rd Army Corps. Called an enlarged Politburo conference, the Ejie Conference might have been overly well-attended.[6] The first action this Conference undertook was the universal condemnation of Zhang Guotao: the resolution castigating him passed without a dissenting vote. Those Party and Army leaders who had been reluctant to criticize Zhang before were eager to denounce him now. Mao, however, mitigating his earlier harshness, insisted that Zhang should not be deprived of his Party membership. Mao was well aware that Zhang was still in control of a dominating number of Red Army troops. Another telegram was sent to Zhang with rather mild words of persuasion. "For the time being the Party Center leads the 1st and 3rd Army Corps to go north," the telegram said, "This is not only for the purpose of realizing its own strategic goal, but for opening a route for the Left Route Army and the 30th and 4th Armies of the Right Route at its own sacrifice, so that they can follow to the north more conveniently."[7] In this way, the telegram expressed the vague hope that Zhang would follow to the north, and it also made an excuse for Mao's unwarranted departure. In contrast with this polite communication, the internal resolution drawn at the Ejie Conference accused Zhang of such misdeeds as defeatism, criminal divisionism, warlordism, Han Chauvinism, and right opportunism, before it concluded:

It is very obvious that if Comrade Zhang Guotao persists in such tendencies, he will separate himself from the Party. For this reason, the Politburo regards it necessary to adopt all concrete measures to correct Comrade Zhang Guotao's serious mistakes, and it calls all the comrades in the Fourth Front Army who are still loyal to the Communist Party to rally around the Party Center, to exert a resolute struggle against these tendencies in order to consolidate the Party and the Army.[8]

Oddly, although it called all comrades in the Fourth Front Army to fight against Zhang Guotao, this resolution was never communicated to the Fourth Front Army. Even in the First Front Army it was only known to the members of the CCP Central Committee. The actual effect of the Resolution was none other than the attainment of solidarity among the top leaders in the First Front Army and the consolidation of Mao's legitimate position in the Party Center.[9]

Far more important than accusing Zhang Guotao was deciding on how to cope with the adverse situation. After Zhang took the bulk of the Red Army away, the KMT enemy's attention shifted to the north and the Central Red Army single-handedly embarked on the northern expedition under unfamiliar and unpredictable conditions. For the Central Red Army and the Party Center, this was the most dangerous and discouraging juncture. The only possibility Mao and the CCP Center could imagine at the time was striving to contact the Soviet Union and asking for temporary asylum. The following record of Mao's speech at the Ejie Conference serves as the best illustration of the adverse situation facing the Party Center, as well as a sketch of Mao's rugged desperate spirit, a part of his personality that showed up only rarely in his life and career.

> The Party Center insists on the previous policy, that is, the policy of continuously going north. The "Supplementary Resolution" requests that we go to the east of the Yellow River. But this policy should be somewhat altered. Now we should apply guerrilla warfare to drive to the Soviet Union border. This is the basic policy. In the past the Party Center opposed such a policy and advocated that, after the union of the First and Fourth Front Armies, we should create a Soviet at the Shaanxi-Gansu-Sichuan border. Now things are different. We only have the main forces of the 1st and 3rd Army Corps of the First Front Army. Therefore, it [our strategy] must be pointed out clearly: to conduct guerrilla warfare, to break through international contact lines, to obtain directions and assistance from the Comintern, to rest and reorganize our troops, and then to expand them . . . It is incorrect to entirely refuse help from others. We are one branch of the Comintern anyhow. We can first open a base area on the border near the Soviet Union, and then develop toward the east. Otherwise, we will have to fight a guerrilla war endlessly, and we will become a turtle kept inside an urn.[10]

With Zhu De gone, Peng Dehuai had become the most important military figure. Following Peng's suggestion at the Ejie Conference, it was decided that the Army structure should be drastically reduced: the General Headquarters was cut to no more than 130 men, and the Political Department to about 60. The division was abolished and each army corps became a 'column'. Each column consisted of four regiments; the battalion too was abolished. Each regiment was directly in charge of four companies. The

First Front Red Army was renamed the Shaanxi-Gansu Branch Brigade of the Red Army, with Peng as the Commander, Mao as the Political Commissar, Ye Jianying as the Chief of General Staff, and Wang Jiaxiang as the Director of the Political Department. A "Five-Man Group" was formed with Mao Zedong, Zhou Enlai, Wang Jiaxiang, Peng Dehuai, and Lin Biao as members. A "Reorganization Committee" was formed with Otto Braun as its director. The basic strategy was to "continue going north" and "break through the international route" from northern Gansu and Shaanxi.[11]

It was obvious that Braun was brought in as the Director of the Reorganization Committee for his symbolic international function which might be useful in contacting and appealing to the Soviet Union. Further, although no definite location on the Russian border was mentioned as that to which the Red Army would head, Mao's speech suggests that the most likely plan was to move across the Yellow River from the Shaanxi-Gansu border, pass through the Gansu Corridor, and approach the Soviet Union from Xinjiang, just as Zhang Guotao had suggested before and the Western Route Army would do later.

After the Ejie Conference the Red Army hurried north and entered Gansu. To go through the high mountains at southern Gansu and reach the flat plain of the Yao River valley, they had to pass the strategic spot of Lazikou. A brief description of the Lazikou battle aids in understanding the morale and capacity of the Red Army as manisfested also in other struggles with the KMT enemy and against the equally (if not more) harsh natural environments.

Literally, Lazikou means the wax-made pass. It is one segment of a narrow valley through which a tributary of the Bailong River flows out between two rows of high peaks. The river was 3 meters deep and 30 meters wide; the steep stone walls on both of its banks were approximately 500 meters high; at the narrowest part of the pass was a wooden bridge with fortifications at each end. In Nie Rongzhen's words, "the whole place was just like one high round mountain made of wax and then chopped into two parts right in the middle." Guarding the pass were two enemy battlions belonging to Lu Dachang, a general of the Gansu provincial army.[12]

The task of capturing the pass was assigned to the 4th Regiment of the 2nd Division of the First Army Corps, famous for its death-defying spirit as a spearhead detachment on the Long March. At first the Red Army men tried five times to seize the pass by unsuccessful attacks from the front. Then they held a so-called "soldier's meeting". As usual, all Party members and Army officers volunteered for the hardest task. Twenty men were selected to form a vanguard squad. A local Tibetan was found to guide them. They tied their belts together to make a cord; the squad leader and the guide climbed up the right peak first, then used the cord to pull the comrades up one-by-one. There they hid themselves on top of the mountain for several hours. Hearing another frontal attack starting soon after the middle night, they threw grenades and shot bullets from the mountain top down onto the enemy. Sounds of firing and the Red Army men's shouts "Surrender or Die" were all over the valley. The KMT troops were shocked and driven back. The Red Army took over Lazikou and chased the enemy deep into its own rear.[13]

The battle at Lazikou was one of the many engagements on the Long March which cannot be discussed in detail, due to the thematic emphasis of this study. As a general rule, it should be noted, the fighting capacity of basic army units was always the most crucial factor in combat. Without this capacity, any commander will fail. Its lack can cause a good strategic commander to lose as much as its presence can help even a bad one win. Furthermore, morale—in both officers and men—was always one of the most crucial factors in determining the fighting capacity, especially in traditional or conventional war. In this respect, the KMT army, either the Central Army or the Provincial Army, were obviously inferior to the Communist troops.

Descending from the south Gansu highland, the Communists landed on the Yao River valley. They arrived at Hadapu on September 20, and rested in this market town for two days to finish the Army reorganization. The Central Red Army was re-named "The Shaanxi-Gansu Branch Brigade," and the 1st and 3rd Army Corps were reformed into three "Branch Teams," as shown in Table 7.1.

It was at Hadapu that the Communists became more certain of the existence of a Soviet base and a Red Army in northern Shaanxi. In his memoirs Nie Rongzhen recalls that he found a KMT newspaper carrying a report on the "red bandit extermination." Of course the Communists knew how to interpret this kind of news report—the bigger a victory the KMT side claimed, the larger the Communists would infer to be the Red Army force in question. Nie sent the newspaper to Mao and this persuaded Mao to turn to northern Shaanxi.[15] The Party cadres and Army officers higher than the regimental level assembled for a rally in a temple at Hadapu. Mao and the other leaders attended the rally and made speeches. In his speech, Mao said:

We are for going north while Zhang Guotao prefers to go south. He calls us opportunists. Who are opportunists indeed? Now Japanese imperialism is invading China; we are going to the north to resist Japan. First we will go to northern Shaanxi where Liu Zhidan's Red Army is. Our line is correct. It is true that now our Northern Vanguard Brigade seems a bit small in size. But that also means our men will draw less attention from the enemy. We need not boast and brag, and we need not be showy. We should not be

Table 7.1 The Central Red Army Reorganization at Hadapu:

The Shaanxi-Gansu Branch Brigade of the Chinese Anti-Japanese Army

General Headquarters	
General Commander	Peng Dehuai
General Political Commissar	Mao Zedong
Chief of General Staff	Ye Jianying
Director of Political Department	Wang Jiaxiang
1st Branch Team	
Commander	Lin Biao
Political Commissar	Nie Rongzhen
2nd Branch Team	
Commander	Peng Dehuai
Political Commissar	Li Fuchun
3rd Branch Team	
Commander	Ye Jianying
Political Commissar	Cai Shufan[14]

pessimistic either. Our troops are still larger now than in early 1929 when we went down from the Jinggang Mountains.[16]

Here Mao seemed a bit reluctant to admit retracting his earlier idea of retreating west to join the Soviet Union. It might have been only as a last resort that Mao thought to appeal to and depend upon a foreign power from the very start. Another point on which Mao did not elaborate was renaming his troops in order to disguise their existence from the KMT army. Since the KMT's attention to the Red Army remained, it might thus be shifted to Zhang Guotao's men in the south, who were still enjoying themselves with the grand title of "General Headquarters of the Red Army."

As a matter of fact, the plan of moving to northern Shaanxi had already been mentioned at the Ejie Conference. But at that time the Communist leaders merely took it as a temporary but necessary step in order to reach contact with the Soviet Union. They had planned neither to fight the Japanese nor to stay in northern Shaanxi for long, but to pass through it to go further northwest. The formal decision to stay and open a new base at northern Shaanxi was not formally reached in Hadapu either. This was done a week later at the Politburo conference at Bangluozhen.

North of Hadapu was the KMT's inner blockade line running from Tianshui along the Wei River westward to Lanzhou. In September 1935, Gansu was governed by Zhu Shaoliang, a general transferred from the South; Shaanxi by Yang Hucheng, a native folk and a general of the provincial army; and military responsibility adhered to Yu Xuezhong, a general of the Northeastern Army recently transferred from Peking as a result of the Japanese invasion.[17] As the Red Army approached, the KMT concentrated a large part of its troops at Lanzhou and Tianshui to protect the big cities at the rear. The leftover forces gathered to protect the county seats. This made it much easier for the Red Army to drive between the county towns of Wushan and Zhangxian through the Wei River blockade line, wade across the river and successfully reach Bangluozhen at the other side of the blockade line on September 27, 1935. The next day another Politburo Conference was held at Bangluozhen—this time only the few members of the Politburo Standing Committee were summoned as participants—to make a decision on their final destination. If they really wanted to go to the far northwest to contact the Soviet Union, they should continue marching north to Ningxia and northern Gansu, from there crossing the Yellow River and then going westward along the Gansu Corridor to Xinjiang. Otherwise, they should turn northeast toward northern Shaanxi and meet the local Red Army there. Now that it had become more obvious that there indeed existed a strong Red Army and a large Soviet base in northern Shaanxi, they opted for the latter course.

So far, there are no written resolutions or records available on the Bangluozhen Conference. Yet it should be clear that the importance of this conference lies in the fact that it formalized the decision, which the Communist leaders had "sensed out" at Hadapu, and resolved to move to northern Shaanxi, not as a temporary stepping board but as a permanent home base. This can be seen from Mao's talk a month later. Referring to the Bangluozhen Conference, Mao once said:

> We broke with Zhang Guotao at the Ejie Conference. Our slogan at that time was to strike into northern Shaanxi in order to contact the Soviet Union by means of guerrilla warfare. The Bangluozhen Conference changed the Ejie Conference's decision. We got new information, got to know there was such a big Soviet area and such a strong Red Army in northern Shaanxi. Therefore we changed our mind and decided to come to protect and expand the Northern Shaanxi Soviet.[18]

Once they forced their way across the Wei River blockade line and defeated the KMT regular troops, the Communists met only local bandits, militia, police and warlords obstructing their way. These local forces did little to deter the Red Army. Although the journey from Bangluozhen to northern Shaanxi may have been as long as 500 li, the Red Army smoothly covered the distance in three weeks. They first brushed away some local troops along two highway blockade lines—one between Huining and Qingning and another between Pingliang and Guyuan—then climbed over the Liupan Mountains to the northeast. The Central Red Army or the Gansu-Shaanxi Branch Brigade reached Weqizhen in northern Shaanxi on October 18 and joined the 15th Red Army Corps a few day later, thus concluding its part of the Long March.[19] The situation grew so promising that Mao's poetic mind was inspired while he stood on top of the Liupan Mountains.

Liupan Mountain—in the *ci* "Qing Ping Le"
(September, 1935)

The sky is high, the clouds are pale.
We watch wild geese flying south until they vanish.
Not true men we will be who cannot reach the Great Wall.
Counting our fingers, we know 20,000 li has been passed.
High on top of the Liupan Mountain,
The west wind is tossing the red flags.
Now that a long cord is held in hands,
When can the grey dragon be finally caught?[20]

For better or worse, classical Chinese poetry always displays a subtlety and vagueness in its expressions. Mao's poem is no exception. What does Mao mean here by saying "Now that a long cord is held in hands"—what long cord and in whose hands? The Party and Army power in Mao's hands? What does "the grey dragon" mean—the Japanese, Chiang, or state power? The romantic tone of the poem seems slightly inconsistent with the official explanation that the last two sentences pertain to a final victory of the Chinese Revolution or emancipation of the Chinese people. Nevertheless, one thing at least should be clear: Mao's firm confidence and strong determination at the end of the Long March.

The Long March of the 25th Red Army

The 15th Army Corps which Mao encountered in northern Shaanxi in October 1935 was in fact a new Red Army group founded only a month earlier as a result of merging the 25th Red Army and the 26th Red Army—

the former having just arrived in the area, the latter being an indigenous Communist force of quite a few years. Both for the purpose of understanding their relationship with the Party Center and the Central Red Army, and for introducing their unique experiences as part of the Communist movement, some introduction of the two Red Armies is necessary.

In October, 1932, while the Fourth Front Army was leaving the Eyuwan Soviet for the western expedition, the KMT pulled its main offensive forces out of this area to fight the Jiangxi Soviet, leaving the provincial and local KMT troops to tangle with the remaining Communist guerrillas. The Communists were thus drawn back to a situation similar to that prior to 1930. The general leadership of the Communist forces in this area was in the hands of the CCP Committee of the Eyuwan Province with Shen Zemin as its Secretary, while the real military forces were the guerrilla troops in the regions of western Anhui (led by Xu Haidong) and eastern Hubei (led by Wu Huanxian). Shen was a returned student and one of the "28 Bolsheviks", versed in Marxist-Leninist doctrines and faithful to the Comintern. His close association with the Party Center leaders helped maintain the eminent position of this Eyuwan Soviet in the eyes of the Party Center, despite its sharp decline in strength after the withdrawal of the Fourth Front Army.[21] Radio communications continued between Shen's Eyuwan Committee and the Party Center for a long time. Shen's revolutionary enthusiasm won him a high respect from the local military leaders, while his seniority in the Party Center made him an authority among the local political cadres. By geographical origin and also by personal character, lower level Communist leaders in this area could be generally characterized as either intellectual cadres chiefly concerned with the Party's political line— and hence more inclined to start anti-counterrevolutionary campaigns to purify their own ranks—or native peasant soldiers who were most interested in military affairs and were generally more enthusiastic and resourceful in partisan warfare.

In November 1932, the Eyuwan CCP Committee decided to gather all the guerrilla troops into one unit under the title of the 25th Red Army. In early 1933 the KMT suppression again tore the Communist troops in two—the 25th Red Army and the 28th Red Army. In 1934, when Shen Zemin died of pneumonia, this Soviet base lost much of the attention by the Party Center. Shen's post as the Party secretary was passed on to Xu Baoshan, and all the troops were once again combined into the original 25th Red Army with Xu Haidong as its commander and Wu Huanxian as its political commissar.[22] As its connection with the Party Center became looser and its political character became weaker, the Eyuwan base became more self-contained and militarily oriented. In late 1934 the 25th Army captured the strategic city of Taihu, destroyed a whole division of the KMT army, and took more than 3,700 prisoners of war in a single battle—this created an impression that they might follow the former pattern of growth of 1931. But the fundamental difference was that after so many years of war, the whole area was physically worn out. The lower positions of the Communist leaders in this area, moreover, made it impossible for them to reach a higher degree of political independence. Their self-containment was not independence in a true sense. Psychologically speaking, local leaders like Xu Baoshan and Wu Huanxian could hardly attain the independence veteran Party Center leaders Zhang Guotao and Zhen Zemin had earlier acquired.

In late July, 1934, when the Party Center dispatched the 7th and 6th Army Corps to fight outside the Jiangxi Central Soviet, it also sent the Eyuwan CCP Committee telegrammed instructions, requiring the them to undertake active operations and shift to fight outside the Soviet. The objective of the instructions might have been to divert the Nationalist troops away from the Central Soviet. Accordingly, Cheng Zihua was dispatched as the Party Center's envoy to the Eyuwan Soviet.[23]

Cheng travelled secretly, starting from Ruijin through Swatow, Shanghai and Hankou, and arrived at the eastern Hubei Soviet in September.[24] In October, when the Party Center decided to break through the KMT blockade and evacuate the Jiangxi Soviet, it again demanded that the 25th Red Army leave the Eyuwan base area for an external expedition. This order stemmed mainly from the Central Red Army's own military concerns at the time. In early November a message from the Provincial CCP Committee, then located in eastern Hubei, was delivered to the 25th Red Army in western Anhui, informing the latter of the arrival of the Party Center's instructions and requesting that the entire army come.[25] On November 6, 1934, the 25th Army set out from western Anhui. It broke through several enemy blockades, travelled several hundred li, and reached eastern Hubei five days later.[26]

A joint conference of the Party and the Army was convened at Huashan in eastern Hubei. Participating at the conference were leaders in the Eyuwan CCP Committee, the 25th Army Headquarters, the Eastern Hubei District Committee, and the Party Center representatives: Xu Baoshan, Wu Huanxian, Xu Haidong, Zheng Weisan, Cheng Zihua and some others. The Party Center's instructions were communicated and unanimously accepted: the 25th Red Army should leave this war-exhausted base and fight outside to create new prospects. Cheng Zihua replaced Xu Haidong as Commander of the 25th Army, and Xu dropped to Vice Commander. One division was left behind, together with local forces, to carry out guerrilla activities—three years later these remnants grew to be one branch of the New Fourth Army in the Sino-Japanese War.[27]

After a few days' preparation, the 25th Red Army, with four regiments and 3,000 men, said goodbye to the Eyuwan base and started on its military expedition under the title "Second Anti-Japanese Vanguard Brigade of the Chinese Peasant and Worker Red Army."[28] They would not consider taking any route other than that which the Fourth Front Army had followed two years before, and their objective seemed rather vague. Whether they were to open a new base somewhere or to join the Fourth Front Army remained a question for the future. For the time being, they struggled through the KMT blockades, hurrying westwards.

There were several factors which might have influenced the 25th Red Army's decision. It had set out on the expedition not due to failure in the battle or loss of its base, but on the Party Center's instructions; and it intended to follow in the steps of its former master, the Fourth Front Army. Thus the Long March of the 25th Army—like those of the 6th and 7th Army Corps—was not an independent operation from the beginning. Because it left the Soviet base on its own initiative, instead of being expelled by ferocious fights, the 25th Army was also not closely pursued by the KMT troops. The provincial armies and local militia in each location it passed through proved to be the most serious military threat.

The 25th Army passed over the Peking-Hankou Railway and entered the Tongbo Mountain region between Henan and Hubei. This was too close to the railway trunk line to be an ideal location for a Soviet base. Instead of proceeding on the westward course as the Fourth Front Army did before, the 25th Army turned north and entered the Funiu Mountain region in Henan in late November 1934. This was a totally new area without any trace of communist or revolutionary influence. The local militias were too stubborn to be easily overcome and the local people too inert to be quickly agitated. The Communist intruders found themselves beaten and on the run, unable to get a solid foothold. Since no political programs seemed possible, and they were mostly ignorant of local military affairs, Cheng Zihua as a newly arrived outsider and Xu Baoshan and Wu Huanxian as political workers all descended to figurehead positions, while Xu Haidong— the native military commander—gradually assumed real control.[29]

Xu was an army man with little formal education but extensive military experience; he was well known for his bold defiance of death. He was more like a Robin Hood than a Communist Party member, with more of the former's cavalier ethic than the latter's dogmatic tenets. There were a half dozen bullets and wounds in his body. His favorite tactic in conducting a battle was rushing himself to the very front amid enemy fire. He was not afraid of death, nor would he tolerate such a fear in his troops. His entire army looked on him with respect and awe. Even the Party leaders recognized Xu's indispensible role under the present conditions. In his memoirs Xu recalled one of the battles the 25th Army fought in the Funiu Mountains in Henan.

In the battle near the town of Dushu our troops were beaten by the enemy both from the front and from the rear. This was the first battle in which we were defeated; and the troops fell into confusion. All those wounded soldiers were lying there, but with few litter men to carry them. I did not eat anything all day. It was raining. I myself carried the litter for five li. The troops were tired out, hungry and cold. The next morning I sent the guard to call for departure. They all kept sleeping there, and nobody got up. I picked up a wooden stick and ran into the village. First I struck those regiment commanders and political commissars; then I struck the lower rank officers and finally the soldiers. Two hundred people were driven out immediately.[30]

In early December 1934, the 25th Army came to Hanzhong and Ankang in southern Shaanxi. Southern Shaanxi at that time had several conditions which favored the Communists: this was a flat and densely populated region; the area had been unstable for many years as a disputed zone between the Sichuan and Shaanxi warlords; and above all, the Fourth Front Army had trampled this area two years earlier and left in the villages some secret Party branches and guerrilla groups, one of which even assumed the title of an army. Even more conveniently, as soon as he heard of the 25th Army's approach, Zhang Guotao dispatched his troops to start the Southern Shaanxi Campaign in January, 1935. This operation attracted the main forces of Yang Hucheng's Shaanxi army, thus making the 25th Red Army in Hanzhong and Ankang comfortable for a couple months. Though it could not rendezvous with the FFA, the 25th Army quickly broke up the KMT encirclement in southern Shaanxi and set up Soviet regimes in two counties and hundreds of villages. The 25th Army now had 4,000 soldiers in addition to four guerrilla detachments in the Henan-Shaanxi border area and six guerrilla detachments in the Shaanxi-Hubei border area, altogether about 3,000 soldiers.[31]

In May 1935, after the Fourth Front Army crossed the Jialing River and moved to western Sichuan, the 25th Army faced military pressure again. Whether out of military necessity or its own strategic decision, this time the 25th Army began large-scale mobile warfare to confront the enemy. The Communist troops struck to the north toward the center of Shaanxi. There they looted a large amount of food, clothes, and ammunition supplies on their way, then pushed back to southern Shaanxi. They won a few battles and temporarily broke the encirclement, but the expedition and fight consumed much of their strength and energy. When another KMT suppression campaign followed, leaders of the 25th Army sensed the potential danger from their previous experiences in the Eyuwan Soviet.[32]

While the leaders of the 25th Red Army were wondering whether they should stick to this place or move to join the Fourth Front Army in northern Sichuan, they learned from the KMT newspapers that the FFA had already shifted to the distant west where it had met with the CRA. This news was soon confirmed by their underground agents. The combined force of the FFA and the CRA, they discovered, were moving to the north. Thus there was no need for the 25th Army to go south anymore. Instead, a unanimous decision was made that it should turn west to southern Gansu and wait for the main forces of the Red Army there. Later, the 25th Army leaders claimed that such a decision was made in order to welcome the Party Center at their own sacrifice. This allegation is true but needs more explanation. In fact, the 25th Army was for their own part desperately anxious to join the main forces and was, as before, obsessively dependent upon the patronage of one Red Army main force or another.[33]

On July 15, 1935, there was an urgent conference of the Party and Army leaders at Fengyukou. They decided that the 25th Army should make another strategic transfer and leave only a few guerrilla squads in the area they presently occupied. The very next day, the 25th Army with its 4,000 men set off on a western march. On August 1 they reached Shangshipu at the Gansu-Shaanxi border, and there they defeated four companies of Hu Zongnan and captured a KMT junior general, from whom they learned that the CRA and the FFA were moving from Songpan down to the north. Under these circumstances, the 25th Army sped up its western expedition, drove toward the Wei River valley and got close to the city of Tianshui. After some unsuccessful engagements with the Nationalist troops along the Wei River line, the 25th Army was compelled to move further north and reached Jingshui in northeastern Gansu in mid-August. They waited there for several days without finding any positive indication of the approach of either the FFA or the CRA. A few clashes with Ma Hongkui's cavalry troops rendered them more losses. When they attempted to cross the Jingchuan River, a fierce fight broke out, in which Wu Huanxian was killed. After this Cheng Zihua became the political commissar and Xu Haidong resumed his position as the army commander. In late August the 25th Army had to turn northeast. After hopelessly trying to join a major Red Army for such a long time, they were unexpectedly driven into the Northern Shaanxi Soviet in early September and ran into a minor Red Army.

The 25th Army of Xu Haidong and Cheng Zihua met with the 26th Army of Liu Zhidan and Gao Gang on September 18, 1935.[34] The two armies soon combined into the 15th Army Corps with Xu as Commander and Cheng as Political Commissar. Liu Zhidan was appointed Vice commander and Gao Gang became Director of the Political Department. The appointments indicate the newcomers got an upper hand and the old hosts fell to an underdog status. The merger took place just one month before the arrival of the Party Center and the Central Red Army.[35]

Communists in Shaanxi Province

Prior to 1935 the CCP had few military forces in North China. Except for the Joint Anti-Japanese Army of Northwest China fighting against the Japanese invaders and their puppet regime in Manchuria, the only visible Communist troops were found in Shaanxi. Among other reasons, this exceptional phenomenon in Shaanxi was largely due to the "Christian General" Feng Yuxiang. Feng applied the support of the Soviet Union and the CCP to his successful participation in the Great Revolution in 1926-1927 and soon afterwards joined Chiang Kai-shek in suppressing the Communists. On the strength of their own anger as well as instructions from the Party Center, the Communists in Shaanxi started a number of vengeful rebellions in the late 1920s. Although these rebellions were quickly put down, the Communist influence remained alive in Feng's troops as well as in some rural areas. In 1930, when Feng lost the war with the KMT central government, his position in Shaanxi was passed to Yang Hucheng, one of Feng's subordinate generals. In the following years, the overall situation in Shaanxi was aggravated by political upheavals and military turmoils, and Communist infiltration in Yang's troops was enhanced rather than retarded.[36]

Located between the North China Plain and the West China Plateau, Shaanxi has been historically called *Guanzhong*, "inside the pass". The Yellow River and the Hua Mountains kept the province somewhat separated from North China, while the Tongguan Pass was the main exit to the east. Leading to the far northwest from Shaanxi is the "Silk Road" or the Gansu Corridor. The province was secluded but not entirely isolated either from China Proper to the east or from China Periphery to the west. The province itself had three main geographic components: the flat and fertile Wei River valley at the center with the southern hilly region and the northern loess highland at the two ends. As a general rule, the rebellious Communists would start from or retreat to the north and the south when they were weak or beaten, and they would venture toward the central region when they became strong or victorious.

One of the most common features of the Communist activities in Shaanxi was the army mutiny, or *bingbian*, as they called it. Employing their agents and friends in the local troops and exploiting the disagreements and conflicts among the Nationalist generals and native warlords, the Communists incited as many as 70 mutinies in this province from 1931 to 1933.[37] A spectacular Red Army force would emerge immediately following a successful mutiny of one or more KMT battalions or even a whole regiment. But the mutineers in general were vulnerable to bribery and threat, and would disband as quickly as they had been created. Consequently, a KMT officer might

become a Red Army commander one morning and be back in KMT rank
the next evening.

Most of the important Communist leaders in Shaanxi were former
students and natives of the province. With few exceptions they came from
families of wealthy landlords or notable gentry. It was strange that the
Communists won the support of the poor peasants by agitating the latter
to rise against landlords and local elite, but meanwhile they were respected
and followed by the poor peasants because of the "name and fame" of
their own higher class origins. Their family background and intellectual
capacity also helped the Communists establish intimate relationships with
the local troops and local governments.[38] In a general rule, they would
risk either an army mutiny or a peasant uprising to set up an armed force,
move to the safer countryside to occupy a base area, then attack for
expansion or retreat for survival, according to the conditions at the time.
Separated from the main trend of the revolutionary movement in the South,
the activities the Shaanxi Communists undertook could just fit into the
pattern, and constitute a part, of local militarism or warlordism. Nevertheless,
they proclaimed themselves Communists and were indeed Communists in
many respects. An interesting phenomenon was that sometimes the more
practically isolated or independent the local Communists were from the
Party Center, the less they could claim a higher degree of ideological or
political independence.

In 1931, the biggest military base was located around Nanliang at the
Shaanxi-Gansu border with a guerrilla force commanded by Liu Zhidan.
The next year, as the provincial army fought the Fourth Front Army in
southern Shaanxi and another mutiny successfully brought two Nationalist
battalions to the Communist side, Liu Zhidan directed his men southward
to Yaoxian and Zhaojin, close to central Shaanxi. There he set up a new
Soviet base and named his troops the 26th Red Army.[39]

In May 1933, the Communists became aggressive enough to attempt a
further southern expedition. Led by Liu Zhidan and Du Heng, the 26th
Army drove into the Wei River valley and hoped to open a "Huawei
Soviet" in the center of the province. Unfortunately, they were defeated
by Yang Hucheng. The whole army was wiped out and only a few top
leaders managed to flee back to Zhaojin. In February 1934, Liu Zhidan and
his men retreated further north to Nanliang, where they fought back and
forth until a new Red Army arrived to revitalize them.[40]

Communist activities in northern Shaanxi were not as visible as those
in the Shaanxi-Gansu border until late 1933. Though mutinies were also
an effective strategy, the Communist efforts in this area bore a clearer mark
of peasant rebellion and rural autonomy. After a few "brewing years," a
dozen locally rooted guerrilla detachments emerged. In early 1934 Xie
Zichang was sent by the underground Shaanxi CCP Committee to take

over the general leadership. Xie gathered all the guerrilla forces into a concerted operation against Jing Yuexiu, the local warlord. This military campaign lasted for four months from August to December, 1934 and ended with a bad wound for Xie Zichang but a big victory for the Communist side. The Communists were happy to exalt their troops with the title of the 27th Red Army.[41]

In February 1935, the CCP Work Committee of the Northwest and the Red Army Military Council of the Northwest were founded to unify the Party and Army leadership throughout the province. Hui Zizun and Guo Songtao were appointed Secretary and Vice Secretary of the Work Committee and Xie Zichang and Liu Zhidan were the Chairman and the Vice Chairman of the Military Council respectively. Their combined troops, though two armies in title, contained only three regiments totaling little more than 2,000 men. Since Xie remained in the rear for treatment and soon died of illness, the military command fell to Liu Zhidan and Gao Gang, Commander and Political Commissar of the 26th Red Army.[42]

In early 1935 the Red Army started fighting with Yang Hucheng in "the Second Suppression Campaign in Northern Shaanxi." After engaging several months, the Communists won a few battles and brought the enemy offensive to a halt. The Shaanxi-Gansu Border Soviet and the Northern Shaanxi Soviet merged into one base. Its territory was expanded to cover 20 counties with a population of 900,000 and a regular force of 4,000.[43] Of course, such successes could not be understood merely as happy chance. In fact, it was the main Red Armies entangling with the KMT army in the South that made possible the rapid growth of the local Red Army in Shaanxi, though neither side seemed quite conscious of this national political balance.

As part of Chiang Kai-shek's nationwide reorganization of anti-Communist activities, Zhang Xueliang was assigned to direct the Xian headquarters. He brought with him his Northeastern Army of about five armies—20 divisions, or about 200,000 men in total.[44] This maneuver was carried out in consideration of the secure situation in the Eyuwan Soviet after the Red Army's double withdrawal and also as a precaution against any possible flight of the CRA and the FFA to the north. At about the same time, Shao Lizi came to Shaanxi to replace Yang Hucheng as the provincial governor, and Yu Xuezhong, one of Zhang Xueliang's generals, moved west to Tianshui in Gansu, presumably to take charge of "suppressing bandit affairs" in the four northern provinces. Zhu Shaoliang's position as the governer of Gansu was thus overshadowed. In sum, this general area of the Northwest fell under the control of Zhang Xueliang in the latter part of 1935.[45]

Zhang Xueliang might have shared Chiang Kai-shek's objective of expelling the Commuists from Shaanxi, but he approached this goal with a different perspective. Zhang was more interested in clearing away the Communists from Shaanxi to set up a personal domain to accommodate his soldiers and Northeasterners who had become homeless since the Japanese occupation of Manchuria in 1931. Soon after his arrival at this new post in July 1935, Zhang started a huge multi-provincial military campaign against the Communists in northern Shaanxi. About 100,000 troops, gathered from several military groups and cliques, were put into the campaign; Zhang's basic combat strategy was to employ Ma Hongkui's Ningxia Army and Yan Xishan's Shanxi Army to check the Red Army at the northern front while his own Northeastern Army would operate at the south as the attacking force.[46]

On the Communist side, the 26th Red Army was deployed in northern Shaanxi and therefore directly encountered the Ningxia and Shaanxi armies. While a few skirmishes occurred in the north and resulted in no major defeat for either side, the Northeastern Army was firmly pressing into the Soviet base from the south. The situation could have been fatal for Liu Zhidan and Gao Gang—their 26th Red Army had been at best only a guerrilla force and so far had never recorded any victory in a large battle. Fortunately, Xu Haidong and Cheng Zihua arrived in northern Shaanxi at this juncture, and their 25th Red Army was better trained and more versed in fighting large-scale mobile war against the regular KMT armies.[47]

On the KMT side, Zhang Xueliang's troops had minimal experience in serious confrontation with the Red Army in the past. They utilized a normal strategy of advancing from several routes toward one central target. Informed of the Red Army's seige of the city of Ganquan, Wang Yizhe, the commander of Zhang's 67th Army, automatically dispatched one division as reinforcements and in this way precisely fell into the Red Army's old trap of "encircling a city to beat the rescuing troops," which the 25th Army had played many times in the Eyuwan Soviet. This division of Wang's army was ambushed at Laoshan by the Red Army. The division was totally annihilated in six hours and the division commander, He Lizhong, was killed. Following the enemy's flight, the Red Army destroyed another regiment of the Northeastern Army and took the regiment commander, Gao Fuyuan, as a prisoner of war.[48]

The victorious Laoshan Battle was a demonstration of the strength and experience of the 25th Red Army coming from an old southern base. This strength constituted a threat to the enemy as well as to the native Red Army in Shaanxi. With the 25th Red Army as a "power checker" to the 26th Red Army, Party leaders like Zhu Lizhi, Guo Songtao, Nie Weijun and Dai Jiying gained more authority, and their ideological orientation gained more weight. The old factionalism in Shaanxi—conflicts such as the Army vs. the Party and the Shaanxi-Gansu Border Base vs. the Northern Shaanxi Base—quickly resurfaced. The ambiguous relationship of the native

Red Army to the local KMT troops, which had contributed to the military successes of the Communists in Shaanxi in the past, led to their political vulnerability now.[49] Some officers in the 26th Red Army, including Liu Zhidan and Gao Gang, were found to have served for or allied with the KMT troops, while other KMT captives claimed themselves to be Red Army agents or aides. According to the strict standard of class origins and revolutionary identification, these phenomena were apparently unforgivable treacheries to the revolution. Right after the Laoshan Battle, Liu Zhidan and Gao Gang were arrested by the CCP Security Bureau headed by Dai Jiying, and a massive anti-counterrevolutionary campaign was immediately under way.[50]

The leaders of Shaanxi CCP Committee and the political cadres of the 25th Army were most active in the anti-counterrevolutionary movement. They might deem themselves executives of the Party Center's authentic revolutionary line, and they might be so to the others, including many of their victims. Only a month later, when Mao and the Party Center arrived, they were shocked to see just the opposite. The Party Center was no longer what they had understood it to be in the previous years.[51]

Consolidation and Expansion of the Northern Shaanxi Base

The Central Red Army arrived at Wuqizhen on October 18, 1935. The next day the Communists started an assault that destroyed one regiment of Ma Hongkui's cavalry army, pursuing the enemy all the way under the slogan, "Don't bring any tail into the Soviet."[52] They gradually moved southeast toward the center of the Northern Shaanxi Soviet. Mao came in person to the headquarters of the 15th Army Corps. He met with Cheng Zihua and Xu Haidong, who had been called back from the front. Mao had a cordial chat with Xu, gave him a radio set and a few operators, then politely asked him to return to the battlefield. At the same time, a message was sent in the name of the Party Center to the Shaanxi CCP Committee asking them to stop the anti-counterrevolutionary campaign and release Liu Zhidan and Gao Gang immediately. Mao was too experienced to neglect either the actual power of Xu's troops or the potential influence of the natives, Liu and Gao. A few days later Mao had another conversation with Xu, consulting him on the Party and Army affairs. When Xu told him that in his 25th Red Army there were still about 300 prisoners and suspects retained for political reasons, Mao replied abruptly: "Set them all free right now and restore their Party membership. Nobody who has undergone the hardship of the Long March can possibly be a counter-revolutionary."[53]

An intimate relationship was easily established between Mao and Xu. Mao liked simple-minded, rough-mannered army officers like Xu; they were useful militarily while politically they were ignorantly obedient. As for Liu Zhidan and Gao Gang, they came out of prison impressed with deep gratitude toward the Party Center. Only the political leaders from the local area might be less happy after the Party Center's arrival, but their relative lack of power made them insignificant, not objects of worry. Dai Jiying, who was among those most responsible for the anti-counterrevolutionary campaign, was thus derided by Zhou Enlai: "If Liu Zhidan were a counter-revolutionary, we would rather like to have many such counter-revolutionaries. If you, Dau Jiying, were a revolutionary, we would not want to have any revolutionaries like you."[54] Even to Zhu, Guo, Nie, and Dai, Mao and the Party Center seemed reasonably lenient. Their revolutionary motives were politely acknowledged, their mistakes mildly scolded, and their authority as local leaders was resolutely diminished—yet appropriately employed, as shown in the "Resolution on the Anti-counterrevolutionary Work of the Northwest Bureau" in November, 1935.[55] Zhu and Guo remained leaders in the local Party because of the former's connection with the CCP Northern Bureau and the latter's influence among the Shaanxi Party cadres. To allow a certain amount of contradiction and conflict among his subordinates would cause Mao no harm, and most probably improve his supervisory status.

In November 11, 1935, the Revolutionary Military Council of the Northwest was formed. This time Mao was made Chairman of the Military Council; Zhou and Peng were the two Vice Chairmen. Peng Dehuai's appointment as vice chairman in the Council and his subsequent inclusion in the Politburo was obviously due to his role as the general commander of the Red Army after Zhu De's departure. Mao remained the Chairman of the Soviet Republic, while the Northwest Office of the Soviet Republic was created (with Bo Gu as its Director) to deal with administrative affairs. In the Party Center, Zhang Wentian was in charge of routine paper work while Mao made the substantial decisions. All in all, it was obvious that the newly arrived Party Center had attained a solid control of the northern Shaanxi base area, and Mao had firmly established himself as the leader of the Party, the Soviet, and the Army.[56]

To both protect the northern Shaanxi Soviet base and consolidate their internal power, the newly arrived southerners needed to launch and successfully complete a battle with the KMT. Mao, more than anyone else, knew it was required. After losing one division at Laoshan, Wang Yizhe halted his operation against the Red Army in the south. But Dong Yingbin, another general of the Northeast Army, kept advancing from Gansu into Shaanxi in the west. Under Mao's direct command, the 1st and 15th Red Army Corps retreated to "lure the enemy deep" while preparing for a decisive conflict. It seemed Dong's troops had not yet learned the tricks of the Red Army from the southern Soviet, and they continued moving forward without much precaution. Finally, Niu Yuanfeng's 108th Division was besieged by the two Red Army corps in Zhiluozhen. In one day's fearsome encounter, this NEA division was utterly destroyed; Niu committed suicide. Mao called the Zhiluozhen Battle the inaugural ceremony to the establishment the 'General Headquarters of the Chinese Revolution in the Northwest'.[57]

Their arrival at Shaanxi helped the Communist leaders learn more about the national and international situations with which they had lost touch in the past year. Soon they resumed contact with the CCP Northern Bureau and heard about the further Japanese invasion in North China, the KMT's ambiguous attitude in the He-Utsumei Agreement, the "local autonomous movements" in Hebei and Chaha'er, and the huge student protest in Peking. The Japanese intrusion into North China became the pre-eminent subject both in view of national defense and the Communists' own survival and growth.[58]

In late November 1935, Zhang Hao (Lin Yuying) came from the Soviet Union via the Mongolian desert to northern Shaanxi. Zhang informed the Communist leaders of the August 1 Manifesto of the CCP Mission to the Comintern, and the Seventh Congress of the Comintern held at Moscow earlier that year—both stressed a new policy of an anti-Fascist united front. This brought the Party Center leaders to a broader political outlook.[59] They were responsive as the Party Center, not as former Shaanxi cadres who were just a local branch without much interest or capacity to connect national and international affairs with their own business. All of the news seemed to inspire Mao and the Party Center. The CCP leaders became astute enough to take all these conditions into account not only for consolidating northern Shaanxi, but also for developing the revolutionary movement in the whole nation. The basic objective was definite: to treat all these objective conditions as favorable factors and employ them to the best advantage for their bid for national power. Soon afterwards, they brought these considerations into their formal resolutions.

In late December 1935, the Communists held an enlarged Politburo conference at Wayaobao. The exact date is not formally recorded. Most probably, the conference consisted of several formal and informal sessions lasting for a number of days before written resolutions were adopted.[60] Ostensibly, this conference marked not only a turning point in the civil war strategy of the CCP—where their policy now involved a national war strategy—but also saw the full maturity of the CCP. Although a basic change in mentality had already occurred in the past year, this conference was a full manifestation of this change in practice.

Taking part in the Wayaobao Conference were Mao Zedong, Zhang Wentian, Zhou Enlai, Wang Jiaxiang, Bo Gu, Liu Shaoqi, Kai Feng, Deng Fa, Li Weihan, Yang Shangkun, Guo Songtao and Zhang Hao. The first seven participants were full or alternate members of the Politburo and legitimate participants; the next two were Central Committee members; Zhang Hao was the envoy of the CCP Mission to the Comintern and Guo the secretary of the Shaanxi CCP Committee.[61] Almost no military commanders participated in this conference. The selection of participants indicated that as soon as the military crisis was over, the political leadership of the Party would become key; it also showed that Mao preferred to use political cadres to keep a power balance with military leaders such as Peng Dehuai and Lin Biao.

The Wayaobao Conference participants produced three important documents: a political resolution of the Conference entitled "Resolution of the Central Committee on the Contemporary Political Situation and the Party's Tasks"; a military "Resolution of the Central Committee on the Military Strategic Problems"; and finally "On Tactics Against Japanese Imperialism", a speech by Mao to the Party activists soon after the Conference.

As an assessment of the general situation at home and abroad, the political resolution declares: "A fundamental change has occurred in the present political situation, and a new era has started in the history of the Chinese Revolution. This change manifests itself in the fact that Japanese imperialism is turning China into its colony, the Chinese Revolution is heading for a giant nationwide upsurge, and we are right at the eve of the world revolution." To cope with this new situation the Party drew a general line:

> Our task is not only to unite all possible anti-Japanese forces, but also all those possible anti-Japanese allies; to make all the Chinese people who have strength deliver their strength; all those who have money deliver their money; all those who have guns deliver their guns; all those who have knowledge deliver their knowledge—not to miss even one single patriotic Chinese—to take part in the fighting against the Japanese. This is the Party's general line, a line of the most broad national united front.[62]

More specifically, the resolution called for the formation in China of a government of national defense and a joint army to resist the Japanese, a change from the Worker and Peasant Soviet Republic to the People's Soviet Republic, and a change in the former policies of class differentiation and social revolution. It stipulated, "No rich peasants' property will be confiscated anymore and they will enjoy equal rights with the others." As for the national industrial and commercial capitalists: "The People's Soviet Republic welcomes them to invest in its territory on the basis of mutual benefit, to run factories and shops. The safety of their life and property will be guaranteed, and their rent and tax will be reduced in order to develop the Chinese economy." The Communist Party would be open to all classes. "All those who are willing to strive for the Communist Party's cause can join the Party, regardless of their class origins. To struggle resolutely for the Party's cause is the main criterion for granting Party membership; the social class background is not the main consideration, though it should be considered."[63]

It is probably impossible to say whether human thought is a reflection of objective conditions or an expression of subjective ones. Is an individual's new opinion on something, formed through further observation, caused directly by actual change in the object or does the change simply exist in the mind of the individual? Did the new policy of the CCP emerge mainly from the Japanese invasion or did it come from the new Communist attitude? The Japanese had been intruding in China since 1931 and had been attempting to make China their colony all the time. There was no change in this respect in late 1935. On the other hand, the CCP Center's attitude toward politics and Chinese politics had undergone a basic change in late 1935. To depend on its own effort and increase its own strength, to utilize all possible factors at hand to gain military power, to give up all bookish dogmas to accord with political reality—it was primarily this change in the CCP's political philosophy that led to the change in policies at the Wayaobao Conference.

Both Japanese imperialism and the KMT government were targets of attacks in the resolution. Chiang Kai-shek was lightly labelled a national traitor. With the bitter experience of the Long March fresh in their minds, the Communists could by no means ignore or neglect their own military strength. The resolution took it for granted that "the Red Army stands as the vanguard force in resisting the Japanese; only by strengthening the Red Army can we win the victory over the Japanese. For this reason we need several million troops in the Red Army, and we should first expand the Red Army to one million. In other words, we must have our own military power. The defeat of the Japanese cannot be achieved without greatly enlarging the territory of the People's Soviet Republic as an anti-Japanese base."[64] It was very clear that, either as a means or as an end, the CCP must increase its military force and expand its territorial base. The anti-Japanese tone was not only a sincere intention, but a skillful excuse. The resolution also called for enrolling hundreds of thousands or even millions of Party members.

Another remarkable statement in the resolution was that "leftist closed-doorism," instead of "right opportunism," was viewed as the most dangerous tendency within the Party. It pointed out the three evil causes of closed-doorism: 1. It does not understand the new political situation and therefore does not understand the necessity of changing our strategy to comply with the new situation; 2. In practical action, it fails to connect the Party's basic slogan and program with the slogans and programs at each moment; 3. Fundamentally, it worships Marxism, Leninism and Stalinism as dead dogmas and is unable to apply them actively to the concrete and specific conditions in China.[65] Here, clearly, expedient political practice in China should be regarded as the most important factor, not revolutionary doctrines. This marked a basic ideological and orientational change, which proved even more important than any single practical issue.

The more urgent measures for the Red Army to take can be seen from the military resolution of the Wayaobao Conference. Though the national war against the Japanese was again emphasized, the real purpose described in this resolution was to preserve and expand the Communist troops, as shown in the following subtle passage: "Our general military strategy in 1936 is to gather strength and prepare for a direct fight with the Japanese. Therefore, our main combat target should be troops of those national traitors. The Red Army should be drastically enlarged to 200,000 men, the First Front Army alone to 50,000."[66]

In the military resolution, the Communist leaders required that the national war be related to the civil war. The Red Army's strategic tasks were to "break through the route to fight the Japanese" and "consolidate and expand the exisiting Soviet area"; it should "take the first goal as the focal task and link it tightly with the second goal." More specifically, they designated Shaanxi at the east and Suiyuan at the north as two directions of the Red Army's operation and the Soviet base's expansion.[67]

The resolution also touched on the problem of a strategic shift from regular warfare to guerrilla warfare in the areas occupied by the Japanese or their puppets. "All the guerrilla brigades should assume names of the national war, and all land revolution should also be carried out under slogans of the national war."[68] It was too early for the Communists to elaborate on this issue but the basic idea was already there. It was not until a couple of years later that the Communist leaders fully realized the advantageous nature of guerrilla warfare to their partisan interests.

Few writings and talks prior to his speech at the meeting of Party activists on December 27, 1935 better illustrate Mao's political capacity and charismatic personality. The speech was made as a colloquial communication of the decisions of the Wayaobao Conference. Mao made his arguments more powerfully and confidently than logically and reasonably. The Long March was regarded as a failure only from the past or Bo Gu's standpoint, but as a victory for the future or Mao's standpoint; no old sayings and wisecracks were spared to deride the former dogmatic leadership. Mao's remarks on international relations are particularly worth noting. In contrast to a few months earlier, when he claimed that the CCP was a branch of the Comintern and raised the possibility of retreat to the Sino-Russian border for support, he now declared: "We Chinese have the spirit to fight the enemy to the last drop of our blood, the determination to recover all our lost territory by our own efforts, and the ability to stand up on our own feet in the family of nations."[69]

The Wayaobao Conference signalled the beginning of the Communists' united front policy, but was more important in indicating the transformation of the Communists' general mentality and orientation. For various reasons, Russian politicians and historians did not realize—and even now do not admit—this obvious fact. They claim that it was only by dint of their direct and indirect influences through Wang Ming at Moscow that the CCP's new policy was established. The following quotation from a book of two Russian official historians published in 1975 is is an exemplary illustration of this attitude.

> Because of the complicated situations at the time, the CCP leaders in China temporarily lost contact with the Comintern and therefore were not unable to jump out of the frame of old policies. At the Maoergai Conference of the CCP Politburo in early August 1935, in which Mao Zedong played a dominating role, no resolution was passed as regards the necessity of a national united front. The August 1 Manifesto and the Resolution of the Maoergai Conference thus reflected two contradictory political lines. It was only through the Comintern's help that the CCP gave up its leftist, factionalist line and turned to the effective anti-imperialist united front policy.[70]

Right after the Wayaobao Conference, Liu Shaoqi left northern Shaanxi to assume the position of Secretary of the CCP Northern Bureau. Liu suggested and Mao approved a formal decision that Communists held in Peking and Tianjun prisons be allowed to write and publish "confessions" in order to be released. Thousands of dissatisfied students were organized to sneak into northern Shaanxi from Peking and Tianjin. Contact between the CCP Center and the Comintern and between the CCP and the Soviet Union became routine in 1936. Early that year, Liu Changsheng arrived from Moscow with a set of secret codes, and radio communication with the Comintern was resumed. Chen Yun was already in Moscow, and Deng Fa was sent to Moscow via Xinjiang as an envoy of the Party Center. Such contacts were necessary for the new leaders to win the sympathy of the Comintern and attain legitimacy as the CCP supreme leadership.[71]

To either implement the new policy of the anti-Japanese united front or consolidate their Army and Soviet, the Communists had to try to reach peace with the surrounding KMT troops. Their present targets were mainly Zhang Xueliang's Northeastern Army and Yang Hucheng's Northwestern Army. After the victorious battle at Zhiluozhen, Mao wrote a polite and modest letter to Dong Yingbin, proposing a truce. Zhang Xueliang was away in Nanking at the time, thus Dong was not in a position to give a definite answer. Simultaneously, personal messages from the CCP leaders were delivered to Yang Hucheng. After a period of warm treatment and careful education, the Communists released all KMT prisoners of war—among them was Gao Fuyuan, an NEA officer captured in the Ganquan Battle. Through Gao's persuasion, Wang Yizhe and Zhang Xueliang agreed to secret negotiations with the Red Army. In February 1936, the Communist Party sent Li Kenong as its agent to meet Wang Yizhe at Yan'an, and they reached an oral agreement of mutual non-encroachment, mutual trade and communication. In March, Li managed to meet Zhang Xueliang in Xian; a month later, Zhou Enlai went to Yan'an to talk with Zhang in person.[72]

Relations between the Communists and Yang Hucheng could be traced back to the Northern Expedition years. Their new contact with Yang Hucheng in North China was therefore opened earlier and closed more easily than that with Zhang Xueliang. Nan Hanchen flew to Nanking for a secret meeting with Yang Hucheng even before the Wayaobao Conference. In December 1935, Wang Feng went to see Yang in Xian again and handed him a personal letter from Mao. After another meeting in Tianjin between Wang Shiying and Yang, both sides finally agreed to exchange a secret delegation, set up secret radio stations to maintain communication, and open a secret route for munition transportation.[73]

The Communists had established a firm foothold in northern Shaanxi, but a foothold was only a foothold. For the time being, no strong enemy troops were likely to bother them, but they problematically needed to bother others. Despite the vast size of the northern Shaanxi base area, it was sparsely populated and hence it was impossible for the Red Army to recruit troops; the whole area was, moreover, extremely poor and it was impossible for them to find adequate material supplies. More fundamentally, in Lenin's words, communist revolution means aggression.

On February 27, the Red Army General Headquarters issued a statement entitled "Declaration of the Eastern Expedition," announcing the formation of the Anti-Japanese Vanguard Army of the Chinese People. By the time the declaration was published, 15,000 Red Army men had already pushed across the Yellow River and plunged into the Shanxi province. The declaration solemnly declared that "the Red Army is crossing the Yellow River and going east to resist the Japanese."[74] Nonetheless, their real purpose proved less clear than that claimed. Of course, Yan Xishan was too experienced to misunderstand the Communist slogan; this old Shanxi warlord had every reason to regard the Red Army's action as an encroachment on his own territory. To the public, the Communists' propaganda was as decently effective as they expected.

There had been controversy among the Communist leaders before this "Eastern Expedition" was organized. Peng Dehuai was among those who objected to this proposal, presumably raised by Mao. Yes, the troops needed clothes, bullets and silver dollars; and yes, they also needed material supplies and new recruits—all these needs Peng could easily understand as a veteran military commander. He did not quite comprehend certain of Mao's philosophical remarks, such as "consolidation can only be achieved through expansion." Peng was not persuaded. While Mao had already become too authoritative to disobey, Peng brought up his own worries: suppose the Red Army moved too far east into Shanxi, what if the rear base in Shaanxi was taken by the enemy, the Yellow River was cut off, and the Red Army could not be guaranteed to turn back; the bitter experience of the Long March—roaming around without a home—should be kept as a fresh lesson. Mao's reply was a vivid expression of his personality: "Guarantee, you said? I cannot offer anything guaranteed." To show his cavalier spirit, Mao declared he would personally lead the expeditionary campaign and leave the Party and government work at the rear to Wang Jiaxiang, Zhou Enlai and Bo Gu.[75]

The Vanguard Army snuck across the River and struck into Xaoyi at the center of Shanxi province. There it was divided into three columns. The 15th Army Corps marched northeast toward the provincial capital of Taiyuan. Then, with Yan's entire army following behind, it turned to northwest Shanxi, attracting the enemy but avoiding serious fighting. Mao and Peng led one regiment with only 500 men at the middle as the command column—Mao's guerrilla experience in Jiangxi Soviet enabled him to manage such an adventure successfully—and the main force of the 1st Army Corps immediately drove straight south along the Taiyuan-Tongpu railway into the wealthy and densely populated Fen River valley. There the Communists defeated some enemy troops, but more importantly, they acquired large amounts of money, grain, munitions and human aid.[76] Yan Xishan and his Shanxi Army were taken in panic. When Chiang Kai-shek eventually transferred his Central Army to Shanxi in early May, the Communists made another eloquent declaration—scolding Chiang Kai-shek and Yan Xishan for blocking them on their way to fight the Japanese and expressing their unwillingness to fight their fellow countrymen—and then hurriedly withdrew with their troops to the western bank of the Yellow River.[77]

In southern Shanxi the 1st Army Corps alone gathered 400,000 silver dollars and recruited 5,000 soldiers, as well as plenty of material supplies. The Communists also founded underground agencies and guerrilla groups; they distributed food to the peasants and provided guns and bullets to the local guerrillas, and thus "planted seeds of revolution" for the future. More practically, all Yan Xishan's troops moved from the western side of the Yellow River back to protect their home province and left the Northern Shaanxi Soviet in an even safer position.[78] In a certain sense revolutionary offensive rose not only from moral commitment but from very practical reasons. Mao the Communist politician had a deeper insight than Peng the military man: only through leading the Army to fight outside could he consolidate his position inside the Party.

Back in northern Shaanxi, a military conference reviewed the Eastern Expedition. This time Mao criticized his own men in the 1st Army Corps for their factionalism, stigmatizing them for being reluctant to support other Red Army troops, especially the 15th Army Corps. Mao was broad-minded enough to realize that this criticism of his own troops would be necessary for him to secure the position as leader of all the Red Army. Mao directed further attacks against "liberalism": some Red Army officers and men had taken the anti-Japanese slogan too seriously; they really wanted to go further east through Shanxi to Hebei to fight the Japanese. They did not understand that "breaking through the anti-Japanese road" was only useful to Mao as a slogan, not a real goal.[79]

A month later, after the Eastern Expedition, Mao called for a "Western Expedition." This action seemed more difficult to explain to the public. If the Eastern Expedition could be justified as attempting to fight the Japanese invaders, it seemed really difficult to justify their attacking the west, where there were no signs of the Japanese at all. Actually, this was no problem at all for Mao and the Communist politicians. In order to prepare for the war against the Japanese, they argued, they had to eliminate those troops of national traitors and reactionary elements who were harassing their rear base. To the friendly Zhang Xueliang, the Communists would confess softly that they were to welcome the Fourth and Second Red Front Armies to join forces with them. This time Peng Dehuai alone was appointed concurrently as the Commander and Political Commissar.[80]

The Western Expedition was formally announced on May 14 under the title, the "Western Field Army of the Chinese People's Red Army." The whole army was divided in two routes: the Right Route consisting of the 15th Army Corps, and the Left Route of the 1st Army Corps. The Left Route Army went through eastern Gansu, occupied Huanxian and Qingyan, and destroyed one brigade of Ma Hongkui's local army. After this it continued marching west into Ningxia and, by the end of August, it reached Haiyuan at the eastern side of the Great Bend of the Yellow River. In the same period, the Right Route followed the Great Wall and captured Yianchi and the three Bians—Qingbian, Anbian and Dingbian. From there they continued west to Tongxincheng, close to Haiyuan.

In three months the Red Army marched about 400 li, occupied a dozen cities and brought nine counties into their Soviet territory. The Red Army showed its combat strength to the Ma Hongkui troops as well as to the Northeastern Army. It smashed four companies of the NEA commanded by He Guozhu. It sent an envoy to negotiate immediately after the battle; eventually He accepted the Communist offer and permitted the Red Army to pass freely through his garrison district.[81]

While striving to consolidate the Shaanxi-Gansu Soviet base and resume contacts with the Comintern and Soviet Union, Mao did not forget to persuade Zhang Guotao to come north. One of the purposes of the Western Expedition was indeed to welcome the Second and Fourth Front Armies, which were on their own Long March toward the north at the time. A unification of all the Communist forces in the North was desired and would be beneficial to Mao and the Party Center leaders in Shaanxi.

By the latter part of 1936 a new Communist stronghold came into formal existence in Northwest China. The Shaanxi-Gansu-Ningxia Border Base covered almost 30 counties with 20,000 Red Army troops and a population of 1,500,000.[82] It looked safe and secure on all four sides: two military expeditions consolidated the eastern and western fronts; secret agreements with Zhang Xueliang and Yang Hucheng guaranteed the southern front; the northern front was the Gobi Dessert, more secure than any man-made fortification. Unless the KMT Central Army planned another giant suppression campaign itself, no provincial or local troops were likely to gain the upper hand over the Communists, let alone exterminate them.

Even more importantly, Mao and his followers in northern Shaanxi had actually become the legitimate and practical center of the Communist revolution in China. They maintained the titles CCP Central Committee, Politburo, Central Military Council, and Central Government of the Soviet Republic; they were acknowledged by the Comintern; their authority in North China was well established and their connection with South China was well under way. The policy of the national united front adopted at the Wayaobao Conference was accepted as the general line of all Communists in China. Although Zhang Guotao might have been among the earliest CCP leaders who sensed the necessity of a less radical line, it was in late 1935 and early 1936—while he was still secluded in the southwest highlands— that Mao and his comrades in the northwest formally established this general line through a series of conferences and documents. What the Communists had achieved in northern Shaanxi with the new leadership and the new political orientation was quite impressive, what they would achieve in the future was staggering.

8

GRAND UNION

From Prospect to Desperation

The secret move of the 1st and 3rd Army Corps from Baxi on September 11, 1935 naturally caused a commotion in the Left Route Army at Aba. Chen Changhao and Xu Xiangquan's telegrams duly arrived to report and protest Mao's secret escape; officers and men of the Fourth Front Army competed with one another in expressing their contempt for the Central Red Army and the CCP Center; in a much cooler manner, Zhang Guotao also expressed anger at Mao for his disobedience to the General Headquarters and for his selfishness in the northern flight. In his memoir, Zhang recalls:

> Mao's ability to take such an action was partly due to the defeatist idea he was obsessed with then and partly because of his Machiavellian philosophy: It is better that others owe me a debt rather than I owe others one. Guided by such a psychological factor, all Communist principles and moral concepts were entirely discarded. Only Mao Zedong could have played such tricks. Now it is clear that ever since the union of the two armies, Mao had always been juggling with political schemes. Those obstinate and naive dogmatists were nothing but tools in his service.[1]

Although he might not have reasoned the full depth of Mao's philosophy either as a Machiavellian politician or as a Marxist revolutionary, Zhang caught one aspect of Mao's personality at this point. Both because Mao's behavior was inexcusable and due to their own politically dependent position as military staff, the commanders of the Central Red Army now staying with the Left Route Army—such as Zhu De and Liu Bocheng—could only follow Zhang Guotao, no matter what they might have thought privately. In fact, these military men normally remained politically neutral, standing between two more extreme sides and moving with the general trend in the central leadership.[2]

In September 13-14, a conference was held at Aba to deal with the new situation. The conference is remembered by some as the Enlarged Conference of the Sichuan CCP Committee, but by others as the Conference of the Party Activists; more simply, it is just called the Aba Conference. Actually, it was more like a mass rally than a formal, high level Party conference. Approximately one hundred people huddled in a lamasery; riotous activity and provocative shouts filled the meeting place. Zhang Guotao was the key figure of the event, and the focal issue was the denunciation of Mao. Mao Zedong, Zhou Enlai, Zhang Wentian, and Bo Gu were all labelled rightist opportunists and their northern march was declared "flightism and defeatism."[3] Zhang Guotao was happy to see some speakers putting pressure on Zhu De, after which he pretended to be a mediator and a defender of Zhu. This time, Zhang was using Huang Chao, a returned student, as his mouthpiece to exaggerate, so that Zhang himself could then propose a seemingly moderate resolution. As a politician Zhang himself followed the same rules of political gaming as Mao often did.[4]

Just as Mao did at the Ejie Conference, Zhang shifted the topic from accusation of his opponent to arrangement of his own maneuver. On September 15, the General Headquarters issued a "Plan of Going South for Political Security." The essential idea was to strike south toward the provincial capital of Sichuan—Chengdu—and establish the whole province as a new Soviet base. In order to raise the morale of his soldiers, Zhang had to use such vulgar slogans as, "Go to Chengdu and eat rice." This secular slogan seemed more enticing to the troops than those of sacred revolution. Accordingly, the 4th and 30th Armies of the Right Route were also ordered to turn south.[5]

In retrospect, Mao's Ejie Conference and Zhang's Aba Conference were quite different in nature. The former was a meeting of senior Party and Army leaders who spent most of their time discussing future military plans, while the latter was more of a mass demonstration in which the military plan was merely a result of commotion. This difference in the styles of Mao and Zhang as politicians constituted one of the reasons for the different destinies of the two Red Army groups under their respective commands.

After a few days of preparation, the Left Route Army, now the 9th, 31st and 33rd Armies of the Fourth Front Army and the 5th and 9th Army Corps of the Central Red Army, took off toward the south under the leadership of the General Headquarters. They went down along the Dajin River and arrived in the Zhuokeji area.[6] There they joined forces with the 4th and 30th Armies of the Right Route Army in early October. The troops amounted to about 80,000 soldiers and 3,000 cadres and officers altogether. On October 5, they held an even more important conference at Zhuomubao to resolve the general political and organizational problems of the new situation.[7]

Communist leaders and historians now face a dilemma regarding the Zhuomubao Conference. They are willing to cite this occasion as evidence to use in denouncing Zhang Guotao's blatant split of the Party Center, but this conference must also be treated with discretion because of the direct involvement of such contemporary CCP leaders as Zhu De, Liu Bocheng, Xu Xiangqian and Li Xiannian. As a result, the documents of this conference are still kept in the Archives of the Central Committee as classified information inaccessible even to Chinese historians. As for Zhang Guotao, he seems reluctant to divulge more details of the Conference in his memoirs, probably because this event plainly reveals his usurpation of Party Center power.[8] The basic significance of the Zhuomubao Conference is clear. This conference proclaimed the founding of a new central leadership in the Communist Party, the Soviet Government, and the Red Army.

At the Zhuomubao Conference, a new Central Committee and a new Politburo were formed, as were a new Central Soviet Government and a new Military Council. Zhang Guotao became the Chairman of the Party Center and the Politburo. A resolution was passed to dismiss Mao, Zhou, Zhang and Bo from their leading posts and expel them from the Party Center. Moreover, they were deprived of their Party membership and declared liable for apprehension.[9] There is no available record indicating the the exact members of the new CCP Central Committee, but no doubt the FFA people controlled a dominant proportion of the top positions. According to Harrison Salisbury's interview with some CCP leaders in China, Wang Ming, Lin Biao, and Nie Rongzhen were on the list of the new Party Center. Zhu De and Liu Bocheng were also probably added to the Party Center as well as the Military Council.[10]

In the meantime, the entire army was thoroughly reorganized and assumed a more centralized leadership. Measures were taken to change some army units and personnel in order to enhance the overall control by Zhang Guotao and his men. Xu Xiangqian was appointed Vice General Commander of the Red Army and Chen Changhao became Director of the General Political Department. Li Zhuoran was seemingly promoted to Vice Director of the Political Department, yet his practical function as the Political Commissar of the 5th Army Corps was replaced by Huang Chao, one of Zhang's followers. He Changgong was also dismissed from his position of Political Commissar in the 9th Army Corps. Furthermore, these two former CRA troops were respectively retitled the 9th and 33rd Army. Thus, in the Fourth Front Army and, in a certain sense, the entire the Party and Army, Zhang Guotao had established his central leadership. He seemed to be in a far more favorable position in October 1935 than ever before.[11]

The military situation did not look bad either. While Mao was still struggling with his 7,000 men to the north, Zhang seemed quite happy with his 80,000 troops in western Sichuan. Hu Zongnan's troops of the KMT Central Army were deployed along the Gansu and Sichuan border while Xue Yue's were at the Sichuan-Shaanxi border—both were there to block the Red Army's northern march. Most of the Sichuan provincial armies were deployed along the Min River at the eastern front, the rest remained further south in the Maogong area. In sum, the KMT troops remained stationary. For a while, the quick move of the First Front Army to the north put the KMT troops at a loss as to the Communists' plans. This strategic uncertainty on the Nationalist side temporarily brought Zhang Guotao to a fairly comfortable position.

There were several alternative directions Zhang could have taken with his troops at the time. In retrospect, he could: 1. follow in Mao's wake to the northeast. This was perhaps ideal, especially in late September, because he could easily have followed the open route to catch up with the Central Red Army and placed all blame for the previous rupture on Mao; 2. go northwest to the Xia River valley as they had planned. The difficulty in this plan was the highland terrain in front of them and the unpredictable future at Gansu; 3. remain in northwest Sichuan area and expand around the Zhuokeji area. The advantage of this option was that they could easily maintain the present level of military security, whereas its disadvantage was the material shortage in this barren region; 4. drive down to the south, as they actually did, to attempt the Chengdu plain, where they might turn central Sichuan into a new base area.

Actually, the political commotion around the Aba Conference led Zhang into quickly taking the last option without careful consideration and adequate consultation with his senior cadres and officers. The combat plans of the Fourth Front Army in the latter months of 1935 were for the most part a direct reflection of political emotion without much military scrutiny. On October 7 the General Headquarters issued the "Combat Plan of Sui-Chong-Dan-Mao," which left two armies to guard the rear of Zhuokeji, while the rest of the troops were divided into two army columns and dispatched to drive south along the Dajin River. Liu Wenhui's Sichuan army at the river proved no match for the Fourth Front Army: the latter easily took over several counties and pushed its front as far as it had been four months before. On October 20, another order for an even more ambitious and aggressive operation entitled "Combat Plan of Tian-Lu-Ming-Ya-Qing-Da" was produced.[12]

The plan was carried out smoothly enough at the beginning. From late October to early November, the Red Army captured most of the designated counties, killed 5,000 of the Sichuan army troops, and reached the edge of the Chengdu plain, as near as 200 li to Chengdu. Had there been no hesitation, the FFA might have swiftly attacked and taken the city.[13] Zhang committed a tactical blunder here. He stayed at the rear and failed to either summon all the troops for a quick strike at the Sichuan army or, even more wisely, hold off the attack indefinitely, waiting for changes in the national situation. Zhang lacked the knowledge and experience in direct military command needed by a political leader with such responsibility.

After working several months, Chiang Kai-shek successfully brought the entire Sichuan province to a state of greater solidarity, and the threat of the Red Army to the provincial center further enhanced the cohesiveness of the Sichuan warlords. Liu Xiang managed to gather together as many as 80 regiments—200,000 men—to check the Red Army's attack. After a few skirmishes, a decisive battle was fought in the Baizhang Pass in Mingshan county from November 12 to 19. Although normally the Sichuan army was not as competent as the Fourth Front Army, this time, thanks to their obvious superiority in numbers and their favorable defensive position, Liu Xiang succeeded in blunting the spearhead of Zhang Guotao's troops. Liu lost 15,000 men and Zhang lost 10,000. More important than this figure is the fact that the Red Army's momentum was stopped and both sides were brought to a standstill. For the Communists, the standstill was a symptom of collapse, whereas for the Sichuan army it meant only a wait for reinforcements.[14]

The temporary truce with Liu Xiang in southwest Sichuan gave Zhang Guotao the illusion that a new military base could be or had already been opened at the Sichuan-Xikang border, where the Fourth Front Army was presently located. On December 5, 1935, he delivered a telegram to the Party and Army leaders with the First Front Army in northern Shaanxi, which demonstrated his political ambitions as well as his poor political judgment. The telegram read as follows:

1. Here we assumed the titles of the Party Center, the Youth League Center, the Central Government, the Central Military Council, the General Headquarters and others. These titles will be employed in drawing up public documents as well as in conducting relations with your side.
2. We demand that you stop using the false title of the Party Center and change it to the CCP Northern Bureau, the Shaanxi-Gansu Government, and the Northern Route Army.
3. The names First and Fourth Front Armies will both be discarded.
4. You should immediately send us a report on the conditions of the Northern Bureau, the Northern Route Army, and the government systems for our approval.[15]

In response to such provocative demands, Mao restrained his temper and did not divulge any emotional expression of protest. The Party Center did not respond to Zhang's challenge until almost two months later. Before this it ignored the titular claim and kept communicating with Zhang on other more urgent and practical issues. In January 16-18, Zhang opened the "Preparatory Congress of the All Sichuan Soviet." He himself gave both the opening remarks and the concluding speech, calling for the implementation of the Soviet system throughout the province. The convocation of such a congress served several purposes: strengthening his position as the legitimate leader of the Party, the Army and the Soviet; encouraging cadres and soldiers in his troops; and inciting local people to join his revolutionary cause—an exhortation he had successfully made in northern Sichuan in early 1933. However, as both the situation of the Communists and that of their enemy had changed considerably, so did the results. Zhang achieved in the Congress nothing more than the gratification of his vainglory, for which he would soon have to pay.[16]

In October 1935, after the Central Red Army arrived at Shaanxi, Chiang Kai-shek called together all his generals in charge of Communist affairs for a discussion of nationwide strategic arrangements. They decided that Zhang Xueliang would run the Xian headquarters which would cope with the Central Red Army in Shaanxi and Gansu; Gu Zhutong would head the Chongqing headquarters which would deal with the Fourth Front Army in Sichuan and Xikang; and Chen Cheng would takeover the Yichang headquarters to fight the 2nd and 6th Army Corps at the Hunan-Hubei-Sichuan-Guizhou border. Since both the First and Fourth Front Armies had moved to the frontier regions, Chiang was more concerned with He Long and Ren Bishi's troops. Xue Yue's four armies, therefore, would be transferred east to the Sichuan-Hupei border where they would suppress the 2nd and 6th Army Corps to the glory of Chen Cheng, as the general commander. The large-scale intrusion of the Fourth Front Army into central Sichuan in late October 1935, however, resulted in a change of this arrangement. Xue was called back on his way to the east and redirected southwest to reinforce the Sichuan army in fighting the FFA.[17]

Xue Yue led his troops to Chengdu in late November 1935. Under his disposal were as ever two columns, four armies, six divisions—altogether 100,000 strong. From mid-December 1935 to February 1936, Xue, together with his generals, Wu Qiwei and Zhou Hunyuan, started the victorious Xinjing Battle to bring the situation under control. The FFA lost about 5,000 men in the fight. In February a military campaign in the Tianquan and Lushan area lasted for a week or so, ending in the disposal of another chunk of the Red Army—2,000 captured and 4,000 killed. With their heavy artillery, air forces, and with rich anti-Communist experience, Xue's KMT Central Army troops were certainly on par with the FFA in terms of combat capacity. Besides, whenever they took over an area, these KMT troops built blockhouses and reorganized the local people, as they had successfully done in Jiangxi. They even learned from the Communists how to treat the captives: retaining those useful personnel for their own service and releasing the rank and file with enough money to travel back to their homes. From March 1936 on, Xue ordered his men to stop for respite and training, leaving the Red Army to suffer the natural hardships on the barren western highlands. Xue Yüe stayed in western Sichuan until June 1936, when the Guangxi and Guangdong revolt broke out and he was called in to cope with the urgent situation.[18]

From the Communist point of view, all Zhang Guotao's mistakes arose from his political strategy rather than from any military blunders. From the very beginning of the southern march, the Fourth Front Army was facing a dilemma: either staying in the Sichuan-Xikang border area around Maogong and Baoxing—where the terrain was tough and the populace small—they were militarily safe but short of material supplies; or fighting forward to the Chengdu plain—rich in material and human resources— where they could possibly obtain food and recruits, but would encounter the superior KMT forces. They were checked by the Sichuan army in November 1935 and defeated by the KMT Central Army in February 1936, after which they lost their offensive momentum and had to retreat to Xikang to survive.

After the Xinjing and Tianjuan battles in late February 1936, Zhang Guotao directed his men first north back to Maogong, where they found to the their disappointment that in their previous four-month-long sojourn, the Communists had consumed almost everything, especially food, in this poor and backward place. In March, they had to turn west. Crossing the Jiajin Mountain and the Dajing River and passing through Danba and Daofu, eventually they reached the town of Ganzi.[19] Though the KMT enemy was left far behind in the south and the east, and though they now occupied a vast region in the Xikang-Tibet border, all the natural and social conditions in this nomadic minority region were dauntingly against them.

In their memoirs or reminiscences, most survivors of the FFA's southern march recall their experience in the Xikang region as a nightmarish famine. Even taking into account possible exaggerations made to denounce Zhang Guotao's erroneous line and express allegiance with the Party Center, their basic account of the FFA's ordeal should assure that it was truly horrific. Zhen Weishan renders a vivid picture of their bitter struggle with the adverse natural conditions in early 1936:

> The biggest difficulty for the Army was shortage of supplies. Winter came after the Baizhangguan battle, and yet there was no way to find padded clothes for the troops. The soldiers tore off barks of palm trees and put it between their shirts just to keep warm. Around the time of crossing the Jiajin Mountains, some troops wore raw skins of cattle and sheep as jackets. Roving among snow mountains and grasslands, and undertaking fierce fights in western Sichuan—lacking food and drink—everybody had a pale and thin face and looked extremely exhausted. Thinking back on the meeting at Maogong with

the First Front Army six months ago, how much we saw that everything had changed! Though we did have a period of respite in Ganzi and Luhuo, this area was vast in land but meagre in people, a nomadic region where all grasses grew but no crops. There was no way to find enough food for these tens of thousands of soldiers. We could only rely on wild weeds to fill our stomaches.[20]

There were other detrimental factors, such as hostile Tibetan tribes and infectious diseases. Zhang Guotao could not find any new prospects and the whole army had lost its vigor and vitality, crucial for revolution or rebellion. Quantitatively speaking, nonetheless, the Fourth Front Army in Xikang in early 1936 had not yet fallen to the so-called "breaking point," nor had Zhang Guotao's leading position in it been challenged. The Red Army troops remained in decent shape. Their army forces had dropped from 80,000 to 40,000 troops. In Ganzi, they went through military training and political education. All headquarters personnel and subordinate units carried on their routine army functions. Propaganda work and entertainment activities proceeded regularly. The Communists strove to overcome shortages by planting crops and spinning wool clothes with their own hands.[21] But these efforts could never amount to anything close to a successful southern expedition, as Zhang later claims.[22] Under such circumstances, an irresistible certainty grew within the troops that they had to shift to another direction as soon as possible. Actually, there had never been any intention of staying in Ganzi for long; while the leaders were pondering a move to the north, two pieces of happy news came out of the blue in June 1936: the Guangdong and Guangxi revolt broke out and drew Xue Yue's Central Army out of Sichuan; and the 2nd and 6th Army Corps were approaching Guizhou and Yunnan, meaning a union with another Red Army group was in sight.[23]

The 2nd and 6th Army Corps Take Off Again

There were quite a few 'unions' of the Communist forces in the general period from 1932 to 1936. The one between the 6th Army Corps led by Ren Bishi and the 3rd Army led by He Long in October 1934 was among those achieved with the least conflict and confrontation. He Long himself recalls, though with a bit of exaggeration, the good relations after the union: "All men of the two troops were cemented into one body. Although there were individual cases of conflict, they were but like single bubbles in a vast sea."[24] Such a situation was not merely due to their common revolutionary allegiance, as He Long tends to believe. It stemmed more from the mutual dependence and mutual utility the troops had for each other or, as Xiao Ke—Commander of the 6th Army Corps—more simply put it, "We needed them and they needed us."[25] After three months' marching and fighting, the 6th Army Corps was reduced from 9,800 to 3,300 men and pushed into a strange land, badly in need of reinforcement and respite. The 3rd Army had outlasted even worse difficulties and sacrifices in the past years in the KMT's suppression campaigns and in their internal anti-counterrevolutionary campaign, so they were also badly in need of material and spiritual reinforcement. Personal dispositions and relations further aided smooth unification. Although Ren Bishi was the indisputable political authority in the 6th Army Corps, he had neither much experience, nor a particular interest, in military command. With the seniority and authority accumulated over years, on the other hand, He Long's military command in the 3rd Army was unchallengeable, but as an army man he hardly aspired to political power in the Party. Thus the two most influential leaders complemented each other in the joint leadership. More importantly, neither the seniority of Ren and He nor the strength of their troops could sufficiently back up a claim for the supreme leadership of the Party and Army. A common sense of inferiority before the central leadership actually drew them closer together.

With doubled strength after the union, Ren and He led the combined troops from eastern Guizhou back to western Hunan in November 1934. At that moment, most of the Hunan army was engaged in the southwest with the Central Red Army—which had just deserted the Jiangxi Soviet and embarked on its Long March. Only the local warlord, Chen Quzhen, was left in western Hunan with about 10,000 men. The Communists had no difficulty driving away this enemy and took over the three county sites of Yongshun, Sangzhi and Dayong, along with their surrounding districts, in less than two months. A new military base thus emerged at the Hunan-Hubei-Sichuan-Guizhou border area.[26]

In the wake of the military victory, Party and Army activists held a conference in which Xia Xi became the target of criticism. He Long initiated this move, revenging the disadvantage of his military authority under Xia's previous political control of the 3rd Army. Ren Bishi's approval of such a move resulted from his attempt to strengthen his own political leadership over the joint army. Xia was ironically labelled as advocating a rightist line against the Party Center's correct line. Ren criticized Xia, but ignored He's demand to dismiss Xia from all leadership. He preferred to keep Xia as a political check on He and the military staff. Xia was transferred to the 6th Army Corps as Director of the Political Department. He Long could neither forget and nor forgive Ren for this lenient treatment even three decades later when he recalled the matter.

Comrade Ren Bishi exerted a leftist line in the past, and did he change his attitude as soon as he reached the Xiang'echuanqian Soviet? One can hardly say so. Then did he not accept the resolution of the Zunyi Conference? We should not say so either. He accepted it, but only slowly. There were crucial errors in his attitude toward Xia Xi. Xia had killed all the cadres but he was still appointed Director of the Political Department in the 6th Army Corps. Was this decided in a small meeting or a big one? I did not know that, neither did Guan Xiangying. . . . We are not like kittens. Kittens cover the shit they lay. What can we possibly do with ours?[27]

He's demand for more serious punishment of Xia was not entirely just. In the previous years, He did not stop Xia from killing Duan Dechang, the founder of the Honghu base and a challenger to He as the leader of the western Hunan-Hubei base. Ren Bishi demoted Xia Xi as a political leader who was threatening his position, but did not eliminate Xia to benefit He. Consciously or unconsciously, these Communists were all involved in a political game. However, this kind of analysis should not so stray from the matter at hand as to ignore the fact that through the criticism of Xia, a stronger and more rational leadership in the joint forces emerged, and disagreements between He and Ren never reached a level of open debate or disruption in their common actions.

The failure of Chen Quzhen, the growth of the 2nd and 6th Army Corps, and the departure of the Central Red Army from Hunan together made it necessary and possible for the KMT to start a suppression campaign in the this area in January 1935. Taking part in this campaign were about 80 regiments, 100,000 men of the Hunan and Hubei armies. They were divided into six assault columns under the general command of He Jian.[28] The news of the planned enemy assault reached the 2nd and 6th Army Corps just as they received a telegram from the Party Center and the Military Council; the latter had just finished the Zunyi Conference and were planning to force their way across the Yangtze River. The telegram dated January 20, 1935, contained a special item concerning the 2nd and 6th Army Corps:

To facilitate the fulfillment of this plan, the 2nd and 6th Army Corps should quickly move to and settle in the general areas of Xiushan, Qianjiang, Pengshui, Songtao, Yinjiang, and Yanhe. It should also dispatch one part to expand into the area of Xianfeng, Laifeng, Xuanen, and Enshi to carry out guerrilla activities in order to create a favorable situation for driving into eastern Sichuan and threatening the land-and-water communications of the lower Yangtze River valley, to check and distract Chiang Kai-shek's new force of encirclement, and to aid this field army and the Fourth Front Army in their effort to take over Sichuan.[29]

Ten days later the Politburo and Military Council sent another telegram to the 2nd and 6th Army Corps, asking them to undertake more active operations, first in western Hunan and western Hubei, then in Guizhou and Sichuan, and "if necessary, to apply the main forces of the Red Army to break through the enemy's encirclement to strike into the broad area of Guizhou and Sichuan."[30] Of course, these plans were all to benefit the Central Red Army. Ren Bishi and He Long, like Zhang Guotao and Xu Xiangqian, could not follow such instructions. In fact, the Party Center itself quickly changed its mind. Failing to cross the Yangtze River and drifting down to the south, it rescinded the above orders. Instead of advancing west to Guizhou and Sichuan, the 2nd and 6th Army Corps withdrew to the east where the enemy was weaker and more vulnerable. There they finally found opportunities to defeat one enemy division in February and destroy another enemy brigade in March. Then they struck back and recovered most of the lost territory. The first suppression campaign ended thus in favor of the Communists.[31]

The KMT's second encirclement started in early June and ended in late August 1935. Although this time the two provinces of Hunan and Hupei cooperated more closely, the Communists still managed to win the battle. They employed the strategies of mobile warfare to wipe out two enemy divisions in the northern border area. The commander of the KMT 44th Division (Zhang Zhenhan) was captured, and the commander of the 85th Division (Xie Chen) was killed. The Communists held Zhang first as an instructor of military technology and then as a hostage for ransom. Later on, they brought him all the way to Yan'an and released him as a bargaining counter at the beginning of the renewed collaboration with the KMT in 1937.[32]

After their victory in the second campaign, the total membership of the 2nd and 6th Army Corps jumped to 21,000, almost three times as many as a year before, when they joined forces in northern Hunan. Once again, they demonstrated that the provincial armies alone could hardly cope with the Red Army's main forces. To win over the Red Army in this region, the KMT needed a unified command and participation of the KMT Central Army.

At the military conference chaired by Chiang Kai-shek at Chengdu in October 1935, Chen Cheng was appointed the head of the Yichang Headquarters to fight with the 2nd and 6th Army Corps. As the 2nd and 6th Army Corps were located in the strategic regions of Central China, Chiang was particularly concerned.[33] In this third encirclement campaign, Chen Cheng employed the provincial armies in Hunan and Hubei—80 regiments altogether—as checking forces deployed to the north, the south, and the west, while he transferred 40 regiments of the KMT Central Army and some northern troops—who had all participated in the military campaigns against the Central Soviet—to attack from the east. The situation of the Communists was most grave. After a few initial unsuccessful encounters, they began to consider a basic change in strategy. For this, He

Long and Ren Bishi consulted with the central leadership, as they were accustomed to do.[34]

The 6th Army Corps maintained constant radio communication with the Party Center from July 1934 to October 1934. They brought all radio equipment to the joint troops after the union with the 3rd Army. In July 1935, their contact with the Party Center was abruptly broken. In late September, 1935, soon after the First Front Army split with the Fourth Front Army, Mao and Zhou tried to reach Ren Bishi and He Long. But since their secret codes were left with the General Headquarters, they could only use open codes. The telegram was delivered in the name of Zhou Enlai, as the former leader of the Military Council and the Red Army Headquarters. Ren replied to Zhou's call in secret codes, of course, and this reply was received by the Red Army Headquarters and passed to the hands of Zhang Guotao. In the name of the Military Council and General Headquarters, Zhang and Zhu responded in secret codes. Although it was Mao and Zhou who first remembered the existence of another Red Army group, Zhang, once reminded, was not so foolish as to ignore the whole matter.[35] In answering the 2nd and 6th Army Corps' question concerning a strategic transfer in face of the enemy's new encirclement, however, Zhang Guotao could only offer a vague and flexible suggestion:

> To stubbornly defend the present area is obviously no good, but to wage a decisive battle for defense is also something which should not be attempted lightly; if you go for a long distance expedition, big losses of troops may once again occur. Therefore, consider just moving out of the enemy encirclement and coaxing the enemy to leave their blockhouses and then concentrating your forces on smashing the enemy troops one by one.[36]

This and other telegrams of Zhang Guotao to Ren Bishi convey a hint that Zhang was not much concerned with the 2nd and 6th Army Corps, and that he was also uncertain about what concrete suggestions to offer. His remarks sound thoughtless. He clearly did not yet fully realize, politically and militarily, the importance of the 2nd and 6th Army as the third biggest Communist force. In October 1935, Zhang was still obsessed with the grandiose idea that his Fourth Front Army alone could take all Sichuan and create a suitable situation there.

As the Red Army Headquarters had already consented to the plan for strategic transfer and, more decisively, as the KMT troops were quickly approaching, a joint conference of the Party and Army of the combined 2nd and 6th Corps was held in early November 1935. They decided to break through the encirclement and fight out of the Soviet base. Initially, their idea was to move only as far as the Hunan-Guizhou border or eastern

Guizhou—He Long's 3rd Army had done this before—but the gravity of the present situation gradually forced them onto another Long March.[37]

On November 19, the two Red Army corps broke across the Li River, guarded by a general of the Hunan army, Li Jue. They marched southeast, crossed the Wan River, and entered the affluent central Hunan area of Xupu and Xinhua. This maneuver distracted the enemy's attention to the southeast and allowed the Communists to gather material supplies and manpower—both necessary for their later shift west to open a new base at the Hunan-Guizhou border. At first, these ploys succeeded. The Communists left central Hunan heading west and captured Zhijiang and Qianyang in late December 1935. As the pursuing Nationalists' five columns drew closer with 14 divisions and 70 regiments, the Communists had to fight and win a decisive battle in order to get a foothold in this border area. But the KMT Central Army commanded by Fan Songpu proved too sturdy for the Red Army Corps. Instead of winning the battle, the Communists lost 1,000 men at Bianshui. They had to run further west.[38] At Jiangkou in eastern Guizhou, they joined forces with Zhang Zhenkun, who had remained at the old base with one division. After the KMT occupied the Soviet base, Zhang could not withstand the pressure; he had to burst out of the base area and run straight southwest to join the main forces.

In mid-January 1936, the Ren and He's troops reached Jiangkou and Shiqian in eastern Guizhou, where they had first met in October 1934. But with substantial enemy armies following closely behind and after their losses in the Bianshui battle, they had to give up their original plan of taking up residence here. At one point the enemy troops they faced totalled as many as 130 regiments. They reached Qianxi, passed through Yuqing, Wongan Xiuwen, Qianxi and Dafang and eventually came to Bijie at the very northwest tip of Guizhou. After several unsuccessful attempts at fighting the pursuing enemy, particularly Fan Songpu of the KMT Central Army, they entered Yunnan province. They avoided the Yunnan army led by Sun Wei, drove south along the Yunnan-Guizhou border, and arrived at the Panjiang River valley in late March 1936.[39]

In the Panjiang River valley, a minor dispute arose between the 2nd and 6th Army Corps and the Red Army Headquarters. The combined troops were thinking of staying in this area and opening a Soviet base. They had fairly plausible arguments: the area was enclosed by three rivers between two provinces, far from any big strategic cities; the local warlord, You Guocai, was weak and had no combat experience; this region had a dense population and a rich supply of grains; and above all, most of the pursuing enemy troops—except the Yunnan army under Sun Wei—were hesitant in military operations either for lack of interest in this frontier area or out of worry about their home provinces right before the Guangdong and Guangxi Revolt broke out. The far-flung expedition of the KMT troops left space for the warlords of the Guangdong and Guangxi provinces to plot a rebellion, which broke out in two months. Ren Bishi reported to the Red Army Headquarters on the situation at that time:

> The enemy forces around us were reduced to only those of Sun, Guo, Li, Fan and Hao—totalling a bit more than 50 regiments. The Sichuan army stayed north of the Yangtze River and a part of the Guizhou army withdrew from the encirclement to strengthen their defense against the Guangxi army on the Guangxi-Guizhou border. All the enemy troops were extremely tired, greatly reduced in number and depressed in morale. No reinforcements were available. Because of the conflicts between Guangdong and Nanking, the Guangxi army was not active, nor were its troops strong; Li and Guo claimed they had lost more than half of their men and kept asking permission to return to Hunan; only Sun Wei seemed a bit more active. All this was favorable for our army. There appeared the most favorable conditions in this expedition. We planned to defeat Sun and Guo, to create a new base and a new prospect.[40]

After three months of expedition, the 2nd and 6th Army Corps still maintained their original force of 18,000 soldiers. Their losses on the way were just offset by their recruitment. This was another favorable factor which made Ren Bishi, He Long, and many others think that they could defeat local warlords and create a new prospect in the Panjiang River valley. Thinking was as good as day-dreaming: they were still not absolutely certain whether to stay or to move. Ren Bishi's telegram to the Red Army Headquarters did not bear a very resolute tone.

It was also in March 1936 that the Fourth Front Army failed in their attack of southeast Sichuan and retreated to Xikang. Zhang Guotao's depressed troops were badly in need of inspiration and reinforcement. A telegram was therefore sent back to the 2nd and 6th Army Corps, suggesting that they cross the Yangtze River and join the Fourth Front Army in the north. Ren Bishi replied to the telegram with mixed views on March 29. First he discussed the possibility of opening a new base in the present area and his wish to do so; then he admitted it was technically possible for his troops to cross the river without much difficulty. Eventually he requested the General Headquarters to make a more definite decision on his behalf. Ren's telegram had a rather suggestive ending.

> Finally, we have not been well informed of current developments of national and international affairs, and therefore cannot exactly estimate whether we should go north immediately or whether we will be plunged into isolation and difficulties if left to the south of the Yangtze River alone. For this reason, we hope that the Military Council can decide and inform us if we should

move north to meet the main forces right now or if we should remain at the present Guizhou-Yunnan border. Please let us know in one or two days.[41]

Among other things, this telegram clearly shows the dependent status of the 2nd and 6th Army Corps as a smaller Red Army group and the gentle character of Ren Bishi as a communist politician. He Long was among those who stood firmly against moving north. In fact, He's most insistent concern at that time was not the general issue of national or international affairs, but rather the independent operation of his own troops. His later account of this episode seemed as bland as his personality.

Why did we go across the Jinsha River? We had argued over this issue. The first telegram (from Red Army Headquarters) required us to prepare ginger, pepper, clothes, and such stuff. We disagreed. The second telegram designated five ferry spots, and the third telegram ordered us to go across the River. We crossed the River according to these orders. A lot of the comrades were unwilling to do that. Their reason was simple: As for the revolution, we should also need to drop some troops in the South.[42]

The 2nd and 6th Army Corps were a minor force in the Army; Ren Bishi and He Long were lower level leaders in the Party Center—they were liable to depend on orders from above to decide their strategic actions. The next day, the General Headquarters, or Zhang Guotao, sent back a telegram of its decision. The introduction of national and international situations which constituted part of the telegram was both pretentious and ambiguous, but there should be little mistake about its essential purpose. While disguising the desperate condition he was facing, Zhang expressed in more eager terms his hope that Ren and He would go north to join his men.

1. As indicated by the national and international situations, the revolution is surging ahead, and the Soviet movement is somewhat developing, but no overestimation should be advisable. The Chiang enemy was weakened, but it is hard to tell when it will topple.
2. It is most desirable for you to take the third or last ferry spot to cross the River and join us to go north together. You can first move to western Yunnan where we would do our best to receive you.
3. If there is too much difficulty you may also stay and operate in the vast area of Yunnan, Guizhou and Sichuan provinces, but you should prepare for a long period of mobile warfare.
4. This order is not binding; you can take your action according to concrete conditions.[43]

Although there had been much hesitation in making their decision, once it was decided, Ren Bishi and He Long quickly took action. They started on April 1, 1936. A three-week-long race took them through central Yunnan via a dozen counties including Qujing, Malong, Xudian, Banqiao, Yuanmu, Yanfeng, Binchuan and Heqing. Each day they covered more than 100 li. On April 24, the 2nd Army Corps reached the ferry spot of Shigu while the 6th Army Corps got to the Judian ferry, ready for crossing. The pursuing enemy was just a short distance behind; there was only one boat in Judian; it could carry only 40 people at a time. To increase its capacity, the Red Army soldiers tied a tree trunk to the boat. Another 20 men could hold the trunk and float in the water behind the boat. Thus, in one day and one night, all the Red Army men were brought to the northern bank of the Jinsha River.[44] On April 29, they arrived at Zhongdian in the northwest corner of the Yunnan province, leaving all the pursuing armies far behind.

They covered the last part of their march to the Fourth Front Army in more than two months through the West China highland with snow mountains, torrential rivers and Tibetan tribes. There were no enemy troops, excepting hostile Tibetan tribes. Hunger and illness were more dangerous than human foes. Up through Zhongdian the two army corps still had 17,000 men, but when they finally reached Ganzi and united with the Fourth Front Army, they were reduced to 14,000. In total, the 2nd and 6th Army Corps lost about 4,000 men in this expedition; among them, 3,000—or three fourths—were left not on any battlefield but on the Tibetan plateau.[45] Summarizing the lessons of this experience, Ren Bishi later reported to the Party Center that, on an expedition like this, the Red Army had to fight and win some battles either for stopping the enemy's pursuit or for setting up a new base, that they had to strive to their utmost to collect material supplies and recruits anywhere they traveled. Ren suggested that the Communists should never lightly enter any barren and vacant lands.[46]

A Necessary Road to the North

Failing to open a new base in western Sichuan, and pushed back to the distant Xikang plateau, the Fourth Front Army was greatly drained, materially and spiritually. The whole army was eager, probably overly eager, to find a way out. The leaders were pondering another strategic move, though they were unsure where and how they would manage it. At the same time, they were trying to coax the 2nd and 6th Army Corps to join them. Ostensibly, these two actions seemed perfectly compatible. As soon as the two Red Army troops were united, they might march together.

The bitter lessons drawn from the unhappy experience with the First Front Army taught the Fourth Front Army the better handling of this second union, at least superficially. On May 5, 1936, at a mass rally to commemorate Marx's birthday, Zhang Guotao warned his men against any verbal disparagement of the 2nd and 6th Army Corps at the forthcoming meeting. "Such education should carry down to every bodyguard and horse groomer," Zhang said, "because even a bit of irresponsible and inappropriate gossips of a bodyguard or a horse groomer may possibly cause undesirable problems for the two armies."[47]

The 32nd Army and part of the 4th Army were dispatched to the south to welcome the 2nd and 6th Army Corps. These FFA troops defeated the KMT army led by Li Baobing and took over Yajiang in mid-April. From there they turned west to the city of Lihua, thus opening a passage for their upcoming comrades through the vast space west of the Yalong River. Zhang Guotao anxiously looked forward to the union. But would this union positively or negatively influence his position within the Fourth Front Army and later within the Party and Army as a whole? This question remained out of the picture at this juncture.[48]

Despite the animosity generated by the abrupt split in September 1935, the First and Fourth Front Armies maintained constant telegram communication. After all, their conflicts were but an internal problem of the Communist Party. Whether in view of their common struggle against the KMT or their attempt to control each other in order to claim legitimacy in the Party and Army, this contact was necessary. Both sides, and especially Mao's, kept a moderate and diplomatic profile in their messages. When, in December 1935, Zhang Guotao proclaimed the founding of his own Party Center and requested the dissolution of the Party Center in northern Shaanxi, Mao and his men were restrained enough not to immediately respond to such an obvious insult. They sent just a personal letter in the name of Zhang Wentian to Zhang Guotao, requesting that he abolish his "false Party Center." Not until February, when the First Front Army firmly took a stand in northern Shaanxi and the Fourth Front Army suffered defeats in western Sichuan, did the Politburo pass a formal resolution denouncing Zhang Guotao.[49]

Ever since his arrival in northern Shaanxi in late November 1935, Lin Yuying—due to his own benevolence as the envoy of the Comintern and also at the encouragement by the Party Center leaders—offered himself as an impartial conciliator between the two sides. The August 1 Manifesto and an excerpt of the Resolution of the 7th Congress of the Comintern were telegrammed to Zhang Guotao, informing him of the new policy of the anti-Fascist united front.[50] Zhang had no difficulty in accepting this less idealistic, more practical policy. Only ten days after the Preparatory Congress of the Sichuan Soviet, in which the policy of the Soviet was the main theme, Zhang spoke in a meeting of Party and Army activists on January 28, 1935, warmly welcoming the new policy of "uniting with all classes, all parties, and all armed forces to form a national front against the Japanese." The slogan of land revolution and Soviet government was consequently withdrawn.[51] This shift to a new line was accepted with such speed and smoothness because of the embracing influence of the Comintern and the nature of Zhang's own political position. Zhang, as well as Mao, had stood against the "radical idealists" in the Party Center for a long time.

As far as the Party leadership was concerned, however Zhang grew even more opposed to Mao. The conflict between the revolutionary idealists and the political pragmatists could be more easily solved because their debate focused on correct and wrong strategy; the conflict among the pragmatic politicians could scarcely be solved, centering as it did over questions of superiority and inferiority in the Party leadership. There could only be one supreme leader. Therefore, at the end of his speech Zhang suggested that a provisional Party Center be established in a suitable location and that organizational disputes be decided at a future Seventh Congress. Before that took place, he further proposed, the CCP mission to the Comintern should assume the responsibility of general leadership under which Mao's side was entitled to the Northwest Bureau and Zhang's side to the Southwest Bureau. Both groups would relinquish their titles of Party Center.[52] This may have sounded like a fair suggestion and compromise; but in fact, Zhang's Party Center had never had the legitimacy that Mao's commanded, even in the eyes of his own followers, perhaps even in Zhang's own view. Now the inferior, under less favorable conditions, he compromised on equality.

This suggestion was neither formally accepted nor formally rejected by Mao. Both sides remained consumed with their own business, aware that their external strength would eventually decide their internal positions. The difference, in the spring of 1936, was that Mao's First Front Army faired well in northern Shaanxi, while Zhang's Fourth Front Army suffered heavily on its southern expedition in Sichuan. Retreating to the Xikang-Tibet border area, Zhang Guotao kept his own Party Center and continued denouncing Mao and his followers. This was done to maintain his own position in the Fourth Front Army and the solidarity of its troops, and not meant as a serious claim to the central leadership of the Party and Army. Thus, at another meeting of the Party and Army activists on April 1, 1936, Zhang said:

> The errors of Mao, Zhou, Zhang, and Bo lie in the fact that, at the time of the union of the First and Fourth Front Armies, the former had just undergone an 8-month long march and was in need of respite and reorganization.

At the same time, the combined force of the two Red Armies would have enabled us to start a counterattack on the enemy. They underestimated such an opportunity and adopted a flightist policy to retreat under the cloak of leftist fallacy. . . . They were used to bragging and boasting, all the time chanting that they had defeated the enemy and they had won victories even after they deserted the Central Soviet, without the most cursory scientific Marxist analyses.[53]

As the 2nd and 6th Army Corps drew close to the Fourth Front Army in the south, however, Zhang Guotao's tone in criticizing the Party Center decreased in severity. With another Red Army group about to arrive, it would be perceived as impertinent to snap at the Mao and the CRA so blatantly and claim his men as the Party Center so arrogantly. Another conference of Party and Army activists in the FFA was held on June 6, 1936, when Luo Binghui's 32nd Army and Xiao Ke's 6th Army Corps met in Lihua. Zhang Guotao offered an interesting speech at the conference, in which he attempted to surprise the audience with two pieces of "happy news." The first was, of course, the union with the 6th Army Corps, and the second one was described by Zhang as follows:

The other happy news I am offering you is that now our Party has reached unification not only organizationally but also politically. In December of last year we adopted a resolution concerning the upsurge of the national revolution and the Party's strategic line according to the instructions of the Comintern. The same resolution was also passed by other groups—the northern Shaanxi side and the 2nd and 6th Army Corps. In this period of revolutionary development, we were all struggling hard for the realization of this resolution and had already achieved remarkable results. Our relations with northern Shaanxi have also improved recently. We have approached the same political line and we have also begun to cooperate in practical operations and military measures.[54]

In more concrete terms, Zhang elaborated on a bilateral agreement reached between the CRA in northern Shaanxi and the FFA in western Xikang. Whether such an agreement actually existed between the two sides, how, if it did, it was made, and in whose name it was approved— these questions remain open. This speech may certainly be burdened with personal and factional biases, but its value as a unique historical source cannot be over-stressed. It continues,

Both sides agree to discontinue their use of the title 'Party Center' and let the Mission to the Comintern temporarily exercise the function of the Party Center. As we all know, the Mission to the Comintern is headed by Comrade Chen Shaoyu; there are other comrades too, and a member of the

Mission, Comrade Lin Yuying, is now back at home in China. On the northern Shaanxi side there are eight members and seven alternate members of the Central Committee, and our side has seven members and three alternate members of the Central Committee. There are about 20 comrades in the Comintern. Thus, the northern Shaanxi side is called the Northern Bureau in charge of the Party and Army work in that area. In addition, of course, there was also the Shanghai Bureau and the Northeast Bureau in the white areas; and we now become the Northwest Bureau.[55]

Standing in an obviously inferior position in terms of Party Center majority and authority and bearing in mind the inferior claim to legitimacy of Party Center he had formed at the Zhuomubao Conference, Zhang was glad to strive for an equal position. However, regarding the Red Army— in which he had the upper hand—Zhang did not offer to share his leadership with anybody—not Mao and his Party Center in northern Shaanxi, nor Wang Ming and his Mission of the Comintern in Moscow. Therefore, Zhang declared in the same speech:

> The unitary leadership in military affairs remains the same and its organization remains the same as what was established at the time of the union of the First and Fourth Front Armies. Comrade Zhu De is Chairman of the Military Council and General Commander of the Red Army; Comrade Zhang Guotao is Vice-Chairman of the Military Council and Political Commissar of the Red Army. Comrade Chen Changhao is Director of the General Political Department. Three front armies are to be formed: The northern Shaanxi side is the First Front Army with Comrade Peng Dehuai as General Commander; the 2nd and 6th Army are the Second Front Army with Comrade He Long as General Commander; and the 4th, 5th, 9th, 30th, 31st, and 32nd Armies still belong to the Fourth Front Army with Comrade Xu Xiangqian as General Commander and Comrade Chen Changhao as General Political Commissar.[56]

Which side is right and which one is wrong? Zhang Guotao could not easily avoid addressing the question of intraparty struggles, which had lasted so long and been debated in so open a manner. In reference to this, Zhang could only glorify himself and his men in the Fourth Front Army as followers of the Comintern line from the very beginning, while deprecating Mao and his Central Red Army as late comers to the Comintern line. "Our struggle against their erroneous line was correct," he said, "but now that the comrades in northern Shaanxi have returned to the Comintern line, we should unite with them to fight our common enemy."[57]

Perhaps these remarks were meant to comfort Zhang's men and Zhang himself. Perhaps they were delivered on the slightest possibility that Mao and his men were listening. As a record of what had happened in the past, there might have been some truth to what Zhang said. Unfortunately, his main purpose in these remarks was not to review the past but to argue for his shaky position at present. For such a purpose, he ought to have been more confident about the current situation, rather than just recalling his glorious past time. It was exactly the current situation which was nagging him. Zhang stubbornly stuck to this attitude until June. The arrival of the third force of Ren Bishi and He Long altered his position, unexpectedly and yet naturally.

In early June, the 32nd Army of the FFA finally met with the 16th Division of the 6th Army Corps in Jiawa, south of Lihua. All the troops of the 2nd and 6th Army Corps followed to arrive at Ganzi, where Ren Bishi and He Long met with Zhang Guotao and Zhu De, at the end of the month. There appeared another happy union of the Red Armies on the Long March. Everything seemed to be going smoothly, but only at the beginning and on a superficial level.[58]

Situated between two strong opposing sides in the Party and Army, Ren Bishi could not have had much independence. But aware of his lack of independence, and because of it, Ren tried to maintain an independent and impartial position as a conciliator and mediator. Perhaps this should be taken as a rule for all "third parties" in the political arena. As the 2nd and 6th Army Corps came near the center of Ganzi, more frequent contacts with the Fourth Front Army brought them not only food and ammunition but also the political propaganda of the party conflict. Some lower rank military leaders, like Xiao Ke, were much more susceptible to Zhang Guotao's persuasion. Xiao soon accepted the Fourth Front Army's stand, and was inclined to believe that the First Front Army had indeed committed serious errors. Ren Bishi proved more prudent politically. Even before the union, he wrote to Gan Siqi, the Director of the Political Department of the 6th Army Corps, giving him special instructions about relations with the Fourth Front Army! No words which might lead to disunion of the Party and the Army were to be accepted from the Fourth Front Army or passed to their own troops. No comments about the split between the First and Fourth Front Armies would be allowed. No documents issued by Zhang Guotao in the name of the Party Center were to be distributed. When the two troops finally met at Ganzi and a joint Party conference was suggested by Zhang Guotao, Ren Bishi balked: Who was to make the general report? Who was to draw the conclusion if disagreements occurred? Under what organizational aegis could the conference be convened?[59] In the face of such objections, Zhang had no choice but to give up his plan of convening a formal Party conference. Ren Bishi's attitude, however, could hardly be taken as evidence of his deliberate support of Mao against Zhang, as many Communist historians would claim later. It was merely a basic requirement of his 'third force' position.

In early July, 1936, a joint conference of the two Red Army groups was held at Ganzi to deal with the situation after the union. The Ganzi Conference was called one of Party and Army activists, without a more formal title. All the leading figures on the two sides attended the conference. There were approximately 15 participants including the Party Committee members of the Fourth Front Army and the Military Sub-Council members of the 2nd and 6th Army Corps, except those, like Xu Xiangqian and Liu Bocheng, who were engaged at the front. Apart from Zhang Guotao, Chen Changhao, Zhu De, Ren Bishi, He Long and Guan Xiangying, other attenders might have been Li Zuoran, Fu Cong, Xiao Ke, Wang Zhen, and others.[60] Throughout the conference, all sensitive topics which might lead to discussion of intraparty problems were avoided; only the most necessary questions, such as unified organization and joint military operations, were treated. To the satisfaction of both sides—but with respective reservations— the 2nd and 6th Army Corps were formally combined into one unit under the title of the Second Front Army with He Long appointed as the General Commander and Ren Bishi as the Political Commissar. The proposal that the Second and Fourth Front Armies should move north without any hesitation or delay received unanimous approval. On the northern march, the Fourth Front Army took the lead in three columns while the Second Front Army followed as one column at the rear.[61]

Although the Ganzi Conference tried not to mention the conflict between Mao's First Front Army and Zhang's Fourth Front Army, or between Mao's Party Center and Zhang's Army Headquarters, it remained the subtext of the meeting. There were problems which could not simply be passed over. For instance, what kind of formal Party organization should they assume themselves to be? After all, they were Communists and they had to have a Communist Party title. Neither the title Party Center nor that of Provincial Party Center seemed appropriate. To attain a legal title to the combined forces, Ren and others proposed formation of the Northwest Bureau, but such a bureau had to be approved by some authority outside themselves. A more profound though less apparent issue was the fact that the military operations of Zhang Guotao and his troops were related not only to the KMT enemy but also to their own intraparty relationships. In other words, their military arrangements had various direct or indirect connections with the Central Red Army at northern Shaanxi.

After June 1936, when the Fourth Front Army and the 2nd and 6th Army Corps were merged, Zhang Guotao seldom let slip any open opinions about the mistakes of Mao and the Central Red Army. Meanwhile, the combination of the two armies subtly shifted the power structure. Since now two military forces balanced each other, political influence would gain an edge over the military strength. More concretely, Zhang Guotao's overall control was roughly shaken, while Zhu De's influence slightly increased;

on the 2nd Front Army side, Ren Bishi's position as the spokesman was more firmly established while He Long's authority was further reduced.[62]

Moreover, the union itself had decided the military operation. Zhang Guotao had neither clearly anticipated nor exactly calculated this effect. His attempt to persuade the 2nd and 6th Army Corps to give up their own base and join the Fourth Front Army was apparently an inspiration for the reinforcement of his baffled troops, but it also preordained his military operation. If the Guangdong and Guangxi Revolt had taken place a few months earlier—i.e., not in June but in April—Zhang might have acquiesced to Ren and He's request that they remain in the south instead of coming north. The two Red Army groups could then have worked as strategically coordinated forces to take advantage of the conflicts within the KMT ranks—Xue Yue's troops at western Sichuan and Wei Lihuang's troops at the Yunnan-Guizhou border would be called back as soon as the Guangdong and Guangxi Revolt happened—and reattempt a successful maneuver in such southern provinces as Sichuan, Guizhou and Yunnan. Under these conditions, Zhang could still have claimed his favorable or equal position to Mao. But now that the 2nd and 6th Army Corps were asked to come north, such a possibility was automatically ruled out. The two Red Armies as a whole now took going north immediately for granted. For a short while, Zhang Guotao was still inclined to stay in the Xikang area for a few more months waiting for any possible change in the current situation before deciding the next step. He was not resolute on this point, and it was also incompatible with the general mood in both the armies, including his own men.

Turning back to the north naturally meant an acknowledgement of Zhang's own failure and a surrender to northern Shaanxi, no matter what slogans or excuses Zhang could create to comfort himself. The combined forces left little possibility for Zhang to impose his own decision. Dragged by the Second Front Army, the Fourth Front Army could hardly repel the Central Red Army's attraction. On their way to the north, the joint troops could not even resist following Mao's previous path toward the northeast, instead of turning northwest as Zhang had preferred.[63]

In early July, the combined forces started from Ganzi with the Fourth Front Army leading the way and the Second Front Army following behind. Zhang Guotao might say that his men went ahead to take the burden of enemy attacks, but He Long and Ren Bishi did not seem grateful. There was little military resistance on the way, but natural conditions more than made up for the lack. The apparent benevolence of the Fourth Front Army seemed more like a scheme against the Second Front Army, for the latter following behind found it harder to find enough material supplies—Zhang's troops grabbed all the food and left nothing for Ren and He's men to eat. The appalling situation is recalled in *Zhang Ziyi's Diary on the Long March:*

Table 8.1 Joint Forces of the Second and Fourth Front Armies

Northwestern Bureau of the CCP Central Committeee

Secretary	Zhang Guotao
Vice Secretary	Ren Bishi
Members:	Zhang Guotao, Ren Bishi, Zhu De, He Long, Chen Changhao, Xu Xiangqian, Guan Xiangying

Fourth Front Army Headquarters (4th, 5th, 9th, 30th, 31st Armies)

General Commander	Zhu De
General Political Commissar	Zhang Guotao
Vice General Commander	Xu Xiangqian
Director of Political Department	Chen Changhao
Chief of General Staff	Liu Bocheng

Second Front Army Headquarters (2nd, 6th, 32nd Armies)

General Commander	He Long
General Political Commissar	Ren Bishi
Vice General Commander	Xiao Ke
Vice General Commissar	Guan Xiangying
Chief of General Staff	Li Da
Director of Political Department	Gan Siqi[64]

July 23, a sunny and clear day.
The 17th Division and the Model Division set off from the Xiqun Temple. Most troops had no food at all and could not gather any along the way; they had to eat wild weeds and then stinking corpse. All were extremely fatigued and exhausted, and 200 men were lost in the 2nd Division alone.[65]

There is one point in this diary which should be particularly noticed. From the literal meaning in Chinese, it would seem that "stinking corpse" referred to a human rather than animal body. Had this been the case, it would have added to the great tragedy or the tragic greatness of the Long March. When Zhang's diary was published, however, the compiler purposefully pointed out that what Zhang described as "stinking corpse" only meant horse bones thrown away by the preceding Red Army troops.

In late July 1936, the Communists arrived at Aba; from there went across the Gaqu River—which had been declared impassable by Zhang Guotao a year before—and reached the Baozuo and Baxi area. There they received a telegram from northern Shaanxi approving the formation of the Northwest Bureau of the CCP with Zhang Guotao as secretary, Ren Bishi as vice-secretary, Zhu De, He Long, Guan Xiangying, Chen Changhao, and Xu Xiangqian as members. Though Zhang might have wondered whether this could really be a decision of the Comintern, or the CCP Mission to the Comintern, or their representative—even Zhang Hao or Lin Yuying's personal freedom seemed questionable in Zhang's eyes—he had to accept this assignment at least for the purpose of controlling the two army forces at present. Accepting this new appointment amounted to abandoning his challenge to the legitimacy of Mao and the Party Center.[66]

In August, the Second and Fourth Front Armies followed the former road of the First Front Army, passed Lazikou and reached Hadapu. An encouraging situation awaited them. They were happy to find rice paddies and warm Han people, and the KMT Central Army was still absent in the south. It was at this juncture that each Red Army group began to operate for its own interest rather than continuing north. They preferred to stay at the present location, taking full advantage of the convenient conditions. On his own initiative, He Long directed his men to the east and quickly occupied four affluent counties in southwest Shaanxi. They obtained a lot of goods and were encouraged by heavy recruitment. They might have gone further into southern Shaanxi if the KMT Central Army had not returned to stop them in early September.[67]

Zhang Guotao led his troops to the west, occupied the Yao River Valley and opened a temporary base of his own in southern Gansu. In the General Headquarters, Zhu De was anxious to continue north to join his own Central Red Army in the name of Western Expeditionary Army under the command of Peng Dehuai; Zhang Guotao was more interested in moving further west; and Ren Bishi was content with the successes of his troops in the east. On September 19, therefore, a conference of the Northwest Bureau was convened in order to organize a concerted operation. The participants at the Minzhou Conference resolved to orchestrate the "Huining and Jingning Campaign," which required the Fourth Front Army to move north for a joint operation with the First Front Army, while the Second Front Army followed at the rear. For several reasons, however, Zhang Guotao was reluctant to move north. If the combat at Huining and Qingning were lost, it would certainly cost his own strength; if it were won, it would mean an expansion of Mao's northern Shaanxi base. Therefore, he was inclined to employ his troops to hunt out new prospects far down to the west. His field commander Chen Changhao seemed more eager to stay at the present location and form a base in southern Gansu, looking askance at both north and west.[68]

The divergence among the three Red Army groups, added to the disagreements within the Fourth Front Army, delayed their military action for a week before another conference had to be called at Zhangxian. Zhu De sent a secret telegram to northern Shaanxi to disclaim responsibility for this delay, as well as his guilt in the past year:

1. The plan of the Huining-Jingning Campaign resolved by the Northwest Bureau has just begun to be executed. But now a few comrades raised disagreement and want to overthrow the whole combat plan.
2. I will call together comrades in the Northwest Bureau to Zhangxian for further discussions and I will inform you about the result later.
3. I myself firmly abided by the original plan. If it could not be realized, it is not my responsibility at all.[69]

Zhang Guotao's factional interest was too set to be dissuaded, but at that same time was too obvious to be supported. The Zhangxian Conference participants again decided that the Fourth Front Army should immediately go north, meet with the First Front Army, and begin a joint campaign to take over Ningxia; the Second Front Army, meanwhile, should operate in the south as a checking force. The conflicts among the three Red Army groups might well have lasted eternally, had they not been stopped by the approaching KMT enemy.

The Guandong and Guangxi Revolt against the KMT central government at Nanking broke up in early June 1936. Though many factors had contributed to this Revolt, the most profound was that the long, large-scale engagement of the Nanking government with the Red Army had allowed the warlord-generals in the southeast to grow strong and ambitious. The combined forces of Chen Jitang of Guangdong and Li Zongren of Guangxi totalled 300,000 troops, and Chiang Kai-shek had to transfer all Central Army forces from anti-Communist fronts to the south to cope with the emerging situation: Xue Yue from western Sichuan, Fan Songpu from eastern Yunnan and Hu Zongnan from southern Gansu.[70] Chiang's careful application of the threat of military force, combined with the lures of money and position, dissolved the revolt by late August 1936. This revolt of KMT local troops was by and large a pure military action without political discipline or ideological orientation; and Chiang Kai-shek was skillful and efficient in handling this kind of factional problem within the KMT.[71]

In early September, Hu Zongnan's KMT Central Army returned from the southern mission to southwest Shaanxi, where the 2nd Front Army was cheerfully expanding influence under He Long's command. Hu Zongnan naturally took He Long's troops as his first target of attack. In less than a week, He lost four consecutive battles and his forces suffered immensely. Later on, he tried to leave all blame with Zhang Guotao:

> Zhang Guotao ran west and the three KMT armies all crossed the river. All the enemy fell upon our heads to strike us. Our four divisions were put onto the battle front but could not win. Tang Xiangfeng surrendered and Yin Xianbing was captured. Zhang Guotao played such a trick on us and caused us such losses. The 17th Regiment was lost. It was only after the Fourth Front Army already left that we were given a notice to take off and turn north. The situation was urgent. We hurriedly crossed the river. The 6th Army was hit from the flank and Yan Fusheng was wounded. We were beaten on our way again and another regiment of the 2nd Army Corps was lost. We suffered another defeat in Haiyuan and I myself nearly got killed by a bomb.[72]

He Long recalled this moment as the most dangerous one in his troops' Long March. In fact, his men had enjoyed both the advantages (in the past) and disadvantages (at present) of being the third force. Depending on others did not always mean a good fortune. The Second Front Army could not have arrived at the town of Jiangjunbao for a union with the First and Fourth Front Armies until late October 1936.

The KMT Central Army's rush from the south actually helped resolve the disagreement among the Communists. Zhang Guotao was pushed to move north and eventually met with Peng Dehuai at Tongxincheng in the Huining County of the Gansu Province on October 10, 1936. This date also recorded the grand union of the three main forces of the Red Army. Although He Long had not yet arrived, Ren Bishi stayed with the General Headquarters as representative of the 2nd Front Army. At the union, the Communist leaders in northern Shaanxi originally planned to conduct a joint military campaign to take over Ningxia. The speedy arrival of Hu Zongnan's troops from the south and the withdrawal of two thirds of Zhang Guotao's army to the far west made this impossible. The Red Army had to retreat east back to their northern Shaanxi base. On the way, all Red Army groups tried to avoid sending their own troops to fight. Finally, the First Front Army had to shoulder the main responsibility in a battle to stop the pursuing enemy—the battle was fought in its territory and for its interest. This battle at Shanchengbao in late October was recalled by Nie Rongzhen, the Political Commissar of the 1st Army Corps of the Central Red Army, as follows:

In confronting the enemy, all those discords arose again. Some of them occurred as a result of defective communication technology at that time; the others were essentially a problem of lack of determination of certain army commanders. I almost got mad when Zuo Quan told me that Yang Dezhi had already driven his 2nd Division into the enemy while other troops had not yet arrived at their positions as scheduled. I had to make an urgent report on this situation to the commander of the First Front Army Headquarters, Comrade Peng Dehuai.[73]

In this manner, the three huge Red Armies finally caught two regiments of Hu Zongnan's KMT army. For the Communist leaders, the Shanchengbao battle was successful enough to be deemed a victory after the grand union. As for the KMT, Hu Zongnan's troops were also suffering from internal problems—the very same disease which had so recently weakened the Communists. No other KMT armies, and especially not the Northwestern Army, were willing to take an active role in fighting the Red Army and sharing the possible damage. Hu had to lead his troops into the pursuit unsupported. His losses at Shanchengbao were not fatal, but were grave enough to make him realize that it would do no good for him to drive deep into the Communist base alone.[74]

Mao had first dispatched Deng Xiaoping, the vice-director of the CRA Political Department, to welcome the newly arrived Red Army comrades. In November, Zhou Enlai came and met with Zhang Guotao, Ren Bishi and He Long at Hungde. This diplomatic Communist leader voiced a simple question: "How should we operate after this union of our three troops?" He Long frankly answered: "Let Peng command them all!" Thus, Ren Bishi was left Political Commissar of the Front Headquarters and Peng Dehuai became General Commander. Zhang Guotao and Zhu De led the General Headquarters back to Bao'an. A Military Council was formed with Mao as Chairman and Zhu and Zhang as Vice Chairmen.[75] In reality, Zhang lost direct touch with the military command both on the front and at the rear. Except for the Western Expedition Army, his political destiny was now dependent on the two conciliatory figures of Lin Yuying and Ren Bishi. Unfortunately, from the very beginning, neither of them seemed dependable enough. But leaving aside Zhang's personal ordeal, the Communist Party and the Red Army as a whole had now successfully completed a great transfer from the South to the North.

9

THE PROWESS OF MAO
AS POLITICAL ENTREPRENEUR

On October 10, 1936, when the three major groups of the Red Army finally joined at Huining in Gansu Province, the CCP Central Committee issued a public statement of congratulation for this jubilant occasion. All Red Army members, from Mao and Zhu down to officers and soldiers, were called national heroes worthy of the highest respect and the warmest greetings. The Central Committee predicted the commencement of a new victorious epoch in the Communist revolution.[1] In a certain sense, the Communists could indeed boast of their achievements in the past two years. Despite the close pursuit of the central and local KMT armies during the Long March, they had survived with the bulk of their military forces intact and had founded a new settlement in the North.

On the same day, coincidentally, Chiang Kai-shek was happily celebrating his 50th birthday. Chiang had left Nanking for Luoyang, presumably to avoid a special birthday ceremony. But he found a big crowd of senior officials and generals following him down to Luoyang. Dressed, respectively, in an army uniform covered with medals, and a mink coat equally decked with jewelry, Generalissimo and Madam Chiang were surrounded by officials and generals who flocking there for music and feasts lasting for three days, commemorating not only Chiang's birthday but their military triumph over the Communists.[2] They too celebrated with just cause. Only two or three years before, the Communists had had 300,000 troops and had occupied nearly 100 counties all over South and Central China. Now they were pressed into the barren Northwest highland and their regular troops were reduced to no more than 40,000 in total. It seemed that the Nationalists were on the verge of final victory over the Communists and Chiang would only need to launch another suppression campaign in the North to deal the Communists a final fatal blow.

Unclear as the status of either the KMT or the CCP might have been at the time, Mao's leadership in the CCP Center and the Red Army was a settled thing, both in title and in practice. The Communist Party was like a nearly bankrupt enterprise and Mao was its newly appointed general manager. Mao's diligence in work and charisma in central leadership are unquestionable. He was used to working day and night and oversaw almost all aspects of general management: external affairs such as negotiation, competition, propaganda and advertisement, as well as internal affairs such as organization, duty assignment and professional education. He knew the importance of proper employment of his subordinates—persuasively rallying everyone under his supervision, and preventing anyone from playing truant at any time. He paid careful attention to investing his assets, maintaining business in slack times and taking hopeful risks for rapid expansion whenever the market was flush. He showed himself a long-sighted, not small-minded, entrepreneur. Besides teaching his men technical skills, he also lectured them on the basic ethic and philosophy of their profession. He cited Marx and Lenin the same way a Protestant merchant cited the Bible—as necessary spiritual inspiration in both occasions—but never believed either Marx or God would bless those who could not take care of themselves.[3]

Toward Allies: The Xi'an Incident

Mao's foremost goal in early 1936 was making peace with the Northeastern and Northwestern Armies. Reaching a truce with these local troops would not only eliminate a grave threat to the Red Army, but provide a buffer to block the KMT Central Army from entering Shaanxi. Mao's direct concern in this moment was the survival and safety of his troops in this new land. As for considering the consequences for the distant future, it seemed too complicated to foresee. Mature and confident, Mao did not flinch from creating complicated situations. The more complicated the situation, the more the opportunities that might arise.

On January 25, 1936, Mao Zedong and Peng Dehuai, in the name of the whole Red Army, issued an open letter to all the officers and men in the Northeastern Army (NEA). The letter recalled the bitter experience of the Northeasterners—either left under the Japanese occupation or made homeless in the past years—and it protested the discrimination against the Northeastern Army by Chiang Kai-shek. "Chiang would transfer the Northeastern Army now to the Eyuwan Soviet and then to Shaanxi and Gansu to exterminate the Communists," the letter stated, "He wants Chinese to fight against other Chinese; he wants the Northeastern Army, whose troops wish to resist the Japanese, to fight the Red Army, whose troops also wish to fight the Japanese. This scheme can only please the Japanese and inflict loss and sacrifice on the Northeastern Army."[4] Applying the most earnest words and the most modest tone, the letter called for an immediate truce between the two Chinese troops.

After patient and careful work, the CCP succeeded in establishing preliminary contacts with both Zhang Xueliang and Yang Hucheng in the spring of 1936. April 9 came as a remarkable day. Zhou Enlai took a secret trip to Yan'an, then under the NEA's control, for a formal meeting with Zhang Xueliang.[5] Zhang, the "Young Marshal", who inherited the NEA troops from his warlord father, flew the airplane from Xi'an to Yan'an by himself. A young man full of romantic ideas but short on political experience, Zhang was so mesmerized with Zhou's diplomatic attractiveness at the meeting that he practically forgot his own position as a Nationalist general. "The KMT is helpless; it's no good any more," Zhang confessed to Zhou, "There are only two ways out for China, either Fascism or Communism."[6] Zhou Enlai was experienced enough to cope with this Young Marshal—outwardly frank and sincere as an individual, inwardly sticking to the interest and principles of the Communist Party and the Red Army. The conference was unexpectedly gratifying from the CCP's standpoint. Zhang not only agreed to stop fighting with the Communists but also promised to open food and ammunition trade with the them. To show his generosity, moreover, Zhang donated 20,000 silver dollars as a personal gift to the Red Army.

To solidify its relations with the NEA, the CCP Center issued an instruction on June 20 deliberating some principles in dealing with the Northeastern Army. The document was circulated within the Party apparatus. As regards a general principle, this paper offers a few noteworthy points:

The main method of winning over the Northeastern Army is to rely on our political work of patient explanation and persuasion, and to draw it politically onto the anti-Japanese front. If we fail to attract it politically and merely resort to intrigues and schemes, we will be unable to make the Northwestern Army become a firm anti-Japanese military force fighting to the very end for the sacred cause of resisting the Japanese and saving the motherland.[7]

In contrast with their attitude in dealing with the Fujian Revolt three years before, the Communists were now remarkably skillful in political negotiation. They kept up a line of patriotic slogans, such as "unite in front of the foreign invaders and fight to save the nation," instead of deluging their possible allies with impregnable revolutionary stance relentlessly insisting on class struggle on the one hand and playing underhanded "petty tricks" on the other hand—as they had done before. This Party Center's instruction did not forget concrete measures either. It called for working on the NEA by "both an upper route and a lower route" and in "both an external way and an internal way." This meant that the Communists were not only to negotiate with the NEA's senior officials but also to agitate within the NEA's rank and file, requiring public propaganda to be sent to the NEA and secret organizations to be set up within it. It insisted that "wherever the NEA troops were deployed, it would become the central work of the Party branches there to win them over" and "all the Party agents within the NEA must be absolutely secret and no parallel contacts among them are permissible."[8] Even more astute in this document was the idea that under necessary and favorable conditions, military actions could be taken against the NEA in order to maintain the alliance. But "these kind of military actions are aimed to enhance our political persuasion, not to destroy the Northeastern Army."[9] Finally, the instruction described the approach of the CCP "manager" Mao to his NEA "customer" as follows:

> The Communist Party is the leader of the Chinese revolution. It stands high above all other parties, and it is far-sighted. No matter how the Northeastern Army behaves itself, we will never stop our work on it in order to win it over. We are not dumbbells, of course, and we cannot just use one and the same method regardless of the Northeastern Army's response, to our own disadvantage. We are going to adopt various methods to deal with the various behaviors of the Northeastern Army.[10]

Once they succeeded in obtaining peace and alliance with the NEA, the Communists started to push Zhang Xueliang forward, not only to consolidate their bilateral relationship, but to extend their influence to the national political arena. The next step of Mao and the Party Center was to remove Zhang Xueliang and Yang Hucheng from Nanking's control and incite them to openly defy Chiang Kai-shek's command. In connection with this situation, it is interesting to note that when their coalition with Zhang and Yang was not yet solidified and the chances of them rising up against Chiang Kai-shek were still slim, the Communists blatantly called for an overthrow of Chiang, but later when the coalition was firmly founded and the possibility of Zhang and Yang rebelling against Chiang were actually established, the Communists toned down their accusations of Chiang. As it proved, this was the most skillful way of inciting Zhang and Yang. This use of the CCP's "political arts"—to use one of Mao's favorite terms—can be seen from a letter of Mao and Zhou to Zhang on October 5, 1936.

> Your honor is the leader of all the troops in Northwest China and you are shouldering the important responsibility of deciding the future of China, either a civil war or an anti-Japanese war. At this moment so critical for the Chinese nation and Chinese history, we beseech your honor to make an immediate decision to stop all KMT armies from attacking the Red Army, and to pass our (your humble servants) opinion to Mr. Chiang Kai-shek and help him make a quick decision to send formal representatives to negotiate with us in concrete terms in order to realize an armistice between us so that we may then fight the Japanese.[11]

Clandestine collaborations with the CCP caused various problems—totally beyond Zhang's imagination but well within Mao's expectation. Zhang was drawn into ever deeper conflicts with Chiang Kai-shek and the KMT Central Government. Among these conflicts, the August 29 Incident and the Shanchengbao Battle were most explosive. As a result of the CCP-NEA coalition, one group of Communists after another flew into the city of Xi'an and joined Yang and Zhang's troops. Their open and secret activities naturally drew the attention of the Shaanxi KMT Committee and the Shaanxi Government. On August 29, KMT policemen detected a Communist agent named Song Li working in Zhang Xueliang's troops and arrested him. On the way to the police station, however, Yang Hucheng's garrison troops detained both the captives and the captor. Zhang Xueliang ordered that Song Li be set free immediately. Fearing the materials and reports the Shaanxi KMT Committee might have filed concerning his contacts with the Communists, Zhang sent troops to the Committee Headquarters to confiscate all the secret archival files there. Afterwards Zhang telegraphed Chiang Kai-shek begging his pardon. As this occurred at the height of the Guangxi-Guangdong Revolt, Chiang had to simply swallow this bitter pill.[12]

During the Shanchengbao Battle in late October 1936, Zhang's troops constituted part of the KMT offensive force, but Wang Yizhe, the NEA general at the front, made all kinds of excuses not to move along with Hu Zongnan in the joint campaign against the Red Army. When one of Hu's divisions eventually fell into the Communist ambush, none of the NEA troops nearby came to the rescue. Wang Yizhe even refused to accept Hu's military telegrams. Again, Zhang had to beg Chiang's pardon for his negligence when Hu brought the issue to Nanking after the battle.[13]

Coming to Xi'an for a final talk with Zhang and Yang in early December, Chiang delineated two possibilities for Zhang and Yang: either move all their troops to the front and fight the Communists, or transfer their troops to other provinces and allow the KMT Central Army come in to fight them. Neither of the proposals could be accepted by Zhang and Yang, who were unwilling to either fight the Communists or concede their own territorial bases. The Xi'an Incident was thus a logical consequence of the CCP-NEA coalition.[14]

In the latter part of 1936, the CCP infiltrated all social circles, especially those of high school and college students, in Xi'an. From September to December, several mass rallies were held—formally sponsored by some student associations but actually manipulated by CCP agents. On December 9, 1936, a huge student demonstration with nearly 20,000 participants took place to petition Chiang Kai-shek at Lintong, about 20 miles east of Xi'an, demanding that the KMT Government stop the civil war against the Communists in order to resist the Japanese. As the students approached Lintong, Chiang ordered his guard battalion to get ready to fire and at the same time called on Zhang Xueliang to dissuade the students. Zhang hurried to catch up with the parade. Moved to tears by such slogans of the students from the Northeastern University as "We'll fight back to our old Northeastern home!" and "We'd rather die on the anti-Japanese battlefield!" the Young Marshal promised the students "a definite reply in action within one week." Now it is clear that this student demonstration was patronized by the underground CCP Northwest Special Committee.[15]

Zhang Xueliang fulfilled his promise. Three days later (on December 12), together with Yang Hucheng of the Northwestern Army, Zhang plotted a military coup, kidnapped Chiang at Lintong, and his aides in Xi'an. This coup is well known in modern Chinese history as the Xi'an Incident. The Communist leaders first knew about the incident from their liaison agent in the Northeastern Army. The next morning, when Chiang was captured in Lintong and brought back to Xi'an, a long telegram from Zhang and Yang was sent to Bao'an informing the CCP of their position and requesting Zhou Enlai to come to Xi'an for cooperation.[16] Naturally, this was a happy surprise to the Communists. Even the top leaders of the Party and the Army could not help leapfrogging and shouting "Kill Chiang," and a mass celebratory meeting was immediately held.[17] But all this emotional reaction could not be taken as the appropriate stance of the CCP Center's handling the situation. The CCP positions at the early stage of the Xi'an Incident can be seen from the telegrams the Party Center sent to the Northern Bureau. The first telegram, issued on December 12, 1936, praised the revolutionary actions of Zhang Xueliang and Yang Hucheng and demanded that Chiang Kai-shek be sent to the people for public trial.[18] Two days later, another telegram said, "We should not place ourselves in opposition to the Nanking Government; we should still pursue the policy of promoting the anti-Japanese sect and the middle sect in the Nanking Government to adopt an anti-Japanese policy."[19] Simply put, the CCP initial positions were: to support Yang and Zhang; to request a public verdict on Chiang; and to win over the Nanking Government. Even at this early stage the Communist leaders realized that Chiang as an individual person was not as important as the Nanking Government as a collective political force. At the same time, the CCP Center sent a telegram to the ECCI in Moscow. The text of this telegram is still not available, but there must have been quite a few words of self-praise, taking the incident as a victory of their own "united front policy", supporting Zhang and Yang's "revolutionary actions" and so on. The Comintern leaders did not send an immediate reply, because they had to wait for—if not totally rely upon—the decision of Stalin and the Soviet Union.

The Soviet Union learned of the Xi'an Incident first from its own men in the Russian Embassy in Nanking, and its response stemmed mainly from its diplomatic interests in East Asia at that time. It did not take much consideration of the CCP and was arrogantly ignorant of the true situation. On December 14, *Pravda* published an editorial, denouncing Zhang Xueliang and the entire event.[20] Three days later this official organ of the Russian Communist Party even went so far as to declare, "From the latest news we received from China, Zhang's rebellion was nothing but another scheme of the Japanese against China; its purpose was to obstruct the unification of China and to sabotage the ever growing anti-Japanese movement."[21] The selfishness and stubbornness of the Russian government toward the Xi'an Incident was so incredible that even the KMT ambassador to the Soviet Union found the labelling of Zhang as a Japanese agent "very funny."[22]

On December 16, the Comintern Executive Committee sent back a telegram under the name Gregory Dimitrov, the General Secretary of the ECCI. This Comintern telegram attempted to bring together the opposite stands of the Soviet Union and the CCP. But the importance of the telegram lies in the fact that it first suggested to the CCP the policy of attempting a peaceful resolution of the Xi'an Incident.

> In consideration of your telegram, we suggest that you should take the following stands:
> 1. No matter whatever motive he may have had, Zhang's action can only be objectively detrimental to the solidarity of all forces in the national anti-Japanese front and encouraging to the Japanese invasion.
> 2. Now that the incident has already happened, the CCP should take the above consideration into full account and try to solve the incident in a peaceful way.[23]

By the time this telegram arrived, the CCP Delegation headed by Zhou Enlai had already been in Xi'an. Zhou left Bao'an on December 15, and arrived at Yan'an the next day. From there Zhou took a special airplane provided by Zhang and landed at Xi'an on the afternoon of December 16, 1936. Zhou kept in mind his limited role and the fact that the Comintern's reply had not yet come. With the arrival of the Comintern's telegram on December 16 or 17 and the CCP Center's instructions on December 18, Zhou took a firm stand in searching for a peaceful conclusion to the Incident.[24]

The Soviet Union and the CCP took different positions for their own political concerns—one against the Xi'an Incident and the other for the Incident. China and the CCP were but one minor dimension of Soviet Union's diplomatic interests; for the CCP, however, the Xi'an Incident was a life and death matter and, therefore, Mao was far more serious and careful in handling it. Eventually, through the Comintern's intervention, both the Soviet Union and the CCP agreed on the quest for a peaceful solution. The problem of how to save Chiang as an individual person had by then become quite easy. The Communists did not mind letting him go free so long as they could get what they wanted for their own political advantage. Zhou Enlai's real mission was not just to release Chiang but to get the best and most from him. All the actions of the CCP from December 16 to December 25 centered on this basic idea.

A romantic and sentimental young man, Zhang Xueliang was the most eager to kidnap Chiang and then the most anxious to release him. Yang Hucheng was a resourceful elder warlord. From the beginning he was worried about the risk of this action and now, fearing Chiang's revenge, Yang was reluctant to free him without his signing any formal promise. But once the CCP lined up with Zhang for Chiang's release, Yang was persuaded to change his mind.[25]

Once again, although Zhang made the practical decision to set Chiang free, the Communists masterminded the event from prelude to epilogue. Their political prowess brought them great benefit, as is outlined in the proceeding section. Zhang Xueliang paid for his political naiveté. His cavalier spirit led him to accompany Chiang back to Nanking and, after some political ceremony and legal ritual, he was sentenced to ten years in custody. In fact, he was incarcerated for life and remains under house arrest in Taiwan even today.

The departure of Zhang Xueliang left Xi'an in great chaos. Revolts within the Northeastern Army were followed by conflicts between the Northeastern and Northwestern Armies. Yang Hucheng and his men were in no position to control the situation. While heated arguments developed as to what means—negotiation or violence—should be taken to rescue Zhang from Nanking, Mao and Zhou's fundamental interest was not to save Zhang as an individual but to reach a peaceful agreement of their own with the Nanking Government. Nonetheless, they took part in all the protests against Nanking and promised to join any military actions, presumably for Zhang's release. This created the impression for the public that all efforts were being ruined by the internal problems of the Northeastern and Northwestern Armies, and not by the passive attitude of the Communist Party.[26]

For Zhang and Yang, the Xi'an Incident meant the destruction of their troops and the end of their political careers. As for the Communists, they obtained from Chiang a promise assuring the peace they dearly desired. They would never have to worry about their physical existence again. On January 7, the CCP issued another internal paper of instructions concerning the Xi'an Incident. Probably composed by Mao, the most essential points of the document are as follows:

1. The Xi'an incident was an internal problem of the KMT Nanking Government, in which this Party never took any part. After the incident this Party immediately called for a peaceful solution.

2. This Party opposes all actions which may lead to a civil war. Therefore, it opposed the Nanking Government's policy of anti-Communist civil war on the one hand, and never supported Zhang and Yang on the other hand. Zhang and Yang might have found a better way to realize their anti-Japanese disposition.

3. As for Chiang's release, Zhang's following Chiang to Nanking, and the Nanking Government's manner of dealing with this case, this Party regards all these as internal affairs of the Nanking Government. This Party stands for a just and fair position, and stands for all measures which can lead to a peaceful resolution of this matter and it is opposed to any civil war to the benefit of Japanese imperialism.

4. In order to realize peaceful unification, and unified resistance to foreign invaders, this Party advocates that the Nanking Government order Zhang to return to Shaanxi to lead his Northeastern Army onto the anti-Japanese front and realize the common goal of both Chiang and Zhang in saving the nation.[27]

The essence of this document should be clear: to excuse the CCP from the censure of the Nanking Government at the expense of Zhang and Yang, while at the same time avoiding any provocation of the Northeastern and Northwestern Armies. What Mao sought from the Nanking Government was not merely a pardon for its present involvement with the Xi'an Incident, but a guarantee not to suppress the CCP in the future. Practically if not formally, Mao and the CCP fulfilled both of these objectives.

The targets of punishment after the Xi'an Incident could only be Chiang's insurgent subordinates. When the Northwestern Army was transferred and dissolved in early February 1937, the CCP did not forget to adopt some of its officers and men into its own ranks, loudly proclaiming its "accommodation of old friends." The Communists took over Yan'an, which became the center of the CCP for the next ten years, and extended their territory to Sanyuan, a dozen miles north of Xi'an. They had won a great strategic success: the fatal threat from the Nationalists to their existence in North China was thus dismissed.[28]

A brief comparison of the Fujian Incident in 1933 and the Xi'an Incident in 1936 reveals the changes in the Communist movement. On the former occasion, where a ready-made advantage was offered the Communists, they refused or failed to take it. During the latter event, which was more complicated and difficult, the Communists successfully exploited the situation and managed splendid achievements. On the first occasion, the Bo Gu Center applied all kinds of Marxist-Leninist doctrines (such as class identity, the third force, the reformist faction and so on) as guiding principles to their practical decisions. During the Xi'an Incident, the Party had better learned how to court its enemy. Although the Mao Center chanted some revolutionary slogans, these followed rather than preceded its practical decisions; Mao never let bookish doctrine drag his feet. The CCP's achievements in the Xi'an Incident were just as much Mao's achievements in the CCP Center. By wisely investing and employing his power, Mao had greatly increased and gathered it.

Toward Comrades: The Western Route Army

In early 1936, while the Fourth Front Army stayed at Ganzi in the Xikang area, Zhang Guotao and other leaders were thinking of moving north. This did not mean they intended to join Mao in northern Shaanxi. Zhang planned instead to go directly north to central Gansu, from there he would to go west to open a new base of his own. Joined by the Second Front Army, Zhang conceded to follow the previous route of the Central Red Army to southeast Gansu. As soon as the Fourth Front Armies landed on the plain region in southeast Gansu in September 1936, Zhang again proposed going west. But Chen Changhao preferred to stay at the present location and found a new base in southern Gansu. Both, however, shared a reluctance to go north and surrender their independence to Mao. With Zhu De and Ren Bishi wedged in the Red Army Headquarters and the KMT Central Army pressing in from the south, Zhang and Chen compromised and directed the Fourth Front Army to northern Gansu. Then Zhang and Chen had to make their final choice: either follow Peng Dehuai to the east or search out their own fortune in the west. Instinctively, they opted for the latter course.[29]

Mao also seemed reluctant to have Zhang and his men come to northern Shaanxi. Zhang's arrival with his title in the Red Army General Headquarters and his superior armed force might shake Mao's authority in this new base area. Besides, there was a practical problem: how would this small, barren base in northern Shaanxi be able to feed a combined army of 60,000 men? Mao and Zhang both had to weigh mixed considerations: their concern with the KMT as their common enemy against their concern with their own positions within the CCP. The situation at that juncture seemed too complicated for either Mao or Zhang to unravel. Mao was happy to see the Fourth Front Army come as reinforcement but felt uneasily that Zhang's men would eat up the little food available in his base, and Zhang himself would encroach upon his power. On his part Zhang also worried about the possible loss of his political independence as well as the shortage of material supplies in northern Shaanxi. Under these circumstances, Mao proposed the Ningxia Campaign in early October 1936. The campaign aimed to destroy the KMT Central Army behind and the Ningxia local army in front in order to take over northern Gansu and Ningxia along the Yellow River. This could then be regarded as both an extension of Mao's old base and the establishment of Zhang's new one. Besides, Mao was eager to open an international route through Ningxia to receive Russian aid, to which Zhang Guotao should have no objections. As a requirement of the campaign and at the suggestion of Zhang Guotao, the Fourth Front Army would move to the western side of the Yellow River. Zhang preferred to lead his own troops cross the Yellow River and drive far west into Gansu and Qinghai; from Mao's viewpoint, it was more than just a concession to let Zhang go.

To carry out the Ningxia Campaign, the Military Council in northern Shaanxi issued the "Combat Project of October" on October 11, 1936. The basic object of this project was to concentrate the three Red Army forces so that they could destroy the KMT troops in northern Gansu, take over Ningxia, and make contact with the Soviet Union from inner and outer Mongolia. The key components of the October Project were as follows:

> It is ruled that all the troops of the Western Field Army of the First Front Army, a part of the First Front Army at Dingyuan and three armies of the Fourth Front Army constitute the offensive force to attack Ningxia at the north. The remaining two armies of the Fourth Front Army, all of the Second Front Army and the independent Fourth Division of the First Front Army constitute the defensive force at the southern front. If necessary and possible, some of the defensive force will also be transferred to attack Ningxia.[30]

The same project further required that within the northern defensive force, the Central Red Army should advance from the eastern side of the Yellow River while the three armies of the Fourth Front Army should advance from the western side. Accordingly, the FFA troops were ordered to prepare for the river crossing by building boats and rafts and seizing the ferry spots between Zhongwei and Qingyuan. All these measures had to be finished in no more than a month.[31]

At the time, the First Front Army was facing the Northeastern Army at the north front, and the Second and Fourth Front Armies were coping with the KMT Central Army led by Hu Zongnan, Wang Jun and Mao Bingwen in the south. On October 22, the Military Council sent a telegram order to the Fourth Front Army, saying that "we are now staying between the southern and northern enemies. . . . Unless we break the enemy in the south, we cannot attack the north."[32] On October 25, the Military Council issued another telegram, stating that "the first step is to concentrate all our attention to defeat the enemy in the south and the second step is to shift our attention to the north."[33] Obviously this was an invitation for the Fourth Front Army to fight the pursuing KMT Central Army, though Zhang Guotao would never do so. While more telegrams came from the Military Council urging the Fourth Front Army to execute the October Plan, Zhang was busily planning for three armies of the FFA to cross the

Yellow River and move further northwest. After the crossing, the 30th and 9th Armies under the command of Xu Xiangqian and Chen Changhao of the FFA headquarters went further west and the 5th Army, a relatively small unit led by Dong Zhentang, was left to guard the ferries and boats. On October 26, 1936, the Military Council ordered: "After the 30th and 9th Armies' crossing, the 30th Army should occupy Yongdeng and the 9th Army should capture the crucial spots north to Hongshui, and get ready to attack and capture Dingyuan. That is the core of the battle."[34] On October 29, Mao and Zhou again telegrammed Zhu and Zhang, "at the suggestion of Zhu, Zhang, Xu, and Chen, in order to seize Ningxia quickly the 31st Army will immediately cross the River and follow the 9th and 30th Army to advance."[35] Mao's basic idea was to use Zhang's men to attack the KMT army, but Zhang sent part of his troops to the western bank of the Yellow River with an equally selfish objective. The Chinese saying "sleeping on the same bed but dreaming different dreams," is an appropriate description of Mao and Zhang's relations at the time.

From October to early November, the KMT Central Army pressed northward. Wang Jun took over all the ferry spots along the Yellow River and Hu Zongnan chased the Fourth Front Army further down to the northeast, dividing the Red Army between the sides of the Yellow River. While Chen and Xu directed the bulk of the FFA to the west, Zhang and Zhu led the remaining troops at the eastern bank around the CRA deployment zone to the north in order to avoid the pursuing troops of the KMT Central Army.[36]

On the basis of the telegram exchanges between the Military Council and the Red Army Headquarters at the time, it appears that the Fourth Front Army's river crossing operation was formally carried out at the order of Mao or the Military Council, and was not just a conspiracy Zhang framed in Mao's ignorance, as later CCP politicians and historians have claimed. On the other hand, it is equally obvious that Zhang Guotao's acceptance and execution of the October Plan was based more on his hopes of using his own troops to gain new territory in the west than on joining the Central Red Army in the Ningxia Campaign. Thus, the river crossing went on well ahead of schedule in late October but the Ningxia project was far behind schedule in early November. The reason was simple: each side tried to avoid sacrifices of its own by shirking military engagements with the KMT troops.

Peng Dehuai recalls that he had proposed an ambush to destroy Wang Jun's pursuing troops twice but Zhang refused each time.[37] Zhang Guotao did this for his own persuasive reasons: first, he could claim that his Red Army Headquarters should have the right to command all the Red Army troops and Peng had no right to operate any battle at all; second, he could argue that since the Fourth Front Army was then in the south and the

First Front Army in the north, any battle with the KMT pursuing troops at the south would simply mean a bigger sacrifice of Zhang's men. As a result of the cleverness and selfishness of both the Red Armies, the Ningxia Campaign was put off and finally given up. Thus the KMT Central Army was able to push into northern Gansu, take back all the ferry spots, and cut the Fourth Front Army into two groups: those who had already crossed the Yellow River at the western bank and those who were left in the east, unable to cross at all.

Party and Red Army leaders issued a series of contradictory decisions from late October to early November 1936. At one time the Military Council wanted the Fourth Front Army to continue sending its troops to the west; at another time it was afraid that Zhang would go west for his own purposes and therefore ordered him to stop crossing the River; Zhang wanted to send out all his troops at one time, then wanted to call them all back at another. Neither Mao nor Zhang seemed serious or sincere in fighting with the enemy. Eventually, all this delay proved detrimental— mainly to the Fourth Front Army and not the Central Red Army, because of their respective positions. Failure to destroy the enemy and to create a new territory would at worst lead the First Front Army back to its northern Shaanxi home base. But the Fourth Front Army had newly arrived and was badly in need of a place to settle down: this failure would cause far more grave consequences. When Zhang's troops were cut into two parts, one merged into the CRA turning back to northern Shaanxi. The other was thrown into the distant west, doomed to destruction. Of course, the other Red Army group to immediately suffer from this factionalist trick was the Second Front Army, which was located even further in the south as a defending force. With both main Red Army forces doing their best to avoid engaging the enemy, He Long's troops became the victim—either due to his faithfulness in a complimentary sense or his foolishness in a less gratifying one.[38]

On November 5, 1936, Chen Changhao and Xu Xiangqian at the FFA Headquarters received a military telegram from the Red Army General Headquarters still controlled by Zhang Guotao. The strategic nature of their being dispatched to the western side seemed totally changed. Instead of a joint attack on Ningxia, Chen and Xu were asked to pursue for another, rather different purpose:

At this moment the most important task of your troops at the northern bank of the river was to destroy Ma Bufang's troops and open an independent prospective situation. You should take the advantageous situation that the enemy did not fully attend to you at this time and firmly take your foot: first capture Daqing, Gulang, Yongdeng and then quickly take over the Liangzhou area if possible and necessary. You should operate swiftly, secretly, firmly and dexterously. . . . You should disregard any obligations whatsoever and fulfill your own goals independently.[39]

Accordingly, the FFA Headquarters produced the "Combat Plan of Bingfan, Daqing, Gulang and Liangzhou" on November 6. Its essential goal was to open a new base by its own effort at the center of Gansu. On November 8, Mao's Military Council issued the "New Combat Project." This time the First and Second Front Armies were supposed to form the Southern Route Army, the two armies of the Fourth Front Army, at the eastern bank of the Yellow River were to form the Northern Route Army and the three armies of the Fourth Front Army in the west were to form the Western Route Army. The Combat Plan specified: "The troops under Cheng and Xu are named the Western Route Army, and its task is to create the Western River Base and to break through to the Distant."[40] In other words, the Western Route Army would go alone to the Gansu Corridor and then go far west to Xinjiang to reach contact with the Soviet Union—"the Distant" as it was called.

This is the brief story of the creation of the Western Route Army. From the very beginning, the Western Route Army's existence was a result of intraparty power clashes, though neither Zhang nor Mao admitted this obvious fact. Until very recently, official historians in China continued to insist that Zhang stealthily ordered his own troops to the west and should be solely responsible for the later tragedy. The real story was certainly less one-sided than this assertion.[41]

The province of Gansu is like a dumbbell, with two thick heads and a narrow slender bar 1,000 li long, the narrowest part of which is less than 100 li wide. The province is located on the Northwest China highland, 4,000 meters above sea level, with a small population of agricultural Han and nomadic Moslems. The Western Route Army was soon to face the reality that they lost all political or revolutionary advantage, and their confrontation with the local Moslem warlords had become armed wrestling whose outcome depended solely on physical attrition.

Chen Changhao and Xu Xiangqian began their western march in early November 1936. They won a series of small clashes and took the strategic location of Gulang at the eastern end of the Gansu Corridor. In late November came the first large battle in Gulang, in which the Red Army destroyed 5,000 of the enemy and lost about the same number of their own troops. The Communists lost the chief of staff of the 9th Army and two division commanders, while the Moslem general Ma Buqing lost his commander of the Front Headquarters. A bad omen for the Communists lay in the fact that they could not deal the enemy a fatal blow and thus had to give up this strategic location. They moved further west and reached the middle of the Corridor in early December. The three armies of the

Western Route Army were scattered over one hundred li between Yongchang and Shandan. The total troops were reduced to 15,000 in one and a half months.[42]

On December 14, news of the Xi'an Incident reached the Western Route Army. At the same time, the Military Council ordered Chen and Xu to get ready to turn back to the east. Mao's purpose was to call them back to reinforce the military position of his alliance with Zhang Xueliang and Yang Hucheng in face of the Nanking Government's attack. The Western Army remained in place for a week or so, waiting for further information.[43] Another order from the Military Council came a few days later, and the plan of returning east was cancelled. The Western Route Army was ordered to resume its western expedition. Mao's telegram reiterated the strategic significance of "breaking through to the Distant" but never admitted the fact that his new enthusiasm for a peaceful resolution of the Xi'an Incident delayed the Western Route Army for almost ten days at this critical juncture. If they had turned east, Chen and Xu could have reached Lanzhou in one or two weeks. The city of Lanzhou was then under the jurisdiction of Yu Xuezhong, a friendly Northeastern general.[44]

Chen and Xu led their men to continue the western march. By New Year's day, they reached the Gaotai area, still more than 400 li from Xinjiang. Did they really need to go to Xinjiang to appeal to the Soviet Union? Or should they just open a base here in the Corridor? Either option was extremely difficult, but hesitating as they did between the two choices proved even worse. While fighting in the west, they kept thinking of the east, and such a situation dragged their feet. The tragedy for Chen Changhao as an individual leader was that he was constantly striving for independence, but was at the same time mentally and practically ill-equipped for independence.

For the Moslem warlords Ma Bufang and Ma Buqing, Gansu and Qinghai were home bases. They would prefer to push all out to eliminate and expel the Red Army from their home, regardless of the state of relations between the Nanking Government and the Red Army.[45] In mid-January, at the peak of the winter, the 5th Red Army commanded by Dong Zhentang was besieged at Gaotai and destroyed by the combined attack of the Ma troops and local militia. All 3,000 men of the Fifth Army died in the battle. Dong Zhentang committed suicide and Yang Keming, the Political Commissar, was killed. The Gaotai Battle marked the breaking point in the temporary standoff; the Western Route Army now fell into serious crisis. Chen Changhao had to call Yan'an for rescue.[46]

After a few days of hesitation, the "Western Reinforcement Army" was formed by the Military Council with Liu Bocheng as the commander and Zhang Hao the political commissar. Presumably rushing to the Western Route Army's rescue, the newly patched troops left Sanyuan in northern

Shaanxi, where there were still 1,500 li away from Gaotai, and reached the eastern bank of the Yellow River in early February.[47] Chen and Xu moved their troops back to the east about 100 li to respond to the Reinforcement Army. They defeated a local police regiment and caught 800 policemen, but it was obviously too late. There were still 700 li—with enemy forces heavily deployed along the way—keeping them from the reinforcement troops. In late February, they were forced to shift west again. The fatal battle finally occurred at Nijiayingzi in western Gansu in early March. All troops of the Western Route Army, except for about 2,000 men, were annihilated. After an emergency meeting at Shiwozi with their senior officials, Chen and Xu abandoned the army and sneaked back to Yan'an, passing the command to Wang Shusheng, Li Xiannian and others.[48]

The remaining troops were divided into two guerrilla squads. Li Xiannian succeeded in leading his small group to pass over the Qilian Mountains into the Gobi Desert, where they were eventually brought to Ulumuchi by Chen Yun in May 1937 and returned to northern Shaanxi after the Sino-Japanese War broke out in September 1937.[49] Wang Shusheng led his group to carry on guerrilla activities in western Gansu until further attacks by the local forces reduced it to less than ten men. Hiding in a cave for a few days, they decided to quit. They destroyed their weapons, changed their uniforms, and dispersed to flee in different directions. Seven of them eventually returned to Yan'an.[50] Thus was the final fate of the Western Route Army, which had started with 21,000 men and ended with less than 1,000 men returning to the Communist ranks.

The Moslem generals of Ma Bufang and Ma Buqing were never hampered by the slightest ethical allegiance, Confucian or Marxist, Nationalist or Communist. After the battle at Nijiayingzi, more than 1,000 Red Army captives were buried alive in Xining; 3,000 were organized into a special regiment to build roads and bridges, toiling 12 hours a day; the old, the weak and the wounded were all killed—buried alive or beheaded with swords to save bullets; about 1,000 were sent to the Nanking Government to fulfill the draft quotas of army conscription; and female Red Army soldiers and nurses were assigned to officers and men as concubines according to their age and appearance. From the loftiest ideals to the cruelest reality, from Communist revolutionaries to professional reactionaries—the fate of the Western Route Army troops was a tragic test of the flexibility and the endurance of human body and soul.[51]

The destruction of the Western Route Army profoundly influenced the power relations within the Communist Party in general and those between Zhang and Mao in particular. Zhang followed Zhou back to Baoan in Northern Shaanxi in early November 1936. Returning to Mao's domain, Zhang found himself in no position to claim general military command. Militarily speaking, there were about 40,000 troops: 20,000 of the First

Front Army, 10,000 of the Second Front Army, and 10,000 of the Fourth Front Army. Clearly, Zhang was no match with Mao in this regard. Zhang was even more inferior in titles: by the end of 1936, Mao held virtually all the supreme positions in the Party, Government, and Army. As for the two mediators, Ren Bishi was left at the front, and Zhang Hao was reassigned to labor union work. The Southwest Bureau or the Northwest Bureau was gone, not even worth mentioning. Mao and his men were busy dealing with all the internal and external affairs, leaving Zhang Guotao "a lonely dog." The last straw in Zhang's power bargaining with Mao was the Western Route Army. If the Western Route Army had been able to reach Xinjiang smoothly, open a new base there, and establish a close contact with the Comintern and Soviet Union, Zhang would still have pulled considerable political weight. If Mao in northern Shaanxi had meanwhile been pushed by Chiang Kai-shek on another long march to the distant west, Zhang might have even regained his superior position.[52]

Had all these happened, the neutral forces of the former Shaanxi Red Army, the former 25th Red Army (originally Zhang's army), Ren Bishi and the Second Front Army, and Zhang Hao as the Comintern envoy might have turned to Zhang Guotao; all the old contradictions between Mao and returned students, between Mao and Zhu and between the 1st Army Corps and the 3rd Army Corps might have been used to Zhang's advantage. All depended on how well or poorly the two Communist factions, one at the east and another at the west, could perform. If both sides did well, a balance of internal party confrontation would have resulted; had both sides failed, the CCP would certainly have been destroyed; and if one side did well and the other did not, that meant a tilt of the intraparty position of Mao over Zhang or vice versa. Mao certainly enjoyed all power and prestige by the end of 1936. This was the justified reward for his effort and success in the past year.

The reality is that the Western Route Army failed completely and Zhang Guotao's fortune as a Communist politician died with it. Mao initiated the criticism of Zhang; he was also the person who finally stood in favor of leniency for Zhang, in the same manner Chiang Kai-shek did for Zhang Xueliang in the Nanking trial.[53] The objective of both politicians was much the same: to deprive his challenger of political influence while maintaining his physical existence. Zhang Guotao recalls the connection between the failure of the Western Route Army and the collapse of his power within the Communist Party as follows:

> The defeat of the West Route troops had considerable effect on the future development of the CCP and the situation in the Northwest at that time. Particularly it brought great blows to me, as leader of the Fourth Front Army. The spearhead of the internal strife of the CCP was pointed at me, hitting

me so hard that it was impossible for me to raise my head. The strife also exposed the extreme savageness of the Mao-type struggle.[54]

An impartial observer would say that although Zhang Guotao's condemnation of Mao as the one who deliberately sacrificed the Western Route Army might be far-fetched, Mao ought to bear heavy responsibility for this tragic debacle in at least one respect: it was under Mao's, not Zhang's, direct military command that the Western Route Army had perished. Zhang never had direct contact with the Western Route Army after his return to Yan'an. It was Mao and the Military Council who kept in daily radio communication with the Western Route Army. At the very least, Mao and the Party Center's selfish interest in the Xi'an Incident delayed and confused the military operations of the Western Route Army, and even the later half-baked "Western Reinforcement Army" contributed to the eventual disaster.[55]

Moral responsibility should not be too impatiently given to Mao. To sacrifice some of his comrades for a more important external purpose and even for a crucial internal power purpose could arguably be justifiable, if not necessary, for an astute politician during a rebellion. Mao happened to be such an astute Communist politician. From late 1936 to early 1937, it was the solution of the Xi'an Incident that critically decided Mao's fortune—perhaps the fortune of the northern Shaanxi base and the Communist Party as well. Mao's negligence and ignorance of the Western Route Army because of his full attention to the Xi'an Incident was possibly understandable and excusable. Here again, politics is like business, a politician like an entrepreneur. He is not the one who never loses anything, but the one who can focus on the key points and lose in order to gain in the long haul. Mao's main concern was, and perhaps should have been, at the east with the Xi'an Incident, not with the Western Route Army.

Despite his accusations against Mao for his selfishness, Zhang's own ambition was equally obvious. First he avoided participating in the Ningxia Campaign just to preserve his own troops, then he sent the bulk of the Western Route Army out to open his own military base and maintained the rest at hand to compete with Mao for supreme leadership. These ideas finally proved not only selfish but also unwise, and thus more blameworthy than Mao's. Zhang's mind was too much engaged with intraparty struggles to realize that only through external successes could internal power be attained.

Furthermore, the Western Route Army presents its own lesson. Although the Communist movement was necessarily in a process of general transference from South China to North China, there must be a limited definition of the term "North." Only through avoiding "going too far north" were the Communists eventually able to set foot in the North. Going to the distant northwestern frontier in Xinjiang, as the Western Route Army intended, would have separated the Communist movement from China Proper and resulted in a total reliance upon the Soviet Union. The CCP would have lost its identity and validity. Such a consequence would seem to stand against the mandate of modern Chinese history—applying a bit of mystery to historical study.

Toward the Competitor:
The Second Nationalist-Communist Collaboration

Despite open snapping at each other, secret contacts between the Communist Party and the Nanking Government can be traced back to as early as November 1935, soon after the CCP Center arrived at northern Shaanxi. Interestingly, the KMT was the first to suggest such a possibility. Moscow and Nanking opened formal diplomatic relations in October 1932. In the following years, Chiang Kai-shek's chief diplomatic concern was improving his relationship with the Soviet Union to check the ever more aggressive Japanese. An appropriate treatment of the CCP was seen as a needed accessory to his appeal to the Soviet Union, as was proved by the first CCP-KMT collaboration ten years earlier.[56]

In early 1935, Deng Wenyi went to Moscow as the KMT Military Attaché to the Soviet Union. When Deng came back home in the autumn of the same year, Chiang learned of the sincere attitude of the Soviet Union in supporting China's resistance to the Japanese. Deng was quickly sent back to Moscow with the special mission of promoting relations with the Soviet Union. In his memoir, Deng recalled:

> After I returned to Moscow in early March, apart from the busy routine work in the Military Attaché's Bureau, I managed to contact a considerable number of Russian generals and officers, who had previously been in China as military advisors and who still had close concerns with China. I also met the representative of the Chinese Communist Party in Moscow, and we had some frank and sincere talks.[57]

During his meeting with Wang Ming, the head of CCP Mission to the Comintern, Deng proposed entering into bilateral negotiations between the KMT and the CCP. Wang Ming replied that as the central committees of both parties were in China, talks had better be held there instead of in Moscow. For this purpose, Pan Hannian was appointed the delegate of the Communist side. Deng and Pan first met in Moscow. Then Pan went back to Shanghai and began further talks with Zhang Chong of the KMT side.[58]

Another channel of communication was opened about the same time. On the KMT side was Zhen Xiaoqin, a senior aide of Zeng Yanji, the Vice

Minister of Railway Transportation in the Nanking Government; above Zhen and Zeng was Chen Guofu, one of the few authoritative figures in the KMT. On the CCP side were Lu Zhenyu and Zhou Xiaozhou of the CCP Committee of Peking, and then Wang Shiying of the Northern Bureau. Both sides negotiated for several months while Chiang and Mao remained behind the curtain. Such covert dealings did not continue for long, as Mao seemed more anxious than Chiang. In January 1936, Zhou Xiaozhou went to Nanking for an informal meeting with Zeng Yangji and handed him a letter from Mao, Zhu, and Zhou to Chen Guofu. Letters from the same Communist leaders were also sent to such KMT leaders as Song Ziwen, Sun Ke, Feng Yuxiang, Cheng Qian, and Song Qingling. Soon afterwards, two secret envoys, carrying the certificate of the Ministry of Finance, were dispatched by Song Ziwen to Xi'an. From there they were escorted by Zhang Xueliang's men to Wayaobao. Mao, Zhou, and other CCP leaders received them warmly, and through them further messages were conveyed to Nanking.[59]

"Semi-formal" talks were held between the CCP and KMT from May onwards. In August 1936, Chen Guofu personally received Pan Hannian at Hangzhou. On behalf of Chiang, Chen told Pan that the antagonistic regime and army of the CCP had to be eliminated; the Red Army could maintain 3,000 men, but all its commanders higher than division level should be dismissed and sent abroad. Pan, naturally, could not accept such a stringent condition. Chen responded, "Neither you nor I have the military authority directly involved in the case. Suppose we let Zhou Enlai come to Nanking and have a personal talk with Chiang."[60]

So far negotiations between the CCP and the KMT had were fruitless, but not entirely in vain—at least for the Communists. They established various contacts with the Nanking Government and obtained a lot of experiences. In the year 1936, the CCP Center headed by Mao was like an octopus, stretching out its tentacles in all directions and searching for all possible targets.

During the Xi'an Incident, while Zhang Xueliang was busily occupied with William Donald, his foreign tutor, and Madame Chiang, his female friend, the CCP delegation was busily exploiting all opportunities to contact various circles in the Nanking Government. This situation can best be seen in the instruction of the CCP Center to Zhou Enlai on December 21, 1936. The first part contained six conditions for Chiang's release; the second part suddenly shifted to seemingly irrelevant matters. Zhou was instructed not only "to open talks with Yan Xishan, Song Ziwen, Yu Youren, the Whampoa left-wing, and any other KMT factions," "to get in touch with the army officers in Shaanxi and Gansu such as Hu Zongnan, Fan Songpu, Dong Zhao and others," and "to invite all those who stand for peace to come for negotiation," but also "to invite British and American advisors to visit Xi'an again, and through them to persuade Britain and America to help make peace in China."[61]

It seems quite clear here that Mao was telling Zhou to regard the Xi'an Incident as golden opportunity to break the ice in their relations with the KMT as a whole, to go beyond Zhang and Yang and create wider and broader prospects for the CCP. In fact, Zhou achieved this goal. Song Ziwen asked the CCP to send special agents to Shanghai and keep secret contacts with him, and Chiang personally invited Zhou to Nanking for more formal bilateral talks.[62]

Instead of taking advantage of the Xi'an Incident to be cocky and demanding, the CCP leaders looked even humbler before the KMT envoy. On February 10, 1937, the CCP Central Committee sent a telegram to the KMT 3rd Plenum with five conditions for a new CCP-KMT collaboration. The KMT would need to "stop the civil war and unite all forces to fight the Japanese; grant freedom to the people and release all political prisoners; hold a national conference of all parties and circles; prepare for an anti-Japanese war; improve the people's welfare." Under such conditions, the CCP would fulfill four promises. It would 1. abolish the CCP rebellious policies against the KMT government. 2. change the Soviet into a special region of the Republic and Red Army as a part of the Nationalist Army. 3. realize a democratic government of the people in a general election. 4. abandon the land distribution policy.[63]

The wording of the telegram was modest and polite, and the general conditions it had addressed seemed reasonable and appropriate. The last two demands were clearly not essential. And the three promises it offered sounded like a radical concession of their past revolutionary line. On February 15, the Party Center issued an internal document, defining the general purpose of this new political line: "The above offers constitute a principle compromise on our part toward the KMT. Our objective is to avoid antagonism of the two regimes in China and to form a united front against the Japanese invasion."[64] However, this internal instruction went on to say:

> The abolition of the Soviet system in the Soviet area and the adoption of a democratic general election does not mean any abolition of the political right already obtained by peasants and workers; rather, we will continue to protect it. The change of the name of the Red Army into the Nationalist Revolutionary Army does not mean any abolition of its main constituency of workers and peasants and its political and organizational leadership by the Party; rather, we will continue to protect it. To stop confiscating the landlord's land does not mean any restoration of the exploitation system; rather, we will protect the land in the hands of the peasants.[65]

In other words, to maintain what the CCP had already gained in substance and to attain a formal legal status from the KMT—these were the basic goals underlying Mao's pursuit of another CCP-KMT collaboration. Thus in February and March, the CCP representatives—Zhou Enlai, Bo Gu and Ye Jianying—were negotiating in more concrete terms with the KMT representatives—Gu Zhutong, He Zhonghan and Zhang Chong—at the city of Xi'an. The Communists requested that the Nationalist Government allow the CCP to operate openly and legally, set free all Communist prisoners, and stop the KMT troops from attacking the Western Route Army. In return, the Communists agreed to 1) rename the Shaanxi-Gansu Soviet the Shaanxi-Gansu-Ningxia Border Region of the Chinese Republic; 2) to hold a general election but subject it to the Central Government's approval—meaning they would control the election; 3) to rename the Red Army the Nationalist Army, and downgrade the three front armies to three divisions, each containing 15,000 men—all together numbering 45,000. In reality, the Red Army barely had so many troops at the time.[66]

The KMT further required 1) that the jurisdiction of the Soviet area should be rearranged and its officials reassigned by the concerned provincial governments; 2) that the Communists should have three regiments instead of three divisions and each regiment should have no more than 5,000 men; and 3) that the Nanking Government should have the right to re-appoint commanders of these troops on all levels as any sovereign government would do. These demands were far beyond the scope of Mao's possible concession. The talks were thus brought to a halt. The CCP refused to talk with Gu and He at Xi'an anymore and requested a direct meeting with Chiang Kai-shek. In late March, Zhou went to see Chiang at Hangzhou. Chiang played the role of a national leader uninterested in concrete details. He avoided reaching any specific terms, but agreed to issue a joint manifesto of the two parties.[67]

On June 4, Zhou went to Lushan to see Chiang again. Chiang suggested that each party nominate the same number of representatives to form a "National Revolutionary Alliance" (with himself as the chairman) to decide all external propaganda and internal programs so that a joint party might be built up to later conduct common relations with the Comintern. The CCP could maintain three divisions, each with 10,000 men. Some Communists could be appointed as division leaders, but Zhou and Mao would have to go abroad and the General Headquarters would need to be assigned by the KMT's Bureau of Political Instruction. The head of the Communist Border Area would be appointed by the KMT Government while the vice-head might be elected by the local people. On his part, Chiang consented to release Communist prisoners, to assemble the CCP guerrilla troops in the South, and to allow the Communists to attend the National Defense Conference.[68]

On June 16 Zhou returned to Yan'an. Ten days later the Communists proposed further concessions. They agreed to found a National Revolutionary Alliance with Chiang as Chairman. For the future, they did not object to the idea of establishing a joint party and joining the Comintern under its name; they agreed that one of the three Nationalists, Zhang Xi, Song Ziwen or Yu Youren could come to govern the Border Area. The only thing they refused to compromise in was the dominant control of the CCP over all its military forces, hence a firm refusal of the appointment of general commanders by the KMT to their troops.[69] In other words, Mao could relinquish all the titles and names but would never surrender his firm control of the territorial base and, above all, of the military force. As the KMT remained too arrogant and yet too passive to concoct any appropriate proposals on their own, it gradually adapted its position to meet the Communists' needs.

On July 15, 1937, Zhou Enlai went to the Lushan Mountain resort yet again to offer concessions on behalf of the Communist Party and the Red Army. Here are Zhou's three demands: 1. Start the national anti-Japanese war and recover the lost territory to achieve national integrity; 2. Hold a National Congress to draft a constitution and make a national salvation policy; 3. Guarantee the people's livelihood. The first and last demands could hardly be debated by the Nationalists; even the second one sounded reasonably moderate, though it implied granting political rights and legal status to all Chinese people including, of course, the Communists. At the same time, the CCP put forth four promises. It would

1. Accept the "three people's principles" as the guiding ideology of the entire Chinese nation;
2. Abolish all rebellious actions and land revolution;
3. Abolish the Soviet system and all its policies;
4. Replace the title "Red Army" with the title "Nationalist Army."[70]

In an interesting arithmetic game, the previous five demands and four promises had now become three demands and four promises. Here Mao seemed to have sold all partisan identity, but actually, he stuck to the principle that never could a single rifle or a single man in his troops be handed out, nor could a single Nationalist be brought in to command or supervise his troops. Except for this matter, Mao was willing to give away everything—even his Marxist-Leninist allegiance!

The tit-for-tat quibbling between the Nationalists and the Communists might have lasted a long time had not the urgent situation emerging in wake of the large-scale Japanese invasion into North China in July 1937 suddenly ended the standstill and shoved the Nanking Government forward. The ever-increasing Japanese encroachment on China and the persistent propaganda and concessions by the CCP kept pushing the Nanking Government along. Eventually, Chiang Kai-shek accepted the Red Army as part of the Nationalist Army and the Soviet area as a part of the Nationalist Government. Although Chiang's suggestion to send a political supervisor to the Communist troops was once again rejected, the Communists accepted the titular subordination of the Red Army to the KMT Northern Combat Zone. The second CCP-KMT collaboration was formally announced on September 15, 1937.

Despite the formal similarities, there were fundamental differences between this KMT-CCP collaboration and the one ten years earlier. In the first collaboration, the CCP constantly insisted on its ideological independence under a practically dependent condition. The new one was just the opposite. The Communists seemed desperately anxious to give up their revolutionary identity and unite with the Nationalist government, but they also firmly held on to their political and military autonomy. They were eager to seek the collaboration at first, but did not care much about it later on. They kept asking for admission into the united front, but once admitted they would never abide by it. Mao, and the CCP as a whole, had learned how to play political games with Chiang and the KMT. The results of the second collaboration were also quite different from those of the first: the first collaboration was a disastrous failure, while the second one proved to be a great success for the CCP as a political party and for Mao as an individual politician.

Toward the Enemy: The Sino-Japanese War

Politics entails paradoxes, not always subject to a simple law of causality. If we say that the CCP-KMT military confrontation invited the Japanese intrusion into China, we may also say that the Japanese invasion promoted the CCP-KMT collaboration. The Sino-Japanese War (1937-1945), which involved all kinds of national and international factors, cannot be taken merely as a fortuitous condition which granted rapid growth to the lucky Communists. Despite all the casual features of the Lugouqiao Incident in Peking on July 7, 1937, and of the Hongqiao Airport Incident in Shanghai on August 9, 1937, there can be little doubt of the aggressive nature of the Japanese diplomacy against China in view of either historical context or contemporary evidence.[71]

The large-scale Japanese intrusion broke the stalemate of the CCP and KMT negotiation. Chiang was eager to have the Red Army move to the front. Informed of the intrusion of the Japanese troops in Shanghai, Chiang immediately summoned and instructed one of his aides, Kang Ze, "Go tell Zhou Enlai, and let him send out his troops at once. Don't wait for reorganization anymore, nor for our vice-commander, political personnel

Territory Bases of the Communist Party in North China in 1938

1 -- Shaanxi-Gansu-Ningxia Border Area
2 -- Shanxi-Charhaer-Hebei Border Area
3 -- Daqing Mountain Area
4 -- Shanxi-Hebei-Henan Border Area
5 -- Northwestern Shanxi Area
6 -- Eastern Hebei Area
7 -- Southern Hebei Area
8 -- Hebei-Shandong Border Area
9 -- Northern Shandong Area

0   200 Miles

and administrative officials."[72] On August 21 and August 23 respectively, the CCP Military Council and the KMT Government formally announced the designation of the Red Army as the Eighth Route Army of the Nationalist Revolutionary Army and the appointment of Zhu De as General Commander and Peng Dehuai as Vice-Commander.[73]

After the Lugouqiao Incident, the CCP kept urging the KMT to declare the anti-Japanese war and demanding that the KMT allow the Communist troops to move east to fight the Japanese. This attitude might have arisen more from a desire to obtain its legal acknowledgment by the Nanking Government than from a serious wish to fight the Japanese. Now that he had finally got what he wanted from Chiang, Mao had to face the real issue of fighting the Japanese. For a while, Mao was hesitant. The Communists needed a special conference. The essential purpose of the Luochuan Conference of the Politburo in late August 1937 was to deal with the new situation after the outbreak of the Sino-Japanese war and the announcement of the formation of the Eighth Route Army. Participating in the Conference were all the Politburo members and some military leaders of the Red Army, all together 22 or 23 men.[74]

For the Communists, it was not difficult to issue new political propaganda or the "Ten Principles of Resisting the Japanese and Rescuing the Nation," the main theme of which was to request the Nanking Government to promote political democracy and people's livelihood. The more troublesome problem for the Communist leaders was how to engage their military forces in the resistance warfare. The timing of the Eighth Route Army's move to the front, the proportion of their troops to be left to garrison the home base, the military strategy in fighting the Japanese, and so on—these were crucial to the CCP's own interest. The focal concern for Mao and the CCP was how to preserve their strength and avoid sacrifice in the national war which they had been calling for so openly and so long.

Mao made the principal report to the Luochuan Conference. His goal was very clear: to protect the strength and independence of his own troops. Mao argued that the Red Army's military maneuvers could only be decided by the CCP and not by the KMT or anybody else. The time and manner of the Red Army's transfer to the front should be appropriately scheduled according to the development of the war, and a considerable portion of the Red Army should be left to guard the rear home base. As for the military strategy in fighting with the Japanese, Mao stressed that the military capacity of the Japanese army should by no means be underestimated, and therefore, guerrilla rather than regular warfare should be taken as the basic strategy; it was impermissible to render the entire Red Army the prey of the Japanese.

There were some mild objections to Mao's proposal, especially from military men and diplomats. Since the national war had started and the

Red Army had become part of the Nationalist Army, there was no reason for the Communists not to fulfill their previous promise to fight the Japanese at the front. It would damage the image of the CCP both domestically and internationally; it would delay or cancel the ammunition and pension supplies from the KMT Government to the Red Army; merely carrying out guerrilla activities without any large engagement with the Japanese army would also damage the reputation of the Party and Army in the eyes of the Chinese people.[75] After several days' scrutiny, the basic principle of self-preservation and self-expansion was reaffirmed, but at the same time a series of more pertinent measures were adopted. On August 25, soon after the Luochuan Conference, the Eighth Route Army officially announced its formation.

The three divisions were sent out from Shaanxi for Shanxi in late August. The 115th Division went to Northeast Shanxi, the 120th Division to Northwest Shanxi, and the 129th Division to Southeast Shanxi. Indeed, the military men of the CCP showed their expertise and morale in the battle. During September and October, they conducted about 100 battles, defeated 10,000 Japanese troops, and captured 1,000 rifles. Their notable victories included one at the Pingxing Pass, Shanxi province, where the 115th Division annihilated a Japanese brigade corps and killed 1,000 Japanese, and another at Yangming, Shanxi, in which the 129th Division ransacked an enemy airport and destroyed 24 airplanes.[77]

These victories were lauded by the Chinese people in general. Chiang as a KMT politician, however, received the news with mixed feelings. He was willing to praise these as victories under his general leadership, but he tried to play down any Communist propaganda. Now he had to provide military supplies to the Communist troops as he had promised. Mao also received the news with mixed feelings of joy and worry. Publicly, he loudly boasted of all these victories as evidences of the CCP's loyalty to the national war, but secretly he warned his military commanders against risking their own forces to wrestle with the Japanese.

The Japanese adopted a "blitzkrieg strategy," attempting to destroy the resistance of the Chinese army in just three months. They did achieve some huge successes. As Mao had expected, if not hoped, the KMT regular troops were quickly defeated, and collapsed in front of the Japanese attacks. By the end of 1937, the Japanese chased the KMT troops southwards, took almost all North China and a large part of the east coastal area, and drove deeply into Central China. Nevertheless, they could only occupy big cities and strategic locations, leaving towns and villages on and below the county level virtually vacant for the Communists to fill in.[78] Nie Rongzhen, the founder of the Shanxi-Chaha'er-Hebei Border Base, recalled the situation like this:

Table 9. 1 The Eighth Route Army in August 1937

General Commander	Zhu De
Vice General Commander	Peng Dehuai
Chief of Staff	Ye Jianying
Director of Political Department	Ren Bishi

115th Division—14,000 men

Commander	Lin Biao
Vice-Commander	Nie Rongzhen
Chief of Staff	Zhou Kun
Director of Political Department	Luo Rongqu

120th Division—6,000 men

Commander	He Long
Vice-Commander	Xiao Ke
Chief of Staff	Zhou Shidi
Director of Political Department	Guan Xiangying

129th Division—6,000 men

Commander	Liu Bocheng
Vice-Commander	Xu Xiangqian
Chief of Staff	Ni Zhiliang
Director of Political Department	Zhang Hao

Rear Garrison Corps—6,000 men

| Commander | Xiao Jinguang[76] |

After the fall of Taiyuan on November 8, 1937, the Shanxi-Chaha'er-Hebei border area fell into a even more chaotic situation. Nearly all the government systems in all the counties had practically dissolved. . . . The officials and staff members in the county government all ran away. In such a broad area no administrative personnel could be found at all. There was an extremely chaotic social condition. The deserted soldiers and local bandits were running amuck, the pro-Japanese Chinese were spreading all kinds of rumors and lies, and the masses were in a state of great fear and shock. A large proportion of the people lost their confidence in the future of the nation, and everywhere was a mood of pessimism or desperation.[79]

Under such conditions, the war between the Japanese and the Nationalists was just like the previous wars between the Nationalists and the local warlords—only on an even larger scale and for a longer period. The revolutionary character of the Communists found its full expression in the early stage of the Sino-Japanese War. Their strict discipline and high morale, their close connection with and skillful organization of the people, their propaganda of national revolution against imperialism and class struggle against local despots and evil landlords—all these made it possible for the Communists to perform a "drama" of rapid growth, with the engagement between the Japanese and Nationalists holding up the "platform."

Instead of concentrating all the Communist troops on one battlefield as required by Yan Xishan, the commander of the Second Combat Zone, Mao proposed that the Eighth Route Army disperse in different rural locations. After the first one or two months' military action, Mao had to re-stress the basic change in strategy from the regular mobile war to the guerrilla war. After September 1937, Mao issued one telegram after another to the General Headquarters of the Eighth Route Army and sometimes directly to the headquarters of individual divisions, reminding them of the guerrilla tactics and warning them against any reckless mobile war actions. On September 21, he telegrammed the Front Headquarters:

Today the Red Army cannot play any decisive role in the war. But we do have a handy trick, which will definitely enable us to play a decisive function later. This is none other than an independent, self-contained guerrilla war in the mountainous regions—not mobile war. To carry out this strategy, we need to have our troops deployed at the flanks and rear of the enemy, to make motivation and mobilization of the masses the main task, to distribute our troops, and not to concentrate on fighting battles as our main task. Concentrate on fighting battles and you cannot carry out any mass work; carry out work on the masses and you cannot concentrate on fighting battles. You cannot have both. Only by distributing our forces to do mass work can we deal a decisive blow to the enemy and support our ally. It will be to no avail just to concentrate our troops in fighting battles.[80]

It is obvious that Mao worried about his generals who might really have their troops fight the Japanese, to the sacrifice of the Red Army. The purpose of this guerrilla strategy was, of course, not merely to avoid fighting the Japanese and preserve his troops, but mainly to move into the vast countryside for growth and expansion. On September 25, while the 115th Division was conducting the Pingxing Pass Battle, Mao delivered another telegram to Zhou, Zhu, Peng and Liu urging them to undertake guerrilla warfare and mass organization. In the telegram Mao issued another strict order, making clear that "All the work in North China should take guerrilla warfare as its sole task. All the work, such as mutiny work, united front, and so on should be centered around guerrilla warfare. If the regular war is lost in North China, we are not responsible; but if the guerrilla war is lost, we must bear a grave responsibility."[81]

Mao was wise enough to publicly boast about the Pingxing Pass victory for propaganda purposes. But after the battle, Mao quickly ordered a split of the 115th Division, transferring the main force of this division to the Taihang Mountains in southern Shanxi while leaving the remaining 2,000 men in the Wutai Mountains. At the same time he also transferred other Red Army troops from the railway line to the distant rural regions, the 120th Division to northeast Shanxi among the Guanqin Mountains and the 129th Division to southeast Shanxi in the Luliang Mountains. All the Communist troops were instructed to hide in the mountains, to carry out "hit and run" guerrilla actions, to agitate the peasant masses, and to expand the CCP military forces; these constituted the key tasks of the Communists in North China. Mao's strategy represented the basic interest of the Communist Party and would sooner or later be accepted by the Party and Army leaders in general. Despite some allegation of Zhou Enlai's disagreement with Mao Zedong over some tactical issues, both Mao and Zhou firmly stood for an rapid independent enrollment of the Red Army troops. In fact, as responsible Communist leaders in power, they could hardly do otherwise. Shortly after the Japanese occupation of Taiyuan, Zhou also sent a telegram to the Party and Army leaders suggesting, among other things, that

> The Red Army should be expanded in order to increase its role as the main force in the national war—this task is far from fulfilled. Hu Fu [alias of Liu Shaoqi] proposed to recruit 100,000 troops in three months. I agree, and suggest that 30,000 be recruited from North China, 5,000 from northern Shaanxi and 15,000 from the old Soviet areas. As for recruitment in North China, please let Zhu, Peng, and Ren issue orders to make concrete arrangements and let local Party and government institutions render support.[82]

Wang Ming and seven members of the CCP Mission to the Comintern flew back to Yan'an in late November 1937. For a while, Wang challenged

Mao's authority and policies. The Politburo held a conference on December 9-14, 1937, in which Wang stressed the slogan "all through the united front" against Mao's slogan "peace, democracy, and resistance."[83] It is true that Wang had first raised the idea of united front against the Japanese two years earlier, so it seemed natural for him to stick to this principle. But more essentially, Wang's position often, if not always, reflected the Comintern's decision and the Soviet Union's interest more than those of the CCP and China. In contrast to Mao, Wang obviously lacked both a sense of CCP's independence and a knowledge of China's political realities. As time passed, Wang's reputation as Comintern commissioner and his eloquent quotations from Marx and Lenin vanished in the face of Mao's practical control of the Party and Army and his concern for Chinese political reality. Wang's challenge to Mao might not have been so serious as has been understood by some historians.[84] In fact, Wang's 'rightist' attitude and activities, like some military men's 'leftist' ones, constituted an integral part of the CCP's general political orientation in 1937-1938, of which Mao was the central representative figure. In other words, both the 'left trend' and the 'right trend' were not only possible but also necessary, because they both had helped make the general line—the 'mean line,' so to speak. Some might take a left wing or radical position; others might take a right wing or conservative position, but so long as Mao, the general manager, could maintain a balance between the left and the right in mind and in action, even a bad thing could sometimes turn into good. To the outsiders, the rightward or the leftward might become a kind of camouflage to cover the CCP's plot to surge forward. The left and the right were like zigs and zags, twists and turns in the path of an entire progressive process, and their possibility and necessity both arose from the need for the general forward direction.

The CCP's staggering growth sharply contrasted the KMT's disastrous collapse in the first year of the Sino-Japanese War. While the regular KMT troops were chased from the North down to the Southwest, the CCP emerged rapidly from the Northwest to the North. By the end of 1938, each of the four Eighth Route Army troops had opened a military base. Their total number grew from 40,000 in early 1937 to 90,000 in late 1937 and 180,000 by the end of 1938.[85] With such exciting successes—not to mention Mao's political dexterity—Mao and his incumbent leadership could not possibly be shaken by Wang Ming and the newly returned leaders. At the CCP Sixth Plenum, convened from September 28 to November 6, 1938, Mao's political and military line was formally adopted by the Party Center; Wang Ming was brushed aside. The importance of the Sixth Plenum lies in the fact that it marked the final establishment of Mao's strategy and authority in the Communist Party.[86]

In a speech on the CCP's overall strategy, which Mao gave to some senior officers in Yan'an at the early phase of the the Sino-Japanese War, he stated frankly: "As for our attention in total, one tenth should be paid to fighting the Japanese; two-tenths to messing around with the Nationalists, and seven-tenths to strengthening ourselves."[87] These remarks may well represent the essence of Mao's strategy throughout the war in general and in its later phase from 1940 to 1945 in particular. For this strategy, Nationalist politicians and historians have rightfully stated that Mao and the CCP were partisan schemers who were interested in clashing with the KMT and expanding their own strength rather than fighting to resist the Japanese invasion.

In reality, the Anti-Japanese War was won through international involvement. Without American and Russian participation, it would have taken many more years for the Chinese to expel the Japanese and recover all lost Chinese territory. To drive the Japanese Guandong Army out of Northeast China seemed far beyond the military capacity of the KMT and the CCP, separately or together.[88] As far as analysis by analogy or hypothesis can be warranted in historical studies, it should also be noted that the KMT Government might more likely have toppled or even surrendered before the Japanese invaders. The Communists were far less vulnerable to the Japanese invasion. The guerrilla warfare of the Communist troops in North China constituted the major obstacle and the biggest nuisance to the Japanese occupiers, and as long as Communist guerrilla activities throughout the countryside existed almost as an integral part of the rural life and society, the Japanese could scarcely claim a total conquest of China. This sweet flattery of the CCP does not mean that, as the Communist politicians and historians often declare, Chiang Kai-shek and the KMT as a whole did not want to fight the Japanese. But in my most emphatic view, I can say no more than that the Nationalist suffered the most but obtained the least in the Sino-Japanese War.[89]

The Communists enjoyed some favorable conditions which the Nationalists could not easily imitate or emulate. The Nationalist troops had to rely on military and provisional supplies from the Government. They were deployed in specific areas; ordered to defend particular locations, they were to conduct a positional war; defeated, they would withdraw; besieged, they would surrender—just as any regular armies would do. For the Communist troops, the "people's army" fighting a "people's war," the situation was entirely different. To resist the Japanese enemy did not only mean directly fighting on the battlefield, and there was also an invisible front. To build up oneself by any means possible also meant to weaken one's enemy. As military men, the Japanese committed strategic errors in confrontation with the Nationalists—they underestimated the resistance of the Nationalist army. As politicians, the Japanese committed even more serious mistakes about the Communists—they never expected that the Communist guerrillas could become their most potent enemy and that all the territory they took over from the hostile Nationalists in North China would become the kingdom of the even more hostile Communists.[90]

10

CONCLUSION: THE LONG MARCH FROM REVOLUTION TO POLITICS

The previous chapters of this book are by and large factual descriptions and explanations of Chinese Communist history in the 1930s. Rather than presenting a simple retrospective by binding together the disparate threads of what has been addressed, as is normally supposed, this concluding chapter attempts to bring the Long March into the broad context of Communist movement and provide some general approaches to Communist politics. In such a painstaking but unlikely rewarding effort, two points come immediately to mind. First, although the significance of any particular historical event can only be fully evaluated in its relation to events beyond the one in question, the broader and deeper discussions go, the more obscure and less definite they necessarily become. It seems that neither ultimate verdict nor final end can be reached in historical studies; historical research is at best a process of passing through endless networks of relationship and countless layers of revelation in depth and breadth, eventually landing nowhere. This situation rightfully leads some historiographers to the belief that history has no meaning in itself and that only historians imbue history with a certain significance.[1]

From my point of view, nonetheless, as long as the insights of historians are broad and profound enough to make a precise judgment of any historical occurrence in question or, in other words, as long as they are broader and more profound than those of the historical figures so that we can reach a more appropriate understanding of what they had done, what they were doing and what they would do, our efforts are fairly justified, and right in such a relative sense lies some absolute criterion of historical studies.

Further, there are a number of controversial questions on CCP history in general and of the 1930s in particular. What caused the CCP's failure and success in China, objectively as well as subjectively? Did the Chinese revolution have more to do with Communism or Nationalism? Was Mao more like a modern Marxist revolutionary or a traditional peasant rebel?

This chapter attends to all these kinds of questions in passing, but tries not to be distracted by any of them from its general course of discussion. In historical research, errors in description are in a certain sense far more persistent than incongruities of general theory. Description is like boxing, where the objective is to knock down an opponent; theory is more like a marathon, where the winner just keeps to his own course and leaves the others to lose by stepping out of bounds, stopping half way, or arriving behind schedule.[2]

The Long March as a Transitional Period

The contrast between the static, introverted, conservative North and the flexible, extroverted, progressive South has loomed large in modern Chinese history. In the modern era, rebellions and revolutions occurred time and time again in South China, while North China remained a reactionary bulwark. But perhaps because intellectuals in the South could find more practical ways to express their insurgent impulses, there was almost no large-scale cultural protest there; in Peking on the other hand—the political center of the North—every few years in this century would witness a new intellectual uproar. It was through the New Culture Movement and the May Fourth Movement in Peking that the doctrines of Marxist theory and Leninist practice were introduced to China in the late 1910s. As Marxism-Leninism gained a more precise political shape, however, it moved south to Shanghai to produce the Communist Party. From there, the Communists went further south to Canton to join the Nationalists in a nationwide revolution.

Decisive battles in the Central South along the Yangtze River between the southern KMT-CCP alliance and the northern warlords ended in the warlords' defeat. It was also in this area that the revolutionary alliance broke apart in 1927: the Nationalists staged the Shanghai Coup and the Communists responded with the Nanchang Uprising. The Communists first intended to direct their troops back to Guangdong to repeat the Northern Expedition, and rested their hopes on the labor unions in Canton and peasant associations in Haifeng and Lufeng. They failed, and could hardly have done otherwise. South China was not prepared for another revolution so soon, either physically or mentally. The Li Lisan Center's call for a full-scale attack on the city of Wuhan was a Communist offensive operation in one sense, but reflected a retreat from the South in another sense. Haifeng and Lufeng were given up, and the 7th Red Army in Guangxi was called back to Jiangxi.

In the wake of the Chiang-Feng-Yan War in 1930, the escalation of the KMT-CCP military confrontation resulted in the five suppression campaigns against the Red Army. Although each Red Army group might have had its own heroic as well as tragic experiences, the Communists as a whole were uprooted from the Central South and pushed all the way up to the Northwest, reducing their influence in South China to a nearly negligible nuisance.

The CCP's burst of growth during the Sino-Japanese War in North China was due in part to the fact that the Japanese intrusion brushed away the hedges of the Nationalist government and left the vast countryside a political vacuum for the Communists to fill. But more substantially, the rural community in North China had not been tackled in the past century and had thus retained a kind of high political potentiality. All its reactionary characteristics were overturned through the revolutionary agitation of the Communist Party during the resistance to Japanese imperialism. By the time the Japanese were defeated, the Communists already had an unconquerable capacity in relation to the Nationalists. Skillfully applying this capacity, they proceeded from the North to take over all of China.

The Long March must thus be seen as a necessary transfer of the Communist movement from the South to the North or, to be more accurate, from the Central South to the Northwest. Of course, such a transfer did not necessarily mean a single, direct process. The Communists had conducted a few other 'long marches' even before the one discussed here. The Nanchang Uprising troops led by Ye Ting and He Long went off to the south for two months in 1927, and ended up failing; Zhang Yunyi directed the 7th Red Army several thousand li from Guangxi to Jiangxi between 1930 and 1931. Although the latter action can now be seen as an indication of the northward retreat, it then constituted a reinforcement of the Communist stronghold in the Central South. The general shift from construction to destruction of Communist forces in the South started with the Fourth Suppression Campaign in 1932. Zhang Guotao's Fourth Front Army and He Long's 3rd Red Army were both driven out of their home bases and pushed to the Southwest, where they enjoyed temporary growth before they were forced to leave again. The Anti-Japanese Vanguard Brigade and the 6th Army Corps both suffered defeats on their expeditions because of their scapegoat missions, though neither Fang Zhimin nor Ren Bishi were quite aware of this status. Their different degrees of failure—Fang's total destruction and Ren's rescue through union with He Long—were due less to their respective command abilities than to their different directions of operation. The Communists in the Jiangxi Soviet might well ascribe their failure in the Fifth Campaign to their own military errors or the superior strength of the KMT side. A more intrinsic reason may be that the Communist movement as a whole could hardly sustain itself in the South. Throughout the Long March, Mao and other leaders in the Central Red Army kept intending to stop and open a new settlement, as they were reluctant to move far away from their southern base. Wherever they arrived, however, they found conditions unsuitable and had to look forward to another, adjacent place. Just as they were on the verge of desperation, they ran into northern Shaanxi and re-settled there. Rather than sheer coincidence, the unintentional arrival of the Central Red Army in northern Shaanxi, as well as that of the 25th Red Army, may be regarded as the embodiment of a sort of historical dictation. In this view, Zhang Guotao's turning back to the South was not merely a tactical mistake, but rather a serious orientational blunder. The fate of Chen Changhao's Western Route Army may also be understood in such a deep sense: since it attempted to leave China Proper, or the Chinese political stadium, for the distant periphery, it could only lead to failure in the political contest in China. In terms of concrete military operations, however, quite another explanation is possible, and we will live to see that it was the Military Council headed by Mao that was directly responsible for the Western Route Army's debacle.

The Communist Party was founded in late July 1921 with about fifty members. It experienced a steady growth in the next two years, but it was not until its collaboration with the KMT in 1924 that the CCP saw an upsurge of growth. Its Fifth Congress recorded nearly 60,000 members in April 1927. But because of the clash between the KMT and the CCP, this figure was sharply reduced to 10,000 in the next three months. The Communists fought back in a series of armed uprisings, then moved to the countryside to regain military autonomy. They gradually gained in strength, claiming 300,000 Party members and 300,000 army men in 1933. Then again, the Fifth Suppression Campaign and the Long March deprived them of nine tenths of their Soviet territory and reduced the Party and the Army to about 30,000 each in early 1937.

The Japanese invasion accompanied the Communist expansion. The year 1937 saw the CCP with 100,000 members and 90,000 troops before its conclusion. The CCP kept rolling and growing like a snowball: by the end of the Sino-Japanese War in 1945 it had 1,200,000 members and regular army forces totalling more than 900,000, in addition to a few millions of *minbing* (people's militiamen). Most of North China fell into the hands of the Communists, and they continued to grow during the Civil War and took over all China between 1946 and 1949. By the time the People's Republic was declared, CCP membership was 5,000,000 and PLA enrollment 4,000,000.

A graphic indication of CCP fortunes during its 28-year-long revolution can be found in the table accompanying the following note.[3] Though these statistics may not be entirely accurate, they should be sufficiently so to support the following generalization: while the CCP generally enjoyed a growth during its revolutionary years, it had suffered two major setbacks, one in 1927 and one between 1933 and 1936; after 1937 it sustained successful growth with little interruption. In this sense, and only in this sense, the Long March represents a demarcation between failure and success in the CCP's revolution.

Many factors contribute to the ups and downs of a political party. Ordinarily, these factors can be categorized in terms of 'objective conditions' and 'subjective performance', although such categorization must immediately invite counter-argument—any political party has an innate nature or inherent features which can hardly be altered even by its own leaders, thus some part of 'subjective performances' is actually 'objective conditions', and because policy choices made by any political leader should take all conditions into account, some 'objective conditions' are actually part of 'subjective performance'.

In a certain sense, the Communists were superior by virtue of their revolutionary character to the Nationalists, just as the Nationalists had been superior by virtue of their revolutionary character to the northern warlords. There is no doubt that the CCP differed fundamentally from the KMT in its Marxist-Leninist doctrines, which stressed global struggle of oppressed nations against imperialism on the one hand and the mass struggle of exploited classes against exploiting classes on the other. While their revolutionary character in general enabled the Communists to maintain high morale and strict discipline, it was mainly those programs of social and economic revolution that gave them vitality and the potential for massive growth. These factors culminated in a situation where, if they encountered no or insufficient containment, the Communists would propagate through their social and economic programs among industrial workers in the cities and peasants in the countryside. This revolutionary character substantially constituted the Communists' superiority over the Nationalists.

But in reality, social and economic revolution are but one part of state politics, and the CCP's social and economic programs were necessarily brought to confront the KMT government's political containment. After all, the CCP was itself a political party. After two years of modest success in building a labor movement in the early 1920s, the CCP faced its first serious political decision: whether it should join the KMT. The Communist leaders were unwilling to participate in the alliance at first, when it was beneficial, nor were they willing to withdraw from it at last when it became detrimental. In fact, CCP policy in this period was masterminded by the Comintern and manipulated by the KMT. Among its grave problems was an inability to conceive of an independent function in contemporary Chinese politics. In the Jiangxi Soviet period, the Communists apparently lost for two reasons: their military adoption of the pure defensive line and their unwillingness to cooperate with the Fujian Revolt. Behind these obvious failures lay a more central deficiency: the Bo Gu Center could not appropriately understand and handle Chinese political reality.

Reviewing these previous failures, Mao correctly surmised that the Communist Party was at that time infantile and naive. The errors of the above periods came from some common roots: too much revolutionary zeal had been combined with too little political savvy; leaders had been involved in politics and yet too revolutionary to qualify as politicians; too much idealism had left behind realism; and too great an insistence on Marxist doctrines had led to the neglect of Chinese affairs.[4]

After the Long March, the basic orientation of the CCP's mentality and practice had changed. The Communists at first earnestly appealed to the KMT for another alliance. But once such an alliance was achieved, they would not allow it to "bind our hands and feet" and remained ready to start "friction" with the Nationalists whenever it seemed advantageous. They talked loudly about combatting the Japanese and were indeed stubborn in doing so, but they also knew how to avoid their own sacrifices in fighting the Japanese, and how to expand their military strength and local dominion under the slogan of the national war. The result was staggering growth during the Sino-Japanese War.

The Civil War was apparently a period of intense military engagement. Despite the unprecedented scale of warfare from 1946-1949, however, the focal issue for the CCP was not war operation but peace negotiation with the Nanking Government. As Mao put it, all that the Communists had obtained in years on the battlefield could be lost at the negotiation table in a single day. Despite the disrespect for or the suspicion of the Communists' strength on the parts of the KMT, the USA, and even the USSR, no one was clearer than Mao on the fact that the KMT could no longer defeat the CCP simply by military means in the year 1946. Therefore, the primary decision Mao made for the CCP was to fight against the KMT to take over state power, and the secondary decision was to talk with the KMT to create all favorable domestic and foreign conditions. Mentally speaking, Mao had the upper hand against Chiang, to say nothing of Stalin and Truman, neither of whom knew Chinese affairs well or took them seriously. The result was that instead of being conquered through negotiation, the CCP took full advantage of its talks with the KMT.[5]

Summing up the CCP's experiences in the 1940s, Mao eloquently stressed "three magic wands" by dint of which the CCP would achieve the final victory in China: Party organization, military struggle, and the united front. It is obvious that these "creative developments of Marxism" by Mao all fall into the category of political 'forms' and not revolutionary 'substance'. If the first 28 years of CCP history, 1921-1949, witnessed a process of transformation from Marxist revolution to Maoist politics, the Long March in the mid-1930s stood as the greatest milestone of this transformation.[6]

Revolution and Politics

This study has alluded so often to the terms "revolution" and "politics" that some questions will naturally come up: What do we think are revolution and politics? How to distinguish them and relate them with each other? The words of revolution and politics are used in so many different ways, academic or not, that no commonly agreeable definitions seem possible. The proceeding theoretical excursion should be considered primarily in relation to the present context, as either an extension of our knowledge of the CCP history in the 1930s or a background from which to reach a better understanding of it.

In a broad sense, politics can be defined as the interactions between man and man or, even better, as the internal relationship of mankind; politics involves several phases of human affairs and several aspects of human behaviors—not merely social administration or state governance.[7] Revolution, on the other hand, can be understood as referring to some drastic change of the present condition—not exclusively in political affairs and/or even human affairs.[8] To make the distinction more apparent, politics represents an area of human affairs while revolution a mode of motion, and there is not necessarily any connection between them. In a narrower or more ordinary sense, however, politics can be understood as the overall operation of social and governmental institutions and revolution as the drastic transformation of such institutions. By dint of these narrow definitions politics and revolution are brought into the same field of study.[9] The above remarks will probably incur arguments and invite disagreements, but each of them has its own worth or truth in the initial terms as well as in the final analyses.

Politics is operation, therefore recognition, of the existing condition, whereas revolution is transformation, therefore negation, of the status quo. Because politics recognizes the status quo, it is more concerned with present reality; revolution denies the status quo, and thus often reflects images of the future. Hence, politics and revolution contrast with one another, yielding the dichotomy of political realism and revolutionary idealism.[10] These remarks may also incur arguments, but each of them may also have its own worth in the initial terms and in the final analyses.

It is only in the sense that revolution stands for an extraordinary type of politics that it contrasts with politics. Hence lies the distinction between as well as connection with revolution/revolutionary and politics/politician. Politicians also demand change, sometimes drastic change. Although all politicians tend to take contemporary conditions as their starting point, few of them are entirely content with the present situation and few governments are not in need of some change. Therefore, the best, most far-sighted politician may become the best, most careful-minded revolutionary, while the worst politician may turn into the worst revolutionary. But ordinary politicians can seldom be ordinary revolutionaries. Similarly, revolutionaries also need internal maintenance and external compromise in order to make a successful revolution. Outstanding revolutionaries can become outstanding politicians and downgraded revolutionaries can become downgraded politicians, while ordinary revolutionaries remain different from ordinary politicians.

Terms like 'overall operation' and 'drastic change' may also be considered to be a bit ambiguous. By the term 'overall', I suggest a dual meaning. It means a general involvement with all the internal aspects of a society, a company, a party, or a state—whatever human institution—but without specific attachment to any particular aspect of it. Externally speaking, 'overall operation' means representation of a society or a state as one entity in relation with other societies or states. By 'drastic', I mean not only something extraordinary in an impersonal sense, but also something beyond human expectation. Revolution comes as a shock or a surprise, perhaps not to the revolutionaries, but definitely to those in the general political arena of which the revolutionaries are only a constituent part and upon which the revolution exerts its impact.

Furthermore, the terms 'operation' and 'change' should also be defined in their own dual sense, either as results of objective observation and reflection of some situation in the past or as as goals of subjective aspiration for some future situation. Politics can be either an art or a science, and people interested in politics can be either political participants or political observers. As a matter of fact, more or less the same type of statement can be made about revolution and people interested in revolution.

Some scholars would claim that revolution differs from politics in two basic ways: the employment of violence to deprive the opponents of power and the transformation of the social and state systems—simply put, violence as a means and transformation as a result; violence distinguishes revolution from reformation or evolution; transformation of the society and the state identifies a revolution as different than a coup or a rebellion.[11] Theoretically as well as practically, however, few revolutions can fulfill both prerequisites at the same time in the same place. To carry out a plan of changing the social order and the state system, for instance, one has to obtain power through either military confrontation or electoral competition or something in between. In other words, one has to operate the governmental apparatus in order to change the state power. Such operation is in essence political and not revolutionary. After becoming the ruling party of the government, all the alleged "revolutionary programs" that the party claims are no longer revolutionary in the sense that they are adopted basically to consolidate, not to overthrow, the overall political order and power. These programs have already become social reforms of a sort, like those of the Russian

Communist Party in 1936 and of the Chinese Communist Party in 1956, and they can hardly be treated as true revolution. Here is a dilemma for revolution and revolutionaries: no revolutionaries can easily dispense with being politicians, and no revolution can separate itself from politics in the long run.

Revolutionaries may, and often do, carry out moderate policies within their own ranks to solidify their own position in order to compete efficiently in a broader arena—from a local or social or partisan basis under their control to bid for power in the whole state, then from a state basis to bid for power in an international or global range. They may talk about revolution for the future as an encouragement to their own comrades or as an inspiration for the masses. After obtaining national power and becoming the ruling party, they may indeed change some social systems partly as necessary fulfillment of their previous promises but mainly for enhancement of their present position. In the long run, any leaders of a new regime will have to face the fact that such operations as "continuous revolution" or "permanent revolution" can but damage the national and partisan interest as well as jeopardize their personal position. It is better even for their own interests to become disloyal, "revisionist" politicians rather than remain diehard, "dogmatist" revolutionaries.

Violence can in this context be considered a pure form of politics, having little to do with revolution. But the opposite allegation may be equally true: violence is in itself a pure form of revolution, having little to do with politics. There are historical cases in which radical changes of social and state institutions occurred without much violence, as in the Industrial Revolution in Western Europe or the Meiji Restoration in Japan; and there are even more historical cases in which violence occurred in the form of rebellion or war without resulting in any apparent social and state transformation. Despite the complexities and subtle interactions which the dichotomy of revolution and politics entails, the following paradigm regarding their differentiation should be of some referential worth.

Politics/Politician	Revolution/Revolutionary
internal relationships of mankind	drastic mode of change
manipulation of social and state institutions	transformation of social and state institutions
change for order's sake	order for change's sake
realism	idealism
poised professionalism	agitating charisma
state power	social force
overall maintenance	factional confrontation

according to rules at hand   according to ideas in mind
stand at the present   look to the future
persuasive, piecemeal   compulsory, holistic
   improvement   renovation

Communism in Transformation

Throughout CCP history Mao seemed to have been the foremost political realist but, ironically and yet reasonably, it is also Mao who appeared to have almost single-handedly preserved the spirit of revolutionary idealism. This situation was most apparent in the post-liberation years, when many formerly idealistic revolutionaries tended to become pragmatic politicians while Mao remained ever resolute as a utopian revolutionary. In reality, the first three decades of the People's Republic under Mao's leadership witnessed the fact that politics had become part of revolution. Hence one political revolution after another occurred in the People's Republic of China (PRC) under Mao's leadership.[12]

The founding of the People's Republic divided the entire CCP history into two clear-cut parts: the years of insurrection and the years of administration. Before 1949, it was the 'end' of the Communists to seize state power; but after 1949, since state power was already in their hands, it had become for them the 'means'. Some questions would naturally arise: What would be the new end? What would be the new orientation for the Party or China—shift to economic construction, keep to political revolution, something else? For Mao as head of the Party and the regime, these questions could be translated into personal psychological terms: what kind of Chinese Revolution had he been thinking about and working for throughout his life and career?[13] Was Mao a man who had played revolutionary games to fulfill his political ambition of becoming another emperor, or was Mao a man who played political games to fulfill his revolutionary ambition of making a utopian China? Aware of the validity of both these views, I would rather think the three decades of the PRC were a period which had demonstrated Mao's revolutionary identity at disastrous political cost to the CCP.

To satisfy his commitment to international revolution, Mao seldom faltered simply to preserve China's national interests. In the 1950s he sponsored participation in the Korean War and rejected any compromise with American imperialism. Through the 1960s, he masterminded the Sino-Russian polemics, relentlessly denouncing Russian revisionism. By the 1970s, the tiny country of Albania was left as China's sole revolutionary comrade, though soon to become yet another "revisionist traitor." Regardless of terrible economic conditions at home, massive amounts of monetary and material aid were poured abroad to support almost any revolution in any place in the world.

This was certainly not just for pursuit of chauvinist expansion in terms of Chinese own benefits, but mainly for making the world revolution at the sacrifice of Chinese national interests.

Domestically, Mao carried out one political campaign after another—every seven or eight years there should be one, and each one should last for seven or eight years, as he put it. He began by eliminating the remnants of former KMT officers and officials; then he started the anti-rightist campaign to suppress the "neutral force" of capitalists, intellectuals and democrats, to whom the Communists owed much of their victory. Eventually, the revolutionary spearhead shifted to point at the Party itself. With almost all of his former colleagues and comrades labelled right opportunists, capitalist roaders, or black gangsters, by his death in 1976, only a small gang of four or five individuals remained in the Party who could claim to be Mao's intimate "co-fighters," against whom Mao also held various suspicions, and who were to become "reactionary intriguers" after Mao's demise.

Up to 1956, the new Communist regime operated generally according to scheduled plans. The distribution of land to the peasants followed by the collectivization of agriculture, and the deprivatization of industrial and commercial enterprises followed by the establishment of state ownership—both completed by 1956—can be understood as true revolutionary actions in one sense and as evolutionary ones in another. After 1956, Mao boldly plunged into inexperienced and unexpected situations. Even the slogan of economic construction, such as the Great Leap Forward (1958), was primarily an expression of revolutionary idealism, hence its failure.[14] The real irony of his position in the Cultural Revolution (1966-76) was that Mao dwelled on top of the bureaucratic pyramid while denouncing the whole bureaucracy; thus the boldness of Mao as a revolutionary was also the absurdity of Mao as a politician. It may be true that, as many writers think, Mao started the Cultural Revolution to further add to his power; but it may be truer to say that Mao was then tired of and wanted to shed his power.

There were certain particular periods of PRC history, certain individual leaders in the CCP, and even certain aspects of Mao's own behavior that reflected an ordinary or moderate political line. The "five principles of peaceful coexistence" implemented by Zhou Enlai in the middle 1950s, the "eight-character policy" of economic rehabilitation pursued by Liu Shaoqi and others in the early 1960s were among the many examples of this concern. These may prove that political reality did exert its influence on revolutionary ideas in the long run, but this political realism actually constituted a deceptive camouflage for the revolutionary idealism of the CCP and the PRC in Mao's era.

Chinese politics still dictated over Mao's revolution, though sometimes in a crooked way. Since the contemporary world order stood as an impossible barrier to his revolutionary adventures abroad, Mao could only shift his revolutionary zeal to domestic affairs under his control, swinging from economic revolution to social revolution to political revolution, and finally to cultural revolution or "revolution of people's minds." In reality, Mao's noblest slogan of revolution had become the most brutal politics: the creation of his one-man dictatorship at the expense of not only the whole nation but his own Party.

Through Mao Zedong's demise, the CCP has awakened from revolutionary nightmare to political daylight. This is a necessary process notwithstanding all the involved personal factors. The current CCP leader, Deng Xiaoping, is commonly considered a pragmatist who "does not care whether a cat is white or black as long as it catches mice." Deng's domestic policy is highlighted as "two systems in one country": an injection into the Communist economy and society of capitalistic elements like private enterprises, market values, and profit incentives. Equally impressive is Deng's new attitude toward foreign affairs; vividly called the "open door policy," it is an invitation of western technology and even culture. For better or worse, these actions constitute a substantial adulteration of Mao's revolutionary line.

The dichotomy of revolution and politics is nevertheless expressing itself to the Chinese Communists in the form of some paradoxical problems. If economic affairs are now supposed to be the major concern of the Party and the nation, how can Communist leaders in China claim their superiority over capitalist America and Taiwan and even over the revisionist Soviet Union—all of which have incomparably higher economic standards? Forced to abandon revolutionary charisma and yet unable to create a new political professionalism, how can the CCP leaders justify their legitimacy as the sole ruling elite in China? More urgently, revolution means idealism, and once revolutionary idealism is dismissed, political corruption will naturally introduce itself. Revolution or corruption—this is a dilemma nagging totalitarian regimes in general and present-day China in particular.

The new Communist leaders keep talking about Marxism-Leninism and Mao Zedong Thought, about the vanguard leadership of the proletarian class, and about socialism and world revolution. They are not merely talking; in a certain sense, to a certain degree, and under certain circumstances, they mean it. Studies of fluctuations between revolution and politics still serve as one of the most convenient emphases in understanding the current developments of the CCP and China. Domestically, anything like policy shift and military division—more chaotic even than the Cultural Revolution—is possible for China. In the international arena, fanatic foreign policies are also possible, as long as the country's economic program fails and its revolutionary legacy remains. Either of these possibilities may once again bring sharp surprises to many casual observers. For the far future, the current economic reform, which the CCP leaders have taken and have to take, may prove a turn for the better. But such a process will probably take place at the expense of the revolutionary heritage and political power of the incumbent Communist leaders and even the Communist Party as a whole. In this one or two decade at least, China will still be obsessed by political rehabilitation and not economic construction; only after this chaotic stage is passed, can a true modernization campaign—probably and hopefully—set forth on its true course.[15]

The ideological inspiration of a classless nation and a nationless world, the practical activities for betterment of the working people's livelihood, and the force of a strictly disciplined party with a strong international background had from its original phase constituted the basic dynamism of the Communist movement, despite its many setbacks which resulted more often than not from various political conditions. Marx himself was a 'scholar-type' without much political experience. The Communist movement has ever since followed a general process of politicization, involving many individual leaders who may be categorized as either 'loyal traitors' or 'treacherous loyalists' of Marx and Marxism.

For quite a few decades in the late 19th century and the early 20th century, the German Communists were the strongest and most promising in the Communist world. And yet, it seemed that time and again they earned their strength through revolutionary propaganda and organization for years and then wasted it all at some critical political juncture. From the 1860s to the 1890s, it was obvious that the Marxian social revolution was overshadowed and overcome by Bismarckian *realpolitik*. In the Second Comintern years at the turn of this century, the German Communists were independent but not united and, coming to the Third Comintern in the 1920s and 1930s, they were united but no longer independent. In a certain sense, the failure of the German Communists promoted and preserved the victory of the Russian Communists, and thus international Communism can better be understood in light of international politics.[16]

In the late 1920s, the imaginary attacks on Soviet Union by the Western powers (hence the slogan "All for protecting the Soviet Union") and the factional struggle of the leftist Stalin against the rightist Zhnoviev dictated to the Third Comintern a line of revolutionary extremism, which deprived each member party in the Comintern of its spiritual independence and practical flexibility as the necessary cost of any decisive success. Emphases on class identity and class struggle, for example, had led the German Communists to regard the German Socialists as their chief enemy and thus to neglect or even support the Nazis for some years. Then Hitler's coup in 1933 totally deprived the German Communists of their vigor and vitality in world Communism once and for all.[17]

The new policy of a united front against Fascism on the one hand and the secret agreement between Stalin and Hitler on the other hand continued to taunt the European Communists in the late 1930s. It was not until after the start of the Second World War in 1939 and, above all, Hitler's attack on Russia in 1941 that the Communists in Europe resolutely threw themselves into the resistance movement for any valid reasons. They did this gallantly in the following years. Except those with the strongest anti-Communist prejudice, few historians would deny the staunch stand and crucial role of the Communists in the resistance. But many historians chose to ignore the fact that the firmness and efficiency of the Communist resistance was directly due to its revolutionary character.

The power division between the Soviet Union and the Western allies led to an international division between the Communist world and the Capitalist world after their common victory in World War II. Some countries would become Communist while others would remain Capitalist. As to which turned what, there were various contributing factors, among which the military strength and political prowess of the Communist party in a particular country were among the most decisive. The Japanese Communists could by no means take state power because of the American occupation, while some Eastern European countries such as Poland and Hungary were turned into Communist regimes because of the Russian occupation. But it was in those European and Asian countries which were not directly under military occupation of either the Soviet Union or the Western powers, and in which Communists had built up some territorial bases and armed forces through the resistance movement but had not yet established any firm control of the national government that the Communist politicians were most seriously tested, and it is those cases which especially interest us here.

The French Communist Party grew to be a most influential force right through the most difficult period of the resistance in the early 1940s. In late 1944, when the British and American troops landed on the Continent and swiftly pushed the Germans northward—already a favorable condition for the Communists, as was proved in China—the French Communist guerrillas obediently followed the military orders of the Allied Headquarters and rendered whole-hearted support to the war, leaving De Gaulle behind to take over and set up the state machinery. After the war, the French Communist Party handed over 100,000 troops in exchange for joining the government and participating in the national election. It won a quarter of the votes at first, while Thorez and a few other Communist leaders assumed ministries in the national government. After a year or so, however, both the Party and its leaders were removed from the government for various reasons—politics is never too stingy to provide a loser with some excuse. The Italian Communists fared much in the same manner. They also disarmed their troops to join the government and were rewarded with speeches of thanks and praise in addition to several cabinet seats. They kept barely active until the late 1940s when the antagonism between the Soviet Bloc and the West in the cold war years naturally created friction between the Communists and the Italian government. They were thrown out of the government in 1947. In the sense that it was basically beyond their expectations, the above occurrences can only be understood as failures for the French and Italian Communist Parties.[18]

The Greek Communist Party is another example—perhaps a more pertinent one. The withdrawal of the Germans in late 1944 left the Balkan Peninsula (i.e., Yugoslavia, Albania and Greece) more or less to Communist guerrilla troops. The Communists took over Yugoslavia and Albania with their overwhelmingly superior military strength, while the Communists in Greece failed due to political errors. In September 1944, the Greek Communists answered the Allied Headquarters' call to participate in the Greek government newly formed in London. They kept politely quiet until the British troops escorted the government to take Athens. Then, offended to learn that the Greek government and the British wanted them to surrender their military troops and territorial bases, the Communists rebelled in December 1944 and reached a stalemate with British reinforcement troops in February 1945. At the peace negotiations, the Communists agreed to give up their troops for a legitimate position. They lost the national election in 1946 and were suppressed afterwards. Once again they gathered their troops to revolt, and were crushed in 1949. The second civil war sealed the Communists' legal status in the government and uprooted their political influence in Greece. The whole process serves as a perfect illustration of the truth that rules of the political game may exert themselves with especial catholicity on those revolutionaries who try to defy them. Comparing the experiences and fate of the Chinese and Greek Communists in the postwar "talk and fight," there is little doubt that the latter failed for lack of political prowess.[19]

Much better—though still not good enough—political savvy was displayed by Kim Il Sung in Korea. Under the persuasion of the Soviet Union, the Korean Communists accepted the general terms of peace in 1946. But enviously watching Mao take over China by force regardless of domestic and foreign opinions, Kim started a belated military action in 1950. The United States stepped in and the Korean War became an international issue. Korea was permanently divided into the Communist North and the Capitalist South. On many occasions, a political game is first played as a heroic success, then repeated as a farcical fiasco.

Despite certain leaders of the Comintern and the Soviet Union's arrogant arguments to the contrary, the CCP's "United Front" policy in the latter half of the 1930s was adopted and implemented primarily by Mao and the Party Center inside China.[20] This was quite different from the situation for most European Communists. The Chinese Communists were manipulating the Comintern whereas the European Communists were manipulated

by the Comintern.[21] During the resistance movement, they were all doing
the same thing and no serious tests confronted them. Their successes were
also just alike, as their revolutionary characters and performances were
identical.

After the war, the differences emerged when the Chinese Communists
proved more independent-minded and politically oriented and, consequently,
more resourceful and successful. The Communists in Italy, France, and
Greece committed serious political mistakes in dealing with the issue of
peaceful negotiation and military confrontation, and they had too many
revolutionary ideals and too few political accomplishments. This may have
seemed merely a matter of postwar global strategy, but a deeper explanation
can be found. One of the profound reasons for this lies in the fact that
before entering the world war, none of them had ever undergone such
complex political experiences as the CCP: the union and split with the
Nationalists, the success and failure in the civil war and, above all, the
dreadful and yet rewarding Long March.

In the contemporary Communist world, positive signs of fundamental
transformation can be identified, though with shifts in balance at particular
times and places. Generally speaking, the Communist world is realigned
more by political norms than by revolutionary fantasy. As regards the most
influential Communist regimes, the Soviet Union has had few basic changes
in its social and political systems since the late 1930s. That is to say, the
Russian Communists lost their central orientation of revolution at home,
and their revolutionary spearhead could only be turned to foreign affairs,
'expansionism' as the West would like to put it.[22] Economic stagnation and
ideological deterioration at home and nationalist dissolution from Eastern
Europe constitute the defensive side of Soviet politics. It is mainly by dint
of steadfast expansion in world politics, notably in the non-European
continents, that the Soviet regime may still claim its revolutionary viability.
At best, this also means that as long as the USSR keeps making progress
in the "world revolution," it can maintain a fairly stable political situation
at home. Although it may also join the Soviet Union in the world revolution,
starker economic backwardness will doom China to a period of "national
shrinkage," which will in turn contribute to bringing a period of political
upheaval. The current reform movements in Russia and China reflect the
same trend of transformation in the Communist world, but their respective
domestic and international consequences can be quite different, a situation
neither Deng nor Gorbachev seems to fully realize yet.[23]

Postwar history shows that the more military strength and political
experience it gathered previously, the more independent a Communist
regime tended to be from the Soviet Union, and only through heated
ideological schism might it eventually reach a lukewarm political relationship
with the Soviet Union—as Yugoslavia and China have done. Countries

like Czechoslovakia and Bulgaria in Europe and Mongolia in Asia are obsessed with authentic Communist doctrines and principles, but they actually tend to become political puppets, helplessly dependent on the Russians. Their lofty revolutionary ideology can only turn into vulgar political mockery, in which even leaders of these countries feel disgusted now and then. Riding between the two extremes are Communist countries like Korea and Romania. Ironically for their moderate stand on international communism, Kim Il Sung and Ceausescu fall back to the monarchical age with their family dictatorships.

In Western Europe, Communists may bring their capitalist countries more communist features, while the Eastern European countries may further loosen their communist systems to appeal to capitalism. This is not just the course they have been pursuing at the present, but the one they will most probably follow in the future. Communist activities in the African and South American continents, which have had less connection with Marxist doctrines and Soviet authority from their very origin, are a unique phenomenon of the present world. While traditional social injustice prompted this movement, economic backwardness relative to the modern international standard represents the root cause. The movement constitutes a challenge to the dominance in world politics of the western powers, rather than a threat to the capitalist economic system.

A general shift of the Communist movement from revolution to politics does not necessarily imply that the western powers can sit contented and just wait for Russia and China to complete "peaceful evolution from Communism back to Capitalism," for at least two basic reasons. First, this study of the Chinese Communist Party should show that when they adhere strictly to their revolutionary ideology, Communists may be most incompatible with their opponents and yet most vulnerable to them; on the other hand, as Communists grow more politically realistic, they may share more common ground with their opponents, but in the meantime become more challenging to them. Second, the Capitalist world—the western world or the free world, whatever one calls it—itself needs and will go through some changes in a profound sense. By now it should be fairly imaginable that, for instance, further setbacks in world politics may cause more domestic strife in the United States. For few political parties and politicians in power, either of Communist countries or of Capitalist countries, can the present study be taken more as a direct encouragement to what they are doing than as an unconditional approbation of what their predecessors have done. Confident in their minds and liberal in their actions, they are all driven along a necessary process of world politics. In this sense, I would say that mankind is still on a Long March.[24]

NOTES

Chapter 1

1. When this footnote was written in early 1986, Marcos, president of the Philippines, had just been dethroned and President Aquino was facing the problem of how to deal with the American Air Force bases and the Communist guerrillas; the South Korean opposition parties were waging a campaign to protest the Chun military regime while Chun used the threat from Communist North Korea to curb opposition activities; President Reagan was escalating his anti-terrorist terror against Qaddafi of Libya; and the USA government was hesitating over military aid to the Contras fighting with the Sandinistas in Nicaragua, while Soviet leader Gorbachev was earnestly carrying out the *glasnost* or open-door policy and calling for reduction and even elimination of nuclear weapons. The linkage of all these international events with the communist-capitalist confrontation can be easily recognized. Negatively, a nuclear war between the superpowers would blow the human race off, and positively, if the arms race were stopped and all the resources and endeavors conducted in peaceful economic development, the general production of the world could be doubled in half a decade—in Khrushchev's words. In this material sense, we really live in an age unprecedented in mankind's history.

2. See Ben Yang, "Long March Survivors Remain in Control of China," in *Mingbao yuekan* (Mingbao Monthly), December 1984.

3. There are a few journalistic works on the Long March, notably Edgar Snow's *Red Star Over China* (1938), Dick Wilson's *The Long March* (1970) and Harrison Salisbury's *The Long March: An Untold Story* (1985).

4. See Shi Ping, "The Heroic Western March," in *Gongchan guoji* (The Communist International), vol.7, No. 1-2, p. 45; also Chen Yun, "Notes for Communicating the Enlarged Politburo Conference at Zunyi," written in February or March 1935, and published in *People's Daily*, January 17, 1985.

5. See Warren Kuo (Guo Hualun), *Zhonggong shilun* (An Analytical History of the Chinese Communist Party) (Taipei, 1969), vol. 3, pp. 9-10, and Cai Xiaoxian, *Jiangxi suqu hongjun xichuan huiyi* (Recollections of the Jiangxi Soviet Area and the Red Army's Western Flight), (Taipei, 1970), pp. 201-205.

6. Xue Yue, *Jiaofei jishi* (A True Record of Bandit Extermination) (n.p., n.d. but obviously 1937), Preface, p. 1.

7. Mao Zedong, "On the Tactics in Fighting Japanese Imperialism," in *Mao Zedong xuanji* (Selected Works of Mao Zedong, hereafter MX) (bound volume, Beijing, 1966), vol. 1, p. 135-136.

8. See *Zhongguo gongnong hongjun diyi fangmianjun changzheng ji* (Records of the Long March of the First Army Corps of the Chinese Worker and Peasant Red Army, hereafter *HJCZJ*) (Beijing, 1958), vol. 2, the appendix.

9. Tetsuya Kataoka, *Resistance and Revolution in China* (Berkeley, 1974), p. 12.

10. Chalmers Johnson, *Peasant Nationalism and Communist Power* (Stanford, 1964), p. 7.

11. Ilpyong Kim, *The Politics of the Chinese Communism: Kiangsi under the Soviets* (Berkeley, 1973), p. 201.

12. Johnson, Preface, viii.

13. Benjamin Schwartz, *The Chinese Communist Party and the Rise of Mao* (Cambridge, Mass., 1979), pp. 189-190.

14. Ibid.

15. Shanti Swarup, *A Study of the Chinese Communist Movement, 1927-1935* (Stanford, 1966), p. 266.

16. Kataoka, pp. 309-310.

17. Quite a number of historians have, directly or indirectly, approached this theme. See Kataoka, pp. 309-311; Swarup, pp. 73-75, 101-104, 259-266; Trygve Lotveit, *Chinese Communism,1931-1934* (Lunt, 1975), pp. 210-211; William Wei, *The Counterrevolution* (Ann Arbor, 1985), conclusion.

Kataoka points out that the Communist revolution cannot be expanded indefinitely regardless of political circumstances. He metaphorizes the CCP as fish and the Chinese masses as water and then characterizes the Long March as a time when the CCP "fish" swam without the masses "water"; Shanti Swarup notes the difference among Mao's revolutionary realism and Li Lisan's revolutionary idealism and then Wang Ming and Bo Gu's revolutionary romanticism; Lotveit alluded to Mao's moderate realistic line in contrast with the previous leaders' overzealous revolutionary line; Wei says that through their experience in the Long March, the Communists learn to be like a supple bamboo which bends over the political winds.

18. For an insightful study of the substance-function debate in the late Qing dynasty, see Joseph Levenson, *Confucian China and its Modern Fate: A Trilogy* (Berkeley, 1968), vol. 1, pp. 59-77.

19. John Fairbank, *The United States and China* (Cambridge, Mass. 1983), p. 547.

20. Derek Waller, *The Kiangsi Soviet Republic: Mao and the Two National Congresses of 1931 and 1934* (Berkeley, 1973).

21. Gong Chu, *Woyu hongjun* (The Red Army and I), (Hong Kong, 1953), p. 389-394. It is bizarre that some ex-CCP leaders denounce their past communist allegiance while at the same time boasting of and even exaggerating their previous positions in the communist movement.

22. John Rue, *Mao Tse-tung in Opposition* (Stanford, 1966), p. 263. It should be noticed that the *pinyin* system in spelling Chinese names is generally adopted in this study except for direct quotations from previous works in English.

23. See Dick Wilson, *The Long March* (New York, 1971), pp. 135-136; Jerome Ch'en, "Resolutions of the Tsun-yi Conference," in *China Quarterly*, October 1969, pp. 18-19.

24. The city of Zunyi was the second largest city in Guizhou. The convocation of the Zunyi Conference was decided by the Politburo and had nothing to do with the military leaders. Mao did not take Zhou's place as Chairman of the Military Council: in fact, Zhou had not had such a position in the CCP Center since the late 1920s. Zhou's power in military command was actually increased, not decreased, at the Zunyi Conference. Ye Jianying was not dropped from his position and he was at that time less Zhou's man than Mao's. Deng Fa was not changed as head of the Security Department. Liu Bocheng became Chief of the Staff before the Long March. Wang Jiaxiang had never been the Political Commissar of the Red Army; Wang was a supporter, not an opponent, of Mao at the Zunyi Conference.

25. Noriyuki Tokuda, Mo Takuto shugi no seiji rikigaku (The Political Dynamics of Maoism) (Tokyo, 1977), p. 5 and pp. 8-127. Tokuda divides Mao's establishment of authority in the CCP into three phases: 1. formation of a certain extent of controlling position—in the Zunyi Conference in 1935; 2. accumulation of authority resulting in tranformation of leading power to authority—in the Sixth Plenum in 1938; 3. Personalized charismatic authority—in the Rectification Movement in 1942. Despite my appreciation of Tokuda's general approach, I am unconvinced of his assumption of Mao's decrease in authority in the 1950s and the 1960s.

26. While most documents used in this study are noted with their inclusion in or quotation by published literature—some of them published internally in China— a few pieces are jotted down from the archives.

27. Schwartz, p. 3.

Chapter 2

1. This observation may be applied to the formation of quite a number of new regimes in pre-modern Chinese history such as the dynasties of Han, Jin, Tang, Sung, Ming and Qing.

2. Li Hanyun, Cong ronggong dao qingdang (From Accommodating the CCP to Purifying the KMT) (Taipei, 1966), pp. 15-21.

3. Hu Qiaomu, Zhongguo gongchangdang sanshi nian (The Past Thirty Years of the Chinese Communist Party) (Beijing, 1951), pp. 20-22.

4. Li Shoukong, Guomin geming shi (A History of the Nationalist Revolution) (Taipei, 1965), p. 465.

5. See Harold Issacs, The Tragedy of the Chinese Revolution (Stanford, 1951), p. 111. Referring to the smooth progress of the Nationalist army on the Northern Expedition, Issacs writes, "the spontaneous rising of the people gave the Kuomintang armies little more to do, often, than occupy territory that had already been secured for them. The bands of political workers which went out in advance of the troops were able, with the slightest touch, to unleash forces which leveled all opposition."

6. The following table of the military cliques within the Nationalist regime in the late 1920s, primarily according to Li Shoukong, pp. 493-494, should be useful for the readers' reference.

Table N. 1 Military Factions Within the KMT in the late1920s

Cliques	Leaders	Territory	Strength
Central Army	Chiang Kai- shek	6 Provinces	600,000
Guangxia Army	Li Zongren	4 Provinces	300,000
Northwest Army	Feng Yuxiang	6 Provinces	420,000
Shanxi Army	Yan Xishang	4 Provinces	300,000
Northeast Army	Zhang Xueliang	4 Provinces	230,000

7. Swarup, p. 72. Though Swarup is right to say that the KMT lost its "touch to the pulse of Chinese revolution" in the 1930s, it may be too farfetched to regard the entire Nationalist agrarian policy as a "suicidal blunder."

8. See Cai Hesen, "History of Opportunism," in Wang Jianmin, *Zhongguo gongchandang shigao* (A Draft History of the Chinese Communist Party) (Taipei, 1966), pp. 483-501.

9. See Dov Bing, "Sneevliet and the Early Years of the CCP," in *China Quarterly*, No. 48, 1971, p. 686.

10. Ch'i Hsi-sheng, *Warlord Politics in China, 1916-1928* (Stanford, 1976), pp. 237-239.

11. See Chen Duxiu et al., "An Open Letter Concerning our Political Opinions," December 15, 1929, in Institute of Marxist-Leninist Studies of Peking University, *Zhonggong dangshi jiaoxue cankao ziliao* (Reference Materials of CCP History, hereafter *DZJX*) (Beijing, 1978), vol. 1, pp. 453-472.

12. Chen Duxiu eventually withdrew from the Chinese political scene. In one of his letters written in his late years, Chen drew a vivid portrayal of his own personality and career: "Faction means limitation. I was always disgusted with the orthodox Way advocated by Song scholars. When I sensed something wrong with Confucianism, I rose to oppose it. When I found something wrong with the Third Comintern, I stood up against it too. So I would do with the Fourth, the Fifth, or any Comintern whatsoever. Mr. Hu Shih once said that I was born a dissident. That is true indeed." See "A Letter to Mr. H and Mr. S," in *Chen Duxiu zizhuan* (Chen Duxiu's Autobiography) (Hong Kong, n. d.), p. 86.

13. It seems necessary to clarify a few points concerning the Nanchang Uprising: 1. The Uprising had a double leadership—the CCP Front Committee headed by Zhou Enlai and the General Headquarters headed by He Long and Ye Ting. Perhaps in this event only, the two institutions generally functioned on an equal basis; 2. It is generally thought that He Long was arrested after the failure of the Nanchang Uprising but was released thanks to his old relations with the the Nationalist Army. Actually, He was released mainly because his troops, the 1st and 2nd divisions of the 20th Army, surrendered to the Nationalist Army; 3. What Zhu De collected of the survivors were not his own troops but Zhou Shidi's 25th Division of the 11th Army. Zhou, as well as many other senior Communists, deserted his own troops and fled to Hong Kong, thus leaving his troops under Zhu's command. See "Notice No. 3 of the Central Committee," (November 1927), reprinted in Wang Jianmin, vol. 2, p. 546; Martin Wilbour, "The Ashes of Defeat," in *China Quarterly*, No. 18, 1964, p. 38; James Harrison, p. 123, et esq.

14. See Zhong Yimu, *Hailufeng Nongmin yundong* (The Peasant Movement in Haifeng and Lufeng) (Guangzhou, 1957), pp. 71-86 and Sima Lu, *Zhonggong dangshi ji wenxian xuancui* (CCP History and its Essential Materials) (Hong Kong, 1977-1982), vol. 6, pp. 193-200; vol. 7, pp. 153-154; and vol. 8, pp. 217-218. Few uprisings on the local level had direct contact with the Party Center and thus left documentary records. In the following introduction of each Communist rebellion and its resultant Soviet base, I will usually cite one or two sources worth noting and then just cite appropriate parts in Sima Lu's work, which is a careful compilation of memoirs and reminiscences published in various newspapers and magazines in China.

15. See CCP Committee of Hengfeng County, *Gandongbei hongqu de douzheng* (Struggle in the Northeast Jiangxi Red Area) (Nanchang, 1980), pp. 15-44. Sima Lu, vol. 7, pp. 162-165; vol. 8, pp. 139-142.

16. Zheng Weishan, "The Red Huangan," in *Xinghuo liaoyuan* (A Single Spark Can Start a Prairie Fire) (Beijing, 1958), vol. 1, part 2, pp. 729-737. Sima Lu, vol. 7, pp. 167-170; vol. 10, pp. 101-114.

17. See He Long and Zhou Yiqun's reports to the Party Center respectively in September 1928 and on September 19, 1929, in the Central Party School of the CCP Central Committee, *Zhonggong dangshi cankao ziliao* (Reference Materials of CCP History, hereafter *DSCK*) (Beijing, 1979), vol. 3, pp. 29-37 and pp. 55-57. Sima Lu, vol. 7, pp. 171-172; vol. 10, pp. 127-135.

18. Peng Dehuai, *Peng Dehuai zishu* (Autobiography of Peng Dehuai) (Beijing, 1981), pp. 87-115; Sima Lu, vol. 7, pp. 95-117; vol. 8, pp. 127-147.

19. Sima Lu, vol. 8, pp. 185-213.

20. Sima Lu, vol. 10, pp. 151-163.

21. See "The Political Resolution of the Sixth National Congress of the Chinese Communist Party," adopted on July 9, 1928, in *DSJX*, vol. 1, pp. 256-281. The resolution states that the most important circumstance leading to the failure in the past year is "the Communist Party's opportunist policies which made the Party unable to maintain its independence, unable to conduct class criticism against its ally and unable to expand its own revolutionary strength."

22. Zhang Guotao, vol. 3, p. 92.

23. See "A Letter of the August 7 Conference of the Central Committee to All CCP Members," adopted August 7, 1927, in *DSJX*, vol. 1, pp. 218-252. The letter condemned the Chen Duxiu Party Center's opportunist attitude in dealing with military affairs. "This attitude prevented the Party Center from making any serious consideration of the possibility and necessity of transforming old armies into new ones and training Party members in military affairs—all these were in fact our most crucial duties."

24. Mao Zedong, "Directives of the General Headquarters of the Chinese People's Liberation Army Reemphasizing the Three Basic Disciplines and the Eight Points for Attention," in *MX*, pp. 1137-1138

25. Zhang Guotao, vol. 3, p. 98.

26. See the Editorial in *Struggle*, February 4, 1933.

27. See "A Letter of the August 7 Conference of the Party Center to All CCP Members," op. cit. The letter says, "the land revolution which includes confiscation and nationalization of all land is the main social and economic content of the Chinese revolution at this moment."

28. This estimation is a general analysis based on scattered sources. See Mao Zedong, "Struggles in the Jinggang Mountains" in *MX*, pp. 57-59; *Wenshi ziliao huibian* (Compilation of Historical Materials) (Beijing, 1982), vol. 62, pp. 41-42. After 1930, in most KMT troops the army became the division and the division in turn became the brigade.

29. This is also a general analysis. The major military groups of the Communist Party at the end of 1929, for example, were approximately as follows: Mao and Zhu's 4th Red Army, 3,000; Peng and Deng's 5th Red Army, 2,000; He Long's 3rd Red Army, 2,000; Xu Xiangqian's 1st Red Army, 1,000; Deng Xiaoping and Zhang Yunyi's 7th Red Army 3,000; and Fang Zhimin's 10th Red Army 1,000. Each group occupied a Soviet base of 2-5 counties as its center and another 5-10 as its zone of influence. Each central county normally had a Red Guard brigade comprising tens to hundreds of native part-time soldiers.

30. Mao and Zhu's army raised "the sixteen-character order," while Peng Dehuai's army used "the stonemill tactic" and Xu Xiangqian' army used "the eight-sentence principle." Of course, it should also be noted that the guerrilla warfare might have variable applications in different Red Armies according to their own conditions and leadership.

31. Peng Gongda, "A Report of the Autumn Harvest Uprising in Hunan," October 8, 1927, in *DSCK*, vol. 3, pp. 7-12.

32. See Hyobom Pak, *Documents of the Chinese Communist Party, 1927-1930* (Hong Kong, 1971), pp. 81-115.

33. Peng Gongda, op. cit.

34. See "From Wuhan to the Jinggang Mountains," in Warren Kuo, vol. 2, pp. 25-29.

35. See *Zhonggong dangshi shijian renwu lu* (Events and People in CCP History, hereafter *DSSRL*) (Shanghai, 1983), pp. 494, 629.

36. Mao Zedong, "Struggles in the Jinggang Mountains," pp. 58-60.

37. Chen Yi, "Report of History and Current Conditions of Zhu and Mao's Army," September 1, 1929, in *DSCK*, vol. 3, p. 52; Edgar Snow, *Red Star Over China* (New York, 1938), p. 153. Mao Zedong told Edgar Snow that since the new line of the Party's Sixth Congress had reached the Jinggang Mountains, disagreements within the Party and Army leadership had disappeared. I would like to add that the harmony between Mao and Zhu was mainly a result of repeated adjustment through their military failures and successes in the latter months of 1928.

38. Chen Yi, pp. 53-54; Peng Dehuai, pp. 113-116.

39. Peng Dehuai, pp. 127-136.

40. A fuller treatment of the Li Lisan leadership is done by this author in an academic paper. See Benjamin Yang, "Complexity and Reasonability: Reassessment of the Li Lisan Adventure," in *Australian Journal of Chinese Affairs*, January 1989.

41. See "A Letter to Comrades Runzhi and Yujie and also the Special Committee of the Hunan-Jiangxi Border Area the Front Committee," February 7, 1929, in *Zhongyang geming genjudi ziliao xuanbian* (Selected Materials of the Central Revolutionary Base, hereafter *ZYGJD*) (Nanchang, 1983), vol. 2, p. 51.

42. Wang Jianying, p. 198.

43. Zhang Guotao, vol. 3, pp. 837-838.

44. See "A Letter of the Executive Committee of the Comintern to the Chinese Communist Party," June 7, 1929, where it is said that "in the Chinese revolution, the most serious threat is the rightist trends," in *Bolshevik*, September 1, 1929. Also see "A Letter of the ECCI to the CCP Central Committee," October 26, 1929, in which it is repeated that "the major danger within the Party at this moment is the rightist opportunist moods and trends," in *Red Flag*, February 15, 1930.

45. See "Xiang Zhongfa's Confession," in Wang Jianmin, vol. 2, p. 159.

46. Schwartz, pp. 127-140.

47. See "The New Revolutionary Upsurge and the Initial Victory in One or More Provinces," in *DSJX*, vol. 1, p. 492.

48. Hsiao Tso-liang, vol. 1, p. 25.

49. See "Resolution on Chinese Affairs, Adopted by the Political Secretariat of the ECCI on July 23, 1930," in Hsiao Tso-liang, vol. 2, pp. 42-45.

50. Xiang Qing, *Gongchan guoji he zhongguo geming guanxi de lishi gaishu* (A Brief Account of the Relations Between the Comintern and the Chinese Revolution) (Guangdong, 1983), pp. 116-117.

51. Sima Lu, vol. 9, pp. 37-43.

52. Peng Dehuai, pp. 134-157.

53. Sima Lu, vol. 9, pp. 50-55.

54. See Harrison, p. 170.

55. See "A Letter to Comrades Runzhi and Yujie and also the Special Committee of the Hunan-Jiangxi Border Area the Front Committee," February 7, 1929, op. cit.

56. See "A Letter of the Front Committee to the Party Center," April 5, 1929, in ZYGJD, vol. 2, pp. 70-72.

57. Zhou Enlai, "A Letter of the CCP Central Committee to the Front Committee of the 4th Red Army," September 28, 1929, in ZX, vol. 1, pp. 29-43.

58. Mao Zedong, "On Correcting Mistaken Ideas Within the Party," MX, pp. 83-93.

59. Mao Zedong, "A Single Spark Can Start a Prairie Fire," January 5, 1930, in MX, p. 101.

60. See "Circular No. 3 of the Front Committee—On the Significance and Policies of Distributing the Troops to Mobilize the Masses," March 18, 1930, in DSCK, vol. 3, p. 61.

61. See "A Letter of the CCP Central Committee to the Front Committee of the 4th Red Army," April 3, 1930, in Warren Kuo, vol. 2, pp. 30-31.

62. See "Public Announcement on Attacking Wuhan and Expanding our Struggles," cited in Ling Yu's article "Comrade Mao Zedong and the Li Lisan Line," in *Dangshi yanjiu* (Studies of the Party History), March, 1982, pp. 79-80.

63. See Mao Zedong, "A Letter to the Party Center," August 24, 1930, cited in Ling Yu, op. cit.

64. Peng Dehuai, pp. 157-160.

Chapter 3

1. Li Shoukong, p. 502. As a historian of Taiwan, Li's account of the Chiang's loss in the war may be a little underestimated.

2. Wang Jianmin, vol. 2, pp. 566-568.

3. See the joint announcement of the Front Committee of the First Front Army and the Action Committee of Jiangxi Province, "Current Situations and Tasks of the First Front Army and the Party of the Jiangxi Province—Strive for Victory in Jiangxi First! Carry out a Decisive Class Struggle!", October 26, 1930, printed in *Zhongyang hongjun wuci fanweijiao ziliao xuanbian* (Materials of the Five Anti-Suppression Campaigns in the Central Red Army, hereafter *WCWJ*) (Shanghai, 1979), p. 3.

4. Ibid, p. 35.

5. See the General Front Committee of the First Front Army, "Eight Favorite Conditions for a Grand Victory," December 22, 1930, in *WCWJ*, pp. 40-42

6. See Xie Muhan, "Chiang Kai-shek's First Suppression Campaign in the Central Soviet Area," in *Wenshi ziliao*, vol. 45, p. 73. Xie was the Director of the Military Bureau of the Jiangxi Provincial Government at that time.

7. Ibid., pp. 73-74

8. Wang Jianmin, pp. 572-573

9. Gong Bingfan, "My Experiences in the Second Suppression Campaign," in *Wenshi ziliao*, vol. 45, p. 83. Gong was then the Commander of the 28th Division.

10. See "Recordings of the Eight Conferences of the General Front Committee," May 25 to June 10, 1931, in *WCWJ*, pp. 105-117.

11. Gong Binfan, pp. 89-90.

12. Ibid.

13. Mao Zedong, "On the Strategic Problems in the Chinese Revolutionary War," in *MX*, pp. 200-203.

14. See "Informational Data of the Enemy in the Third Anti-Suppression Campaign,"in *WCWJ*, p. 163.

15. See "Recording of the 9th Conference of the General Front Committee," June 22, 1931 at Kangdu, in *WCWJ*, p. 137.

16. Ibid., p. 140-141.

17. Mao Zedong, op. cit.

18. Cao Boyi, pp. 259-260.

19. Mao Zedong, op. cit.; Wang Jianmin, vol. 2, p. 577; Sima Lu, vol. 9, p. 100. Apart from the obvious partisan reasons, the differences of the CCP and the KMT in accounting the participating troops in the military campaigns are due to the fact that the Communist statistics include all the KMT troops in this general combat area while the Nationalist statistics only count the KMT troops directly involved in the battles.

20. See "Xiang Zhongfa's Confession," op. cit.

21. As for the serious damage of CCP underground organizations in the cities, see Warren Kuo, vol. 2, pp. 251-253.

22. Yang Yunruo, *Gongchan guoji he zhongguo gemin guanxi jishi* (Records on Relations of the Comintern and the CCP, 1919-1943) (Beijing, 1983), p. 100.

23. Sheng Yueh, *Sun Yat-sen University and Chinese Revolution*, pp. 263-269.

24. See "Circular No. 2 of the Central Bureau—Resolution on the Futian Incident," in Hsiao Tso-liang, vol. 2, p. 108.

25. The CCP History Institute of the Party School of the CCP Central Committee, *Zhonggong dangshi gao* (A Draft History of the Chinese Communist Party, hereafter *DSG*) (Beijing, 1983), vol. 2, p. 144.

26. See "Resolution on Acceptance of the Comintern Instructions and the Resolution of the Party Center's 4th Plenum—No. 1 Resolution of the First Enlarged Conference of the Central Soviet Bureau," in *ZYGJD*, vol. 2, pp. 299-330; and "Resolution on the Futian Incident—No. 4 Resolution of the First Enlarged Conference of the Central Soviet Bureau," April 16, 1931 in *WCWJ*, pp. 97-98.

27. Wang Jianying, p. 160.

28. See *Zhongong dangshi dashi nianbiao* (Annual Records of Big Events in CCP History, hereafter *DSNB*), pp. 41-42; Kim, pp. 65-68.The official date of the Party Center's arrival at the Jiangxi Central Soviet is early January 1933.

29. Sheng Yueh, p. 251.

30. See Zhang Guotao, "A Comprehensive Report to the Politburo on the Eyuwan Base Area," May 24, 1931, in Yu Jinan, *Zhang Guotao he "Wode huiyi"* (Zhang Guotao and his Memoirs) (Chengdu, 1982), p. 112.

31. See "A General Report of the Eyuwan Sub-bureau to the Party Center Regarding Current Situations of the Eyuwan Base Area," October 9, 1931, in the Political Academy of the CPLA, *Zhonggong dangshi ziliao* (Materials of CCP History, hereafter *DSZL*) (Beijing, 1982), vol. 7, p. 6.

32. Zhang Guotao, "Carry out the Party's Line and Intensify the Two-Line Struggle," in *Shihua* (Honest Words), March 5, 1931.

33. Zhang Guotao, *Wode huiyi*, vol. 3, p. 938.

34. See "Zhang Guotao's Report on Behalf of the Eyuwan Sub-bureau Regarding the Victorious Anti-counterrevolutionary Movement," November 25, 1931, in Yu Jinan, p. 117.

35. Xu Xiangqian, *Lishi de huigu* (Retrospect of History) (Beijing, 1984), vol. 1, pp. 146-151.

36. See "Report of Xu Xiangqian and Zeng Zhongsheng to the Party Center Regarding Conditions and Combat Plans of the 4th Red Army," August 20, 1931, in Yu Jinan, p. 122.

37. See "A Letter of the Party Center to the Eyuwan Sub-bureau," November 3, 1931, in Yu Jinan, p. 131.

38. Zhang Guotao, *Wode huiyi*, vol. 3, p. 1006.

39. See "A General Report of the Eyuwan Sub-bureau," op. cit., pp. 6-10.

40. Chen Changhao, "Detailed Report on the Anti-counterrevolutionary Campaign," November 22, 1931, in Hsiao Tso-liang, vol. 2, pp. 471-472.

41. See *DSRSL*, p. 175.

42. Chen Changhao, "A Brief Account of Heroic Struggles of the Fourth Front Army," July 25, 1933, in *Chuan-Shan geming genjudi lishi wenxian xuanbian* (Selected Historical Materials of the Sichuan-Shaanxi Revolutionary Base, hereafter *CSGJD*) (Chengdu, 1982), vol. 2, p. 750; also, Xu Xiangqian, vol. 1, pp. 182-186.

43. See the Ministry of Defence of the Taiwan government, *Jiaofei zhanshi* (Combat History of Exterminating Communist Rebels) (Taiwan, 1967), vol. 4, pp. 523-524.

44. Wang Jianmin, vol. 2, pp. 207-208.

45. Zhang Guotao, vol. 3, p. 1034.

46. Xu Xiangqian, vol. 1, pp. 205-207. Recalling Zhou and Mao's instructions, Xu can only note coldly: "It would have been nice, had we got it at the beginning of the campaign."

47. Zhang Guotao, vol. 3, p. 1039; Xu Xiangqian, vol. 1, p. 209.

48. Zhang Guotao, vol. 3, p. 1040; Xu Xiangqian, vol. 1, pp. 209-211.

49. Zhang Guotao, vol. 3, p. 1045; Xu Xiangqian, vol. 1., p. 215.

50. See *Jiaofei zhanshi*, vol. 4, p. 561.

51. See "A Letter of the Party Center to the Eyuwan Provincial Committee," March 15, 1933, in Yu Jinan, p. 177. This number may be a bit exaggerated. According to Zhang Guotao himself, the deserted wounded and sick soldiers amounted to about 1,000.

52. Zhang Guotao, vol. 3, pp. 1049-1050.

53. See "The Party Central's Instruction to the Eyuwan Sub-bureau Requesting That the Fourth Front Army Open a New Base Area on the Hubei-Henan-Shaanxi Border," November 27, 1931, cited in Xu Xiangqian, vol. 1, pp. 225-226.

54. Zhang Guotao, vol. 3, pp. 1071-1072.

55. Zhang Guotao, vol. 3, p. 1073; Xu Xiangqian, vol. 1, pp. 227-228.

56. Zhang Guotao, vol. 2, p. 1049; Xu Xiangqian, vol. 1, p. 231.

57. Xu Xiangqian, vol. 1, pp. 232-233.

58. See "Report of the Eyuwan Provincial Committee to the Party Center Concerning the Fourth Suppression Campaign and the Following Struggles," January 5, 1933, in Yu Jinan, p. 176.

59. See "Letter of the Party Center to the Provincial Party Committee of the Eyuwan Soviet Area," March 15, 1933, in Yu Jinan, p. 177.

60. Pi Dingxiu, "Three Times' Entry into the Honghu Base," in *Huiyi He Long* (Reminiscences of He Long) (Beijing, 1980), p. 287.

61. See *Jiaofei zhanshi*, vol. 4, pp. 537-538.

62. He Long, "Recalling the Second Front Red Army," in *Jindaishi yanjiu* (Studies of Modern History), No. 1-2, 1981, p. 10.

63. Pi Dingxiu, pp. 291-292.

64. Wang Miaosheng, "Studies of Causes Leading to the Loss of the Xiangexi Base," in *Zhongguo xiandaishi* (Contemporary Chinese History), September 1983, p. 117.

65. Xu Guangda et al., "Reminiscence of the Xiangexi and Xiangechuanqian Bases," *People's Daily*, February 1, 1962.

66. He Long, pp. 23-25.

67. Xu Guangda, op. cit.; He Long, op. cit.

68. Li Guoliang, "Old Marshal He, Red Guard Veterans of the Honghu Cherish a Memory of You," in *Huiyi He Long*, p. 247.

69. Sheng Yueh, p. 266.

70. He Long, p. 27; also "Report of the Xiangexi Sub-bureau," September 15, 1934, in *DSZL*, vol. 7, pp. 89-92. This important document offers detailed statistics of the four anti-counterrevolutionary campaigns in the Xiangexi Soviet.

71. Li Guoliang, p. 250.

72. See "Open Letter to All Brothers in the Celestial Army," in *Qianshan hongqi* (Red Traces Left in The Guizhou Mountains) (Guiyang, 1980), p. 255.

73. Wang Jianying, pp. 161, 163, 164.

74. See the Central Military Council, "A Military Order on Attacking Ganzhou," January 10, 1932, in *WCWJ*, pp. 178-182.

75. Ma Kun, "Personal Experience in the Chiang Army Defending the City of Ganzhou," in *Wenshi ziliao*, vol. 45, pp. 141-148.

76. See Lin Biao and Nie Rongzhen, "Detailed Report on the Battle at Longyan and Zhangzhou, April 1-30, 1932," in *WCWJ*, pp. 186-191; Nie Rongzhen, *Nie Rongzhen huiyi lu* (Nie Rongzhen's Memoirs) (Beijing, 1983), vol. 1, p. 186.

77. See Snow, p. 165; also Huang Shaojun, "The Timing of the Ningdu Conference," in *Dangshi yanjiu ziliao* (Materials of the CCP History Studies), January 1984, p. 69.

78. Huang Shaojun, op. cit.

79. Wang Jianmin, pp. 577-578.

80. See Zhou Enlai's telegram on behalf of the Red Army General Headquarters to the Party Center, January 30, 1933, in *ZX*, vol. 1, p. 62.

81. See Sun Ruike, "Recall of the Fourth Suppression Campaign in the Central Soviet," in *Wenshi ziliao*, vol. 45, p. 159.

82. Ibid., pp. 160-166. Also see the military reports of Teng Daiyuan and Peng Dehuai of the 3rd Army Corps and Dong Zhendang and Zhu Rui of the 5th Army Corps about the Huangpi Battle, February 28-March 1, 1933, in *WCWJ*, pp. 213-236.

83. Nie Rongzhen, vol. 1, p. 190.

Chapter 4

1. Cao Yibo, p. 505. In fact, this slogan was first raised during the Fourth Suppresion Campaign, then perfected in the Fifth Suppression Campaign.

2. Li Shoukong, pp. 559-560.

3. Cao Yibo, pp. 605-609, 629-630.

4. F. F. Liu, *A Military History of Modern China, 1924-1949* (Princeton, 1956), pp. 91-99.

5. Cao Yibo, op. cit.; Li Shoukong, op. cit.

6. See Chiang Kai-shek's speech at the military training program, in *Jiaofei wenxian* (Materials on the Bandit Extermination) (Nanking, n.d.), vol. 3, p. 5.

7. Yang Botao, "A Brief Account of the Fifth Suppression Campaign of the Chiang Army," in *Wenshi ziliao*, vol. 45, p. 183.

8. See "Informational Data on the Enemy in the Fifth Anti-Suppression Campaign," in *WCWJ*, pp. 325-326.

9. Dick Wilson, p. 79.

10. Dai Yue, "My Suggestion to Chiang Kai-shek for the Blockhouse Policy," in *Wenshi ziliao*, vol. 45, pp. 171-180.

11. Ibid.

12. See *Wenxian he yanjiu* (Documents and Studies), No. 6, 1984, pp. 20-21. According to the official statistics of the Nationalist Army at that time, 14,294

blockhouses had been built in and around the Central Soviet by the end of the Fifth Campaign in October 1934.

13. Cao Yibo, pp. 596-602.

14. Ibid.

15. Luo Ming, "Some Suggestions on Our Work," reprinted in *Zhonggong dangshi ziliao* (Materials of the Party History), February 1982, p. 275; the quotation here is from another article by Luo Ming, "A Report to the CCP Committee of the Fujian-Guangdong-Jiangxi Province on the Current Situations in Shanghang and Yongding Counties," extensively cited in Zhang Wentian, "What is the Luo Ming Line?" in *Struggle*, February 18, 1933.

16. Zhang Wentian, op. cit.

17. See Luo Ming, "Reminiscence on the Anti-Luo Ming Line," in *Zhonggong dangshi ziliao*, op. cit., pp. 246-253. Luo recalls, "In fact, we did not dare oppose the recruitment drive by the Red Army main forces, but only required that there should be some difference in policies between the central areas and the border areas."

18. Zhang Wentian, op. cit. and Bo Gu, "Support the Party's Bolshevik Offensive Line," in *Struggle*, Feburary 23, 1933.

19. Warren Kuo, vol. 2, pp. 383-397.

20. Ibid.; Kitada Sadao, "The Struggle Against the Luo Ming Line in the Jiangxi Soviet," in *Ajia kenkyu* (Asian Studies), vol. 23, No. 1, 1973, p. 47.

To realize that in a final sense the anti-Luo Ming line was aimed by the newly arrived Party Center leaders at the veteran cadres (Mao included) in the Army and the Soviet government is one matter, and to claim that this movement directly plotted against Mao is quite another. Kitada concludes, "As regards the personal relationships, the Luo Ming liners or those who supported the Luo Ming line, especially in Jiangxi province, were either Mao's acquaintances or people close to this kind." As a matter of fact, among the people attacked in the movement, perhaps only Mao Zetan and Gu Bo had some personal attachment with Mao at that time, while all the others—like Deng Xiaoping, Lu Dingyi, Xiao Jinguang, Tan Zhenlin and Luo Ming—as yet had no direct affiliation with Mao.

Another notable fact is that the anti-Luo Ming movement in the Central Soviet never reached the level of intensity and cruelty it did in some other Soviet areas. After the movement, Luo Ming was transferred to the Academy of the Red Army as the Director of its General Affairs Department; Deng Xiaoping was moved to be Chief Editor of the Army newspaper, *Red Star*; and only a few months after being bitterly criticized, Mao Zetan was publicly honored for his active role in Red Army recruitment. More concrete investigations into this interesting phenomenon are beyond the scope of the present study.

21. See Trygve Lotveit, pp. 154-179; Warren Kuo, pp. 409-419; and Mori Kazuko, "The Land Revolution During the Period of the Jiangxi Soviet: the Factors Leading to the Land Investigation Movement and the Factors Hidden Behind," in *Ajia kenkyu*, vol. 19, No. 4, 1973, pp. 60-70.

Kuo is mainly interested in deriding the absurdity of "Communist bandits" from a Nationalist viewpoint. Lotveit attempts to stress the Party Center's leftist line in the Movement which broke the "harmonious relationship between the people and the regime." Mori rightfully points out that Mao and the Party Center all wanted the Land Investigation Movement at its initial stage and disagreements occurred between them only later on. Here we can see the varying depth of historical studies of this subject. The fundamental theme of the CCP's agrarian policy in its revolutionary years in general and the Land Investigation Movement in the Jiangxi Soviet in particular is whether to treat the land reform as a revolutionary means to promote political ends (as Mao did) or to treat it as the revolutionary end in itself (as the Bo Gu Center actually did). In other words, there had not been a definite criterion for a correct agrarian policy in view of the agarian policy itself; the criterion was whether and to what extent an agrarian policy could facilitate the rebellious warfare under existing conditions. This is the key to assessing the land policies of the CCP from 1927 up to 1949.

22. See "Resolution of the CCP Central Committee Concerning the Fifth Campaign of Imperialism and the Kuomintang, and the Tasks of Our Party," July 24, 1933, in *Struggle*, August 12, 1933.

23. See "Combat Plan of the First Front Red Army," October 14, 1933, in *WCWJ*, pp. 287-291. The plan requires that "before the enemy's attacking arrangements are completed, and in order to break one route of the enemy and join forces with the northwest Jiangxi Red Army, we should take it by surprise and quickly and simultaneously annihilate the enemy troops in Jianning, Taining, and Lichuan, and capture all these places." Another noteworthy point in this document is that it was cosigned by "Zhu De as the General Commander, Mao Zedong as the General Commissar, and Zhou Enlai as the Acting General Commissar."

24. Cao Yibo, p. 523 .

25. The best quote by Mao on this is the speech at the Wayaobo Conference in which Mao laughed off the Party Center leaders, saying that "even when shaking hands with Cai Tingkai, they would at the same moment curse him as a reactionary." See Mao Zedong, "On the Tactics in Fighting the Japanese Imperialism," in *MX*, p. 140; also see Honjo Hisako, "The Fujian Revolt and the Chinese Communist Party," in *Kindai chugoku kenkyu senta iho* (Reports of Modern China Studies), No. 15, 1971, p. 6.

Honjo's view is no more than something like the assertion that Mao first held his own positive stand toward the Fujian rebels and then had to surrender to the Party Center's negative attitude. I discussed this subject with Hu Hua, the most authoritative CCP historian. Professor Hu said "Mao's criticism of the Fujian People's Government in his speech at the Second Soviet Congress was not his own view, but the Party Center's official stand." Progresses can be found in the studies of this subject, but they are not yet fully satisfactory. The problem stems, I am inclined to think, not only from shortage of documentary sources but also from a shortage of analytical insight.

26. Gong Chu, pp. 392-397.

27. Peng Dehuai, pp. 182-183.

28. "The Anti-Japanese, Anti-Chiang Preliminary Agreement," October 26, 1933, in *Red China*, February 14, 1934.

29. Mao Zedong, "On the Strategic Problems in the Chinese Revolutionary War," in *MX*, pp. 219-220. Note that Mao raised the suggestion "two months after the

commencement of the Fifth Anti-Suppression Campaign," that is, in December 1933.

30. Otto Braun, A Comintern Agent in China, 1932-1939 (translated by Jeane Moore, Stanford, 1982), p. 62.

31. See, for example, "The Second Statement of the CCP Central Committee on the Fujian Incident," January 26, 1934, in Red China, January 1934 and Struggle, February 1934.

32. See Cai Tingkai, Cai Tingkai zizhuan (Autobiography of Cai Tingkai) (Har'erbin, 1982), p. 317.

33. Braun, p. 49.

34. See "Resolutions on the Current Situations and the Tasks of the Party," January 18, 1934, in Struggle, February 16, 1934.

35. Wang Jianying, p. 190.

36. Waller, pp. 84-85.

37. Braun, p. 54. Braun recalls that most of the guests of the Congress did not show up and the auditorium itself could only hold a few hundred people.

38. Waller, pp. 84-98.

39. See "A Letter of the CCP Mission to the Comintern to the CCP Politburo," September 6, 1934. The letter says that Mao's speech "is a very significant historical document. We and comrades in the Comintern regard it as a record of achievements of the Chinese Soviet movement and progresses of the Chinese Communist Party. It also reflects the rich experiences of Comrade Mao Zedong."

40. Waller, op. cit. Among the people named here, Xiang Ying and Bo Gu may be regarded as Mao's antagonists. As for the others, the most we can say is that they were neither for nor against Mao. Waller does not give any evidence to his classfications. I am inclined to think that he takes Fang Zhimin, for example, as a Maoist simply because Fang was also a local Soviet leader and he had been mentioned in some of Mao's articles and speeches. If so, it is certainly not adequate for drawing a conclusion that Fang was Mao's man in terms of intraparty relationship.

41. See Zhongguo renmin jiefangjun zhanshi jianbian (A Brief Combat History of the Chinese People's Liberation Army, hereafter PLAZS) (Beijing, 1983), pp. 105-106; Nie Rongzhen, vol. 1, pp. 192-193.

42. See Braun, p. 33 and p. 46. Braun arrived at Ruijin in October 1933, and he got hold of military command in about December of the year. "Before that time, the Front Headquarters acted on its own initiative," Braun says.

43. Peng Dehuai, p. 188.

44. Cao Yipo, pp. 549-551.

45. Wang Jianying, p. 200.

46. Peng Dehuai, pp. 189-190.

47. Braun, p. 69.

48. Su Yu, "Reminiscences of the Anti-Japanese Northern Expeditionary Vanguard Brigade of the Red Army," in Jiefangjun bao (People's Liberation Army Daily), July 26, 1981.

49. See "Declaration of the Central Government of the Chinese Soviet Republic and the Revolutionary Military Council of the Chinese Worker and Peasant Red Army Concerning the Northern Expedition of the Anti-Japanese Vanguard Brigade of the Red Army," July 15, 1934, in Red China, August 1, 1934.

50. Braun, p. 74.

51. See Zhang Yi, "The Start and the End of the Anti-Japanese Northern Expeditionary Vanguard Brigade," in *Zhongguo xiandai shi* (Modern Chinese History), January 1983, p. 110.

52. Su Yu, op. cit.

53. Zhang Yi, p. 112.

54. Su Yu, op. cit.

55. Shi Zunfei et al., "Fang Zhimin and the Northwest Jiangxi Soviet," in *Zhonguo xiandai shi*, January 1983, pp. 224-225. Also see *Fang Zhimin zhuan* (Biography of Fang Zhimin) (collectively compiled, Nanchang, 1982), pp. 212-213.

56. Wang Jianying, p. 204.

57. Shi Zunfei et al., p. 227.

58. Ibid., p. 228.

59. Wang Yaowu, "My Combat Experience in Blocking Fang Zhimin's Anti-Japanese Northern Expeditionary Vanguard Brigade," in *Wenshi Ziliao*, vol. 24, December 1961, pp. 190-191.

60. Su Yu, op. cit.; *Fang Zhimin zhuan*, pp. 241-242.

61. Fang Zhimin, *Wo congshi gemin douzheng de lueshu* (A Brief Account of My Revolutionary Life) (Beijing, 1980), p. 91.

62. Wang Yaowu, p. 203.

63. Fang Zhimin, p. 99.

64. Gao Jun, *Weida de zhanshi Ren Bishi* (Ren Bishi the Great Fighter) (Beijing, 1980), p. 61.

65. Li Jue, "Reminscences of He Jian's Troops Blocking the Red Army's Long March," in *Wenshi ziliao*, vol. 62, p. 64.

66. See "An Order of the Secretariat of the CCP Central Committee and the Central Military Council to the 6th Army Corps and the Hunan-Jiangxi Military District," July 23, 1934, in *Hongjun guo Guangxi* (The Red Army Marched Through Guangxi, hereafter *HJGGX*) (Nanning, 1986), pp. 57-61.

67. Xiao Ke, "Reminiscences of the Second Front Army," in *Jindaishi yanjiu*, No. 1, 1980, p. 666.

68. Wang Jianying, p. 210.

69. Xiao Ke, pp. 666-668.

70. Li Jue, pp. 66-67.

71. See "A Letter of the Central Military Council to the 6th Army Corps Regarding its Operations and Tasks in the Future," September 8, 1934, in *HJGGX*, pp. 61-63.

72. Li Jue, op. cit.

73. Xiao Ke, pp. 673-674 and Gao Jun, p. 63.

74. Li Jue, p. 68.

75. See "Instructions of the Central Military Council to the 6th Army Corps," October 4, 1934, in *Qianshan hongji*, p. 43.

76. See "Telegram of Ren, Xiao, and Wang to the Central Military Council Concerning the Ganxi Battle," October 10, 1934, in *Qianshan hongji*, p. 43.

77. See "Telegram to the Party Center After the Union of the 6th and 2nd Army Corps," October 25, 1934, in *Qianshan hongji*, pp. 44-45; Wang Jianying, pp. 215-217.

78. Warren Kuo, vol. 2, pp. 469-471; and Gong Chu, pp. 537-544.

79. Hsiao Tso-laing, vol. 1, p. 350.

80. Braun, p. 76.

81. See Lin Biao, "On the Short, Swift Thrust," and Peng Dehuai, "A Letter to a Certain Division Commander," in *Revolution and War*, respectively on June 17, 1934 and August 14, 1934.

82. Braun, p. 76.

83. Zhou Enlai, "A New Victory in a New Situation," August 18, in *Red Star*, August 20, 1934.

84. Braun, op. cit.

85. Zhang Wentian, "All for the Defense of the Soviet," September 26, 1934, in *Red China*, September 29, 1934.

86. In fact, the subtle divergence between Zhang Wentian and the Bo Gu Center can be traced back even earlier. For a further discussion of this issue, see Zhang's articles in *Struggle* (May 1, 1933, and November 26, 1933) and in *Red China* (May 1, 1934 nd May 25, 1934). All these articles were aimed against leftist adventurism.

87. Braun, p. 78.

88. Sheng Zhongliang (Sheng Yueh) was the Secretary of the CCP Central Bureau of Shanghai. He was arrested in early October 1934 and betrayed to the KMT. The radio stations of the underground Communists were all discovered and confiscated, and thus the contact between the CCP Center and the Comintern was broken. See Shen Yiqin, "Some Information of the Shanghai Central Bureau Formed in 1933," in *Dangshi ziliao congkan* (Serial of CCP Historical Materials) (Shanghai), No. 1, 1981, p. 170.

89. Gong Chu, p. 397.

90. John Rue, p. 263.

91. At the very least, Mao was involved with the conferences making decision of the Fujian Incident, review of the Guangchang battles, and arrangement of the general evacuation. As for the impact of Zhang Wentian's appointment as Chairman of the Council of People's Commissars, it is also much complicated. Zhang recalled this episode as follows: "As a concrete measure (of Bo Gu) to expel me from the Party Center, I was assigned to work in the Central Soviet Government after the Fifth Plenum. . . . This was actually a one-stone-hitting-two-birds trick. It squeezed me out of the Party Center on one hand and also squeezed Mao Zedong out the Soviet government on the other." See Wang Wentian, "From the Fujian Incident to the Zunyi Conference," in *Zunyi huiyi wenxian* (Documentray Material of the Zunyi Conference) (Beijing, 1985), pp. 78-81.

92. See *Poems of Mao Tse-tung*, (translated and published in Hong Kong, 1960), p. 26.

93. See "Comrade Mao Zedong Talks About the Current Situation and the Anti-Japanese Vanguard of the Red Army," in *Red China*, August 1, 1934.

94. See Wu Jiqing, *Zai Mao zhuxi shenbian de rizi li* (The Days When I Was with Chairman Mao) (Nanchang, 1982), pp. 146-156.

95. I would suggest that Mao's sojourn in western and southern Jiangxi in the summer of 1934 was rather intentional. It was something like Yuan Shikai's retirement to Zhangde in 1909-1911 and that of Chiang Kai-shek to Fenghua several times

from 1927 to 1949. They all had a similar purpose: waiting for the later appeal and reappearence. See Otto Braun, p. 71, "After the Guangchang battles, Mao increasingly avoided meetings of the Military Council in order to continue the factional struggle in secret."

96. Gunther Stein, *The Challenge of Red China* (New York, 1975), p. 118.

97. Braun, p. 70.

Chapter 5

1. Benjamin Yang, "The Zunyi Conference as One Step in Mao's Rise to Power: A Survey of Historical Studies of the Chinese Communist Party," in *China Quarterly*, June 1986.

2. See "Political Directives of the General Political Department of the Red Army," October 9, 1934 and "An Order of the Central Revolutionary Military Council," October 10, 1934, in *DSZL*, vol. 7, pp. 148-150; also Wu Yunpu, "Diary of the Long March," in *Wenshi ziliao*, vol. 72, pp. 1-2. The Military Council and the Party Center left their office quarters in Meikeng on October 11, reached and stayed at Yudu, and marched quickly toward Gupi and Xintian on October 21. Also see the appendix of daily itinerary in *HJCZJ*, vol. 2, p. 423. The 1st Army Corps left its camp on October 16 and captured Xintian on October 21.

3. See Zhou Enlai, "Lessons Learned from Party History," June 10, 1972, in *People's Daily*, January 17, 1985; Braun, p. 81; and *DSRSL*, p. 188.

4. Wang Jianying, pp. 228-231.

5. Robert Payne, *Mao Tse-tung* (New York, 1969), p. 148.

6. Lian Chen, "Following the Red Army on the Western March" in *HJCZJ*, vol. 1, pp. 5-6 (Lian Chen is a penname of Chen Yun); also Peng Dehuai, pp. 193-194; and Nie Rongzhen, vol. 1, pp. 216-217.

7. Yan Daogang, p. 10.

8. See Chiang Kai-shek's order of appointment on December 12 1934 and He Jian's announcement on duty on December 14, 1934, in *Hongjun zhuanzhan Guizhou—Jiuzhengquan dangan shiliao xuanbian* (The Red Army Fighting in Guizhou: Selected Archival Documents of the Nationalist Regime, hereafter *HJZGZ*) (Guiyang, 1984), p. 77.

9. Braun, pp. 89-90.

10. See Chiang's telegram order "Outline Project of the Joint Campaign of Hunan, Guangxi, and Guizhou," in *HJZGZ*, pp. 77-79; also see Xue Yue, Part 3, p. 14.

11. See Zhu De, "Order to Lin, Nie, Peng, Yang and others," November 25, in *HJGGX*, pp. 79-80.

12. Nie Rongzhen, vol. 1, pp. 221-222.

13. See "Telegram of the 1st Army Corps to the Military Council," November 30; also "Telegram of the Central Military Council to the 1st and 3rd Army corps," December 1, in *HJGGX*, pp. 85-87.

14. Nie Rongzhen, op. cit.

15. Braun, p. 90.

16. Jerome Ch'en, *Mao and the Chinese Revolution* (London, 1965), p. 189. Ch'en estimates that the Red Army lost 50,000, or more than half, of its troops in the Xiang River battle. Ch'en seems to have ignored the fact that the Red Army did not start with 100,000 men and that it suffered losses while overcoming the first two blockade lines. Therefore, its reduction to about 40,000 men does not simply mean a loss of 40,000 or 60,000 in this one battle.

17. Based on the military reports on the KMT part, we can confidently assume that the Central Red Army lost about one third or 20,000 of its troops in the Xiang River Battle. See *HJGGX*, pp. 523-526, 561-565.

18. Yan Daogang, pp. 11, 14.

19. Nie Rongzhen, vol. 1, pp. 234-235.

20. See Chiang Kai-shek's telegram orders on December 18, 24 and Xue Yue's reply telegram on December 26, in *HJZGZ*, pp. 84, 85, and 86; also Xue Yue, Part 2, p. 22.

21. See Braun, pp. 92-93; also see "Resolution of the Politburo on Founding a New Base at the Sichuan-Guizhou Border," December 18, 1934, in *Qianshan jongji*, pp. 218-219; Chen Yun, "Notes."

22. Wang Jianmin, vol. 2, p. 641. Wang quotes the phrase "setting the tiger free to the mountain," to describe the smooth motion of the Red Army in Guizhou in late December 1934.

23. Wang Jialie, "Reminiscences of Checking the Central Red Army on the Long March," in *Wenshi ziliao*, vol. 62, p. 86.

24. Hou Hanyou, "Failure of Hou Zhidan's Troops in Defending the Wu River," in *Wenshi zilaio*, vol. 62, p. 97.

25. See "Resolution of the Politburo of the Party Center Concerning the New Tasks After Crossing the River," in *Qianshan hongji*, pp. 223-224.

26. Ibid.

27. See Zhu De's telegram to Lin, Nie, Peng, Yang, and others on January 1, 1935, in *Qianshan hongji*, p. 229. Zhu says, "Guarding the southern bank of the Wu River are three regiments of Hou Zhidan. They can by no means defend the ferry spots along the 100 li river bank." On the KMT side, Hou Hanyou, who was in charge of the river defense, recalls, "At that time we thought the Red Army was 100,000 strong, and my troops were only 5,000 or 6,000. How could we possibly win?" See *Wenshi ziliao*, vol. 62, p. 97.

28. Warren Kuo, vol. 3, p. 13; Cai Xiaoxian, p. 281.

29. See "A Public Order of the General Political Department on Entering Zunyi," signed by Li Fuchun, the Acting Director of the General Political Department, in *Qianshan hongji*, pp. 235-236.

30. Cai Xiaoxian, pp. 282-284.

31. See Dieter Heizig, "Otto Braun's Memoir and Mao's Rise to Power," in *China Quarterly*, April-June, 1971, p. 280.

32. This telegram is exhibited in the Memorial Hall of Chairman Mao in Beijing.

33. Wu Xiuquan and Wu Jiqing both recall that most sessions of the Zunyi Conference were held deep in the night. Wu Xiuquan, "My Memoirs," in *Zhonggong dangshi ziliao* (Historical Materials of the CCP), February 1982, p. 171; Wu Jiqing, pp. 196-197.

34. See Zou Aiguo, "Newly Discovered Materials about the Zunyi Conference," in *Liaowang zhoukan* (Watchtower Weekly), March 5, 1984, p. 41. As an official Communist version, Zou's list includes Deng Xiaoping and Wu Xiuquan.

35. Braun, pp. 99-104.

36. Wu Xiuquan, pp. 173-174.

37. Wu Jiqing, pp. 199-200. While the Zunyi Conference was still in session, Mao sent Wu to console and consult Deng Yingchao, who was sick at the time.

38. Peng Dehuai, p. 195.

39. See "Military Bulletins of the Guizhou Army on January 17, 18," in HJZGZ, p. 528.

40. Chen Yun, "Notes."

41. See the telegrams of the Central Military Council to the Army Corps leaders during this period, in *Wenxian he yanjiu*, January 1985, pp. 20-25.

42. See *Qianshan hongji*, pp. 236-252; English translation of this document by Jerome Ch'en is found in *China Quarterly*, October 1969. A unique analysis is given in Warren Kuo, *A Study of the "Resolutions of the Tsunyi Conference"* (Taipei, n.d.), pp. 9-10.

43. See *Qianshan hongji*, pp. 266-268; English translation of this document by Benjamin Yang is found in *China Quarterly*, June 1986.

44. Many Chinese historians think the second document is a summary of the first for the purpose of communicating the Zunyi Conference on a lower and broader level. But an obvious contradiction here is that this document bears the real name of the accused and not symbols such as XX and XXX as in the first document. See Benjamin Yang, p. 262.

45. See "Outline Resolution," p. 268.

46. Ibid.

47. See "Resolution on Some Historical Problems," adopted by the CCP Center in April 1945 and included in Hsiao Tso-liang, vol. 2, pp. 787-803.

48. After the Huili Conference in May 1935, Chen Yun was dispatched to Shanghai to reorganize the Party's underground work. From there Chen went to Moscow in June 1935.

49. See "Summary Resolution," in *Qianshan hongji*, p. 237.

50. See "Outline Resolution," in *Qianshan hongji*, p. 266.

51. Chen Yun, op. cit.

52. Ibid.

53. Braun, pp. 81-83.

54. See "Summary Resolution," p. 239.

55. Mao Zedong, "On the Strategic Problems in the Chinese Revolutionary War," in MX, pp. 219-220.

56. In the Fourth Campaign, the Central Red Army reached contact with the 10th Red Army. The Party Center at that time called the 10th Army to join the Anti-Suppression Campaign in the Central Soviet. In fact, the 7th Army Corps was founded on the basis of the 10th Army in 1933. Later on Fang Zhimin gathered his local troops remaining in the Northwest Jiangxi Soviet and reorganized them into another army also entitled the 10th Red Army. The new 10th Army was ordered to unite with Xun Huaizhou's 7th Army Corps to carry the anti-Japanese

expedition into the KMT rear areas in October 1934. Even from this episode, two points arise: first, the Party Center and Central Red Army used to take their own interests as priority; second, neither calling in nor sending out of Red Army troops could directly result in any guaranteed victory in the Central Soviet.

57. Peng Dehuai, pp. 247-248.

58. Mao Zedong, op. cit.

59. See "Summary Resolution," pp. 238-239.

60. This list of contrasts between the two military lines is drawn on the basis of Mao's "On the Strategic Problems of the Chinese Revolutionary War," op. cit.

61. Wu Tien-wei, p. 2.

62. See "Outline Resolution," p. 267.

63. Nie Rongzhen, vol.1, pp. 213-214.

64. Later Braun was entrusted with other positions, but none of them could compare with the Fifth Campaign so far as his military function was concerned.

65. Zhou worked with Li Lisan for several years, but when Li was attacked by Wang Ming and Bo Gu in 1931, Zhou, rather than being weakened, strengthened his position. A similar situation can be found with Zhou and Liu Shaoqi in 1966. This does not mean, however, Zhou was a two-faced politician. Actually, Zhou's ability and hard work had made him indispensible to all in power, and when anyone higher than him in rank in the past later lost power, this would naturally grant him a promotion.

66. Braun, p. 104.

67. Xue Yue, Part 3, p. 25.

68. The Red Army General Headquarters, "Combat Plan of Crossing the River," January 20, 1935, in *Qianshan hongji*, pp. 260-262.

69. Ibid.

70. See Liu Xiang's telegram reports to Chiang Kai-shek on January 29, 30, and 31, 1935, in *HJZGZ*, pp. 99-100. It is reported that more than 2,000 Red Army men were killed or captured. Also see "Experience of Liu Xiang's Troops in Blocking the Red Army in the Sichuan-Guizhou-Yunnan Border Area," in *Wenshi ziliao*, vol. 62, pp. 114-118.

71. Chen Yun, "Notes"; "Order of the Military Council on Reduction of the Army Corps," in *Wenxian he yanjiu*, No. 1, 1985, p. 34.

72. See Zhu De and Zhou Enlai's telegrams to the Army Corps leaders, Lin Biao, Nie Rongzhen, Peng Dehuai, Yang Shangkun, and others, February 10, 17, and 18, 1935, in *Wenxian he yanjiu*, No. 1, 1985, pp. 35-36.

73. See Wang Jialie's "self-accusation" telegram to Chiang Kai-shek on March 5, and Chiang's "consolation" telegram back to Wang on March 6, 1935, in *HJZGZ*, p. 114; Wei Jianxiang, "Witnesses as a Subordinate of Xue Yue in Pursuing the Red Army," in *Wenshi ziliao*, vol. 62, pp. 52-56.

74. Although the "General Headquarters" and "Central Military Council" sounded more authoritative, obviously they could not control any other Red Armies than the First Front Army at the time. Now that the Front Command Headquarters was put in charge of all the army corps there, the General Headquarters was left with only some guarding units and non-combatant troops.

75. See "Order of the Military Council Regarding Establishment of the Front Headquarters and the Appointment of Zhu De as Commander and Mao Zedong as Political Commissar," March 4, 1935, in *Wenxian he yanjiu*, No. 1, 1985, p. 40; also "Order of the Front Command Headquarters," March 5, 1935 at Yaxi, in *Qianshan hongji*, p. 280.

76. See Zhou Hunyuan's telegram on March 13, 1935, in *HJZGZ*, p. 120; Xue Yue, Part 3, pp. 29-30. Zhou reported that the Red Army searched for a battle in vain yet Xue recorded two small victories: one in Lubanchang on March 14 and another at Fengxiangba on March 15.

77. Wang Jialie, pp. 93-94; Yan Daogang, pp. 19-26.

78. Nie Rongzhen, vol. 1, p. 256.

79. Based on the numerous reports of the KMT generals such as Xue Yue of the Central Army, Pan Wenhua of the Sichuan Army, and Sun Du of the Yunnan Army, we can certainly reach the judgment that the Central Red Army under the new leadership did not win any decisive battles in March-April 1935. See *Hongjun changzheng zai Guizhou* (The Long March of the Red Army in Guizhou, hereafter CZZGZ) (Guiyang, 1983), pp. 636-684; *Guomindang zhuidu hongjun changzheng dangan shiliao xuanbian* (Archives Materials of the KMT's Pursuing the Red Army on the Long March, hereafter *GMDDA*) (Chengdu, 1986), pp. 123-129.

80. Braun, pp. 114-116; Nie Rongzhen, vol. 1, pp. 258-259; Peng Dehuai, pp. 198-199.

81. In this and other places of Nie's book, there are prejudicial accusations of Lin Biao. In reality, Nie also joined the protest against Mao's new leadership at the end of April, 1935. A telegram cosigned by Nie with Lin and dated 22:00 hours, April 25, complained to the Military Council that "we have lost all possibilities of returning to Guizhou, nor have we been able to open any new prospect in eastern Yunnan," and demanded that "this field army should change its current strategy immediately." See *Wenxian he yanjiu*, No. 1, 1985, p. 62.

82. See "Instructions of the Central Military Council Regarding the Red Army's Immediate Crossing of the Jinsha River and Opening a Soviet Area in Western Sichuan," April 29, 1935, in *Qianshan hongji*, p. 284.

83. Nie Rongzhen, op. cit; Peng Dehuai, op. cit.

84. Nie Rongzhen, vol. 1, p. 260.

85. Braun, p. 121.

Chapter 6

1. Braun, p. 123.

2. Kuang Shanji, "The Surtax and Pretax Systems under the Warlord Rule in Sichuan," in *Sichuan daxue xuebao* (The Sichuan University Journal), No. 1, 1981, p. 79; More or less the same description can also be found in *Sichuan shengqing* (Information of Sichuan Province) (Changdu, 1984), p. 6.

3. The following table should produce a general sense of the grave social and economic situation in Sichuan.

Table N. 2 Sichuan Warlords and Their Pretaxes in Some Counties in 1934

County	Location	Army	Warlord	Year
Nanchong	Central	20th	Yang Sen	1965
Jianwei	Southeast	21st	Liu Xiang	1975
Yuezun	Southwest	24th	Liu Wenhui	1985
Guanxian	Northwest	28th	Deng Xihou	1991
Anxian	Northeast	29th	Tian Songyao	1983

Source: Kuang Shanji, pp. 82-83.

4. See *Sichuan nongcun jingji* (Rural Economy in Sichuan) (Shanghai, 1936), p. 136.

5. See "Overview of the Upheavals in Sichuan," in *Minguo yilai Sichuan dongluan shiliao bianji* (Selected Materials of the Chaotic Conditions in Sichuan in the Republican Period) (Hong Kong, 1977), vol. 2, p. 117.

6. Robert Kapp, *Szechwan and the Chinese Republic* (New Haven, 1973), p. 88.

7. Zhang Guotao, vol. 3, pp. 1053-1061, pp. 1071-1079.

8. See "Monthly Events in the Sichuan-Shaanxi Revolutionary Base," in *CSGJD*, vol. 2, pp. 764-767.

9. Kapp, pp. 88-89; also "Laws of Soviet Organization in the Sichuan-Shaanxi Province" and "How to Distribute Land?" in *CSGJD*, vol. 1, respectively p. 143 and p. 590. The first document contains such leftist allegations as "The village Soviet is the basic organ of the Soviet system. It is elected by all the people in the village except the landlords, the rich peasants and those elements deprived of citizenship." In the second document, very radical policies can be found as follows:

> Question: Can children and wives of rich peasant households be assigned with any good land or not?

> Answer: No. Give them the worst land and let them till and farm it. If they are unable to work, they can swap labor with others or ask their relatives for help. We don't really care.

10. Zhou Kaiqing, *Minguo chuanshi jiyao* (Important Events in Sichuan in the Republican Period) (Taipei, 1974), pp. 501-502; Kapp, p. 90.

11. See *CSGJD*, vol. 2, pp. 769-770; Zhou Kaiqing, pp. 504-507. Some of the dates in these two sources are a bit different perhaps because the delays of reports by the KMT.

12. Zhou Kaiqing, op. cit.

13. Cheng Shicai, "The Grant Victory at Kongshanba," in *Kunan de licheng* (Experiences of Hardship and Heroism) (Beijing, 1984), vol. 1, p. 392; Xu Shiyou, *Wozai hongjun shinian* (Ten Years' Experience in the Red Army) (Beijing, 1983), p. 227.

14. Kapp, pp. 90-91; *CSGJD*, vol. 2, p. 780. Several times in his book, Kapp refers to a city of Suiting, which is obviously a mistake for Daxian where the warlord Liu Cunhou's headquarters was located.

15. Wang Jianmin, vol. 2, pp. 211-214.

16. Yu Jinan, pp. 180-184.

17. Zhang Guotao, "Fundamental Mistakes of the Rightists," in *Ganbu bidu* (Cadres' Manual), August 31, 1933; "Land Distribution and Soviet Construction," in *Soviet*, October 20, 1933.

18. Zhou Kaiqing, p. 523; CSGJD, vol. 2, p. 779.

19. Xu Xiangqian, vol. 1, p. 92.

20. See CSGJD, vol. 2, pp. 792-793; and Zhang Caiqian, "Reminiscences of the Fight Against the Six-Route Encirclement," in *Kunan de licheng*, vol. 1, pp. 452-468.

21. Zhou Kaiqing, pp. 536, 544.

22. See Zhang Caiqian, p. 448.

23. Zhou Kaiqing, p. 545

24. See "Combat Plan of the Military Council for Crossing the River," in CZZGZ, p. 56.

25. See "Telegraph of the CCP Politburo and the Central Military Council to the Fourth Front Army Concerning the Red Army Main Forces' Entering Sichuan," in CZZGZ, p. 57.

26. Zhang Guotao, vol. 3, pp. 1103-1104; Xu Xiangqian, vol. 1, pp. 95-96.

27. Yu Jinan, p. 193; Zhang Guotao, vol. 3, p. 1101.

28. See "Arduous Struggles," p. 243.

29. See "Proclamation of the Founding of the Northern Federate Government of the Chinese Soviet Republic," in *Zhang Guotao wenti zilaio* (Documentary Materials on the Zhang Guotao Issue, hereafter ZGTWT) (Chengdu, 1982), p. 451.

30. Ibid.; also Zhang Guotao, vol. 3, pp. 1113-1114.

31. See ZGTWT, p. 449.

32. See "No. 1 Declaration of the Northwest Federate Government," cited in Yu Jinan, p. 449.

33. Zhang Guotao, vol. 3, p. 1102; Xu Xiangqian, vol. 1, p. 95.

34. Zhang Guotao, op. cit.

35. Yang Chengwu, *Yi changzheng* (Reminiscence of the Long March) (Beijing, 1982), pp. 150-151; Han Dongshan, "The Seizure of Maogong and the Union at Dawei," in *Kunan de licheng*, vol. 2, pp. 50-51; Harrison Salisbury, pp. 239-240.

36. Han Dongsheng, pp. 53-55; Yang Chengwu, 152-153.

37. See "Arduous Struggles," p. 245.

38. See "Declaration to Protest the Japanese Annexing North China and Chiang Kai-shek Selling the Nation," June 15, 1935, in DSG, vol. 2, p. 183.

39. Braun, p. 121.

40. "Telegram of the Central Military Council to the Fourth Front Army for Establishment of Soviet Regimes in Sichuan, Shaanxi and Gansu," June 16, 1935, in DSZL, vol. 7, p. 179.

41. Yu Jinan, p. 203.

42. Ibid.; Cai Xiaoxian, pp. 341-342; Harrison Salisbury, p. 240.

43. Zhang Guotao, vol. 3, p. 1121.

44. Zhang Guotao, vol. 3, pp. 1123-1127.

45. See Zhang Guotao, "Political Report at the Conference of Party and Government Work of the Fourth Front Army," November 11, 1934, in ZGTWT, pp. 405-410.

In this speech, Zhang told his men that the Chinese Soviet Republic had a vast territory of more than 100 counties, that it had 10 big Soviet bases—theirs was only one of them—and one million Red Army troops. In the Central Soviet there were five Red Army Corps, that meant five times as big as theirs. The CCP altogether had 380,000 members all over the country, and so on. Zhang Guotao's bragging and bluffing here was to exalt the Party Center in order to inspire his men's morale and to enhance his own prestige. But at the same time, he also created a kind of quasi-religious faith among his men in the Fourth Front Army toward the Party Center and the Jiangxi Central Soviet.

46. See *Zhongguo gongchandang lici zhongyao huiyi ji* (Important Conferences of the Chinese Communist Party, hereafter ZGHY) (Shanghai, 1982), vol. 1, p. 150. Here 16 participants are named: Mao Zedong, Zhang Guotao, Zhu De, Zhou Enlai, Zhang Wentian, Bo Gu, Wang Jiaxiang, Liu Shaoqi, Liu Bocheng, Deng Xiaoping, Lin Biao, Peng Dehuai, Nie Rongzhen, Lin Boqu, Li Fuchun.

Zhang recalls that six Politburo members participated in the Conference in addition to Liu Bocheng, the Chief of Staff. Braun says that he himself attended the Lianghekou Conference but no outsiders—Braun did not deem himself an outsider—were invited. It is impossible to establish an accurate and comprehensive list without more documentary sources. But it seems likely that due to the sensitive relationship of the First and Fourth Front Armies at that time, Mao and the Party Center could not have been so rude and unwise as to cram all their own army men into this Politburo conference and not to allow in anyone from Zhang's side.

47. Ibid.; Zhang Guotao, vol. 3, pp. 1130-1134 and Warren Kuo, vol. 3, p. 58.

48. See ZGHY, vol. 1, p. 159.

49. Ibid.

50. Braun, p. 124; Zhang Guotao, vol. 3, p. 1134.

51. See "Resolution of the CCP Politburo on the Military Policies after the Union of the First and Fourth Front Armies," June 28, 1935, in *DSZL*, vol. 7, p. 180. That the resolution was drafted some days after the Conference can be seen from the attached date to this document.

52. Wang Jianying, p. 236.

53. Kapp, p. 95.

54. Zhou Kaiqing, pp. 557-559, 570-572; Kapp, pp. 99-101.

55. Yan Daogang, p. 32.

56. There are other versions on the strength of the First and Fourth Front Armies when they first met in westen Sichuan. The following are some I noted in my research:

	1st Front Army	*4th Front Army*
Otto Braun	15,000–20,000	50,000
Cai Xiaoxian	8,000–10,000	70,000
Warren Kuo	10,000	70,000
Zhang Guotao	10,000	45,000
Edgar Snow	45,000	50,000

57. Ouyang Qin, "Chairman Zhu Was with Us Together," in *Xinghuo liaoyuan*, vol. 3; Harrison Salisbury, pp. 312-313.

58. Zhang Guotao, vol. 3, p. 1133; Braun, p. 121.

59. See *DSG*, vol. 2, p. 185.

60. Ibid.

61. Yu Jinan, p. 211.

62. See *DSG*, vol. 2, p. 186 and Peng Dehuai, p. 201. In his memoirs (vol. 3, pp. 1156-1158), Zhang Guotao refers to a joint conference of the Party and the Army, which most probably pertains to the Luhua Conference.

63. Wang Jianying, p. 236.

64. Yu Jinan, op. cit.

65. See ZGHY, vol. 1, pp. 164; Zhang Guotao, vol. 3, pp. 1159-1160.

66. See ZGHY, vol. 1, p. 164-165.

67. Zhang Guotao, vol. 3, pp. 1160-1161.

68. See "Resolution of the Central Committee on the Political Situations and our Tasks After the Union of the First and Fourth Front Armies," in *DSZL*, vol. 7, pp. 183-184.

69. Ibid., p. 185.

70. Ibid., p. 186.

71. See "Arduous Struggles," p. 247.

72. Wang Jianying, pp. 236-237. Some sources say that the 33rd Red Army was dismissed and combined into the 9th Army Corps.

73. Peng Dehuai, p. 201; Wu Yunpu, "Diary on the Long March," in *Wenshi ziliao*, vol. 72, pp. 34-35.

74. Wu Yunpu, op. cit. Wu was the political commissar of the Third or Communication Bureau in the Red Army General Headquarters.

75. See ZGHY, vol. 1, p. 168.

76. See "Supplementary Resolution on the Strategic Policy at Present," August 20, 1935, in *DSZL*, vol. 7, pp. 187-188.

77. Ibid.

78. See "Report of the Staff Office in the Chiang Kai-shek Headquarters on Pursuit of the Red Army on the Long March, June-September 1935," in *GMDDA*, pp. 281-296.

79. Peng Dehuai, p. 201; Nie Rongzhen, vol. 1, p. 284.

80. See Cheng Shicai, pp. 123-129; Xu Shiyou, pp. 318-320; Warren Kuo, vol. 3, p. 63; "Report of the Staff Office in the Chiang Kai-shek Headquarters on Pursuit of the Red Army on the Long March, June-September 1935," op. cit.

81. Wu Yunpu, p. 37. Wu's diary serves to correct some errors in Zhang Guotao's memoirs. The area that the Left Route Army marched through from Zhuokeji to Aba in late August 1935 was not the real grassland but a hilly area of mixed grasses and woods.

82. See Jiang Lixin, *Zhang Guotao de panghuang yu juexing* (Wavering and Awakening of Zhang Guotao) (Taipei, 1981), p. 311.

83. Zhang Guotao, vol. 3, p. 1171; Wu Yunpu, p. 38. From the evidence of Wu's diary there should be no doubt that the Left Route Army was indeed deluged with three days of heavy rain from August 30 to September 1, 1935, and this rain directly caused Zhang Guotao's decision to turn back.

8/31   Heavy rain.

9/1   Heavy rain; the river in front flooded over a thirty li long distance;
      impossible to wade across.

9/2   Stayed at spot.

9/3   Clear; Stayed at spot.

9/4   Failed to build up bridges over the river and turned back to Aba.

84. "Telegram of the Red Army Headquarters to the Right Route Army,"
September 3, 1935 in Yu Jinan, p. 218.

85. Yu Jinan, p. 219.

86. See Kai Feng, "What Are the Differences Between the Party Center and
Zhang Guotao?" written on Feburary 27, 1937, in ZGTWT, pp. 34-35.

87. See "Instruction of the Party Center on Implementing its Strategic Policy
and Ordering Zhang Guotao to Go North Immediately," September 9, 1935, in
DSZL, vol. 7, p. 189.

88. There has been an interesting debate between an old Army officer and a
young Party historian. See Lu Liping, "Reply to 'Suspicion and Questions Concerning
Zhang Guotao's Secret Telegram of Dispensing of the Party Center with Force',"
Dangshi yanjiu ziliao, May 20, 1982, and Wang Nianyi, "One More Discussion on
Zhang Guotao's Secret Telegram of Dissolving the Party Center by Force," Danshi
yanjiu ziliao, June 20, 1985.

Lu claimed that he was a staff member in the Left Route Army Headquarters
at that time and personally read the telegram, while Wang interviewed the directors
of the radio stations of the Left and Right Route Armies at the time and concluded
that no such a telegram was remembered. The debate finally ended when the central
authority demanded that Wang Nianyi refrain from any further discussion.

89. Peng Dehuai, pp. 202-204; Zhang Guotao, vol. 3, pp. 1171-1173; Braun, pp.
137-139. Though Braun and Bo Gu were very suspicious of Mao's assertion that
Zhang Guotao intented a coup d'etat, neither could help following Mao's proposal
to flee.

90. See ZGHY, vol. 1, p. 172.

91. See "Another Telegram of the Party Center on Implementing its Strategic
Policy and Ordering Zhang Guotao to Go North Immediately," September 11, 1935,
in DSZL, vol. 7, p. 190.

92. Yan Jiesan, "My Personal Witness of the Capture and Release of Li Te,"
Wenshi ziliao, vol. 72, pp. 160-163. Yan recalls that Mao jokingly said something
like "You cannot tie the bride and the groom together at their wedding, and you
cannot incite a family feud. Those wishing to go north may just go north, and
those wishing to stay may stay."

93. Xu Xiangqian, "Always Keep to the Principle that the Party Leads the Army,"
in People's Daily, September 19, 1977.

94. See Yu Jinan, p. 218. Yu's blunt accusation of Zhang for making up the
weather condition merely as an excuse is not just. According to Wu Yunpu's diary,
there was indeed heavy rainfall and the Left Route Army did try to set up bridges
to cross the Geju River. On the other hand, Zhang Guotao could certainly have
found one way or other to overcome this kind of obstacle and go north, if he was
serious in his intention to do so.

95. See Zhang Guotao, "Announcement to All my Fellow Country Men," June
5, 1938, ZGTWT, p. 621. Zhang admitted that his strategy at the time was to stay

in western Sichuan or Xikang to reach a truce with the KMT Central Army, while Mao stood for turning north to open a new Soviet base.

Chapter 7

1. Peng Dehuai, p. 203.

2. Yang Dinghua, "Marching over the Snow Mountain and the Grassland," in *HJCZJ*, vol. 1, pp. 314-316.

3. Snow, p. 432; Salisbury, p. 272.

4. See Yan Daogang, pp. 34-35; also see *Gansu jiefangqian wushi nian dashi ji: 1898-1949* (Important Events in Gansu in the Fifty Years Before the Liberation: 1898-1949) (Lanzhou, 1982), p. 159.

5. After their union, two regiments of about 4,000 men of the Fourth Front Army were added to the First Front Army, thus making the total First Front Army of the 1st, 3rd, 5th and 9th Army Corps have about 18,000 men. The later split took away the 5th and 9th Army Corps of about 6,000 troops, and one half of the Fourth Front Army men previously incorporated into the First Front Army, leaving the latter with only about 10,000 on its way to the north.

6. See ZGHY, vol. 1, p. 174.

7. Kai Feng, p. 35.

8. See "Resolution on Comrade Zhang Guotao's Mistakes," passed by the CCP Politburo on September 12, 1935, in *DSZL*, vol. 7, p. 191.

9. Ibid.

10. See the record of the Ejie Conference, cited in Wang Zhixin, "More Discussions on the Destination of the Long March," in *Dangshi tongxun*, December, 1984, p. 39.

11. Ibid.

12. Zhang Juezeng, "Failure of Lu Dachang's Troops at Lazikou," in *Wenshi ziliao*, No. 62, pp. 191-192; Yang Chengwu, pp. 206-207.

13. Yang Chengwu, pp. 207-219; Nie Rongzhen, vol. 1, pp. 288-289.

14. Wang Jianying, pp. 239-240.

15. Nie Rongzhen, vol. 1, p. 290.

16. Ibid.

17. See "Appointment Notice of Yu Xuezhong and Others," in *Dagong bao* (Great Public Daily), June 7, 1935.

18. See the record of the Bangluozhen Conference, cited in Wang Zhixin, p. 43.

19. Nie Rongxhen gives the date of the Red Army's arrival at Wuqizhen as October 18, 1935, but the appendix in the *HJCZJ* gives it as October 21, 1935. See Nie Rongzhen, vol. 1, p. 293 and the latter book, vol. 2, p. 439.

20. Mao Zedong, *Poems of Mao Tse-tung*, pp. 38–39.

21. Zhang Guotao, vol. 3, p. 1039.

22. Hu Hua et al., *Zhonggong dangshi renwu* (People in CCP History) (Xian, 1982), vol. 5, pp. 227-231.

23. Ma Yuqing, *Hongjun changsheng zhongde qici huishi* (Seven Times of Reunion on the Long March) (Lanzhou, 1982), pp. 15-16.

24. Cheng Zihua, "Strive to Hold Military Forces for the Party," in *Red Flag*, August, 1978; Harrison Salisbury, pp. 291-292.

25. See Hu Hua et al., vol. 5, p. 234; also see *Zhongguo renmin jiefangjun dashi ji* (Important Events of the Chinese People's Liberation Army, hereafter *PLADS*) (Beijing, 1983), p. 94. Cheng claims—and so many CCP historians believe—that he was sent by the Party Center to the Eyuwan Soviet to guide the local Red Army for the Long March. That is not quite true. Cheng left Jiangxi in July 1935 and arrived at the Eyuwan base no later than August or September. The decision to start the 25th Army on a long-distance expedition did not occur until sometime in early November. In all likelihood, there must have been newer instructions from the Party Center or more practical reasons of the Eyuwan CCP leaders which were directly related to such a decision.

26. Xu Haidong, *Wode zishu* (My Memoirs) (Beijing, 1983), pp. 35-36.

27. Ibid. Xu's claim that on his own initiative he handed over command to Cheng Zihua because "Cheng was formerly a division commander in the Central Red Army" should not be accepted without further testimony. In fact, Cheng never assumed so high a position in the Jiangxi Central Soviet, and Cheng's—as an envoy from the Party Center—replacement of Xu as the commander of the 25th Red Army might have come from a decision of the Eyuwan CCP Committee rather than from Xu's personal generosity.

28. Zhang Lin, *Xu Xaidong jiangjun zhuan* (Biography of General Xu Haidong) (Beijing, 1982).

29. See Xu Haidong, pp. 36-38.

30. Ibid.

31. Ma Yuqing, pp. 20-21.

32. Ibid.

33. See *Xinminzhu zhuyi geming shiqi Shaanxi dashi jizhu* (Important Events in Shaanxi During the Period of the New Democratic Revolution, hereafter *SXDS*) (Xian, 1980), pp. 255-256.

34. Ibid.

35. See *PLADS*, p. 106.

36. Wu Tien-wei, *The Sian Incident: A Pivotal Point in Modern Chinese History* (Ann Arbor, 1976), p. 22; Also Wu Zhiping, "Reminiscence of the United Front Work in the Sichuan-Shaanxi Region," in *Geminshi ziliao* (Materials of Revolutionary History), No. 3, 1981, p. 134.

37. *SXDS*, pp. 190-191.

38. Most of the major Communist leaders in Shaanxi, such as Liu Zhidan, Xie Zichang, Gao Gang, Yang Guodong, Guo Songtao, Nan Hanchen, Pan Zili and Wang Bingnan, were from local landlord or gentry families. This situation was particularly due to the fact that the earlier Shaanxi Communists were mostly students who could afford to travel to the South and be converted to communism there.

39. *SXDS*, pp. 202-206, 221-222.

40. Ibid. pp. 228-232.

41. Ibid., pp. 243-244; Li Chiran, "The Three Anti-Suppression Campaigns in the Northern Shaanxi Revolutionary Base," in *Geming huiyi lu* (Reminiscences of the Revolution), vol. 5, pp. 86-93.

42. *SXDS*, pp. 248-249.

43. Ibid., pp. 250-252; Li Chiran, pp. 94-123.

44. *SXDS*, pp. 253-254.

45. Li Chiran, pp. 124-125; He Jinnian, "Record of the Third Anti-Suppression Campaign in Northern Shaanxi Revolutionary Base," in *Shaanxi wenshi ziliao* (Historical Materials of Shaanxi) (Xian, 1983), vol. 10, p. 32; Shen Shuming et al., "The Story of the 109th Division of the Northeastern Army's Annihilation in Zhiluozhen," *Wenshi ziliao*, vol. 62, pp. 205-206.

46. He Jinnian, pp. 33-37.

47. Ma Yuqing, p. 27; Li Chiran, p. 126.

48. Zhou Zuyao, "My Witness to the Destruction of the 110th Division of the Northeastern Army at Laoshan," *Wenshi ziliao*, vol. 62, pp. 32-36; He Jinnian, pp. 38-41.

49. See "Resolution of the Northwestern Bureau on Investigation of the Anti-counterrevolutionary Work," November 26, 1935, in *DSZL*, vol. 7, p. 229; also Gao Gang, "Review of the CCP Historical Problems in the Border Area," November 1942, cited in Warren Kuo, vol. 3, pp. 96-97. Gao emotionally recalled the conflict between the Party and the Army in Shaanxi and the impact of the 25th Red Army's arrival in northern Shaanxi on intraparty relationships.

50. He Jinnian, p. 42; Li Chiran, 130.

51. Warren Kuo, op. cit.

52. Wu Xiuquan, *Wode huiyi: 1908-1949* (My Memoirs: 1908-1949) (Beijing, 1984), p. 101.

53. Xu Haidong, pp. 104-105.

54. Zhang Lin, p. 345.

55. See "Resolution of the Northwestern Bureau on Investigation of the Anti-counterrevolutionary Work," op. cit.

56. Wang Jianying, pp. 242-248.

57. Nie Rongzhen, pp. 296-300; Xu Haidong, pp. 108-109; Shen Shumin, pp. 209-214.

58. It should be noted that for a long time the Shaanxi CCP Committee was one chapter of the CCP Northern Bureau. Zhu Lizhi himself was the secretary of the Northern Bureau in 1934 before he came to Shaanxi as representative of the Northern Bureau. Partly due to his special connection with North China, Zhu remained unattacked by the Party Center and indeed played an active role later in the contact between the Party Center and the Northern Bureau.

59. Zhang Hao is the alias of Lin Yuying, Lin Biao's uncle.

60. See *DSNB*, pp. 52-53; *DSG*, vol. 2, p. 225; *ZGHY*, vol. 1, p. 179.

61. See *ZGHY*, vol. 1, pp. 179-180.

62. "Resolution of the Central Committee on the Contemporary Political Situations and the Party's Tasks (the Wayaobao Conference)," passed by the Politburo on December 25, 1935, in *Liuda yilai: dangnei mimi wenjian* (Since the Sixth Congress: Collection of Secret Documents of the CCP) (Beijing, 1980), vol. 1, pp. 734-745.

63. Ibid.

64. Ibid.

65. Ibid.

66. "Resolution of the Central Committee on Military Strategies," passed by the Politburo on December 23, 1935, in *DSZL*, vol. 7, p. 288-289.

67. Ibid.

68. Ibid.

69. Mao Zedong, "On the Tactics against Japanese Imperialism," in *MX*, p. 147.

70. B. M. Leibzon and K. K. Shirinia, *Povorot v politike komiternia* (A Turning Point of the Comintern's Policy) (Moscow, 1975), p. 288.

71. See the Institute of Party History of the CCP Central Committee, *DSNB*, pp. 51- 52; Zheng Yuyan, "Reminiscence of Comrade Liu Changsheng," in *Shanghai wenshi ziliao* (Historical Materials of Shanghai) (Shanghai, 1982), vol. 10, pp. 68-69; Hu Hua et al., vol. 1, pp. 359-360.

72. See *DSG*, vol. 2, p. 233.

73. Ibid., p. 234.

74. Warren Kuo seems to have mistakenly considered "Announcement of the Eastern Expedition" the same document as "Announcement of the Central Government of the Chinese Soviet Republic for Convocation of the National Congress of Resisting the Japanese and Saving China" issued on February 21, 1936. See *DSNB*, p. 53; *DSG*, vol 2, p. 238; Warren Kuo, vol 3, p. 129.

75. Peng Dehuai, pp. 211-214.

76. Ibid.; Nie Rongzhen, vol. 3, pp. 308-309.

77. Before leaving Shanxi to return to Shaanxi, the Communists did not forget to lodge another protest, "Manifesto of the Vanguard Brigade of the Chinese People's Red Army Regarding the National Traitors, Chiang Kai-shek and Yan Xishan, Blocking its Way in Going East to Fight the Japanese and Disturbing its Rear Base," April 5, 1936, in *DSZL*, vol. 7, p. 752. Back in Shaanxi, they issued "Manifesto on Ceasing Fire for Peace Talks and Uniting Against the Japanese," on May 5, 1936, in *Liuda yilai*, vol 1, p. 762.

78. Nie Rongzhen, op. cit.; *DSG*, vol 2, pp. 238-240.

79. Nie Rongzhen, vol. 1, p. 314-316; Li Chiran, "The 81st Division of the 27th Red Army in the Eastern and Western Expeditions," in *Shaanxi wenshi ziliao*, vol. 10, p. 58.

80. Peng Dehuai, pp. 214-215; Nie Rongzhen, vol. 1, pp. 316-322.

81. Ibid.; *PLAZS*, pp. 188-190.

82. In the autumn of 1935, the northern Shaanxi base area loosely spread into 20 counties with a population of 900,000. Then, during the Western Expedition in the summer of 1936, the Communists captured 15 counties and could achieve solid control in 10. The regular troops of the 26th Red Army in Shaanxi were about 4,000. The arrival of the 25th Red Army added some 4,000 soldiers while the Central Army brought in 7,000. Altogether, there should have been 15,000 Communist troops. They lost 2,000 but gained 7,000 in the Eastern Expedition. Therefore, the CCP's territory can be roughly accounted to be 30 counties and its military strength 20,000 troops in the year 1936. See *SXDS*, pp. 252, 264.

Chapter 8

1. Zhang Guotao, *Wode huiyi*, vol. 3, p. 1172.

2. There is a great controversy over Zhu De's attitude in the Mao-Zhang rift. Some describe him as a purposeful follower of Zhang; others would believe that he was kidnapped by Zhang, while Zhu made such strong protests against Zhang as "Even if you chop me to halves, you cannot cut off my relationship with Comrade Mao Zedong." I think Braun's judgment is closer to the truth, when he writes, "According to my knowledge, Chu followed Chang as he followed Chou before." This situation can also be seen from Smetley's recalling Zhu's reluctance to mention his experience in western Sichuan after the split later on. See Zhang Guotao, vol. 3, pp. 1172-1173; Yu Hongda, "Going South Leads to Nowhere," in *Hongqi piaopiao*, vol. 21, pp. 18-19; Braun, pp. 138-139; and Smedley, pp. 330-331.

3. Yu Hongda, op. cit.; Wang Weizhou, "My Reminiscences," in *Geming huiyi lu*, vol. 1, pp. 119-120; Wu Yunpu, p. 39.

4. Yu Hongda, loc. cit.; Ouyang Yi, p. 375.

5. See Kai Feng, p. 31.

6. See Yu Jinan, p. 250; "Arduous Struggles," p. 250; and Zhang Guotao, vol. 3, p. 1182.

7. There are different statistics of the strength of the Fourth Front Army at the time. "Arduous Struggles" reports it as 80,000, while *PLADS* says 100,000. I believe the former is more accurate.

8. See Zhang Guotao, vol. 3, pp. 1176-1178.

9. Yu Jinan, op. cit. This is the only place where I find this document partially presented.

10. Salisbury, pp. 311-312. In a later speech of Zhang Guotao, however, he referred to the Party Center as being composed of eight members and seven alternate members from the CRA side, seven members and three alternate members from the FFA side and some others from the Mission to Comintern. Following this line of research, I think, it will be possible to reach better information on this kind of historical fact than by accepting the allegations of any incumbent Communist leaders. Needless to say, the final judge is the evidence of original sources, if any exist.

11. Wang Jianying, pp. 251-253.

12. *PLAZS*, pp. 167-168; "Arduous Struggles," pp. 251-252.

13. "Arduous Struggles," op. cit.

14. See "Report of the Chongqing Headquarters on Pursuing the Red Army on the Long March," in *GMDDA*, pp. 326-328.

15. See *DSZL*, vol. 7, p. 187.

16. Zhang Guotao, vol. 3, p. 1182.

17. Yan Daogang, pp. 40-41.

18. Xue Yue, Part 4, p. 87; "Telegrams of the Sichuan Army and the Central Army Regarding Counterattack of Ming, Ya, Tian, Lu, and Bao Counties," in *GMDDA*, pp. 341-350.

19. See "Arduous Struggles," pp. 253-254.

20. Zheng Weishan, "Embarking on the Road Illuminated by Mao Zedong's Thought," in *Xinghuo liaoyuan* (Bejing, 1982), No. 3, pp. 383-384. The adverse conditions facing the FFA is confirmed by the KMT military reports in *GMDDA*, p. 354.

21. Zhang Guotao, vol. 3, pp. 1192-1194.

22. See Zhang Guotao's speech at a conference of Party activists on April 1, 1936, entitled "Prospects of the Chinese Soviet Movement and our Tasks at the Present Time." There, Zhang did not spare vulgar agitations such as "There is a woman available, why don't you grab her as your wife?"—to metaphorize the Chengdu Plain as attractive treasure just to pluck up his troops' morale; see *ZGTWT*, pp. 539-540.

23. Zhang Guotao, loc. cit., p. 545; Zhang Guotao, *Wode huiyi*, vol. 3, p. 1192.

24. He Long, "Recalling the Second Front Red Army," p. 31.

25. Xiao Ke, "At the Time of Union of the Second and Sixth Army Corps," in *Zhonggong dangshi yanjiu wenxuan* (Selected Articles on CCP History Studies) (Changsha, 1983), vol. 2, pp. 680-681.

26. *PLADS*, pp. 93-94; *PLAZS*, p. 148.

27. He Long, p. 34.

28. Xiao Ke, pp. 679-689.

29. See "Combat Plan of Crossing the River," January 20, 1935, in *CZZGZ*, pp. 53-55.

30. See "Instructions of the Politburo of the Central Committee and the Central Military Council to the Second and Sixth Army Corps on Smashing the Hunan-Hupei-Guizhou Suppression Campaign," February 1, 1935, in *Qianshan hongji*, p. 265.

31. Xiao Ke, op. cit.

32. Ibid.

33. Yan Daogang, p. 41.

34. Ren Bishi, "Outline Report of Experiences of the Second and Sixth Army Corps on the Long March from Hunan-Hupei Border to Northeast Xikang," written in July 1936, printed in *DSZL*, vol. 7, p. 235.

35. He Long, op. cit., p. 35.

36. Cited in Ren Bishi, p. 236. It should be noted that what Ren referred to as the Central Military Council throughout his report was actually the Red Army General Headquarters controlled by Zhang Guotao.

37. Xiao Ke, p. 692.

38. Ren Bishi, pp. 236-237; He Long, pp. 34-35.

39. Ren Bishi, pp. 237-238.

40. See the telegram of the Second and Sixth Army Corps to the Military Council, issued on March 27, 1936, at Panjiang, cited in Ren Bishi, op. cit.

41. See the telegram of the Second and Sixth Army Corps to the Military Council, issued March 29, 1936, at Panjiang, cited in Ren Bishi, p. 239.

42. He Long, op. cit.

43. See the telegram of the Military Council to the Second and Sixth Army Corps, issued on March 30, 1936 and cited in Ren Bishi, op. cit.

44. Xiao Ke, p. 698; Ren Bishi, pp. 239-240.

45. Ibid.

46. Ren Bishi, p. 241.

47. See "Comrade Guotao's Speech at the May 5 Commemoration Rally," in *Cadres' Manual*, May 16, 1936; also in *ZGTWT*, p. 572.

48. Zhang Guotao, vol. 3, p. 1197. .

49. Although the Resolution contains such strong protests as "The action of Comrade Zhang Guotao is a de facto betrayal of the Party and the Revolution," this document was not sent to Zhang at all. See "Resolution on Comrade Zhang Guotao's Establishing another CCP Central Committee," January 22, 1936, in *ZGTWT*, p. 6.

50. Zhang Guotao, vol. 3, pp. 1147-1149.

51. Zhang Guotao, "Report on the Upsurge of the National Revolution and the Strategy and Tactics of the Party," January 28, 1936, in *ZGTWT*, p. 486; also Zhang Guotao, "Comrade Guotao's Report at the First Provisional Conference of All Sichuan Soviet Congress," January 18, 1936, in *ZGTWT*, p. 462.

52. Zhang Guotao, "Report on the Upsurge," p. 513.

53. Zhang Guotao, "Prospects of the Chinese Soviet Movement and our Tasks at Present Time," on April 1, 1936, in *ZGTWT*, p. 540.

54. Zhang Guotao, "Speech at the Conference of the Central Column Activists," June 6, 1936, in *ZGTWT*, pp. 581-584.

55. Ibid.

56. Ibid.

57. Ibid.

58. Wang Zhen, "A Loyal Fighter and a Brilliant Life," in *Jiefangjun bao* (The PLA Daily), July 28, 1977; Zhang Guotao, vol. 3, p. 1205. Zhang recalled, "The previous lessons (union and split of the FFA with the CRA) kept in our mind, we were very cautious this time."

59. He Long, p. 36; Zuo Qi, "On the Long March," in *Wenshi ziliao*, vol. 92, p. 94.

60. See Yu Jinan, pp. 248-249.

61. Ibid.; "Arduous Struggles," p. 257.

62. Zuo Qi, op. cit.; Yu Hongda, op. cit.

63. Zuo Qi, p. 95; "Arduous Struggles," p. 257.

64. Wang Jianying, pp. 251-255. Wang's inclusion of Wang Zhen into the Northwestern Bureau seems questionable to me.

65. Zhang Ziyi, "Diary on the Long March," in *Zhonggong dangshi ziliao*, No. 3, 1982, p. 480. Literally, the Chinese term *xiushi* for stinking corpse sounds more like human bodies than animal ones.

66. See Kai Feng, p. 55. In one of his telegrams to Zhang Hao, Zhang Guotao even raised the soft question "Elder Brother Hao, are you permitted to telegraph me freely or not?"

67. He Long, p. 37; also Zhang Ziyi, pp. 487-493.

68. Zhang Guotao, vol. 3, pp. 1214-1215.

69. This telegram is exhibited in the Museum of the Chinese Revolution in Beijing.

70. See Xue Yue, Part 4, p. 108; Yan Daogang, p. 41; Zhou Kaiqing, pp. 510-512.

71. Ibid.

72. He Long, p. 37.

73. Nie Rongzhen, vol. 1, pp. 329-330. Obviously Nie is complaining here about the Second and Fourth Front Armies.

74. Peng Dehuai, pp. 217-218; Yang Daogang, pp. 45-46.

75. See *DSG*, vol. 2, p. 197; *PLADS*, pp. 117-118.

Chapter 9

1. See "The Party Center's Announcement on the Grand Union of the 1st, 2nd, and 4th Front Armies," October 10, 1936, in *DSZL*, vol. 7, p. 262.

2. Zhang Guowei, "Reminiscences of the Birthday Celebration of Chiang Kaishek in Luoyang," in *Wenshi ziliao*, vol. 18, 1963, pp. 163-165.

3. As for Mao's hard working style and all-round responsibility in the Communist Party and Red Army, see Edgar Snow, p. 72 and Zhang Guotao, vol. 3, p. 1236. For the interactions between Christian belief and Capitalist practice, see Max Weber, *The Protestant Ethic and the Spirit of Capitalism* (New York, 1958), particularly the chapter on Luther's concept of the calling, pp. 79-92.

4. See "A Public Letter to all Officers and Men of the Northeastern Army Concerning the Red Army's Willingness to Unite with the Northeastern Army to Resist the Japanese," on January 25, 1936, in *Liuda yilai*, vol. 2, p. 746.

5. See "Telegram of Mao Zedong and Peng Dehuai to Zhang Xueliang and Wang Yizhe," in *Xian shibian ziliao* (Materials on the Xian Incident, hereafter *XASB*) (Beijing, 1978), vol. 1, p. 41; and also Song Enfu, "A Historical Meeting of Zhou Enlai and Zhang Xueliang," in *Lishi zhishi* (Historical Knowledge) (Beijing, 1985), No. 1, pp. 1-3.

6. Song Enfu, op. cit.

7. See "Principal Instructions of the Party Center on Works with the Northeastern Army," June 20, 1936, in *XASB*, vol. 1, pp. 44-53.

8. Ibid.

9. Ibid.; also Nie Rongzhen, vol. 1, p. 321. Nie Rongzhen recalls how the Red Army fought with the Northeastern Army on the one hand and made friends with it on the other. Nie uses the term "fight to unite" to describe the Communist strategy.

10. Ibid.

11. See "Letter of Mao Zedong and Zhou Enlai to Zhang Xueliang," on October 5, 1936, in *XASB*, vol. 1, p. 73.

12. Luo Ruiqing et al., *Xian shibian yu Zhou Enlai dongzhi* (The Xian Incident and Comrade Zhou Enlai) (Beijing, 1978), p. 27.

13. Yan Daogang, p. 46.

14. Luo Ruiqing et al., p. 30; Wu Tien-wei, *The Sian Incident: A Pivotal Point in Modern Chinese History* (University of Michigan, 1976), p. 69.

15. See "Zhang Xueliang's Speech to All Staff Members in the Bandit Extermination Headquarters of Northwest China," on December 13, 1936, published in *Liberation Daily*, on December 16, 1936; also *SXDS*, pp. 269-270 and Wu Tien-wei, pp. 72-73.

16. See "About the Telegram of Zhang Xueliang and Yang Hucheng to the CCP Central Committee," December 12, 1936, in *XASB*, vol. 1, p. 131.

17. Warren Kuo, vol. 3, p. 169.

18. See "Telegram of the General Secretariat to the Northern Bureau," December 12, 1936.

19. See "Telegram of the Central Committee to the Northern Bureau," December 14, 1936.

20. See the Editorial in *Pravda*, December 14, 1936.

21. See the Editorial in *Pravda*, December 17, 1936.

22. Jiang Xiaotao, "Diplomatic Response of the Government of Soviet Union to the Xian Incident," in *Lishi ziliao*, No. I, 1985, pp. 20-21.

23. See A. M. Grigoriev and A. B. Reznikov, "Greogry Dimitrov and the Anti-imperialist United Front," in *Greogry Dimitrov, voshchi meshdunarodnovo komunichiskovo dvishrenia* (Greogry Dimitrov, Leader of the International Communist Movement) (Moscow, 1972), p. 394.

24. Fang Detian, *Zhang Xueliang yu Xian shibian* (Zhang Xueliang and the Xi'an Incident) (Beijing, 1980), pp. 112-113; Shen Bochun, *Xian shibian jishi* (Personal Experiences in the Xian Incident) (Beijing, 1979), p. 114.

25. Luo Ruiqing et al., p. 47. To understand CCP's change of position in the early days of the Xian Incident, please see the two editorials of *Jiefang ribao* on December 16 and 17 entitled respectively "Scandalous Positions of the Nanking Government after the December 12 Incident" and "Exclusively Stop the Civil War."

26. See Wu Tien-wei, pp. 156-178.

27. See "Instruction of the Central Committee on the Propaganda Policy on the Xi'an Incident," January 7, 1937, in *XASB*, vol. 1, pp. 168-169.

28. According to *SXDS*, p. 271, the CCP established Party branches in 21 counties around the city of Xian and enrolled 1,350 Party members in late December 1936.

29. Zhang Guotao, vol. 3, p. 1214. Zhang himself admitted that the Fourth Front Army decided to send Zhang to northern Shaanxi to bargain within the Party Center while Chen Changhao was left with the troops as military support.

30. See the telegram of the Central Military Council, "The Combat Plan of October," on October 11, 1936, cited in Cong Jin, "Several Problems of the Western Route Army," in *Dangshi yanjiu ziliao*, No. 5, 1982, pp. 27-30.

31. Ibid.

32. See Zhang Yimin, "Refute the Fallacies of Zhang Guotao in his Memoirs," in *Dangshi yanjiu*, No. 1, 1982, p. 61.

33. See the telegram of the Military Council on October 25, in Yu Jinan, p. 256 and Zhang Yimin, p. 61.

34. See the telegram of the Military Council on October 26, cited in Cong Jin, p. 28.

35. Yan Shi, "Studies on Some Historical Facts of the Western Route Army," in *Dangshi yanjiu*, No. 1, 1982, p. 67.

36. Zhang Guotao, vol. 3, p. 1215-1216.

37. Peng Dehuai, pp. 216-217.

38. He Long, pp. 37-38.

39. See the telegram of Red Army Headquarters to Xu Xiangqian and Chen Changhao on November 5, 1936, cited in Cong Jin, p. 29.

40. See the CCP Central Committee and the Central Military Council, "The New Combat Plan," on November 8, 1936; also "Telegram of Zhang, Zhou, Bo and

Lin to Zhu, Zhang, Peng, He and Ren," on November 10, 1936, cited in Yu Jinan, p. 259 and Cong Jin, p. 30 and also *DSNB*, p. 58.

41. Of the four historians quoted above, Yu and Zhang support the traditional version that the Western Route Army was secretly formed by Zhang Guotao against the wishes of the Party Center while Cong and Yan represent the liberal view that the formation and operation of the Western Route Army was approved and appointed by the Military Council and the Party Center. Both sides apply some documents to back up their views yet for various political and academic reasons, but neither is able to study the subject in a broader, deeper sense. This can be regarded as an exemplary case of studies on CCP history in China.

42. Chen Yigui, "A Fierce Battle at Gulang," in *Kunan de licheng*, vol. 2, pp. 265-269; Zhang Yimin, p. 63.

43. Cheng Shicai, *Beizhuang de licheng* (A Heroic but Tragic Experience) (Shenyang, 1959), pp. 12-14; Li Xinguo, "Bloodshed along the Western Expedition," in *Kunan de licheng*, vol. 2, p. 256.

44. Cheng Shicai, op. cit.

45. Ma Buqing, "A Decisive Battle in the Gansu Corridor," in *Jinri dalu* (The Mainland Today), Taipei, No. 146, October 1961.

46. Dong Hanhe, *Dong Zhentang* (Biography of Dong Zhentang) (Lanzhou, 1981), pp. 132-137.

47. See *DSG*, vol. 3, p. 194; *PLAZS*, p. 204.

48. Cheng Shicai, pp. 29-54; Yu Jinan, p. 265.

49. Cheng Shicai, pp. 55-70; Zhou Chunlin, "Our Commissar Li Xiannian," in *Kunan de licheng*, vol. 2, pp. 281-284.

50. Li Xinguo, pp. 96-100; Li Tianhuan, "Marching out of the Qilian Mountains," in *Kunan de licheng*, vol. 2, pp. 444-448.

51. See the Qinghai Political Consultative Conference, "Birth and Death of the Ma Family Troops in Qinghai," in *Wenshi ziliao*, No. 27, 1962, pp. 159-161.

52. See ZGHY, vol. 1, pp. 186-193.

53. Zhang Guotao, vol. 3, pp. 1259-1265.

54. Ibid.

55. I assume that the tens of telegrams of the Military Council to the Western Route Army Headquarters from November 1936 to March 1937 held in the Archives of the CCP Central Committee may soon be released to Chinese historians and will hopefully verify this assumption.

56. Li Haiwen, "The Formation of the Second CCP-KMT Collaboration," in *Watchtower Weekly*, No. 45, 1984, pp. 36-37.

57. Deng Wenyi, *Congjun baoguo ji* (I Joined the Army to Serve the Motherland) (Taipei, 1979), p. 261.

58. Li Haiwen, p. 37.

59. See *DSG*, vol. 2, p. 237.

60. Li Haiwen, op. cit.

61. See "Telegram of the Central Committee to Zhou Enlai for Peaceful Solution of the Xian Incident," December 21, 1936, in *XASB*, vol. 1, p. 166.

62. Zhou Enlai, "Report of Results of my Talk with Song Ziwen and Song Meiling," December 25, 1936, in ZX, vol. 1, p. 73.

63. See "Telegram of the CCP Central Committee to the KMT 3rd Plenum," February 10, 1937, in *XASB*, vol. 1, pp. 236-237.

64. See "Outline Propaganda and Explanation of the CCP Central Committee on the Peaceful Resolution of the Xian Incident and the Party Center's Letter to the KMT 3rd Plenum," February 15, 1937, in *XASB*, vol. 1, pp. 236-237.

65. Ibid.

66. *DSG*, vol. 2, pp. 259-261; Wang Pei et al., *Zhongguo kangri zhanzheng shigao* (A Draft History of the Anti-Japanese War) (n. p., 1983), vol. 1., pp. 94-100.

67. Ibid.

68. *DSG*, op. cit.; Wang Pei et al., op. cit.; Kang Ze, "My Experiences in Negotiating over the Second CCP-KMT Collaboration," in *Wenshi ziliao*, No 71, pp. 20-21; Zhou Enlai, "On the United Front," in *ZX*, vol. 1, p. 195.

69. Ibid.

70. Zhou Enlai, "Announcement of the CCP Central Committee Regarding the CCP-KMT Collaboration," July 15, 1937, in *ZX*, vol. 1, pp. 76-78.

71. See Johnson, p. 33; Kataoka, p. 48; Li Shoukong, p. 570; Wang Pei et al., pp. 72-73; and particularly Wu Xiangxiang, *Di erci zhongri zhanzheng shi* (A History of the Sino-Japanese War) (Taipei, 1974), vol. 1, pp. 361-370. Johnson and Kataoka both believe that the Lugouqiao Incident occurred as the measured response of a Japanese troop being fired upon "by elements of General Sung Cheyuan's 29th Army" (Johnson) or "from unknown sources" (Kataoka) while on their routine exercise. This is obviously questionable for the sole usage of Japanese military sources to describe an international event.

72. Kang Ze, pp. 21-22.

73. Wang Pei et al., p. 101.

74. See ZGHY, vol. 1, pp. 200-205; also Zhang Guotao, vol. 3, p. 1296; Warren Kuo, vol. 3, pp. 231-233. At the Luochuan Conference, Zhang Guotao, Zhou Enlai, Zhu De, and others might have stood for a mild attitude toward the KMT and called for fighting against the Japanese—as Zhang and Kuo allude to—but two basic issues are worth noting: the Party and Army leadership as a whole already held a stance represented by Mao Zedong and all radical or moderate shifts constituted some part of this general direction.

75. Ibid.

76. See the Central Revolutionary Military Council, "An Order for Reorganizing the Red Army into the 8th Route Army of the Nationalist Army," cosigned by Mao Zedong as Chairman and Zhu De and Zhou Enlai as Vice Chairmen on August 25, 1937, in *Mao Zedong ji* (Works of Mao Zedong) (Tokyo, 1984), Supplementary Volume 5, pp. 101-102; Wang Pei et al., pp. 130-131; *PLAZS*, pp. 240-241. There are some flaws in Johnson's list of the Eighth Route Army's organization in 1937 as shown in Table 3, p. 96. Wang Jiaxiang was already in Moscow and could not be appointed Political Commisssar of the 8th Route Army; Deng Xiaoping was Vice Director of the Political Department of the 8th Route Army and not Political Commissar of the 129th Division until early 1938. In fact, the entire political commissar system was temporarily abolished at the beginning of the Anti-Japanese War.

77. Wang Pei et al., pp. 134-137.

78. As for the swift intrusion of the Japanese and the quick collapse of the KMT in North China, see Johnson, pp. 33-35; Wang Pei et al., pp. 107-112.

79. Nie Rongzhen, vol. 2, pp. 350-355.

80. See Mao's telegram to Peng Dehuai "On the Principle of Independent, Autonomous Guerrilla Warfare in the Mountains," September 21, 1937, in *People's Daily*, July 7, 1981.

81. See Mao's telegram to Zhou Enlai and others "All Work in North China Must Take Guerrilla Warfare as its Sole Orientation," September 25, 1937, in *People's Daily*, July 7, 1981.

82. Zhou Enlai, "Fight Against Compromise and Appeasement, and Persist in the Anti-Japanese War in North China," in ZX, vol. 1, p. 80.

83. See ZGHY, vol. 1, pp. 206-213.

84. Warren Kuo, vol. 3, pp. 251-263. Kuo may have tried too hard to deride Mao in his book. He says that Mao had to "bow down" before Wang Ming in late 1937. Even at the December Conference, Mao was elected the Chairman of the Preparatory Committee for the Seventh Congress; and no general resolution was reached partly because of Mao's objection. As for the potential power of Mao, Wang was incomparably weak. Wang Ming went from Moscow to Yan'an on November 27, 1937.

85. The Communist troops increased from 40,000 in August 1937 to 90,000 in the year 1938. With such obvious success, neither Wang nor anybody else could have changed Mao's line of leadership.

86. See "The Sixth Plenum of the Sixth Congress of the CCP, September 29-November 6, 1938," in ZGHY, vol. 1, pp. 214-220.

87. Warren Kuo, vol. 3, pp. 222-223.

88. In 1945, Japan still had one million troops in China Proper and half a million in Northeast China. In the Anti-Japanese War, there were only a few victorious battles on China's side. In the Pingxingguan Battle, which is boasted as a "giant victory" by the Communists, about 2,000 Japanese were lost, while in the Taierzhuang Battle, which is bragged loudly by the Nationalists, about 20,000 Japanese were defeated. From 1939 on, there were half a dozen battles in which China lost more than 100,000 men but almost no battles in which Japan lost 10,000 or more. At any rate, it would have taken a long time for the Chinese army, either Nationalist or Communist or both together, to drive Japan out of China without any international intervention.

89. While it is true that, from the military point of view at least, the Nationalist Government suffered far more than the Communist Party during the Sino-Japanese War—the former lost about one million troops and one hundred generals while the latter lost few troops and only one military commander ranked equal to the general—this fact can hardly be taken as glory for the Nationalists. Just think of the fact that most of the puppet governments and armies in the Japanese occupied areas were former Nationalists, that Wang Jingwei, the No. 2 leader of the KMT, surrendered to the Japanese, and Chiang Kai-shek also conducted some secret contacts and negotiations with the Japanese; think of the fact that quite a number of nationalist governments in other Asian and European countries surrendered to or cooperated with the Japanese, German, and Italian invaders, and we can infer

that the KMT, by its nature and position, was more vulnerable than the CCP in face of the Japanese. For the secret contacts between the KMT and the Japanese, see Wu Xiangxiang, vol. 1, pp. 532-541.

90. Mao Zedong claimed that during the Sino-Japanese War his Communist troops were resisting about 65 percent of Japanese troops and 95 percent of the puppet troops. Despite his apparent exaggeration, the Communist troops, both regular and irregular, certainly constituted a major potential challenge to the Japanese invaders. On the one hand Mao may be blamed for shirking his responsibilities in fighting with the Japanese in order to preserve and increase his own strength, but on the other hand he is to be admired for searching into the deep grassroots to mobilize the broad masses against the Japanese. See Mao Zedong, "On the Coalition Government," in MX, p. 944.

Chapter 10

1. See Karl Popper, *The Open Society and Its Enemies* (London, 1966), vol. 2, the last chapter.

2. G. W. F. Hegel, *System der Philosophie. Erster Teil. Die Logik* (Stuttgart, 1929), preface to the second edition. Here Hegel cites, with due admiration, a famous quote from Spinoza: The criterion of truth lies in the truth itself; but it at the same time serves as the criterion of falsehood.

3.   Table N. 3 Overall Growth of the CCP and the PLA, 1921-1949

Year	Party	Army
1921	50	0
1923	400	0
1925	1,000	0
1927.4	58,000	0
.8	10,000	30,000
.10	—	8,000
1928	40,000	10,000
1930. 1	—	50,000
.6	—	100,000
.10	—	80,000
1933	300,000	300,000
1936	—	40,000
1937. 1	400,000	30,000
.12	—	90,000
1938	—	180,000
1940	800,000	500,000
1941	—	440,000
1944	—	780,000
1945	1,200,000	900,000
1946	—	1,200,000
1947	2,700,000	2,000,000
1948	—	3,000,000
1949	4,500,000	4,000,000

Source: DSSRL, pp. 707, 733; PLAZS, p. 468; and other scattered information.

4. See Mao Zedong, "Reform our Studies," in MX, pp. 753-754. What Mao pertained to as application of Marxist theory to Chinese reality was actually transformation of Marxist ideology into Chinese politics.

5. The CCP's attitude in the postwar years was clear: to wage a civil war to overthrow the KMT government and to use negotiation only to win over the domestic and international sympathy and support. The Soviet Union signed a peace agreement with the Nationalist Government in August 1945 and stood against the CCP's military adventure, and the United States sent one envoy after another to help reach a peaceful resolution to the Nationalist-Communist conflicts; but all these efforts, sincere or insincere, became a smoke screen to cover the Communists' ever determined intention to employ military means to take over the state power. See "Notice of the Party Center on the Chongqing Talks," in *Chongqing huitan jishi* (True Records of the Chongqing Talks) (Chongqing, 1983), p. 15; Mao Zedong, "Talks about the Chongqing Negotiation," *Chongqing huitan jishi*, p. 300; Zhou Enlai, "Last Year's Negotiation and its Future," December 18, 1946, in ZX, vol. 1, pp. 260-261, and "Report on the Issue of Peace Negotiation," in ZX, vol. 1, p. 314.

6. See Mao Zedong, "Foreword to the *Communists*," October 4, 1939, in MX, pp. 565-577.

7. It is almost impossible to reach a consensus in defining a general term like politics, nor is it the main purpose of this study to attempt such. Nevertheless, it should be agreed that there are some "extensive relations" between politics and other fields of human phenomena and human behaviors, and that there are some "intensive relations" within the field of politics such as family, society, state, and so on. As for the definition I have raised here, refer to Harold Lasswell and Abraham Kaplan, *Power and Society* (New Haven, 1950). Lasswell and Kaplan define politics as "the relationship through which one person or groups of persons influences the behavior of others." Obviously, they should have taken family relations as a part of politics.

8. See Crane Brinton, *The Anatomy of Revolution* (New York, 1957), pp. 1-27. There have been a variety of revolutions such as the Industrial Revolution, Cultural Revolution, technological revolution, ecological revolution, and cosmological revolution. Even women's hair styles can enjoy a revolution or revolutions.

9. There may be various expression of the same idea in a narrow definition of politics and revolution. Lasswell himself, for example, makes such an attempt, as his other influential book, *Politics: Who Gets What, When, How* (New York, 1936) suggests.

10. See Shanti Swarup, pp. 73-105, where the author alludes to the disparity between revolutionary idealism and revolutionary realism; and also see John Herz, *Political Realism and Political Idealism* (Chicago: the University of Chicago Press, 1951), pp. 17-42. What I attempt here is to bring to focal attention the dichotomy of political realism and revolutionary idealism.

11. Hugh Seton-Watson, *Neither War Nor Peace* (New York, 1960), pp. 188-193.

12. See Lucian Pye, *Mao Tse-tung: the Man in the Leader* (New York, 1976), pp. 36-37; Pye described Mao's "contradiction in nature of a tiger image with conquering power and a monkey image with changeable spirit"; Stuart Schram, *The Political Thought of Mao Tse-tung* (London, 1963), pp. 81-84. Schram attributes to Mao a

contradictory personality of romantic individualism and realistic collectivism; Frederic Wakeman, *History and Will* (Berkeley, 1973), Preface. Wakeman describes Mao's mixed minds of objective history and subjective will; Ross Terrill, *Mao* (New York, 1980), p. 430. Terrill points out Mao's insecure mentality and zig-zagged behavior, especially in his later years.

Remaining aware of the inadequacy of applying abstract concepts in describing historical events and figures, I would nevertheless propose that the dichotomy of revolutionary idealism and political realism and the demarcation of his life before and after the year 1949 should be taken as the very basic ground from which to understand Mao. Furthermore, I would like to pinpoint the fact that in the rebellious years when he was supposed to be a revolutionary, Mao showed himself among his comrades to be an outstanding politician, while in the postliberation years when he was supposed to be a politician, Mao distinguished himself as a unique revolutionary.

13. See Roderick MacFarqhuar, *The Origins of the Cultural Revolution* (New York, 1980), vol. 1, Introduction.

14. Ibid. MacFarquhar also takes the year 1956 as an uniquely important time for the People's Republic of China and the Chinese Communist Party. But I am not quite sure that what I understand of the importance of that year fully accords with his view.

For many years—even now they do not clearly deny it—the Chinese Communists have theoretically divided their political history into two stages: the democratic revolution and the socialist revolution. According to this allegation, the year 1949 seems not as important as the year 1956 because the former only marked a change of the state power or the political form while the latter recorded a real change of social contents or a transition from the democratic revolution to socialist revolution. In other words, the Communist regime cannot legitimately claim itself a socialist state of proletarian dictatorship until after 1956.

Of course, there is a lot of illogical jargon involved with the above topic and the Chinese Communists have never put this kind of theoretical allegation in any clearer terms. From a political point of view, nobody should believe that 1956 is more important than 1949. What I try to stress here is the fact that the year 1956 marked completion or conclusion of the CCP's scheduled orientation.

15. Now there are generally two extreme approaches—an optimistic one and a cynical one—toward the recent economic reforms in China. Here I would bring attention to the situation that, for better or worse, China is facing another era of political revolution and not economic construction.

16. Franz Borkenau, *World Communism* (Ann Arbor, 1962), especially pp. 376, 418.

17. Ibid.

18. Hugh Seton-Watson, *From Lenin to Khrushchev* (New York, 1960), pp. 210-227.

19. Ibid., pp. 291-301.

20. See Ben Yang, "Behind the Anti-Japanese United Front," in *The Quest*, Nos. 33, 34, 35, 1986.

21. In July 1936, Dimitrov, the General Secretary of the Executive Committeee of the Comintern, derided the stubbornness and immaturity of the Chinese

Communists which "delayed their shift to the Comintern's new policy of the anti-imperialist united front for two or three years"; Cherepanov, the Russian military advisor to China in the Anti-Japanese War, wrote that "Before the Japanese started their large scale invasion, the Chinese Communists had almost been wiped out by the Chinese reactionaries, and their remaining troops were scattered in the barren mountainous regions in North China. In fact, it was mainly due to our internationalist policy in China that it resulted in the formation of the united front that saved the CCP from the verge of destruction and created all favorable conditions for the CCP to resume and increase its strength." See Leibzon and Shirinia, p. 287; Alexandr Cherepanov, *Zapiski voenovo sovetnika v kitae* (Memoirs of a Military Advisor in China) (Moscow, the Science Press, 1976), p. 603.

Now it seems obvious that Cherepanov is but a spokesman of Stalin and the Russian Communist Party—for their unfair arrogance they were to pay after Mao and the CCP came to power in China—and that Dimitrov had no right to boast of "political maturity" before Mao and Chinese Communist leaders at all—for his own lack of political maturity, he and his home country were also to pay. Dimitrov died in Moscow in 1948 with a wishful idea of creating a socialist confederation of all Eastern European countries. Had Dimitrov lived into the 1950s, he might very likely have had to face two equally tough choices: either to give up his own political life to somebody else or to give up the political independence of his party and nation to the Russians.

22. It should be clear that there have been no radical domestic changes of social and economic structures in the Soviet Union since the late 1930s, particularly the year 1936 when the 2nd Five-Year Plan was fulfilled, the 8th Party Congress was held, the Soviet Constitution was promulgated and, above all, the collectivization of agriculture and industry was completed.

See the Central Committee of the All Union Communist Party, *Istoria vsiesoyuzkoi komunisticheskioi partii—bolshevikov* (A Concise History of the All Union Communist Party—Bolshevik), (Leningrad, 1950), pp. 320-330. This book admits, "The economy of the USSR completely changed in the year 1936. By that time, all capitalist elements had been eliminated and the socialist system had won victory in all circles of people's economy." For the Russian Communists, however, it means that they can hardly boast of revolution in a domestic socioeconomic sense any longer. Their residual adherence to revolutionary propaganda has gradually degenerated into an effort to conserve their invested interests and established rule at home and to pursue international expansionism. A true revolution may occur someday when they stop talking about revolution.

23. I believe Deng's reform will lead to political confusion and division within China, while Gorbachev's reform will eventually fall back to world expansionism of the Soviet Union. Neither of them will achieve what he expects for sure.

24. Even a quick glance over the words of historical prediction by some great minds in the past may lead to a fairly discouraging conclusion as regards our ordinary selves. Few can forsee far enough into the future. The only thing for us to hope is a resolution to the current confrontation of communism vs. capitalism, the Soviet Union vs. the United States and the like in a manner neither violent nor revolutionary.

Necessarily, these problems will be solved in one way or another through historical developments. We are still living in an age of revolution and politics but hopefully future generations will not. Revolution as something standing against mankind's expectation and plan and politics as something restraining mankind's focal concern to its internal relationship should and will be gone.

CHRONOLOGY

(This chronology is compiled especially to indicate the political and military interactions relevant to the Chinese Communist Party during the period of the Long March and to establish some historical facts not so clearly provided in the previous writings.)

1930

April 28, Jiang-Feng-Yan War breaks out, lasting for four months, covering a dozen provinces and involving nearly two million troops.

June 11, Li Lisan chairs the CCP Politburo conference in Shanghai to adopt the resolution calling for an immediate victory in one or more province.

July 27, Peng Dehuai's 3rd Army Corps captures Changsha and holds the city until August 5.

August 23, First Front Army is founded with Mao Zedong as general political commissar;

August 24-September 12, the second attack on Changsha takes place without success.

September 24-28, Qu Qiubai chairs the 3rd Plenum of the CCP Central Committee to check the Li Lisan adventure.

October 30-November 1, Luofang Conference is held; Mao's military strategy is accepted in the First Front Army.

November 25, Li Lisan is formally expelled from the CCP Politburo.

December 30, First Front Army wins the Longgang Battle and subsequently breaks up the First Suppression Campaign.

1931

January 7, 4th Plenum of the CCP Central Committee convenes in Shanghai under the supervision of Pavel Mif, who arrives in China in late December 1930. The CCP Bureau of the Central Soviet is formed with Zhou as secretary; Xiang Ying, the active secretary, arrives in the Jiangxi Soviet shortly before that time.

April, Wang Jiaxiang, Gu Zuolin and Ren Bishi leave Shanghai for the Jiangxi Central Soviet; Zhang Guotao, Sheng Zemin and Chen Changhao leave for the Eyuwan Soviet; and Xia Xi and Xu Zenggen for the Xiangexi Soviet.

April 16, First Enlarged Conference of the Central Soviet Bureau convenes in Ruijin.

May 16-30, First Front Army breaks the Second Suppression Campaign.

June 22, Xiang Zhongfa, the general secretary is arrested, and killed on the 24th.

July 10-September 15, First Front Army breaks the Third Suppression Campaign.

September 18, Japanese invade Northeast China.

November 1-5, Gannan Conference or the First Conference of CCP in the Central Soviet Bureau convenes; Zhou remains as secretary of the Bureau.

November 7-20, First Congress of the Chinese Soviet Republic convenes; Mao is appointed Chairman of the Chinese Soviet Republic.

November 7, First Congress of the Eyuwan Soviet is held with Zhang Guotao elected chairman; the Fourth Front Army is founded with Xu Xiangqian as general commander and Chen Changhao as political commissar.

November 25, Central Military Council of the Chinese Soviet Republic is formed with Zhu De as chairman. The headquarters of the First Front Army is dismissed, so is Mao's position as its political commissar.

December 14, Ningdu Revolt occurs, in which 17,000 KMT troops join the Red Army.

December, Zhou Enlai arrives in the Jiangxi Soviet at the end of this month.

1932

January 9, CCP Center adopts resolutions once again calling for taking over one or more province.

January 21, He Long's Third Army takes offense and wins one victory in Longwangji and another in Xiaogan on the 25th.

February 4-March 7, Peng Dehuai commands the Red Army to encircle and attack Ganzhou without success.

March 21-May 2, Fourth Front Army wins a grand victory in the Sujiafu Battle.

June, KMT Government starts the Fourth Suppression Campaign against the Eyuwan Soviet and the Xiangexi Soviet.

August 8, Mao is reappointed as political commissar of the First Front Army.

August 15, Fourth Front Army loses a battle in Qiliping.

August 30, Third Army loses a battle in Honghu.

October 8, Ningdu Conference of the Central Soviet Bureau is held; Mao is bitterly criticized; on the 23rd, Zhou replaces Mao as the political commissar of the First Front Army.

October 11, Fourth Front Army leaves the Eyuwan to begin the western march.

October 19, Fourth Front Army reaches the Henan-Hupei border and loses a battle at Zaoyang.

October 25, 3rd Army withdraws from the Honghu Soviet.

November 11, Fourth Front Army suffers another loss in the Manguan Battle before being pushed into Shaanxi; on the 27th, it receives from the Party Center an order to stay in southern Shaanxi instead of running further west.

December 12, Soviet Union and the KMT Government resumes diplomatic relations.

December 25, Fourth Front Army captures Tongjiang to get settled in northern Sichuan.

December 30, Third Army arrives at Hefeng in western Hunan-Hubei border area.

1933

January, Party Center headed by Bo Gu and Zhang Wentian moves to the Jiangxi Soviet and combines with the Central Soviet Bureau.

January 3, Japanese takes Shanghai Pass to invade North China.

February 26-28, First Front Army wins a victory the Yihuang Battle, and another one in the Caotaigang Battle on March 21; the Fourth Suppression Campaign in the Central Soviet is thus broken.

February 15, Anti-Luo Ming Movement begins in the Jiangxi Central Soviet.

May 21-24, Fourth Front Army conducts the victorious Kongshanba Battle with the local warlord, Tian Songyao, in northern Sichuan.

May 31, KMT Government signs the Tangguo Agreement, admitting the Japanese occupation of Chinese territory in the north of the Great Wall.

June 1, Central Government of the Chinese Soviet Republic decrees the Land Investigation Movement.

July 18, Chiang Kai-shek opens the Lushan Military Training Program.

September, Fifth Suppression Campaign starts against the Jiangxi Central Soviet; on the 28th, First Front Army loses Lichuan, which shows an ominous sign.

October, Otto Bruan, the military advisor of the Comintern to the CCP, arrives in the Jiangxi Central Soviet.

October 4, Liu Xiang summons all Sichuan warlords to announce the "Six Route Suppression Campaign" against the Fourth Front Army.

October 26, Red Army and the 19th Route Army signs a secret agreement.

November 20, Fujian Incident takes place.

1934

January 15-18, 5th Plenum of the CCP Central Committee is held; Mao becomes a member of the CCP Politburo.

January 22-February 3, Second Congress of the Chinese Soviet Republic opens at Ruijin; Mao is elected the Chairman of the Central Government and Zhang Wentian the Chairman of the Committee of People's Commissars.

January 15, Fuzhou is taken by the KMT Central Army, which precedes collapse of the Fujian Revolt.

April 4, Xianfeng Conference of the Xiangexi Sub-bureau decides that the Third Army drive to the Hubei-Sichuan border area.

April 28, Central Red Army loses the Guangchang Battle.

June 19, Fengxiangxi Conference of the Xiangexi Sub-bureau is held; radical policies are corrected to cope with reality in eastern Guizhou.

July 7, 7th Army Corps or the Anti-Japanese Vanguard Brigade leaves Ruijin to embark on the northern expedition.

July 23, 6th Army Corps leaves the Hunan-Jiangxi border for the western expedition.

August 9, Fourth Front Army wins a victory in the Wanyuan Battle and proceeds to defeat Liu Xiang's Six-Route Suppression Campaign.

September 4, 6th Army Corps crosses the Xiang River.

September 12, 25th Army starts the long march from the Eyuwan Soviet.

September 20, 6th Army Corps captures Liping; on the 26th, it loses a battle in Jianhe.

October 7-10, after another defeat in Ganxi, the 6th Army Corps turns north; on the 25th, it meets with the Third Army in Yinjiang.

October, CCP organization in Shanghai is exposed and distroyed; communication between the Comintern in Moscow and the CCP Center in Ruijin is disconnected.

October 21, Long March of the Central Red Army commences.

October 23, Central Red Army breaks through the first blockade line.

October 24, 6th Army Corp and the Third Army are incorporated.

November 3, Central Red Army breaks throught the second blockade line.

November 4, Anti-Japanese Vanguard Brigade joins the 10th Army Corps under the general leadership of Fang Zhimin to resume the northern expedition.

November 11, KMT's third blockade line is overcome by the Central Red Army.

November 12, Fang Zhimin's troops are badly defeated in the Tanjiaqiao Battle.

November 29, Central Red Army passes through the the Xiang River or the fourth blockade line, though with a heavy loss of troops.

November 26, Party Committee and Military Council are founded of the Xiangechuanqian Base Area with Ren Bishi and He Long as leaders respectively.

December 11, CCP Politburo holds the Tongdao Conference, and then the Liping Conference on the 18th; the idea of going north to meet the 2nd and 6th Army Corps is cancelled.

1935

January 1, CCP Politburo holds the Houchang Conference on the southern bank of the Wu River.

January 15-18, Zunyi Conference convenes; the Central Red Army decides to go across the Yangtze River and open a new base in southern Sichuan.

January 22, CCP Center telegraphs the Fourth Front Army, requesting military cooperation.

January 24, Fourth Front Army moves north to start the Southern Shaanxi Campaign, which lasts for a month.

January 24-26, Central Red Army loses the Tucheng Battle with the Sichuan army; on the 29th, it turns west to cross the Chishui River.

February 5, Communist guerrilla in Shaanxi grows to two armies, and the Military Council of the Northwest is formed with Xie Zichang as chairman and Liu Zhidan as deputy chairman.

February 8, Central Red Army arrives at Weixin in Yunnan. Zhang Wentian replaces Bo Gu as person in charge of general responsibilities in the CCP Center.

February 18-19, Central Red Army crosses the Chishui River the second time to return to northern Guizhou; February 28-March 1, it wins a military victory in the Tongzi-Zunyi region.

March 4, Front Command Headquarters is formed with Zhu De as commander and Mao Zedong as political commissar.

March 16-17, Central Red Army crosses the Chishui River the third time to attempt at the west.

March 21-22, Central Red Army returns across the Chishui River and then drives down south to central Guizhou and eastern Yunnan.

March 28, Fourth Front Army crosses the Jialing River and leaves northern Sichuan for the Sichuan-Xikang border.

May 1-9, Central Red Army crosses the Jinsha River to enter Sichuan.

May 5, Zhang Guotao proclaims founding of the Confederate Government of Northwest China.

May 12, Huili Conference of the CCP Politburo is held; the anti-Mao mood is overcome.

June 13, First and Fourth Front Armies unite at the foot of the Jiajin Mountains.

June 26, Lianghekou Conference of the Politburo is held; on the 29th, the Military Council draws the "Plan for the Songpan Campaign".

July 25-August 20, 7th Congress of the Comintern convenes in Moscow, in which the general policy of anti-Fascist united front is adopted.

July 28, Zhang Guotao replaces Zhou Enlai as General Political Commissar of the Red Army.

August 1, CCP Mission to the Comintern headed by Wang Ming publishes in Moscow the August 1 Manifesto, advocating a national united front against the Japanese invasion.

August 6, Shawo Conference of the Politburo is held to solve political divergences between the First and Fourth Front Armies.

August 20, Maoergai Conference of the Politburo is held to reaffirm Mao's military strategy.

September 9, Mao runs the Emergence Conference of the Party Center at Baxi; they manage a secret flight.

September 12, Ejie Conference of Mao Zedong decides to go north; Aba Conference of Zhang Guotao decides to go south.

September 16, 25th Army completes its long march and meets the 26th Army in Yongping, northern Shaanxi; on the 18th, the two troops are incorporated into the 15th Army corps.

September 27, CCP Politburo holds the Bangluozhen Conference, resolving to head for northern Shaanxi.

October 15, Zhuomubao Conference of the Fourth Front Army convenes, resulting in another CCP Center headed by Zhang Guotao.

October 19, Central Red Army reaches Wuqizhen in the Northern Shaanxi Base.

October 24, Fourth Front Army starts the Tianquan-Lushan-Mingshan-Ya'an Campaign.

November 18, 2nd and 6th Army Corps takes off again; the 21st, they force across the Wan River to start a westward expedition.

November 21, Zhang Hao or Lin Yunan, the Comintern envoy, comes from Moscow to northern Shaanxi.

November 21-22, Central Red Army and the 15th Army Corps cooperates to win the Zhiluozhen Battle.

December, CCP Politburo holds the Wayaobao Conference late this month to adopt a new policy of national united front.

1936

January 1, 2nd and 6th Army Corps reach Yuping in eastern Guizhou; after a loss in Jiangkou they move further west to Shijian on the 11th.

January 6-14, Zhang Hao and Zhang Guotao exchanges telegrams.

February 11-23, Fourth Front Army retreats from Tianquan in western Sichuan to Ganzi in the Xikang-Tibet border.

February 17, Central Red Army declares the Eastern Expedition.

March 18, Zhang Xueliang flies to Yan'an for a secret talk with Zhou Enlai.

March 28, 2nd and 6th Army Corps reach Panjiang at the Guizhou-Yunnan border and receive telegrams from the Red Army General Headquarters encouraging them to go north.

April 28, 2nd and 6th Army Corps cross the Jinsha River.

May 5, Central Red Army withdraws from the Eastern Expedition; on the 14th, it starts the Western Expedition.

May 28, Guangdong and Guangxi armies revolt against the KMT Central Government.

June 3, 2nd and 6th Army Corps meet the Fourth Front Army in Lihua.

July 2, Leaders of the 2nd and 6th Army Corps and the Fourth Front Army hold a joint conference at Ganzi; the two Red Army groups set out for the north.

July 18, Guangdong and Guangxi Revolt is pacified by the Nanking Government.

September 19, Minzhou Conference of the CCP Northwest Bureau decides to continue moving north to join the First Front Army.

September 27, Zhu De telegraphs the Party Center. Shortly afterward, the Zhangzhou Conference of the CCP Northwest Bureau once again decides to go north.

October 8, First and Fourth Front Armies meet in Huining.

October 21, First and Second Front Armies meet in Jiangjunbao.

November 10, Western Route Army is formed with Xu Xiangqian as commander and Chen Changhao as political commissar.

November 16-18, Western Route Army conducts the Gulang Battle without success.

November 21, Peng Dehuai leads the joint troops to beat part of the KMT Central Army in the Shanchengbao Battle.

December, Mao writes "On the Strategic Problems in the Chinese Revolutionary War".

December 7, Mao assumes a position as Chairman of the Central Military Council.

December 12, Xi'an Incident happens; on the 16th, the Comintern's telegram instructs the CCP Center for a peaceful solution; on the 25th, Zhang Xueliang accompanies Chiang Kai-shek back to Nanking.

1937

January 12, Dong Zhentang's 5th Army of the Western Route Army is annihilated at Gaotai.

February 10, CCP Center issues a letter by telegraph to celebrate the 3rd Plenum of the KMT Central Committee, proposing for another KMT-CCP collaboration.

February 26-March 11, battles in Nijiayingzi destroys the Western Route Army.

March 12, Zhou Enlai returns to Yan'an from his unsuccessful negotiation with Gu Zhutong in Xi'an.

March 27-30, CCP Politburo opens the Yan'an Conference to criticise Zhang Guotao.

May 2-14, CCP Conference of All Soviet Areas is held in Yan'an.

June 16, Zhou Enlai returns to Yan'an from his successful talk with Chiang Kai-shek in Lushan.

July, Mao lectures "On Practice" and "On Contradiction".

July 7, Marco Polo Bridge Incident marks the beginning of the Sino-Japanese War.

August 13, Japanese attack on Shanghai.

August 23-24, CCP Poliburo holds the Luochuan Conference to make strategic arrangements in the Sino-Japanese War.

August 25, Formation of the Eighth Route Army is announced by the Central Military Council.

August 26, Soviet Union and China sign a mutual non-aggression treaty.

September 22, Joint communique of KMT-CCP collaboration is published.

September 25, 115th Division wins the Pingxingguan Battle; Mao telegraphs Zhou, Zhu, and Peng to warn against regular positional warfare and stress guerrilla activities.

October 2, New Fourth Army is founded with Ye Ting as commander and Xiang Ying as vice-commander and political commissar.

November 7, Jin-Cha-Ji Military District comes into being.

November 8, Taiyuan, the provincial capital of Shanxi, is lost to the Japanese.

November 12, Mao attends the conference of Party activists, emphasizing on the independent stance of the CCP in relation with the KMT.

November 27, Wang Ming flies from Moscow back to Yan'an.

December 9-14, CCP Politburo holds the December Conference, in which Wang Ming shows as the upper hand over Mao the underdog but no formal resolution is reached.

1938

January 11, Minor part of the 115th Division led by Nie Rongzhen founds the Jin-Cha-Ji Base Area.

February 27-March 1, Politburo holds the March Conference, in which Mao and Wang reach a stalemate and no formal resolution is agreed on.

March 18, Main part of the 115th Division led by Luo Rongqu creates the Southwest Shanxi Base Area.

March 16, Ren Bishi leaves for Moscow as CCP representative to the Comintern.

April 1, 120th Division headed by He Long and Guan Xiangying opens the Jin-Sui Base Area.

April 27, 129th Division headed by Liu Bocheng and Deng Xiaoping opens the Jin-Ji-Yu Base Area.

April 4, Zhang flees out of Yan'an to join the KMT side.

May 26, Mao publishes "On Protracted War".

September 14, Wang Jiaxiang returns from Moscow to Yan'an, bringing with him the instruction of the Comintern that Mao Zedong, not Wang Ming, should be the Party boss.

September 26-November 6, Sixth Plenum of the CCP Central Committee convenes; Mao's authority and strategy are generally accepted.

BIBLIOGRAPHY

Part One: English Books

Borkenau, Franz, *World Communism* (Ann Arbor: University of Michigan Press, 1962).

Braun, Otto, *A Comintern Agent in China, 1932-1939* (translated by Jeane Moore, Stanford, 1982).

Brinton, Crane, *The Anatomy of Revolution* (New York: Vintage Books, 1957).

Chen, Changfeng, *On the Long March with Chairman Mao* (Beijing: Foreign Language Press, 1972).

Ch'en, Jerome, *Mao and the Chinese Revolution* (London: Oxford University Press, 1967).

Ch'i, Hsi-sheng, *Warlord Politics in China, 1916-1928* (Stanford: Stanford University Press, 1976).

Fairbank, John, *The United States and China* (Cambridge, Mass.: Harvard University Press, 1983).

Harrison, James, *The Long March to Power* (New York: Praeger Publishers, 1972).

Herz, John, *Political Realism and Political Idealism* (Chicago: University of Chicago Press, 1955).

Hsiao, Tso-liang, *Power Relations within the Chinese Communist Movement, 1930-1934* (Seattle: University of Washington Press, 1962).

Issacs, Harold, *The Tragedy of the Chinese Revolution* (Stanford: Stanford University Press, 1951).

Johnson, Chalmers, *Peasant Nationalism and Communist Power* (Stanford: Stanford University Press, 1964).

Kataoka, Tetsuya, *Resistance and Revolution in China* (Berkeley: University of California Press, 1974)

Kim, Ilpyong, *The Politics of the Chinese Communism: Kiangsi under the Soviets* (Berkeley: University of California Press, 1973).

Kuo, Warren, *A Study of the "Resolution of the Tsunyi Conference"* (Taipei: Institute of International Relations, n. d.).

Lasswell, Harold, *Politics: Who Gets What, When, How* (New York: Meridian Books, 1958)

Lasswell, Harold, and Abraham Kaplan, *Power and Society* (New Haven: Yale University Press, 1950).

Levenson, Joseph, *Confucian China and its Modern Fate: Trilogy* (Berkeley: University of California Press, 1968).

Liu, Po-cheng and others, *Recalling the Long March* (Beijing: Foreign Language Press, 1978)

Li, Tien-min, *Chou En-lai* (Taipei: Institute of International Relations, 1970).

Liu, F. F., *A Military History of Modern China, 1924-1949* (Princeton: Princeton University Press, 1956).

Lotveit, Trygve, *Chinese Communism, 1931-1934* (Lund: Studentlitteratur, 1973).

MacFarquhar, Roderick, *The Origins of the Cultural Revolution* (New York: Columbia University Press, 1974).

Mao, Zedong, *Poems of Mao Tse-tung* (Translated by Wong Man and published in Hong Kong: Eastern Horizon Press, 1966).

Pak, Hyobom, *Documents of the Chinese Communist Party, 1927-1930* (Hong Kong: Union Research Institute, 1971).

Payne, Robert, *Mao Tse-tung* (New York: Weyside & Talley, 1969).

Popper, Karl, *Open Society and Its Enemies* (London: Routledge & K. Paul, 1966)

Pye, Lucian, *Mao Tse-tung: the Man in Leader* (New York: Basic Books, 1976).

Rue, John, *Mao Tse-tung in Opposition* (Stanford: Stanford University Press, 1966).

Salisbury, Harrison, *The Long March: The Untold Story* (New York: Harper & Row, 1985).

Schram, Stuart, *The Political Thought of Mao Tse-tung* (London: Pall Mall Press, 1963)

————— , *Mao Tse-tung* (New York: Penguin Books, 1977).

Schwartz, Benjamin, *Chinese Communism and the Rise of Mao* (Cambridge, Mass., Harvard University Press, 1979).

Seton-Watson, Hugh, *From Lenin to Khrushchev* (New York: Praeger, 1960).

————— , *Neither War Nor Peace* (New York: Praeger, 1960).

Sheng, Yueh, *Sun Yat-sen University in Moscow and the Chinese Revolution: A Personal Memoir* (Lawrence: University of Kansas Press, 1973).

Smedley, Agnes, *The Great Road, the Life and Times of Chu Teh* (New York: Monthly Review Press, 1956).

Snow, Edgar, *Red Star Over China* (New York: Random House, 1938).

Stein, Gunther, *The Challenge of Red China* (New York: Da Capo Press, 1975).

Swarup, Shanti, *A Study of the Chinese Communist Movement, 1927-1935* (London: Oxford University Press, 1966).

Terrill, Ross, *Mao* (New York: Harper & Row, 1980).

Wakeman, Frederic, *History and Will* (Berkeley: University of California Press, 1973).

Waller, Derek, *The Kiangsi Soviet Republic: Maso and the Two National Congresses of 1931 and 1934* (Berkeley: University of California Press, 1973).

Wang, Ming, *Mao's Betrayal* (Moscow: Progress Publisher, 1975) translated by Vic Schneierson.

Weber, Max, *The Protestant Ethic and the Spirit of Capitalism* (New York: Charles Scribner's Sons, 1958).

Wei, William, *The Counter-Revolution* (Ann Arbor: University of Michigan Press, 1985).

Wilson, Dick, *The Long March* (New York: Avon Books, 1971).

Wu, Tien-wei, *The Sian Incident: A Pivotal Point in Modern Chinese History* (Ann Arbor: University of Michigan Press, 1976).

————— , *Mao Tse-tung and the Tsunyi Conference* (Washington, D.C.: Association of Research Libraries, 1974).

Part Two: Non-English Books

Cai, Tingkai, *Cai Tingkai zizhuan* (Autobiography of Cai Tingkai) (Har'erbin, Heilongjiang People's Press, 1982).

Cai, Xiaoxian, *Jiangxi suqu hongjun xichuan huiyi* (Recollections of the Jiangxi Soviet and the Red Army's Western Flight) (Taipei: CCP Study Press, 1970).

Cao, Boyi, *Jiangxi suweiai zhi jianli ji bengkui, 1931-1934* (Establishment and Collapse of the Jiangxi Soviet, 1931-1934) (Taipei: National University of Politics, 1969).

Cherepanov, Alexandr, *Zapiski voenovo sovetnika v kitae* (Memoirs of a Military Advisor in China) (Moscow: Science Press, 1976).

Chen, Duxiu, *Chen Duxiu zizhuan* (Chen Duxiu's Autobiography) (Hong Kong: Modern Culture Press, n. d.).

Cheng, Shicai, *Beizhuang de licheng* (A Heroic but Tragic Experience) (Shenyang: Spring Wind Press, 1959).

Chongqing tanpan jishi (Documental Records on the KMT-CCP Talks at Chongqing) (Chongqing: Chongqing People's Press, 1983) collectively compiled..

Chuan-Shan geming genjudi wenxian xuanbian (Selected Documents and Materials Concerning the Sichuan-Shaanxi Revolutionary Base) (Chengdu: Sichuan People's Press, 1982) collectively compiled by the University of Sichuan and others.

Deng, Wenyi, *Congjun baoguo ji* (I Joined the Army to Serve my Motherland) (Taipei: Zhongzheng Press, 1976).

Dong, Hanhe, *Dong Zhentang* (Biography of Dong Zhentang) (Lanzhou: Gansu People's Press, 1981).

Fang, Detian, *Zhang Xueliang yu xian shibian* (Zhang Xueliang and the Xian Incident) (Beijing: People's Press, 1980).

Fang, Zhimin, *Wo congshi geming douzheng de lueshu* (A Brief Account of my Revolutionary Life) (Beijing: People's Press, 1980).

Fang Zhimin zhuan (Biography of Fang Zhimin) (Nanchang: Jiangxi People's Press, 1982) collectively compiled.

Gandongbei hongqu de douzheng (Struggles in the Northeast Jiangxi Soviet Base) (Nanchang: Jiangxi People's Press, 1980), compiled by the CCP Committee of Hengfeng County.

Gansu jiefangqian wushinian dashi ji: 1898-1949 (Big Events of Gansu in the Fifty Years before the Liberation: 1898-1949) (Lanzhou: Gansu People's Press, 1982) collectively compiled.

Gao, Jun, *Weida de zhanshi Ren Bishi* (Ren Bishi the Great Fighter) (Beijing: Chinese Youth Press, 1980).

Gong Chu, *Woyu hongjun* (The Red Army and I) (Hong Kong: South Wind Press, 1954).

Grigoriev, A. M. and A. B. Reznikov, *Greogry Dimitrov, voshchi voshdunarodnovo komunichiskovo dvishrenia* (Greogry Dimitrov, a Leader of the International Communist Movement) (Moscow, 1972).

Guomindang jun zhuidu hongjun changzheng dangan shiliao xuanbian (Selected Materials of KMT Archives on Pursuing and Blocking the Red Army on the Long March) (Beijing: Archives Press, 1986).

Hatano Kenichi, *Chugoku kyosanto shi* (History of the Chinese Communist Party) (Tokyo: Jiji Tsushin Press, 1961).

Hegel, G.W., *System der Philosophie. Erster Teil. Die Logik* (Stuttgart, 1929).

Hongqi piaopiao (Red Flags Fluttering) (Beijing: Chinese Youth Press, 1958 onwards).

Hongjun changzheng guo Guangxi (The Long March of the Red Army in Guangxi) (Nanning: Guangxi People's Press, 1986).

Hongjun changzheng zai Guizhou (The Red Army's Long March in Guizhou) (Guiyang, 1983).

Hongjun zhuanzhan Guizhou—Jiuzhengquan dangan shiliao xuanbian (The Red Army Fighting in Guizhou—Selected Archival Documents of the Nationalist Regime) (Guiyang: Guizhou People's Press, 1984), compiled by the Archives of Guizhou Province.

Hu, Jiaomu, *Zhongguo gongchandang sanshinian* (The Chinese Communist Party in the Past Thirty Years) (Beijing: People's Press, 1951).

Huiyi He Long (Reminiscences of He Long) (Shanghai: Shanghai People's Press, 1979).

Istoria vsiesoyuzkoi komunisticheskoi partii—bolshevikov (A Concise History of the All Union Communist Party—Bolshevik) (Leningrad: Official Press of Political Literature, 1950), compiled by the Central Committee of the All Union Communist Party.

Jiang, Lixin, *Zhang Guotao de panghuang yu juexing* (Wavering and Awakening of Zhang Guotao) (Taipei: Young Lion Press, 1981)

Jiaofei zhangshi (Combat History of Exterminating Communist Rebels) (Taiwan: Chengwen Press, 1976), compiled by the Ministry of Defence of the KMT Government in Taiwan.

Jiaofei wenxian (Materials on the Bandit Extermination) (Nanking, n. d.).

Kunan de licheng (A Road of Bitter Struggles) (Beijing: People's Press, 1984) collectively compiled.

Kuo, Warren, *Zhonggong shilun* (Analytical History of the CCP) (Taipei: National University of Politics, 1969).

Leibzon, B. M. and K. K. Shirinia, *Povorot v politike komitern* (A Turning Point of the Comintern's Policy) (Moscow: Press of Thought, 1975).

Li, Hanyun, *Cong ronggong dao qingdang* (From Accommodating the CCP to Purifying the KMT) (Taipei: Elite Press, 1966).

Li, Shoukong, *Guomin geming shi* (A History of the Nationalist Revolution) (Taipei: Weiwu Press, 1965).

Liuda yilai: dangnei mimi wenjian (Since the Sixth Congress—Collection of Secret Documents of the CCP) (compiled by the Secretariat of the CCP Central Committee in 1941 and reprinted in Beijing: People's Press, 1980).

Luo, Ruiqing, et al., *Xian shibian yu Zhou Enlai tongzhi* (The Xian Incident and Comrade Zhou Enlai) (Beijing: People's Press, 1978).

Ma, Yuqing, *Hongjun changzheng zhongde qici huishi* (Seven times of Reunion of the Red Army on the Long March) (Lanzhou: Gansu People's Press, 1982).

Mao, Zedong, *Mao Zedong xuanji* (Selected Works of Mao Zedong) (Beijing: People's Press, 1969)

Mao Zedong ji (Works of Mao Zedong) (Tokyo: Soso Press) compiled and published in Chinese.

Mingguo yilai sichuan dongluan shiliao bianji (Selected Materials of Chaotic Conditions in Sichuan in the Republican Period) (Hong Kong: Great East Press, 1977).

Nie, Rongzhen, *Nie Rongzhen huiyi lu* (Memoirs of Nie Rongzhen) (Beijing: Soldiers' Press, 1983-1985).

Peng, Dehuai, *Peng Dehuai zishu* (Peng Dehuai's Autobiography) (Beijing: People's Press, 1981).

Qianshan hongji (Red Traces Left in the Guizhou Mountains) (Guiyang: Guizhou People's Press, 1980).

Shen, Bochun, *Xian shibian jishi* (My Experience in the Xian Incident) (Beijing: People's Press, 1979).

Sichuan nongcun jingji (Rural Economy in Sichuan) (Shanghai, 1936).

Sichuan shengqing (Handbook of Sichuan Province) (Chengdu: Sichuan People's Press, 1984) collectively compiled by the Research Institute of CCP Sichuan Provincial Committee and others.

Sima, Lu, *Zhonggong dangshi ji wenxian xuancui* (CCP History and its Essential Materials) (Hong Kong: Zilian Press, 1977 onwards).

Tokuda, Noriyuki, *Mo Takuto shugi no seiji rikigaku* (The Political Dynamics of Maoism) (Tokyo: Keio tsunshin, 1977).

Wang, Jianmin, *Zhongguo gongchandang shigao* (A Draft History of the Chinese Communist Party) (Taipei: 1966).

Wang, Jianying, *Zhongguo gongchandang zuzhishi ziliao huibian* (Compilation of Materials on CCP Organization) (Beijing: Red Flag Press, 1981).

Wang, Pei et al., *Zhongguo kangri zhanzheng shigao* (A Draft History of the Chinese Anti-Japanese War) (n. p.: Hubei People's Press, 1983).

Wu, Jiqing, *Zai Mao zhuxi shenbian de rizili* (The Days When I Was with Chairman Mao) (Nanchang: Jiangxi People's Press, 1982).

Wu, Xiangxiang, *Dierci zhongri zhanzheng shi* (A History of the Sino-Japanese War) (Taipei: Scooper Monthly Press, 1973).

Wu, Xiuquan, *Wode licheng: 1908-1949* (My Memoirs: 1908-1949) (Beijing: PLA Press, 1984).

Xian shibian ziliao (Materials of the Xian Incident) (Beijing: People's Press, 1980) compiled by the Modern History Institute of the Academy of Social Sciences.

Xiang, Qing, *Gongchan guoji he zhongguo geming guanxi de lishi gaishu* (Brief Account of the Relations between the Comintern and the Chinese Revolution) (Zhaoqing: Guangdong People's Press, 1983).

Xinghuo liaoyuan (A Single Spark Can Start a Prairie Fire) (Beijing: Soldiers' Press, 1958 onwards).

Xinminzhu zhuyi geming shiqi Shaanxi dashi jishu (Big Events in Shaanxi in the Period of the New Democratic Revolution) (Xian: Shaanxi People's Press, 1980).

Xu, Haidong, *Wode zishu* (My Memoirs) (Beijing: People's Press, 1983).

Xu, Shiyou, *Wo zai hongjun shinian* (Ten Years in the Red Army) (Beijing: Soldiers' Press, 1983).

Xu, Xiangqian, *Lishi de huigu* (Retrospect of History) (Beijing: PLA Press, 1984).

Xue, Yue, *Jiaofei jishi* (A True Record of Bandit Extermination) (n. p., 1937).

Yang, Chengwu, *Yi changzheng* (Reminiscences of the Long March) (Beijing: Soldiers' Press, 1982).

Yang, Yunruo, *Gongchan guoji he zhongguo geming guanxi jishi, 1919-1943* (Records of the Relations between the Comintern and the Chinese Revolution) (Beijing: Science and Relics Press, 1983).

Yu, Jinan, *Zhang Guotao he "Wode huiyi"* (Zhang Guotao and his Memoirs) (Chengdu: Sichuan People's Press, 1982).

Zhang, Guotao, *Wode huiyi* (My Memoirs) (Hong Kong: Mingbao Monthly Press, 1973).

Zhang, Lin, *Xu Haidong jiangjun zhuan* (Biography of General Xu Haidong) (Beijing: Press of PLA Literature, 1982).

Zhang Guotao wenti ziliao (Documentary Materials on the Zhang Guotao Issue) (Chengdu: Sichuan People's Press, 1982), compiled by Sheng Renxue and others.

Zhonggong dangshi cankao ziliao (Reference Materials of CCP History) (Beijing: People's Press, 1979), compiled by the Party History Institute of the Party School of the CCP Central Committee.

Zhonggong dangshi gao (Draft History of the CCP) (Beijing: People's Press, 1983) compiled by the Party History Institute of the Party School of the CCP Central Committee.

Zhonggong dangshi jiaoxue cankao ziliao (Teaching Materials of CCP History) (Beijing, 1978), compiled by the Institute of Marxist-Leninist Studies of Peking University.

Zhonggong dangshi dashi nianbiao (Annual Records of Big Events in CCP History) (Beijing: People's Press, 1981), compiled by the Institute of Party History of the CCP Central Committee.

Zhonggong dangshi shijian yu renwu lu (Events and Peoples in CCP History) (Shanghai: Shanghai People's Press, 1983) collectively compiled.

Zhonggong dangshi yanjiu wenxuan (Selected Articles on CCP History Studies) (Changsha: Hunan People's Press, 1983).

Zhonggong dangshi ziliao (Materials of CCP History) (Beijing, PLA Press, 1982) by the Political Academy of the Chinese People's Liberation Army.

Zhonguo gongchandang lici zhongyao huiyi ji (Important Conferences of the CCP) (Shanghai: Shanghai People's Press, 1982) collectively compiled.

Zhongguo gongnong hongjun diyi fangmianjun changcheng ji (Records of the Long March of the 1st Army Corps of the First Front Army of the Chinese Worker and Peasant Red Army) (Beijing, People's Press, 1958).

Zhongguo renmin jiefangjun dahsi ji (Big Events of the Chinese People's Liberation Army) (Beijing: Military Press, 1983) compiled by the Institute of Military Science of the PLA.

Zhongguo renmin jiefangjun zhanshi jianbian (A Combat History of the Chinese People's Liberation Army) (Beijing: PLA Press, 1983), compiled by the Academy of Military Science.

Zhongyang geming genjudi ziliao xuanbian (Selected Materials of the Central Revolutionary Base) (Nanchang: Jiangxi People's Press, 1982), compiled by the Archives of Jiangxi Province.

Zhongyang hongjun wuci fan "weijiao" ziliao xuanbian (Collection of Documents Concerning the Central Red Army's Five Anti-Suppression Campaigns) (Shanghai: Fudan University Journal, 1979), compiled by the History Department of Fudan University.

Zhong, Yimu, *Hailufeng nongmin yundong* (Peasant Movements in Haifeng and Lufeng) (Guangzhou: Guangdong People's Press, 1957).

Zhou, Enlai, *Zhou Enlai xuanji* (Selected Works of Zhou Enlai) (Beijing: People's Press, 1980).

Zhou, Kaiqing, *Minguo chuanshi jiyiao* (A Basic Account of Sichuan Affairs in the Republican Period) (Taipei: Sichuan wenxian, 1974).

Zhu, Jianhua and Song Chun, *Zhongguo jinxiandai zhengdang shi* (A History of Political Parties in Modern and Contemporary China) (Har'erbin: Heilongjiang People's Press, 1984).

Zunyi huiyi wenxian (Documents on the Zunyi Conference) (Beijing: People's Press, 1985).

Part Three: Periodicals and Newspapers

Ajia kenkyu (Asian Studies), Japanese journal, Tokyo.

Buersaiweike (Bolshevik), organ of the CCP in the 1930s.

China Quarterly, English journal, London.

Dagongbao (Great Public Daily), newspaper in the 1930s.

Dangshi yanjiu (Studies of Party History), monthly journal in Beijing.

Dangshi yanjiu ziliao (Materials of Party History Studies), journal sponsored by the Museum of Chinese History and Revolution, Beijing.

Dangshi tongxun (Communication on CCP history), journal published once every two months, Beijing.

Douzheng (Struggle), organ of the CCP in the 1930s.

Ganbu bidu (Cadres' Manual), organ of the Fourth Front Red Army in the 1930s.

Gemingh huiyi lu (Reminiscences of the Revolution), serial of volumes published by the People's Press in Beijing.

Gemin yu zhanzheng (Revolution and War), organ of the Red Army in the 1930s.

Gongchan guoji (the Communist International), organ of the Third Comintern in Chinese in the 1930s.

Hongji (Red Flag) or *Hongji zhoukan* (Red Flag Weekly), organ of the CCP in the 1930s.

Hongji (Red Flag), organ of the CCP Central Committee, Beijing.

Hongse zhonghua (Red China), organ of the Soviet Republic in the 1930s.

Jiefangjun bao (People's Liberation Army Daily), official newspaper of the PLA, Beijing.

Jiefang ribao (Liberation Daily), official newspaper of the CCP in the 1940s.

Jindaishi yanjiu (Studies of Modern History), journal sponsored by the Chinese Academy of Social Sciences, Beijing.

Jinri dalu (Mainland Today), journal published in Taiwan.

Kindai chugoku kenkyu sebta iho (Report of Modern China Studies), Japanese journal, Tokyo.

Liaowang zhoukan (Watchtower Weekly), journal published in Beijing.

Lishi zihishi (Historical Knowledge), journal published in Beijing.

Mingbao (Mingbao Monthly), Chinese journal, Hong Kong.

Pravda (Truth), official newspaper of the Russian Communist Party.

Renmin ribao (People's Daily), official newspaper of the Chinese Government.

Shaanxi wenshi ziliao (Historical Materials of Shaanxi), serial of volumes sponsored by the Political Consultative Conference of the Shaanxi Province.

Shanghai wenshi ziliao (Historical Materials of Shanghai), serial of volumes sponsored by the Political Consultative Conference of Shanghai.

Shihua (Honest Words), organ of the Communist Youth League in the 1930s.

Sichuan daxue xuebao (Journal of the University of Sichuan), published in Chengdu.

Suweiai (Soviet), journal of the CCP in the 1930s.

Tansuo (Quest), Chinese journal published in New York.

Xinghuo liaoyuan (A Single Spark Can Start a Prairie Fire), monthly journal in Beijing; not the books bearing the same title.

Wenshi ziliao huibian (Collections of Historical Materials), serial of volumes published by the National Political Consultative Conference, Beijing.

Wenxian he yanjiu (Documents and Studies), journal published once every two months in Beijing.

Zhonggong dangshi ziliao (Materials of CCP History), serial of volumes published in Beijing; not the books bearing the same title.

Zhonggong dangshi renwu (People in CCP History), serial of volumes compiled by Hu Hua and others and published by the Shaanxi People's Press.

Zhongguo xiandaishi (Contemporary Chinese History), monthly compilation of academic articles by the Chinese People's University, Beijing.

INDEX